I'r dair sy'n llonni fy nghalon
Nerys, Betsan a Ffion

Secret Sins

Sex, Violence and Society in Carmarthenshire 1870-1920

Secret Sins

Sex, Violence and Society in Carmarthenshire 1870–1920

RUSSELL DAVIES

UNIVERSITY OF WALES PRESS
CARDIFF
2012

First published 1996
Reprinted 1997, 2004, 2012

British Cataloguing-in-Publication Data.
A catalogue record for this book is available from the British Library.

ISBN 978–0–7083–2556–8
e-ISBN 978–0–7083–2557–5

www.uwp.co.uk

Printed by CPI Antony Rowe, Chippenham, Wiltshire

Contents

List of Illustrations *viii*

Acknowledgements *ix*

Preface *xi*

Introduction: Private Lives, Public Witnesses: The Individual and Society in Carmarthenshire 1

1 A Sense of Place 14

2 A Psychic Crisis? The Social Context of Mental Illness and Suicide 89

3 'Secret Sins': Crime and Protest 112

4 Sexuality and Tension 156

5 Spiritual Skeletons: Religion, Superstition and Popular Culture 186

6 Conclusion: Carmarthenshire and Welsh Society 231

Notes 240

Index 324

List of Illustrations

1. Pen-y-groes, *c.* 1930: a typical industrial village of south-west Wales 17
2. All members of the family had to contribute to the work of the farm 39
3. One of Carmarthenshire's great landowners, Sir J. Hills-Johnes in *c.* 1914 43
4. Generally the children of the gentry enjoyed easier childhoods. Here the children at Glanbrydan take the dog out boating 50
5. A typical Carmarthenshire cottage, *c.* 1906 63
6. Pantglas, home of Gerwyn Jones, High Sheriff of Carmarthenshire in 1887 68
7. "The House of the Mad", or the Joint Counties Lunatic Asylum which opened in 1865 103
8. Leonard Worsell and John John, the two Llanelli men shot by the military in 1911 145
9. Too late – police in Llanelli decide to guard a goods truck that has been ravaged by looters 147
10. The boisterous life of the Victorian public house 177
11. Women at Work in Carmarthenshire market in *c.* 1870 185
12. The "Wonderful Woman of Carmel": Sarah Jones and her family at home in 1906 200
13. The Llandeilo Literary Society 222
14. The Regulars of the Cross Inn Hotel, Ammonford, begin their outing 227
15. The sinister products of the Pen-bre munitions factory 238

Acknowledgements

In view of the disturbing nature of some of the evidence which is contained in this book, it is probably sensible to begin with the statement that I was born and raised in the county of Carmarthenshire. The people we will encounter in the book, saints and sinners, are my people. I can think of no better birthplace for a Welsh social historian than the terraced house into which I was born in Pen-y-groes. Outside our front door stretched the beauty of rural Wales. At the back door lurked one of the most poignant symbols of modern Wales – an abandoned coal mine. Our road, Norton Road, could be regarded as a dividing line, it separated industrial and rural Wales, the natural world from the man-made, the fragrant and the foul. When I was a boy my mother could always tell which door I had used to leave the house by the mess on my clothes upon my return. Green, ochreous grass stains indicated departure through the front door for a game of cowboys on the closest farmer's horses. But black, oleaginous stains testified to the fact that I had stolen quietly out of the back door to be an adventurer, a downhill skier or a mountaineer on the slopes of the coal tip. Looking back, I realize with gratitude that a tender family nurtured me through my turbulent youth.

In the preparation of this book I have incurred many debts and it is a pleasure to record my indebtedness here. The staff at the Hugh Owen Library at the University of Wales Aberystwyth, the Carmarthenshire Records Office in Carmarthen and the National Library of Wales all combine courtesy and professionalism to such an extent that it is a delight to use these institutions. Illustrations 2, 3, 4, 5, 6, 13, 14 and 15 by permission of Llyfrgell Genedlaethol Cymru/The National Library of Wales.

I have benefited greatly from the advice and guidance of a number of people. Marian Davies, Mr David Harries, Mr Gareth Williams and Emeritus Professor Ieuan Gwynedd Jones were inspiring and stimulating teachers. Professor Merfyn Jones and Dr Ian Salmon made valuable suggestions on early drafts of this book. Professor Geraint H. Jenkins and Dr John Davies examined the work with characteristic accuracy and thoroughness. I am deeply aware that this book would not have been deemed worthy of publication without their astute advice and wisdom. The errors of fact and interpretation which remain are mine, and mine alone.

The Trustees of the Sir David Hughes Parry Trust at the University of Wales Aberystwyth have generously provided financial support for various projects which are incorporated in this book. The Welsh Arts Council met the costs of publishing this book. For this generosity and support I am particularly grateful. The editors of *Llafur* and *Cof Cenedl* have kindly allowed me to republish some material which appear in sections of this book. It is a pleasure to record such kindness. Unusually for a work of history, parts of this book have been dramatized and televised. I learnt much from Ms Bethan Eames and Teliesyn regarding the visual presentation of the human stories contained in this work.

The University of Wales Press proved a model publisher, Susan Jenkins a model editor. Gillian Parry transformed pages of impenetrable handwritten scrawl into a presentable typescript. No one can write a general history such as this without leaning heavily upon the efforts of other historians. I am conscious of my many exactions, and trust that every footnote will be held indicative of my gratitude and esteem.

My family have provided a continuous source of support and encouragement. Without my wife, Nerys, and my daughters Betsan and Ffion, life would have little of its joys and pleasures, but then this book would have been finished much sooner. It is to them that I dedicate this book.

Russell Davies
July 1996
Aberystwyth

Preface

The opportunity to provide a new preface for *Secret Sins* evoked the Biblical warning 'as a dog returneth to his vomit, so a fool returneth to his folly' (Proverbs 26:11). The fear was, however, tempered by the recollection that *Secret Sins*, judging from a number of responses that the author received, did capture the affection of a wide readership around the world. That it is being republished by the University of Wales Press almost two decades after its first publication indicates, hopefully, that there is still a demand for a history that seeks to engage with wider concerns of humanity than just the political. The emotional, the sexual and the personal lives of people provide a different perspective from which to view the world and its woes.

Revisiting the work after so much time, the author was struck by much of the youthful exuberance and enthusiasm that went into its writing. Inevitably, even this author has acquired a modicum of wisdom with age. Certain infelicities of phrase or particular sweeps of generalization now appear at best unfortunate, at worst unwise. Therein arose a difficult decision. Should one re-write or re-phrase much of the original? To do so would have been quite an onerous task, and one would be producing not a new edition of an old book but, essentially, a new work. This would probably have been a clumsy and unprofitable attempt to force new wine into old bottles. More worryingly, the special character of the old vintage which had engendered such a warm reception among its readership could have been lost. The book was written at a time when a few of the author's acquaintances who remembered some of the events that feature in it were still alive. Some recalled the winds of wrath that blew during the religious revivals and seeing the angels who gathered to mark the passing of the revivalists –

those fascinating characters, part St John the Baptist, part Valentino. Others remembered dark tales of deadly battles with water bailiffs or police, the pubs of the wild wasted boyos that never closed, or the 'canwyll corff' (corpse candle) that still shone despite the warnings of air raid wardens. Re-editing might have lost the elegiac echo of the voices of those loved and loving people, which can be heard on occasion in the book. And that would have been the greatest loss.

Secret Sins thus appears, once more as it did originally in 1996, with all its flaws and failings. Like us all, it is a child of its time, a product of its age. Many of the themes discussed in the book were further considered by this author in *Hope and Heartbreak: A Social History of Wales and the Welsh 1776–1870* (University of Wales Press, 2005). These included the links between religion and superstition, the private committal of sin and its public condemnation, the ways people sought to bring joy and happiness into their lives, and the friction between love and lust. Since 1995, a few other authors have also ventured into examining the criminal and sexual lives of the Welsh people. Dr Kate Fisher has published on birth control practices and policies in south Wales, while Richard Ireland has published extensively on the misdeeds and misdemeanours of my forefathers in Carmarthenshire.

Hopefully, *Secret Sins* still has something of relevance to say. The period concerned in the book, 1870–1920, is often viewed as a golden age. The world that we have lost – allegedly rejoicing in high morality and Victorian values – was an eternal summer, only eventually finished with the 'death of innocence' and the roaring guns of August 1914. *Secret Sins* offers a gentle corrective to this view in suggesting that there was also loneliness and isolation, drink and drunkenness in astonishing amounts, violence and social ways that were coarse and even bizarre. The people featured in the book, who are a fine people, are my people, and they were not wholly bad or good.

Russell Davies
The Ides of March, 2012
Aberystwyth

Introduction

Private Lives, Public Witnesses: The Individual and Society in Carmarthenshire

At the turn of the twentieth century, Carmarthenshire was portrayed in contemporary literature as a beautiful, unspoilt Arcadia. One author, viewing the county from the windswept, wild hills above Rhandir-mwyn, saw a promised land – 'the milk and honey lands of Carmarthenshire'.[1] Rhys Davies, the author of several classic short stories, recalled Carmarthenshire as 'the county of my childhood years, everlastingly green in my broken nose'. He regarded the town of Carmarthen as 'the cows' capital of Wales . . . prosperously lactic'.[2] To Gwenallt, crossing the boundary into the county was a thrilling experience, an embrace with nature's immemorial, natural order.[3] In poetry and prose Carmarthenshire is celebrated as the symbol of tranquility, stability and the ancient pastoral past.[4]

This obsession with the bucolic negates a major feature of Carmarthenshire society. Through the distorting filters of personal recollections and the necessities of literary creativity, the industrial experience of Carmarthenshire has, as Bryan Martin Davies recorded, been suppressed. It has become 'y graith a geisiwn ei chuddio, y celwydd cyfleus a sgubwn o dan y carped'.[5]

But the reality was different. In the south-eastern parishes of Carmarthenshire, owing primarily to the mining of anthracite coal and the manufacture of tinplate, the society which evolved by the 1870s shared many of the characteristics of the communities of industrial south Wales.

It is this duality, being both industrial and urban, agricultural and rural, which makes Carmarthenshire such a fruitful area for historical research. Carmarthenshire, the largest administrative county in nineteenth-century Wales, experienced not only the bitter and harrowing experiences of rural communities, but also rapid industrialization and its accompanying social dislocation.[6] In some respects Carmarthenshire was a frontier society straddling within its boundaries the new 'American' Wales of industrial productivity and mass culture and the old agricultural 'Welsh' Wales. The county can serve as a microcosm for the macrocosm of south Wales. Within the confines of one administrative unit the profound economic and social forces which transformed south Wales in the forty years leading up to the First World War can be analysed, examined and understood. To understand the county is perhaps to understand the forces that transformed south Wales at the turn of the twentieth century. It is important to remember that industrialization was not a sharp, sudden or alien intrusion into the green and pleasant land of Carmarthenshire. On the contrary, industrial enterprises had been an intrinsic part of the county's history for a considerable period. 'In or about the year 1536–39' John Leland had recorded that coal was being mined in the county.[7] The metallic, mineral and woollen resources of Carmarthenshire had also been exploited from an early period.[8] But what was new in the late nineteenth century was the extent and intensity of industrial activity in Carmarthenshire. It is this acceleration of industrial activity which marks the period 1870–1918 from the earlier history of the county. The new towns and villages which developed during the years leading up to the First World War, though they maintained many of the characteristics of the older 'traditional' communities, were substantially different in their social structure and organization. By 1914 the people of Carmarthenshire were housed in a plurality of contrasting communities.

The historiography of south Wales has tended to concentrate either on the history of the urban and industrialized south-east, or on the history of the agricultural south-west. As a consequence, the modern history of south Wales has sadly become polarized, with the emphasis being placed on the contrasts between urban east and rural west. The dominant images are of the Anglicized grey, industrialized communities in 'the valleys' and the rosy, idyllic, rural settlements in the Welsh west. Two communities, worlds apart.[9] As with many cliches, there is much truth in this view. However, this study attempts to show not only the contrasts but also the interrelationships and interdependencies which existed between rural and industrial communities. In south Wales, as in the rest of Britain, there was a continuum between farm, hamlet, village, town and city.[10] Communities in Carmarthenshire, different as they were in social structure and organization, reacted to both urban and rural stimuli.

This continuum can be clearly seen in the history of the Teifi Valley. Though it is set in the heart of rural west Wales, in the late nineteenth century the valley was a centre of significant industrial activity. The woollen industry, and the communities which depended upon it for work in the period 1870–1914, shared many of the experiences of industrial south Wales. The introduction of powered machinery from the 1870s, and the replacement of small, paternalistic mills with factories organized and structured on industrial principles, led to an increase in labour consciousness and calls for the protection of workers' rights.[11] The ideological attachment to south Wales was strengthened with the improvement of communications in the 1880s and 1890s. The opening of the Teifi Valley Railway in 1895 served not only to cement relations and contacts with south Wales; it also increased the perception of people in rural west Wales that they too were living in an age of change.[12] Gwyn Thomas, with characteristic sarcasm, scornfully dismissed the railway service in west Wales as possessing 'the gentlest train in existence, the only railway on earth designed not to disturb the pollen in the lush paradise around'.[13] But his response fails to recognize the vital importance of rural railway lines in quickening the pulse of life in the countryside of west Wales. Until the arrival of these lines men had been at the mercy of horse-drawn transport. Most journeys, even the simplest, involved a day's travel. From the 1890s the people of the isolated parishes of west Wales became members of the modern age, the railway age.[14] To many contemporaries the speed and rapidity of change was bewildering.

Yet perhaps the strongest link between rural and industrial Wales was human. The majority of the first generation of migrants into industrial south Wales came from the western counties.[15] These people brought their attitudes, beliefs and traditions with them into their new industrial homelands. Despite the geographic distance, many of these people naturally maintained strong links with their kin and kith in rural west Wales. It is this innate traditionalism which accounts for the preference of south Wales workers for particular goods and produce, such as the butter of Tywiside and the cloth of Teifiside.

This study commences with an examination of the changes that occurred in the demographic, economic and social structure of Carmarthenshire between 1870 and 1920. The growth and development of industry and the condition of agriculture in the county are discussed in order to identify the modes of production which operated in Carmarthenshire's economy. Their effects on the distribution of population, on social organization and structure are analysed in order to provide the background for the human activities which are discussed in later chapters. Having examined the demographic, economic and social changes which occurred in Carmarthenshire between 1870 and 1920, an attempt is then made to assess the impact of these changes on the lives of individuals. The study aims to go beneath the generalizations of economics and the social sciences in order to capture the particular experience of the individual person, to rescue the individual from what E. P. Thompson termed 'the enormous condescension of posterity'.[16] The fears, hopes, aspirations, anxieties, ambitions, loves, hatreds, phobias and desires that were the dominant forces in an individual's life are studied in order to question commonly held generalizations. To attempt this we have to examine not only the political, educational, religious and cultural history of Carmarthenshire but also the psychological, psychic, criminal and sexual history of the people. These latter subjects are frequently regarded as too perverse and obscure to be of concern to the serious historian. Sadly, too many historians have regarded these areas as the prerogative and preserve of the psychologist or the prurient. But although they are fraught with complexity, compassion and passion, they allow the historian to peel away layers of significance from the respectable façade of society, revealing something of the pathos of the human condition. The historian can thus recapture the secret hidden world of the individual and encounter the nobility of human suffering in the grand drama of life. The problems which are examined in this book are not trivial or obscure. They constitute some of the timeless problems created by the principal constants of conflict in the condition of mankind – the confrontation between men and women, old age and youth, society and individual, humankind and God.[17] If it appears at times to be a chronicle of woe, individual wretchedness and personal humiliation, then this is testimony to the fact that many Victorians were in several respects stupid, vulgar, unhappy and unsuccessful. Despite this, it is hoped that something of the spontaneity, joy and laughter of Victorian Carmarthenshire will also show through the gloom, for to be amused does not necessarily spell disaster for Victorian historical studies.

Through studying a wide range of topics the enormous variety and complexity of human experience becomes apparent. Social experience is fragmented and more complicated than historians and sociologists have allowed.[18] Theories, ideologies, and firm, pre-conceived sociological concepts are inadequate when applied to the complexity of human society and experience. It is only through studying many different aspects of human experience that we can glimpse the totality of human society. It is only through examining the particular experiences of individual people in the context of the general experience of their society that we can begin to capture something of the totality of Carmarthenshire society in the late nineteenth and early twentieth centuries.[19]

But the historian cannot, of course, capture the totality of a community's experience. To include everything is impossible. Such an approach would fail to distinguish between the important and the negligible, the significant and the insignificant. It would also negate the central task of the historian, which is to analyse the evidence which has survived from the past. Many of the historians who have bravely pioneered the total history of their chosen communities point to the importance of Walter Benjamin's maxim that 'nothing that has taken place should be lost to history'.[20] Whilst accepting the validity of this maxim, the intention of this study is more modest; it is simply to provide an impression of life in Carmarthenshire at the turn of the twentieth century. Though many suggestions are made in the course of this study on the sexual life of the Welsh, the state of their mental health, their occasional predisposition to despair, and the survival amongst them of paganistic beliefs, it is stressed that these suggestions need to be analysed in greater detail, on a national scale and over a longer time period before firm conclusions can be drawn. This is a tentative study designed to put forward deductions that may be proved wrong and to suggest further lines of approach that may be regarded as misguided. Above all the intention is to show the infinite variety of human life as it was experienced by the people of Carmarthenshire between 1870 and 1920.

The evidence used in this study has been drawn from as wide a range as possible. Personal papers, autobiographies, private memoirs, letters, government reports, the records of police courts, petty and quarter sessions, mental hospitals, and local health authorities, and medical officers of health reports, are amongst the most important. But the perceptive reader will detect the overwhelming importance of the local newspaper as a source for much of the evidence presented in this study. The newspaper, owing perhaps to the gross excesses of the tabloid press in the 1980s and 1990s, has become justifiably suspect as an historical source.[21] The dangers of relying on newspapers are obvious. The bias, selectivity, vindictiveness and malice of editors and reporters are legendary. Newspapers are often the vehicle for political propaganda, with many topics receiving a superficial or over-simplified approach so that the facts of a particular issue or event are either distorted, misrepresented or ignored. For many editors the temptation to perpetuate and promulgate petty gossip was and is irresistible. The reports and details given in the press are selective. Indeed, the historian, too conscious perhaps of the importance which some events have gained through hindsight, is often surprised and frustrated to find scant coverage of many events in the newspapers. For newspapers were surprisingly and irritatingly inconsistent in the events they reported. In order to redress some of the difficulties inherent in using the press, the present author has attempted as far as possible to cross-reference the press reports with the more 'official' records. To give one example: the press reports of affiliation order proceedings are cross-referenced to the written depositions and records contained in the petty sessions papers in the Carmarthenshire Records Office. Where detailed depositions are available, it is this source that is used in this study. However, sadly more often than not, the official record contains no more than the names of the mother and the alleged father involved in the case. One example can be used to illustrate the point. The official record for May Jenkins notes that she won a case against Ernest Treharne for the paternity of a child.[22] However, the press report provides a wealth of detail on the human vice of curiosity in rural areas, and offers valuable insights into popular behaviour, morality, courtship customs, and the raucous youth culture of west Wales and the relative roles of women and men.

The historian of west Wales is particularly fortunate in that the area was well served by a number of newspapers. This enables the historian of Carmarthenshire to test the selectivity of newspapers in reporting or neglecting to report those events which were detrimental to the good standing of their locality. Thus the Tory *Carmarthen Journal* and the Liberal *Welshman*, both published in Carmarthen, are consulted in conjunction with the Liberal *South Wales Press* published in Llanelli. Their communal rivalries and jealousies ensured that stories which were excluded from one paper, because they were harmful to the reputation of the town, were included in the rival paper's coverage of the week in Carmarthenshire. Despite their enormous limitations, newspapers are amongst the most valuable evidence which the social historian has available. Often, as Michael Foot found in his biography of Aneurin Bevan, they are the only sources which offer evidence on a number of aspects of social life.[23] They offer such conflicting, contrasting and contradictory evidence on all aspects of daily life that one's initial response is to feel overwhelmed by a sense of incoherence and disorder. But it is the newspapers of Carmarthenshire which enable the historian to present information and impressions which are not included in the official reports. They provide descriptions as to the character of people and particular areas, offering the views of contemporaries regarding the significance of certain events and on the social regard or disregard in which individuals were held. This is doubly important when we remember that many of the people encountered in this study left no other record. The newspapers offer the flesh to place on the skeletal details of prison records, quarter and petty sessions papers and other official records. For a description of the atmosphere and mood, the special milieu of a particular place or period, and for character and local colour, the newspaper is an almost unrivalled source. Its wide-eyed immediacy, chronologically noting the passing of the years, is invaluable to the study of a local society. The willingness to accept the press, despite its serious limitations and deficiencies, opens up a wealth of evidence for the social historian to use in the sullen task of capturing the teeming variety of social life.

The focus on the personal experiences of the individual raises a number of important historiographical questions. Can an individual's particular experience be representative of society's general experience? Are the experiences of individuals typical or exceptional? Can personal experiences, whether bitter or sweet, be representative of the experiences of society or are they simply a collection of curiosities, an assembly of anecdotes? The difficulty of answering such questions is compounded when we note that a number of individuals encountered in this study lived beyond the outer margins of Carmarthenshire society in the late nineteenth and early twentieth centuries. Many of the life stories encountered here are those of people ostracized by society because of their sexual immorality, intemperate and bad habits, or their mental illness. Given that the author's approach is an almost shameless eclecticism, borrowing ideas and concepts from the other branches of the social sciences with the morality of a thieving magpie, it would be both impertinent and presumptuous to attempt to defend the work from some of the above charges. But it is pertinent to offer an explanation of the motives and methodology which underpin this study.

In this context it is relevant to note the argument of a number of historians who have, through the influence of anthropology, accepted the notion that 'history in the ethnographic grain . . . the anthropological mode of history . . . begins from the premise that individual expression takes place within a general idiom'.[24] One of the many dangers inherent in pursuing the individual further into the elusive secrets of his, or her, private life, is that of producing another example of what has become a despised genre of historiography – the series of anecdotal books on 'Everyday Life in'. But there is importance in the particular experience of the individual's life story – bristling and jumping with novelty.[25] Such anecdotes are useful in helping the historian to distinguish a true picture of the customs and character of any given period. Indeed, as Eugen Weber has argued, all history is exemplary.[26] Curiosities do exist in society and this work notes quite a few of them, but historical anecdotes properly treated are full of insights and meaning. Provided we are willing to listen sympathetically and attune ourselves to the special circumstances of our chosen historical period we might realize that it is often in the realm of the exceptional that we can sometimes discern a ray of truth. One of the main intentions of this work is to cumulate individual life stories in order to reveal some of the recurrent factors in the general experience of society. Thus in the discussion on criminality and sexuality the author has selected examples which can be considered to be representative of several. For the average truth of a period can be gleaned in what is 'current and ordinary in the repetition of gestures, images and fragments of discourse among the majority of people'.[27] The records used in this study do not only present the exceptional; the 'normal' experiences of society are there as well. In seeking to balance the two extremes we may discover sections of contemporary reality which otherwise might be lost to us in the overworked terrain of our knowledge of south Wales at the turn of the twentieth century. The approach is thus occasionally comparable to that adopted by a number of French historians who have pioneered 'serial history'. Taken together in a serial way the life stories recounted in this study can be appreciated as being more than mere anecdotes. When organized together in a structured way, eliminating repetition, this evidence can be construed as being part of a wider historical discourse. Their value is that they provide evidence for the beginning of a new kind of social history for Carmarthenshire – a social history which is neither enchained in the rigidity of the view from above nor the equally misleading view from below. Such evidence, taken from across the social classes, is representative of the experience of Carmarthenshire people who lived at the turn of the twentieth century. It is not a simple one-dimensional montage of anecdotes.

The value of the life stories cited in this study is that they reveal the hidden moments and moods of Carmarthenshire society at the turn of the twentieth century. Their importance derives from the light they throw upon the hidden, forgotten, dark areas of society's experience to reveal layers of reality which are traditionally ignored by historians. People, often simple uneducated people, emerge from this marginal twilight world to communicate a message which has a significance for whole areas of society's characteristics and experiences.[28] Such insights can only be captured by studying the type of evidence and adopting the methodology used in this study. Gradually, through the accumulation of individual experiences, we can look into the hearts and minds of the people themselves, hear the whisperings of their voices and capture part of the secret history of the common people. We can also transcend the condescension of those historians who would argue that such life stories are simple descriptions of simple lives in which nothing of any significance ever happens. These people, ostracized from society, forgotten by history, shared one profound fact with all other members of Carmarthenshire society – their common humanity. If only for this fundamental reason their life stories deserve to be told. Through their fears, phobias and passions, we can view the wider fears, phobias and passions of their society. From the margins we can view the hypocrisies, double standards and sheer callous disregard of suffering that were a part of the complex and contradictory character of Carmarthenshire society.

Though the focus is on the individual, it is essential that we do not lose sight of the wider forces which were operating within society as a whole. The argument advanced here is that the study of the individual does not undermine the significance of important events; rather it helps us to realize that there are alternative ways of looking at events and that the traditional view is not necessarily the only tenable one.[29] There is nothing new in this approach. Despite the attention given to the innovations of the 'new history', the basic message was expressed eloquently by Sir Lewis Namier as long ago as 1931 in an essay on 'The Biography of Ordinary Men'. When working on the history of the crowd, Namier wrote:

> The student has to get acquainted with the lives of thousands of individuals, with an entire ant-heap, see its files stretch out in various directions, understand how they are connected and correlated, watch the individual ants, and yet never lose sight of the ant-hill.[30]

Thus, in this study, the particular experience of the individual is related to the general experience of Carmarthenshire society. One of the advantages of such an approach is that it enables us to realize that the boundaries traditionally established by empirical historians between subjects have been too inflexible. The boundaries, for example, between religion and irreligion, Christianity and superstition, traditional and modern attitudes have been too firmly drawn. The evidence that emerges from the individual's viewpoint indicates that a single life could consist of various phases of faith and doubt.[31] This is perhaps one of the most obvious factors in explaining the vicissitudes in the fortunes of Welsh religious life and the tradition of the renewal of religious strength through revivals. An additional complication is that not only did periods of faith and doubt take place within an individual's life but that, at the same time, the person who attended chapel also subscribed to a number of beliefs and practices which dated back to pagan times.

People appear to have operated different time-scales for different aspects of their lives.[32] The period under study, 1870 to 1920, was a period of rapid educational, scientific and technological change. It was a period during which Wales was hailed as one of the most religious countries in the world. But it was also a period in which large numbers of people were preoccupied with survivals from pagan and medieval times. Horoscopes, fortune-tellers, superstitions, folk medicine and healing, and other vestiges of paganistic folk-beliefs were more common and widespread than has been acknowledged. Corpse candles, phantom dogs and fairies continued to disturb unsuspecting, nervous and sensitive travellers on the highways and byways of Carmarthenshire. Despite the Methodist Revival, the continued advancement of Nonconformity and scientific and technical developments of the nineteenth century, primitive beliefs continued to have widespread social relevance at the outbreak of the First World War.[33]

The major advantage of adopting a wider approach is that it allows new perspectives and questions to emerge to test the validity of the accepted generalizations of Welsh history. The family, for example, traditionally regarded as the cornerstone of Welsh society,[34] was also the theatre of considerable tension and violence. Tensions within families were stretched tight by the clashes between age and youth, between ambition, authority, duty and love, whilst profound tensions were created by inadequate financial resources. The pressure generated by these tensions was normally suppressed and curtailed by an arsenal of defence mechanisms which individuals built around themselves, but frequently the pressure exploded and caused vicious and savage cases of child abuse and assaults, wife-beatings, inter-family fights and even murder. The police court provides the historian with an indication of the problems which simmered under the placid façade of family life and offers glimpses into a dark and depressing underworld that existed in the reality of south-west Wales. Envy, cruelty, hatred, malice and spite were often the dominant emotions in a savage, vicious world. It is clear that even at the most intensely religious period in Welsh history there was a beast in Welsh man, and in his heart there remained the pagan darkness. These dark, sombre episodes should not be exorcized like evil spirits from our history. They should be acknowledged as an integral part of the total social context and studied in order to attempt to gain an understanding of the human responses to economic and social change.[35]

The political and religious history of Wales in the nineteenth and twentieth centuries has been brilliantly and extensively explored and explained by Welsh historians during the past two decades.[36] The study of politics and religion provides a mass of documentation which allows the historian to scrutinize behaviour in greater detail and in a more comprehensive way than is possible in the study of some of the topics discussed in this study. But politics and religion did not dominate people's lives as much as some contemporaries believed, or as political and religious historians have subsequently assumed. Despite the attempts of nineteenth-century reformers to bring as many men as possible within the pale of the constitution, many were still excluded and a large number chose not to involve themselves with either politics or religion. Moreover, one human gender was effectively excluded by law from the political life of the community. Many historians have noted the apathy and indifference which many people showed towards politics and religion. But, to many people, the business of living, of maintaining a tenuous grip on existence had more relevance than involvement in a political cause.[37] Why, for example, were women and children willing to play no part in the political life of the nation?

Education has long been regarded as the ladder of progress which the Welsh people eagerly grasped and climbed in order to escape the confines and restrictions of their social position. In Carmarthenshire the personification of this heroic tradition of Welsh educational development was Sir John Williams.[38] His life story is another example of the *locus classicus* of Welsh educational development, the cottage-bred boy who reached a prestigious post through educational achievement. But education also created new divisions in Welsh society. If success in examinations opened new doors for some, it effectively closed doors to others. It is the successful who have attracted the attention of historians. The experience of the few has obscured that of the many. A different picture emerges when the historian examines the log-books of the elementary schools of Carmarthenshire. It becomes clear that, even at the beginning of the twentieth century, education was actually regarded by many people as being of secondary importance to the requirements of the agricultural calendar. A whole social transformation had to occur before people grasped the potential which education offered to them. The old order had to change. People's perception of the world had to change. Those transformations occurred in the period between 1870 and 1920. It is with the interplay between the forces that brought about such a transformation and their effect on the lives of individuals that this study is concerned.

1

A Sense of Place

1. People and Places

Decline, stagnation and expansion are obvious, but appropriate, descriptions for the demographic experience of the different counties of south Wales during the period 1870–1920. Decline was the tortuous experience of rural Cardiganshire. Between the censuses of 1871 and 1921 the county had experienced a painful decrease of 18.5 per cent of its population. The decline in the coastal sea trade, the collapse of the leadmining industry and the prevailing gloom over the future of agriculture combined to drive people out of Cardiganshire. In Pembrokeshire the same problems prevailed to a lesser degree. Thus there was little change in the county's population over the decades down to 1921.[1] In marked contrast the population of Glamorgan, boosted by the spectacular development of the south Wales coalfield, expanded at a phenomenal rate. The 397,859 people who lived within Glamorgan's borders in 1871 had swollen to 1,252,451 by 1921. In Carmarthenshire, though the growth in population was less spectacular than that of its dynamic neighbour and the pace of immigration was less intense, it was still significant. In 1871 the county's population had reached 115,710. By 1921 it had increased to 175,073. Superficially this would seem to indicate that the population history of Carmarthenshire was more closely tied to that of Glamorgan than its western neighbours. However, these county-wide statistics conceal significant local variations in the demographic experience of different communities. Whilst some areas of Carmarthenshire, most notably the south-eastern parishes, witnessed rapid growth in population in the years down to 1921, other communities experienced a painful haemorrhage of people during the fifty years between 1871 and 1921. An analysis of the population history of Carmarthenshire on a local level thus reinforces the county's value as a centre for the study of the wider trends occurring in south Wales at the turn of the twentieth century.

The growth of population was concentrated in the south-eastern parishes of Ammanford, Betws, Burry Port, Cwmaman, Kidwelly, Llanelli, Llangennech, Llan-non, Llangyndeyrn, Llanedi, Llandybïe, Llanarthne, Llanfihangel Aberbythych, Penbre and Cwarter Bach. Collectively these parishes contained under a quarter of the area of the county and 33.0 per cent of the population of Carmarthenshire in 1871. Their share of the total population had risen to 45.6 per cent by 1907, 52.5 per cent by 1911, and 55.1 per cent by 1921.[2] The level of population growth varied from decade to decade, and also from parish to parish. The population of the parish of Llan-non, for example, which contained the mining community of Tumble, increased by 206.3 per cent between 1871 and 1921; it rose from 1581 in 1871, to 1684 in 1887, 2104 in 1891, 2634 in 1907, 4103 in 1911 and 4842 in 1921. The peak period in the population growth of the parish of Llan-non – the decade 1901–11 – coincided with the expansion of the Great Mountain Colliery Company's mining activities in Tumble.[3] In a similar way, the population of Llandybïe, another anthracite mining parish, expanded most rapidly, from 4,388 to 6,393 (an increase of 45.7 per cent), in the period 1891–1907. These were the years which saw the founding of the Emlyn Colliery at Pen-y-groes, the Caerbryn Colliery, and the expansion of Pencae'r Eithin in Pentregwenlais.[4] For each of the parishes of south-east Carmarthenshire, the period 1871 to 1921 saw an almost uninterrupted growth in population. During the period 1871 to 1921, the parishes of the south-east experienced population growth ranging from 40.6 per cent in Llangyndeyrn, to 98.1 in Cwarter Bach, to 153.9 in Llangennech and up to 206.3 in Llan-non.

There was another group of parishes, spread across the county which, although primarily agricultural in composition, also experienced population growth between 1871 and 1921. The growth was less dramatic and intense than that experienced by the previous group. The level of growth varied from Pendine (0.1) to Castelldwyran (2.2), Llandeilo (3.7), Llanfihangel Abercywyn (5.6), Merthyr (7.1), Llanfallteg East (9.3), Penboyr (11.4), Llangeler (12.2), St Ishmael (15.6), Llanddarog (18.6), Llanpumsaint (37.2) and Llangan East (76.5). Local pockets of industry serve to explain the growth in the population of these parishes. The population of the parishes of Castelldwyran, Llangan East and Llanfallteg East grew because of quarrying in Rosebush and other slate quarries. The population of the parishes of Llangeler and Penboyr grew because of woollen manufacturing, and Llanddarog because of coal mining.[5]

In contrast to these parishes are fifty-three parishes which experienced an absolute decline in population between 1871 and 1921. The decline ranged from 0.5 per cent in Laugharne to 54.0 per cent in Llanfihangel-ar-arth. It is a sad fact that forty-three rural parishes in Carmarthenshire reached their peak of population before 1877.[6] Thereafter these rural parishes experienced an absolute decennial decline in population. While the population of Carmarthenshire increased by 51.3 per cent between 1871 and 1921, that of Llandyfeisant declined from 225 in 1871 to 109 in 1921, and Llanfynydd from 1,132 to 691 – reductions of 51.5 and 38.9 per cent respectively.

In 1871, 77 per cent of Carmarthenshire people lived in seventy-one rural parishes. By 1907 the percentage share had declined to 54.5 per cent and by 1921 under half of the county's population (44.9 per cent) lived in the agricultural parishes of the county. In fifty years, the forces of industrialization had transformed the distribution of population within Carmarthenshire. While noting this rural population decline, we should note that industrial communities also experienced variations in loss and gain by migration. For example, in the decades 1881–91, 1891–1901, 1901–11, Pen-bre experienced losses as a result of the migration of 161, 979 and 918 people respectively. This was due to the fact that the growth in bituminous coal mining was comparatively slower than the growth in anthracite mining, which took place inland. The parish of Pen-bre was an exporter of people despite its industrial base.[7] Llanelli also experienced mixed fortunes. Between 1881 and 1891 the town experienced a net gain of 1,681 people. Following the imposition of the McKinley Tariff by the United States government in 1893, the tinplate industry

Pen-y-groes, c. 1930: a typical industrial village of south-west Wales (By permission of National Museum Wales)

was devastated. 2,740 people migrated from Llanelli. The industry had recovered by 1898, with the consequence that 1,722 moved into the town in the period 1901–11. In contrast, the parish of Llandybïe, as a result of the continued expansion of anthracite mining, experienced gains in each of the decades 1881–91, 1891–1901, and 1901–11 of 471, 1,385 and 595 respectively. It is worth noting that Llandybïe experienced its highest gain by migration during the decade of greatest expansion in mining in the 1890s, but that both it and Llanelli gained substantially through immigration in 1901–11. This was the period when the south Wales coalfield was second only to the United States as a centre for migration. During this remarkable decade, the economic pulse of Carmarthenshire, Glamorgan and Monmouth beat to the rhythm of the Atlantic economy. For the first time Wales became a net importer of people. In Carmarthenshire, the loss between 1881–91 of 7,870 people, and between 1891–1901 of 8,588 people, was largely nullified through the immigration of 10,664 people in 1901–11.[8] Although the figures are not available for inter-parish migration during this period, it is probable that much of the influx into the industrial areas came from the rural parishes of Carmarthenshire. It is this movement of population within the county and not from the county that accounts for the fact that 70.9 per cent of the people born in Carmarthenshire still lived in the county in 1891, and that 84.0 per cent of those born in the county continued to live within its borders in 1901.[9] These factors, as we shall see, had important effects for the maintenance of the Welsh language in the county.

Thus the strong Welsh character of Carmarthenshire was preserved throughout the period 1871 and 1921 perhaps confirming Brinley Thomas' argument that industrialization, at least in its formative stages, was not detrimental to the Welsh language. In the linguistic census of 1891, 112,947 of Carmarthenshire's population of 126,166 were returned as Welsh speaking. Of these 44,901 were monoglots speaking only the rich Carmarthenshire dialect. In 1891 the number of people in Carmarthenshire who could speak English stood at 81,064, of whom only 12,018 were monoglot English speakers.[10] When he mapped the geographic distribution of the Welsh language across the country in 1901, J. E. Southall noted that only '5,499 or 4 per cent are foreign born' and that throughout the county '90 per cent of the population are able to speak the National language'. In Newcastle Emlyn the figure was as high as 99 per cent.[11] This should not blind us to the fact that powerful forces were at work to the long-term detriment of the Welsh language. Anglicized influences were particularly strong in the administrative, commercial, industrial and market centres of Carmarthenshire. The number of English speakers had risen significantly in the town of Llanelli. Throughout Carmarthenshire cultural, economic, educational and technological changes led to a marked reduction in the number of monoglot Welsh speakers. Thus an increased bilingualism was the major linguistic characteristic of Carmarthenshire by the second decade of the twentieth century. These influences permeated into rural Carmarthenshire. In Llandeilo, for example, the social pretence and the refined, gentle graces of the town's tone was in sharp contrast to the 'mountain manners' of the surrounding countryside.

There is an additional sexual dimension to the demographic history of Carmarthenshire which should be noted in passing.

Though it has been described, like war, as a 'total' social experience, industrialization, initially at least, was a process that overwhelmingly involved men. Men were the first to move to the industrial centres of Carmarthenshire spawned by the development of tinplate mills and collieries. Wives and families usually followed. This process created an imbalance in the distribution of men and women across Carmarthenshire. An analysis of fourteen parishes reveals that, while in the rural parishes there was a ratio over the period 1887–1921 of 870 men for every 1,000 women,[12] in the industrial parishes of the south-east there was a ratio during the same period of 1,023 men for every 1,000 women. It is noticeable that in some rural communities, for example Llandyfeisant, the ratio was 767 men to every 1,000 women, perhaps confirming that the men were the people primarily drawn out of the rural areas by the lure of industry. The male-dominated character of coalmining communities is also noticeable in the mining parishes of Llan-non, Llandybïe, Betws and Cwarter Bach. In 1911 there were 1,223 men for every 1,000 women in Llan-non, 1,134 in Betws, 1,202 in Llandybïe and 1,120 in Cwarter Bach.[13] This reflects the fact that productivity in Welsh mining was dependent upon the number of miners employed. In the period between 1902 and 1911 the number of coal miners working in the Aman Valley increased from 2,874 to 4,862.[14] The lower ratios in Pen-bre of 982 men per 1,000 women, and Llanelli at 1,008 men per 1,000 women, indicate that employment opportunities were available to women in these areas in the tinplate trade and services retail trades.[15]

The redistribution of population within Carmarthenshire consequent upon rapid industrialization from the 1880s created a new dynamism in the urban life of the county. The most obvious manifestation of this was the creation of centres of population in the south-eastern parts of the country in an arc stretching from Burry Port to Ammanford and the Aman Valley following the old carboniferous limestone outcrop which bordered the rich veins of anthracite. The influx of people into the south-eastern parishes of Carmarthenshire created new communities which were permeated with a sense of innovation and excitement. In 1892, a writer in the *Llanelly Mercury* described Tumble as 'a miniature Rhondda valley' and noted the animation and activity in the town after 600 men arrived to work the Stanllyd vein:

> The old order of things had given way to the new and where the peace and quietude attendant upon country life had predominated before, prosperity, progress and enterprise were the ruling power now.[16]

In 1860 the small hamlet of Cross Inn was described as a pleasantly situated village in the valley of the Amman.[17] By 1899 this hamlet had been transformed into the brash and bustling town of Ammanford. 'Veritas' in a 'prize essay' described how 'The place seemed as if awakening from an unconscious slumber and to shake off the drowsiness which had over hung it for several years'.[18]

Though contemporaries were struck by the rapid transformation of rural to urban communities, the pace of development was not as breakneck as experienced further east in Glamorgan. These new communities rapidly developed the basic retail infrastructure which underpins urban life. The histories of the villages of Llandybïe and Pen-y-groes are illustrative of the wider trends at work in the urbanizing process in Carmarthenshire. The village of Llandybïe down to the 1890s had been a small grouping of houses and two pubs centred round the parish church.[19] Following the establishment of three collieries in the locality of the village it expanded rapidly into an active community. At Pen-y-groes, before the opening of the Emlyn and Caerbryn collieries, there had been only some scattered farms and a few thatched cottages. By 1893 both Llandybïe and Pen-y-groes had developed into significant colliery towns typical of those which developed in the anthracite coalfield. The domestic needs of the inhabitants were well served by the wide variety of retail outlets which developed. *Kelly's Directory* of 1920 noted that the population of 5,607 in 1911 was served by twenty-four shopkeepers, ten tailors/drapers, six confectioners, four builders, a bazaar, eleven publicans, twenty-one grocers, a refreshment room, two cycle agents, three butchers, two water millers, six boot and shoe makers, a flannel agent, an insurance agent, a fried fish dealer, a photographer, a fruiterer, two tobacconists, three fishmongers, a watch repairer, a tool handle maker, a surveyor, an auctioneer, two ironmongers, a bookseller, a stationers, a hairdresser, an electrical engineer, an electricity supply company, a blacksmith, a butter merchant, a painter, and a stone and marble mason.[20] The medicinal requirements of the two villages were met by two doctors, a chemist and three resident midwives. Only seventeen women were named in the list of 133 commercial enterprises presented in the *Directory*. Three of these, unsurprisingly perhaps, were midwives, the remainder were engaged in shopkeeping, confectionery, drapery and flannel sales whilst one ventured into the supposedly all-male domain of public house keeping.

The harsh domestic, social and urban problems which blighted the industrial communities of Glamorgan were not as intense in eastern Carmarthenshire. Nevertheless, these new communities came increasingly to resent what they regarded as the disregard of the basic requirements of civilized life by the existing structure of local government. The same pungent whiff of sewage which fuelled the mid-nineteenth century drive for urban powers to counter insanitary conditions can be seen to be at work in the local politics of the new coalmining communities of eastern Carmarthenshire. Ammanford, Cwmaman and Burry Port moved quickly towards the establishment of urban sanitary and local authority powers so that the grievances which people perceived in their town could be addressed and remedied.[21]

In 1902 Carmarthenshire County Council finally agreed to the demands of the inhabitants of Ammanford that the town be granted urban powers because of the failure of the Llandeilo Rural District Council to provide a water supply and adequate lighting.[22] Two weeks later, the council granted Burry Port urban powers after disclosures that Llanelli Rural District Council had failed to provide decent water and sanitary facilities.[23] Tied in with these demands for the provision of the basics of dignified human life were the hopes and ambitions of the people for their community. In August 1900 Tom Wilkins of The Bungalow, Burry Port, had expressed concern that, although the medical officer of health had shown a link between the high incidence of disease in the area, the council had resolved to do nothing, and had ignominiously failed in its duty towards Burry Port. He lamented that 'If Burry Port only had urban powers, it would become in a very short time, a second Naples. Llandrindod and other such places of less size than Burry Port which have urban powers, would in my opinion, not be in it'.[24]

The sense of grievance people harboured at the inability of the existing local authority structure to deal with their needs ushered in a new force into the political life of Carmarthenshire. By the end of the First World War there had been a significant shift away from Liberal allegiance to the new Labour movement in almost all of the industrial communities of eastern Carmarthenshire.

In contrast to the thriving optimism of these new communities the old market and administrative centres of Carmarthenshire appeared almost moribund. Places like Llandeilo, Llandovery, Llanybydder and Newcastle Emlyn owed their status in the urban pattern of south-west Wales to their central locations for road and rail transport, their administrative and educational functions, and their commercial services.[25] Many observers reported that these towns only came to life on market and fair days when their quietude was shattered by the noise and activity of rural commerce. At Llandovery, for example, the weekly market was held on Friday while there were separate, monthly, fairs for the sale of horses, cattle, sheep and pigs. Throughout the remainder of the week these communities retreated into a rural peace of almost Arcadian simplicity.

The new dynamism which industrialization created in the urban history of Carmarthenshire in the period 1870–1914 caused profound tensions in the always strained relationship between the county's largest towns, Carmarthen and Llanelli. They had always been bitter rivals but by the turn of the twentieth century the dislike had been transformed into deep mutual aversion and hatred.[26] By 1920 it was clear that Carmarthen and Llanelli were not only different in history and topography; they were also profoundly different in personality and character. Yoked together in an uneasy alliance in a parliamentary constituency, their mutual jealousies and animosities were expressed at every opportunity in the local press and on every conceivable public occasion. At times the relationships between the two resembled that of a family being torn asunder by intergenerational tensions – Carmarthen, the slightly doddery, elderly figure whose gnarled hands held the purse strings; Llanelli an overgrown, muscular youth impatient to grasp the inheritance.

In 1897 the Llanelli paper the *South Wales Press* noted with the disdainful scorn which characterized all its discussions of its hated neighbour, that 'all the primitive inhabitants (of Carmarthen) can ever hope to boast of is its past'.[27] In many respects there was considerable truth in the spiteful aside. Between 1831 and 1921 the population of the town had increased by only 56 people, from

9,955 to 10,011. The town thus retained much of its early character.[28] In 1920 it still extended for about a mile and a half along the slope of Penlan Hill, on the northern bank of the Towy. The houses were irregularly built and converged towards the castle. The views from the town across the Towy Valley were striking, particularly so from the Parade, an area much resorted to by visitors and townspeople because of the salubrity of the air and the beautiful shaded walk. Coracles were still seen on the river and, provided the spring tides were sufficiently high, vessels of 300 tons could sail upriver to offload at the town's quay. Woollen weaving, rope-making and ironfounding on a substantially reduced scale were the major trades undertaken by the town at the end of the First World War. Carmarthen's major function however was as an administrative, educational and commercial centre for the surrounding agricultural districts. Within the town's boundaries there were the South Wales and Monmouthshire Training College, the Presbyterian College, a grammar school, the County Girls' School, the Carmarthen High School for Girls, a school of art and six primary schools. The town was the centre for the assizes, the quarter and petty sessions, a rural and urban district council, the Poor Law union, a prison, a hospital and the Joint Counties Mental Hospital. Along the streets in the town's centre around Nott Square a plethora of over 300 retailers provided the commercial requirements of the town and hinterland. Though some noted that the market was well run, others were more scathing. One correspondent in the *Carmarthen Weekly Reporter* described the typical scene on market day in September 1897:

> 'Blackberry Fair' was held in the streets last week, and anybody . . . would see in it an exhibition of barbarism which would be more in place in Matebeleland than in Wales. Horses, cattle, and men bellowing, neighing, shrieking, and tearing at each other, elbowing, kicking, hustling, jostling and goring each other . . . Windows get smashed and the citizens are made to clear off the footpaths at the bidding of any brute driving half-a-dozen horned animals which show more signs of rudimentary intellect than he does himself. St Peter's Church stands on an island surrounded by a green sea, ankle deep in green foul smelling manure . . .?[29]

The activities described are clearly distasteful to the writer's refined sensitivities. This is illustrative of the duality which was present in the town's character. A sense of deep civic pride was displayed by the town when the Carmarthen Improvement Act was passed by Parliament in 1896. But the most notable and persistent trait which is discernible in the town's municipal history in the period from 1890 to the First World War is that of corruption. Local elections were often the occasion for bacchanalian excesses when candidates would purchase drinks for prospective voters in the low, lewd and loud public houses along Priory Street. In 1892 the editor of the *Carmarthen Journal* noted that:

> Carmarthen in the days of Town Council elections is a regular pandemonium and is a disgrace to civilisation. Corruption and bribery reign supreme, and are practiced openly and defiantly in their worst and most degrading forms. . . . Total abstainers when they stand appear to pour forth on these occasions all the drink they have saved for years past by their own abstentioness.[30]

The municipal corruption extended to the parliamentary level. The 1895 general election in the Borough seat was described as 'the drunken election' with 'free booze all round for all and sundry' by the *South Wales Press*.[31] Amidst uproar in October 1898, Gwilym Evans, probably the most famous chemist in nineteenth-century Wales, the creator of quinine bitters whose efficacious qualities were proclaimed in every newspaper, resigned as a parliamentary candidate. The reason he gave was that he could no longer afford to meet the financial favours people expected from a candidate.[32]

In comparison with the stagnant demographic experience of Carmarthen, that of Llanelli was positively explosive. Between 1831 and 1921 the population of the town had increased from 4,173 to 36,520. In contrast to the bucolic splendours of the views over the Towy Valley which Carmarthen enjoyed, Llanelli was permeated by the grey, billowing smoke and the night and day rattle of its industrial enterprises. By 1920 the town was home to steel, chemical, brick, tile and earthenware works, steam sawmills, two breweries and several foundries. But the town's major activities were coalmining and the production of tinplate which gave the town its proud title of 'Tinopolis'.[33] Thus Llanelli developed as an significant port but, because of natural restrictions in the harbour, it never attained the status which it so passionately aspired to. In 1913, 1,136 vessels of a total tonnage of 403,338 tons visited the port exporting coal, tinplate and galvanized sheets valued at over £128,602 and bringing in pig and scrap iron, timber and copper valued at £203,508.[34] These disparate activities provided considerable contrasts in the character of various sections of the towns. The seaside area around the four docks was, compared to the rest of the town, a cosmopolitan area home to sailors and mariners of several nationalities and the vice consuls of France and Spain. Further north the internal stratifications and divisions of tinplate workers and coalminers were exemplified in the subtle differences in the type and quality of houses – terraced, semi-detached and bay-windowed.

Llanelli, like Carmarthen, had administrative, educational and cultural functions to perform for its inhabitants. Of these the major function was to serve as a commercial and retail centre. In 1917 the Borough Shops Inspector reported that 1,063 premises were registered with the Borough Council.[35] This 'shopocracy', together with over four hundred residents of private means, created a significant middle class in the town which provided an active civic leadership. They were prominent in the establishment in 1894 of an urban district council and in its replacement in 1913 by a charter which established a corporation for the government of the town. Thus, much to the chagrin of the newspapers of Carmarthen, Llanelli seemed to prosper; its civic pride evidenced in its new Town Hall erected in 1894 in a 'free Classic style' and in its own *Who's Who* of 1910. Llanelli's reputation appears to have been less tarnished with the taint of corruption than Carmarthen's.[36] Each success of the sons and daughters of Llanelli was eagerly and gleefully reported in the pages of the local press. On one notable occasion, large crowds gathered to welcome the bard Elfed back to Llanelli following his victory at the 1894 National Eisteddfod.[37] The position of the town, at least in the inhabitants' eyes, was unassailable. As the *South Wales Press* noted on May 2 1895, Llanelli was home to 'A Queen's shooting prize winner, a world champion quoiter, a tiptop football team, a brass band that beats creation, and the finest choir in the world . . . Floreat Llanelli.'[38]

But others, particularly Carmarthen people, were less inclined to marvel at Llanelli's achievements. The *Carmarthen Weekly Reporter* noted in 1899 that the Assizes had visited the 'region of the swelled head':

> To gratify the morbid vanity of the place, they actually expect the Grand Jurors and everybody else attending the Assizes . . . to be compelled to come not to a central place like Carmarthen – but to an out of the way place on the Glamorganshire borders, which is just as convenient for county business as would be Cynghordy or Pencader, or Pontarddulais or Whitland. Because Judge Brace accepted the High Sheriff's invitation to look over the new Llanelli Town Hall, the simple folks of Llanelli think that all this is going to come about. Such child-like faith is very touching on the verge of the twentieth century.[39]

Elsewhere within Carmarthenshire the tensions which existed between rural and urban communities do not seem to have been as severe or virulent as the rivalry which existed between Carmarthen and Llanelli. Carmarthenshire's contrasting communities existed alongside each other in a complex symbiotic relationship. The lights and the noise of industry were the magnets which drew people out of the old rural darkness. As Enoch Rees, the historian of one of the towns located on the frontier between rural and urban Wales, Brynaman, remarked 'Aeth goleuni tân y gweithfeydd fel toriad dydd dros y bryniau i ddefro gwyr Gwynfe i groesi'r mynydd.'[40]

At the turn of the twentieth century it was clear that people believed in the bright lights, in the promise of a better future in the world of work which the light held out to them.

2. *The World of Work*

The sanctity of work was one of the central tenets of Victorian society. Work provided status and prestige, it endowed some people with respectability, reinforced the Victorian obsession with separate spheres for different aspects of life and provided society with an ethos which stressed diligence, discipline and order. But above all work secured, at its most basic level, the means for people to achieve a living.[41] The condition of the county's economy was thus of central importance to the inhabitants of Carmarthenshire. At the turn of the twentieth century Carmarthenshire's economy presented a mirror image of the startling contrasts which existed within the wider Welsh economy. The economic optimism of the industrial areas was in stark contrast to the disenchantment and depression which seemed to pervade rural Carmarthenshire.

In the period after 1870 Carmarthenshire experienced dramatic industrial expansion based primarily upon two industries: the manufacture of tinplate and the mining of coal. Local supplies of coal, limestone, sulphuric acid and water together with a number of convenient ports for the import of iron ore and tin, and of course for the export of finished goods, gave south-west Wales a distinct advantage as a centre for the manufacture of tinplate. These natural advantages were supplemented in the 1870s by a further set of fortuitous circumstances. The iron industry in south-east Wales was too heavily involved in the production of rails to even consider producing a second product, whilst the exhaustion of home supplies of iron ore necessitated a move away from the historic inland centres of iron production towards the coastal towns. The decline of the traditional charcoal, iron and copper industries in south west Wales provided a pool of skilled and experienced labour with no competing industry. Thus when, in 1875, Siemens developed a process to produce good quality steel for tinplate manufacture at the Landore Steel Works in Swansea, the scene was set for the concentration of the tinplate industry in south-west Wales.[42]

Pre-eminent amongst the towns which thrived in tinplate production was Llanelli. By 1851 the Dafen and Morfa works were in full production, and were joined by the Western Works in 1863, the Old Castle in 1867, the Burry Works in 1875 and the Old Lodge Works in 1880. By 1880 there were six tinplate works in operation in Llanelli, and the town, to confirm its position as the capital of the industry, christened itself 'Tinopolis'.[43] In 1880 forty-one of the works in south Wales were west of Port Talbot and only twenty-three were to the east. By 1890, new tinplate works had been founded in Brynaman, Glanaman, Pontarddulais, Pantyffynnon, the Gwendraeth Valley, Burry Port, Bynea, Ammanford, Llangennech and Hendy.[44] Many of these areas, lacking the range of industries which Llanelli possessed, were in effect one-industry towns, their retailers and service industries being dependent upon the fortunes of tinplate manufacturing.

The industry was dependent upon the export market, with 76.4 per cent of British production being exported in 1891. Only 138,000 tons of the total production of 586,000 was used in the domestic market. Most of the tinplate produced was shipped to the United States, where the agricultural products of the Midwest and the oil industry required a durable, cheap and disposable container.[45] By 1891, of a total of 448,000 tons of tinplate exported, the United States received 72.5 per cent.[46] Dependency on the export market made tinplate production vulnerable to fluctuations in the trade cycle. Periodically, these fluctuations in trade wreaked havoc in the tinplate communities of south-west Wales. It is important to remember that the industrial experience of Carmarthenshire is not a picture of uninterrupted development. Periods of acute depression and suffering punctuated those of advance and prosperity. The imposition of the McKinley Tariff by the American Congress, restricting the importation of foreign tinplate, led to a severe depression in the industry in south-west Wales. With the loss of the American market, several small works suspended production, while others closed.[47] With a general upturn in economic activity in the late 1890s, the industry only gradually began to recover. Recovery was assisted by an increase in the range of foods requiring canning abroad – salmon in Canada and the United States, beef in North and South America, mutton and fruit in Australia, fruits, oysters and lobsters in the United States, sardines and peas and other vegetables in France, Spain, Italy and Portugal, pineapple in Mauritius and Singapore, and milk in Switzerland. Though several of these countries had their own tinplate industries, their domestic productivity was unable to meet demand. The development of the petroleum industry added substantially to the demand for tinplate. At the turn of the twentieth century the increased foreign demand coincided with a substantial rise in the British need for domestic and dairying utensils. This situation produced rapid developments in the Carmarthenshire tinplate industry. Seven new works were established in the Llanelli district in the period 1897–1913.[48] This period also witnessed the supremacy in the tinplate industry of Richard Thomas and Co. By 1911, the South Wales Steel and Tinstamping Works had ten tinplate works under its control, and in that year added a further eight mills to its capacity.[49] Such large capitalistic groupings were, however, exceptional. The majority of the tinplate industry was undertaken in relatively small-scale factories where the relationship between capital and labour was generally good.

The late nineteenth century was also a flourishing period for the county's other principal industry, coalmining. The Royal

Commission on Coal of 1919 was informed that the export of anthracite commenced in 1884, when Mr Frederick Cleeves visited France and Germany, and Mr Andrews, the President of the Swansea Chamber of Commerce, visited Sweden. Their mission was to distribute free samples of newly-graded anthracite coal in order to prove its superiority over other coals.[50] Whether because of their inspiring missionary work, or because of the pure quality of their samples, the effect on the anthracite industry was spectacular. In 1886 Swansea exported 740,000 tons of anthracite and Llanelli 80,000 tons. By 1890 Swansea was exporting over one million tons of anthracite and Llanelli 195,000.[51] The principal markets of Llanelli were France, Germany, Sweden, Holland and the Channel Islands, with lesser amounts being exported to Denmark, Spain, Portugal, Norway, Russia and Italy.[52] Between 1904 and 1911 Llanelli exported over 1.2 million tons of anthracite, while Swansea exported over 13.3 million tons.[53] As with the tinplate industry, over-reliance on the export market would prove damaging in the future but in the buoyant years of the late 1880s the industry's thoughts were purely on expansion.[54]

In view of the demand, the production of anthracite in south Wales increased rapidly, rising from 1.5 million tons in 1896 to 2.2 million tons in 1900, 3 million tons in 1906, 3.5 million tons in 1907, and to over 4 million tons in 1910.[55] From 1905 south Wales was responsible for over 90 per cent of the United Kingdom's annual production of anthracite. During this period almost half of the south Wales anthracite coal was mined in Carmarthenshire.[56]

Though bituminous coal continued to be mined in the area around Llanelli, it was the inland anthracite areas which experienced rapid developments. In the last decade of the nineteenth century and the first decade of the twentieth, new collieries were established annually in an arc stretching from Pontyberem, Tumble, Cross Hands, Pen-y-groes, Llandybïe, Betws, Pantyffynnon and Ammanford, Garnant, Glanaman, Brynaman and into Gwauncaegurwen and the upper Swansea Valley. The development of coalmining transformed the landscape of eastern Carmarthenshire. Pit-head winding gear dominated the architecture of these towns and the dismal spoil heaps squatting like black pyramids dominated the horizon. 'Gwlad y Piramidau'

– 'The land of the pyramids' – was the colloquial description of the area.[57] The mining towns, like the new tinplate towns, were essentially one-industry towns, with their prosperity dependent upon the fortunes of coal. The number of collieries in the Carmarthenshire anthracite district doubled from twenty-two in 1888 to forty-four in 1913.[58] The number of miners employed in the Gwendraeth Valley almost doubled in the decade between 1896 and 1905 and almost doubled again in the five years between 1905 and 1910. This area, comprising pits such as California and Pontyberem in the Gwendraeth Valley and the Great Mountain, New Cross Hands and Emlyn Nos. 1 and 2 on the summit of the Great Mountain, which were sunk in the 1890s, was the foremost mining area in the Carmarthenshire anthracite field by 1910. It was closely rivalled by the upper Aman Valley, where the number of miners employed doubled between 1896 and 1905 and almost doubled again by 1920.[59] In the two decades between 1896 and 1915 employment in collieries in the Gwendraeth Valley increased by over 190 per cent, in the lower Aman Valley by over 72 per cent, and in the upper Aman Valley by 135 per cent. In the same period, growth in employment in the steam coal areas around Llanelli was virtually static at 3 per cent per annum.[60]

Because of the geological difficulties and the sharp faulting in the region, pits were small in comparison with those of the steam coal industry of eastern Wales. But despite the difficulties, the trend was towards the concentration of companies into larger sized capitalistic groupings through takeovers and expansion. Between 1888 and 1913, collieries which employed fewer than a hundred miners declined from 73 per cent of the pits in Carmarthenshire to 29 per cent in 1913.[61]

The growth in tinplate manufacture and coal mining led to an increase in the activity of Carmarthenshire's ports. In 1914 Burry Port was exporting over 7,000 tons of coal and over 400 tons of tinplate and other local products a month.[62] To facilitate trade, improvements were made – 5,000 tons of mud were dredged from the East Dock, a new engine house was erected and new dock gates installed at a cost of £1,936.[63] But the most dramatic increases occurred in Llanelli. By 1913 Llanelli was exporting 68,849 tons of tinplate and 211,106 tons of coal in its total of 320,944 tons of exported goods.[64] In order to cater for the increase in exports in the 1890s, a New Dock was constructed and opened on 23 December 1903, with a capacity to handle an additional 40,000 tons of coal for export per annum.[65] Over a thousand ships carried the coal, testifying to the fact that local shipping was flourishing. However, despite the industrial development of its hinterland, Llanelli, unlike Swansea, never came to rank as one of the major ports in south Wales. This was due to a number of historic and geographical factors. Firstly, Llanelli was never suited by location to be a major port. In the early nineteenth century, Isambard Kingdom Brunel had declared that 'Nature has not done much to fit Llanelli for a port'.[66] And what nature had not provided could not, for once, be created, even by the ingenuity of the nineteenth-century ironmasters and coalowners. The problem was compounded by the failure of engineers to site the docks so that the River Lliedi could achieve an effective scouring action. With shifting sands in the harbour and the treacherous Cefn Sidan sands outside in the estuary, large ships were well advised to sail clear of Llanelli. The difficulties of the Llanelli docks persuaded industrialists to export their coal from Swansea. In this they were assisted by the rail network, which, with the linking of the Aman Valley to Pontardawe by rail, enabled collieries in the Great Mountain region to send their coal to Swansea.[67] It is noteworthy that out of the eighteen collieries in the Great Mountain and lower Aman Valleys, named by the Llanelli Harbour Commissioners to the House of Lords as possible users of the proposed new Llanelli dock, only two pits – Pen-coed and Great Mountain – actually chose to export their coal through Llanelli.[68] Swansea had captured Llanelli's hinterland and without it Llanelli would never achieve the greatness as a port to which the town's people so ardently, passionately and naïvely aspired.

To serve the tinplate and coal industries, a number of smaller industries were established, providing specialist equipment, goods, and general services. Small companies fringed the tinplate and iron and steel works to supply castings and moulds and other engineering needs. From 1887, the produce of the Nobel explosives factory at Pen-bre helped to give credibility to Britain's expansionist foreign policy. The Boer War and the First World War and the petty skirmishes of Empire provided a continuing and growing demand for its grim products.[69] Stimulated by the growth in population, the building and construction industry, served by several brickworks, also expanded rapidly.

Population growth and industrial activity also promoted the development of the service industries of gas, electricity and transport. Having received parliamentary authority in 1882 to supply electricty to the town, the Llanelly and District Electric Lighting and Traction Co. Ltd. had expanded by 1914 to offer an extensive tramcar service over 7.5 miles in Llanelli.[70] In 1886, the historian of Llanelli, James Lane Bowen, noted how the 'tramways have annihilated the distance between New Dock and the town'.[71] By 1914, Burry Port and its satellites were included in the route. Catching the last tram home on a wet Saturday night from Vent's Picture Palace became part of the modern folklore of the town. The advent of the motor car, and, in particular, motor omnibuses, proved more efficient at eroding the friction of space than had railways or trams.[72] Garages were established throughout the county, offering services from the sale of petrol to the hiring of a charabanc for Sunday school outings. The growth in population caused a phenomenal increase in the demand for food and drink. The produce of Buckley and Felinfoel breweries quenched the thirst of the adult population, while Corona and a host of smaller aerated water producers served younger and more temperate palates. Retailing, as we have seen, also expanded rapidly. By March 1914 there were over a thousand shops in Llanelli, ranging from the hold-all emporia and bazaars to more specialized wholesalers, and the 'friend of the poor', the pawnbroker.[73] Similar service industries developed in other leading towns such as Ammanford, Carmarthen and Llandeilo, each concern tailoring its specialities to the needs of the local population and the staple industries.

It would be easy to portray Carmarthenshire as comprising two very different communities. In the east was industrial Carmarthenshire, thriving, advancing economically, and buoyant with the optimism of Edwardian south Wales, while in the west was rural Carmarthenshire in almost medieval simplicity. As one prejudiced contributor to the *Carmarthen Journal* wrote in 1888, 'Carmarthen is a dead-alive place which can boast little or nothing of commercial life . . . Wild Wales is a hundred years behind the times.'[74]

But such views are misleading. Every society in every age experiences change. The level and intensity of that change, of course, varies, but no society remains totally static. Carmarthenshire's industrial and agricultural communities were symbiotically tied to each other. Indeed, in the heart of rural west Wales there was real industrial activity. For example, communities of miners mined high quality anthracite in the area around Saundersfoot.[75] But, as we have already noted, the interaction between the rural and urban communities is clearly seen in the fortunes of the county's oldest staple industry, woollen manufacturing.[76]

The period after 1870 saw revolutionary changes in woollen manufacturing. The loss and dislocation of the markets which had enabled mid Wales to dominate the industry, together with changes in technology, led to the shift of the industry to the Teify Valley and, in particular, to an area around Dre-fach Felindre, Pentre-cwrt, Henllan and Llandysul. So rapid was the growth that the historian of Llangeler and Penboyr noted in the 1890s:

> Nid oes yn awr o bosibl ddau blwyf yng Nghymru yn troi allan gymaint o wlaneni Cymreig a'r plwyfi hyn . . . Mae yma fwy o wehyddion nag erioed, a'r rhan fwyaf ohonynt mewn cyflawn waith. Mae bron holl nerth gallofyddol ei nentydd a'u hafonydd wedi eu ffrwyno i yru peiriannau ynglŷn â'r gelfyddyd. Nid oes braidd ysmotyn ar lan afon ynddynt lle y gellir yn gyfleus i osod ffatri na melin ychwanegol.[77]

The introduction of power machinery in the 1860s laid the foundation of the industry's prosperity for sixty years. Skilled and sophisticated labour migrated to the area from mid Wales, providing the necessary experience to develop the industry on more commercial lines. The development of a rail network was also instrumental in the expansion. The railway from Carmarthen to Lampeter was completed in 1864, and by 1895 a new line had been completed between Pencader and Newcastle Emlyn.[78]

Behind the success of the factories of Alltcafan and Derw at Pentre-cwrt, and the other large mills which often employed over a hundred people, was the traditional and conservative demand of Welsh colliers, many the sons of rural Wales, for the underwear and woollen shirts produced in the Teifi Valley.[79] Though often portrayed as unimaginative people, the woollen manufacturers were in fact highly innovative. Advised by experts from the University College of Wales at Aberystwyth, the mill owners experimented with new dyes in an attempt to extend their range of products.[80] Large mills had marketing agents who visited the main centres of south Wales to sell their products. The expansion of coalmining in south Wales in the period up to 1914 meant that growth was rapid and that the Teifi Valley boomed. Indeed, the First World War added substantially to the prosperity of the area as large government orders for uniforms were placed with the local mills.[81] The over-dependence on industrial south Wales was tragically shown in the 1920s when, as a result of the south Wales miners' strikes of 1921 and 1926, the demand for the industry's produce disappeared. The implications of 'Black Friday' reverberated throughout the Teifi Valley and rural west Wales also had cause to remember 1926.[82] Twenty-one factories were closed, never to reopen, whilst others, unable to compete in a fashion market of savage fickleness, were pulled into a spiral of decline.

Hard times were not new to rural Carmarthenshire. It was an endemic trait of farmers to voice concern at the hard, unprofitable life which went with working on the land. Revisionist historians have questioned the severity, even the existence of a depression in late nineteenth-century agriculture. Some have argued that political motives led to an exaggeration of the problems which confronted Welsh agriculture.[83] Whatever the merits of these bitterly conflicting views, the characteristics of agriculture in Carmarthenshire are clear and it is apparent that agriculture experienced profound changes between the 1880s and the outbreak of the First World War.

Agriculture in Carmarthenshire was predominantly pastoral. In 1887, out of a total farming area of around 470,000 acres, 31,000 was given over to rough pasture, whilst 442,000 acres was cultivated land. Of this 442,000 acres, 333,000 was given to permanent grass – 261,000 for grazing and 71,300 for hay. Of the 109,400 acres of arable land, 34,100 acres was given to rotation grass and 75,131 to the main crops of wheat (9,080 acres), barley (14,994 acres), oats (38,120 acres), potatoes (4,386 acres) and turnips and swedes (5,048 acres). By 1912 the total farming area had increased to 506,500 acres and the figure devoted to rough grazing had more than doubled to 68,000 acres. Whilst the total cultivated area had declined to 438,500 acres the acreage given over to permanent grass had increased to 360,500 – 265,900 acres being used for grazing and 94,600 for hay. The acreage of arable land had decreased dramatically to 77,900 acres, of which 24,500 was given to rotation grass, and 53,397 to the main crops wheat

(6,645), barley (11,533), oats (24,900), potatoes (3,204) and turnips and swedes (3,921).[84]

The county's agriculture was geared to the raising of livestock, in particular cattle. In the thirty years between 1887 and 1917 the number of cows and heifers in milk and in calf increased from 53,222 to 56,229, and the number of other cattle increased from 61,681 to 75,530. No other Welsh county had as many cattle as Carmarthenshire. It was indeed, as Rhys Davies claimed, 'the cows' capital of Wales'.[85] The number of sheep also increased substantially from 217,322 to 299,538. The growth in the number of sheep took place against the backcloth of the abandonment of many small upland holdings. In the remote areas above Caeo, Llanfair-ar-y-bryn and Llanfihangel Rhos-y-corn, heaps of stones mark out the boundaries of what used to be homes – testimony that determination, resilience and all the ancient human virtues could not draw life out of a stone.[86]

The number of horses also increased from 19,445 to 24,989. The only animal population which declined was that of pigs, which decreased from 31,746 to 28,474.[87] The south Wales rail network profoundly influenced the type of farming adopted in parts of Carmarthenshire, particularly the Tywi Valley.[88] The growth and expansion of coalmining in south-east Wales, and the consequent rise in population, led to an increased demand for meat, butter, cheese and milk, a demand which could not be met by local agriculture.[89] The opening of the railway in 1853 provided Carmarthenshire dairy produce with a buoyant market in the industrial regions. Such was the high quality of this produce that it was claimed that Carmarthenshire produce was advertised as such by leading London retailers.[90] Not only did Carmarthenshire butter have geographical advantages over the butter of other countries, customers actually preferred it. Colliers, many of them from Carmarthenshire, were said to appreciate the saltier taste of Carmarthen butter.[91] The growth in the acreage devoted to hay suggests that Carmarthenshire farmers, in addition to keeping greater numbers of milk cows, were also fattening cattle at home rather than exporting them elsewhere, as had been the case in the past.

This livestock was spread across a system of farming which was remarkable for the large number of smallholdings which operated within it. In common with Cardiganshire and the other counties of south and mid Wales, where the tradition of *gavelkind* had operated, the county was dominated by smallholdings.[92] The 'Second Domesday Book' of 1873, though its verdicts were not as reliable as the first,[93] revealed that two peers and thirteen 'great landowners' owned 175,575 acres of land in Carmarthenshire. Fifty 'squires' owned 85,000 acres, and 695 'greater and lesser' men owned 183,000 acres. Thus, over 83 per cent of the land of Carmarthenshire was owned by 760 individuals. In contrast to these were the 2,093 'small properties' and 'cottagers', 7,261 individuals who owned 64,975 acres, representing only 12.3 per cent of Carmarthenshire land.[94]

The estates of the peers and the great landowners were units of ownership and management, not of agricultural production. Land beyond the home farms and demesne was let to tenant farmers. Thus the number of people involved in the farming of land was far greater than the number who owned land.[95] In the 1920s the smallholding continued to be a notable feature of agriculture in Carmarthenshire.[96] An analysis of all the parish rate books showed that there were, in 1923, 7,121 individuals holding land in Carmarthenshire. Of the 7,121 individual holdings, 4,087 (or 57.4 per cent) were under 50 acres in size, and of these 44.4 per cent were owned or mainly owned by the occupiers, while 55.6 per cent were rented or mainly rented.[97]

These factors gave rise to particular forms of farm and community organization and practice. The occupation of small-holdings frequently meant that farmers had to supplement their income from other means. Of the 4,087 holdings under 50 acres in 1923, 1,905 occupiers had employment outside agriculture. The vast majority were coalminers or general labourers, but there were also significant numbers of carpenters, road labourers and publicans.[98] It can be seen, therefore, as one historian has concluded 'that this area demonstrates the principle that the development of coalfields and their industries does encourage and afterwards fosters the small holding as an unit of the landscape.'[99]

In the pre-omnibus age, farmer colliers would 'tramp' to the local collieries and return at the weekend to their smallholding. When work was not available at local collieries, they would journey, often on foot, to the Rhondda and 'the coal mountains' for employment, returning home for the harvest.[100]

The pattern of land ownership gave rise to one of the dominant features of Welsh agriculture. This was the participation of the whole community in farm work at certain times of the year, most notably harvest times.[101] The farms of Carmarthenshire were not self-contained or self-sufficient units. Smallholders had to rely on the larger farms for the essential services of bulls and stallions, animals which were too expensive for smallholders to maintain. In return for these services, larger farmers were reliant upon cottagers and smallholders for their labour at harvest time.

The operation of this system of interdependence at harvest times can be seen in the 200-acre farm of Henry Jones-Davies, chairman of the Carmarthenshire County Council.[102] Although the main activity of the farm was dairying, a proportion of the total acreage was given over to corn, hay, wheat, and oats. David Jenkins, in his classic study of the rural community of south-west Wales, has estimated that, using a scythe, a worker would take one day to cut an acre of corn.[103] Thus the farmer required a number of days of labour identical to the acreage under corn in order to harvest his crop. Corn cut by scythe lay on the ground in swathes and had to be bound into sheaves by hand. Wheat was bound by a woman following the scythesman and making the 'bindings' for securing each sheaf out of the straw as she went along. Thus as many days of labour were required to bind the wheat into sheaves as were required to cut it. Thistles, though lending a romantic purple hue to the harvest fields, cut the hands of the binders, so that the time taken to bind the crop depended upon the presence or absence of thistles. Again the historian of Welsh agricultural practice, David Jenkins, estimates that to cut and bind the crop of a 220-acre farm took some seventy to seventy-five working days. In addition, twenty to twenty-five working days were required to stack the crop. David Jenkins's estimation is based upon an ideal harvesting season, which in view of the vagaries of the climate of south-west Wales, were few in the 1880s and 1890s. Henry Jones-Davies recalled that 1887 was a very bad year, as were the 1900s. During such years the overabundance of rain or its paucity created difficult conditions needing more days of labour at the harvest.[104]

Henry Jones-Davies's farm employed nine workers – the first servant, second servant, two labourers, two lads and three maids, 'y forwyn fawr', 'yr ail forwyn', and 'y forwyn fach' – which was clearly insufficient to meet the demands of the harvest.[105] In order to meet these demands, farmers co-operated with each other and with smallholders and cottagers. In return for their labour, smallholders received the use of Jones-Davies's land to grow crops such as potatoes, an allocation of manure from the farm for the crops, the services of a bull or stallion in the breeding season, the loan of a horse and cart to carry coal and lime from the railway station, and many other services and produce which the cottagers and smallholders could not provide for themselves.[106]

As the historian of Llangeler and Penboyr noted, favours and services rendered by farmers to cottagers throughout the year counted towards their harvest debt:

> Talu dyled cynheua y gelwid hyn. Yr oedd y bobl gyffredin yn nyled y ffermwr dros eu pen a'u clustiau yn yr ystyr hyn. Yr oeddynt wedi cael rhai llwythi o ddom tato ac ychydig rychiau ar ei dir i osod tato ynddynt, yr oedd hefyd, wedi eu cwen eu tanwent-llwyth o gôd o'r allt ac ychydig lwythi o fate a thwarch o'r rhos, ac wedi spario berfa neu ddwy o dô i doi y tŷ. Yr oedd llawer stened o faidd ac ambell un o lathenwin wedi eu cyfranu ganddo, a mil o gymwynesau mân o bob math yn ystod y flwyddyn, ac yr oedd y cwbl yn ddyled cynheua.[107]

The services received were strictly tied to the number of days of labour which the cottagers and smallholders had provided and were expected to provide during the harvest. Around Llanybydder, for example, four days' work was owed per Winchester bushel of seed potatoes. The growth of industry did not automatically signal the end of community co-operation at the potato harvest. In the Pontarddulais area, for example, colliers set out potatoes in return for help at the hay harvest.[108] The importance of the potato crop to the agricultural community of Carmarthenshire is seen in the fact that the school October half-term is still referred to as 'wythnos dato'.[109]

It was universally acknowledged that although the lives of the cottagers and labourers of rural Wales were exceptionally hard and gruelling, those of the tenant farmers were infinitely harsher. This comes through quite clearly from the eloquent testimony presented to the Royal Commission on Land in 1896. As Nathaniel Williams told the Commissioners assembled at Llandeilo, 'No labourer would think of living or working so hard as the hill farmers do. They rise early and work late, and yet it is as much as they can do to get any sort of living.'[110] The families of the hill farmers, the wives, sons and daughters, were not spared

All members of the family had to contribute to the work on the farm (By permission of Llyfrgell Genedlaethol Cymru/The National Library of Wales)

these hardships: 'The women have a particularly hard lot, their duties being never ending and even the children have to start working at a very early age, earlier even than the children of farm labourers.'[111] Tenants, as one witness explained, were acutely aware of their predicament: 'Our present position is most deplorable and peculiar. We work hard, we live thriftly and frugally, get most of our labour done for nothing, serve very plain food and scant clothing for our children . . . We live on the charity of our landlords.'[112]

The point that produce was sold to pay the rent rather than retained for the use of the family was stressed by several witnesses:

> Cattle, sheep and dairy produce are our chief dependence to pay our rents[113]

> Farmers very seldom touch butcher's meat, but generally live on bread and cheese, potatoes, and some salted meat. They sell nearly all their cattle, butter and eggs and all the best things in order to pay the landlord. In fact they would almost prefer to die of starvation than fail to pay the landlord.[114]

Since the whole family was involved in the work of the farm it was no surprise to learn from one witness that the local farmers' 'houses – I emphasise this sentence, the houses about here are more like workshops than homes'.[115]

This perceptive comment upon the dual function of the houses of rural Carmarthenshire provides a useful reminder that the middle-class expectation that separate spheres should operate between home and work was an impossibility in the constricting realities of working-class life. It should also serve as a reminder that the most significant single occupation in Carmarthenshire was neither industry or agriculture, but the forgotten toil of housework.

3. *Property and Status*

In Victorian and Edwardian Carmarthenshire work and property were the two most important factors in determining the social status and value of individuals. The duty of men to work was almost universally accepted across all sections of Carmarthenshire society. The ability to work diligently, honestly and hard was an integral part of the contemporary description of manliness. Alongside this belief was the acceptance that the institution of property underpinned all social institutions. Brilliant authors have bravely grappled with the complex questions of social class, property and status. The fluidity of the concepts, the shifting and contradictory nature of human society, have meant that, despite their best efforts, their conclusions are often unconvincing, their results inconclusive. It is as if they have tried to lift quicksilver with a fork. This study does not intend to provide a detailed analysis of the class basis of Carmarthenshire society. Rather the intention is to provide a snapshot across different social groups to provide an illustration of the gradations which existed in Carmarthenshire society at the turn of the twentieth century.

In the nineteenth century the possession of land conferred special status and prerogatives.[116] In the words of Archdeacon Grantly from Anthony Trollope's *Barchester Chronicles*: 'Land gives so much more than rent. It gives position and influence and political power, to say nothing of the game.'[117] In Carmarthenshire, as we have seen, the ownership of land was concentrated in a few select hands. The amount of authority, prestige and power derived from land ownership varied according to the size of the estate. In differing degrees the estates which were spread throughout the county built up, during their existence, networks of debt, loyalty and animosity which were part of the fabric of rural society.[118]

Pre-eminent amongst the families of Carmarthenshire were the earl of Cawdor of Stackpole Court and Golden Grove, and Lord Dynevor of Dynevor Castle, Llandeilo.[119] Earl Cawdor, educated at Eton and Oxford, owned 33,782 acres in Carmarthenshire, valued in the early 1870s at £20,780 per annum. Cawdor was also a great landowner in Pembrokeshire, where he owned 17,735 acres valued at £14,207 and Nairn in Scotland, where he owned 46,170 acres, valued at £7,882 per annum.[120] Lord Dynevor had also been educated at Christ Church, Oxford, indicating that there was perhaps as much brains as brass in the aristocracy of Carmarthenshire. From his hilltop citadel above Llandeilo, Lord Dynevor surveyed an estate of 7,208 acres valued at £7,253. In addition, the 3,299 acres he owned in Glamorgan yielded an additional £5,000 per annum.[121] Sir James Williams-Drummond possessed 9,287 acres of land, centred on his Edwinsford home and valued at over £6,000 per annum. These magnates shared the enjoyment of the prestige and authority of major landowners with eleven other gentlemen who each owned over 3,000 acres, yielding rental income valued at over £3,000 per annum.[122] Prominent in this group was Morgan Jones of Llanmilo, St Clears, whose 11,031 acres in the west of the county yielded £5,867 per annum, Sir Arthur Keppel Cowell-Stepney of Llanelli, who held 9,841 acres valued at £7,047 per annum, F. A. G. Jones of Pantglas, Carmarthen, the owner of 8,280 acres at an annual value of £5,384 and J. W. Gwynne-Hughes of Tre-gib, Llandeilo, who owned 6,797 acres valued at £3,990 per annum. Beneath them, in terms of the amount of land owned, but not in social pretension, were a group of twenty-nine landowners, each of whom owned over 2,000 acres. Prominent among them were such men as William Yelverton of Whitland, William Peel of Taliaris, Llandeilo, Henry Lavallin Puxley of Llangan, St Clears, William Harries-Campbell-Davys of Neuadd-fawr, Llandovery, Llewelyn Lloyd of Glangwili, Carmarthen, and Sir Marteine Owen Mowbray Lloyd of Bronwydd, Llandysul. To this group, perhaps more so than the great landowners, the charisma of their name and ancestry was sacrosanct and frequently stressed so that ancient prestige added verisimilitude to contemporary pretensions.[123] In that Indian Summer before the First World War, these people had the sensitivity of raw sunburn to matters of honour, precedence and protocol.

The advance of the Liberal Party after the *annus mirabilis* of the 1868 election and the erosion of the landlords' powers as county governors by the establishment of the county councils in 1888 and parish councils in 1896 brought an end to the political domination of landed wealth. But if their real political power had been eroded and the magnates had become marginalized, in social terms the gentry of west Wales still exercised considerable influence. Their estates continued to be the foci of fealty, locales of loyalty. This was seen at its clearest on the occasions of the rites of passage of landed families. The coming-of-age of the eldest son was an occasion of special social significance. In August 1890,[124] at the coming-of-age of E. C. Richardson, 350 guests, many of them tenants of the Glanbrydan estate, enjoyed a sumptuous menu.[125] The entertainment at the coming-of-age of Miss Peel of Danyrallt included a male voice choir and a marquee on the lawn.[126] Special trains were arranged to bring the tenants of the Dynevor estate to the demesne for the coming-of-age celebrations of Walter Fitzuryan Rice in September 1894.[127] Following their wedding in April 1899, Mr and Mrs Powell, Maes-gwyn, were escorted by thirty-six mounted tenants to church to the accompaniment of a brass band. At Llanboidy, resplendently decorated for the occasion, a community shy of public speaking but conscious of the value of physical strength, expressed its appreciation by unharnessing the horses and manually pulling the carriages into the town.[128] The return of elder sons from heroic escapades in the Boer War provided tenants with the opportunity to express their awareness of the realities of the deferential system[129] which, despite the inroads made into the political authority of the gentry, continued to operate in south-west Wales up to the First World War. Deference also operated in the industrial communities of Carmarthenshire, as the celebrations at the christening of Stafford Vaughan Stepney Howard in October 1915 show. His father's tenants turned out decorated with with sprigs of yew – 'symbols of immortality'.[130] At his coming-of-age, Richard Thornton Nevill was presented with a gold watch by the workmen of the Wern Foundry.[131]

One of Carmarthenshire's great landowners, Sir J. Hills-Johnes in c.1914 (By permission of Llyfrgell Genedlaethol Cymru/The National Library of Wales)

Ensconced in the mansions of south-west Wales, great landowners and squires enjoyed the pleasures of landed wealth. In Carmarthenshire, up to the First World War, the financial pressures which led to the decline, decay and disintegration of many great estates and the rise of freehold farming do not appear to have been as severe as they were elsewhere in Wales.[132] Though they lived in west Wales, the tastes, habits, language[133] and life experience of the landowners was very different from that of the majority of the populace. Their lifestyles were lavish and luxurious. Their houses were frequently resplendent, with the oak panelling on the walls symbolic of the intended longevity of the owner's authority, prestige and status. Portraits of the family, by talented and famous artists, hung on these solid walls. Edwinsford was notable in laying claim to a Van Dyck.[134] Other families expressed equal pride in souvenirs acquired over generations. At Dolau Cothi, for example, the Roman gold chain and clasp and the 'Abyssinian Bible' which had been found by Sir James Hills-Johnes in the King's Wigwam at Malaga after the storming of the fort and the killing of King Theodore, were treasured.[135] Boudoirs, such as that of Lady Drummond, were centres of privacy, often of sensuality and individuality, and crammed with the bric-a-brac of decadent and ostentatious fashion.[136]

When they were in residence, the social and leisure time of the gentry was spent in the Guild Balls of the principal towns of south-west Wales – Carmarthen, Newcastle Emlyn, Llandeilo and Llanelli. On pampered green lawns the gentry played gentle refined games. H. M. Vaughan, the gentle chronicler of the gentry of south-west Wales, recalled:

> The Lawn-tennis club at Newcastle Emlyn formed a convenient centre for meeting. On the shady lawns by the swift-flowing Teify, the gentry of the Tivyside collected every Tuesday throughout the summer months to play tennis and croquet, to gossip, to drink tea, to flirt, to quarrel and generally to disport themselves. Jealous and exclusive, the club was confined to the gentry and their visiting friends.[137]

But the gentry's main sport was hunting, and in south-west Wales the unspeakable passionately pursued the uneatable. The larger estates had their own packs of hounds, and many, such as Glansevin, also maintained their own pack of otter hounds to safeguard their fishing.[138] In the south and west of the county, the Tivyside and W. R. H. Powell's Hunt were dominant, while in the north and east, the Irfon and Tywi Hunt were pre-eminent.[139] The interest in hunting and horses did have beneficial effects. They led to the establishment of the United Counties Hunter's Show of which Lord Emlyn was President, and to attempts to improve the quality of the county's horses.[140] Racing was also a gentry passion. W. R. H. Powell was influential in the resurrection of the Llanboidy races in the 1870s and the point-to-point races at Carmarthen enjoyed the patronage of the whole county.[141]

When they tired of the delights of local society, many took themselves off to the Continent and to London. In the 'Society and Personal' notes of the *Carmarthen Journal* it was reported in May 1890 that 'Viscount Emlyn and his family left Golden Grove on Monday for London where they will remain for the rest of the season'.[142]

The lesser gentry and squires participated in the country house life-style, though some of the lesser squires of Carmarthenshire added to the sports of the gentry the new mass-activity sports of cricket and rugby. Charles Prytherch Lewis, MA, JP, of Llandingat near Llandovery acquired these sporting interests while at the Cathedral School, Gloucester, Llandovery College and Jesus College, Oxford. A member of the MCC and an Oxford double blue in 1882, 1883, and 1884, he also captained the Welsh Rugby Union team.[143]

It is useful and important to remember that landed estates played an important part in the development of industry in Carmarthenshire. Earl Cawdor and Lord Dynevor owned extensive acreages in the parishes of Llandeilo Fawr and Llandybïe. It was Lord Dynevor's willingness to grant quick leases which explains the very rapid growth of towns such as Llandybïe and Ammanford.[144] The estates of Sir James Howard and Sir Arthur Stepney were of central importance in the development of industry in Llanelli.[145] But in the towns which developed rapidly in Carmarthenshire during the closing decades of the nineteenth century, it was the men of the new wealth, men of a commercial and professional background, who held power. It was around men of this background, clear-sighted businessmen, that new patterns of deference and loyalty began to crystallize.[146] These were men such as William Howell, a solicitor of New Lodge, Burry Port, who worked his way up from being an articled clerk with J. W. Phillips of Haverfordwest to the post of clerk and solicitor to Burry Port Urban District Council and the Llanelli and the Pen-bre Parish Council, and his own substantial and flourishing legal practice.[147] William Buckley Roderick, also a solicitor, was educated at Marlborough and Bath. By 1907 he was coroner, registrar and high bailiff of Llanelli County Court, vice-consul of Spain, a member of the Llanelli Local Board for Health, a harbour commissioner, and a senior partner in the firm of Roderick, Richards and Williams. His multifarious duties necessitated his relinquishing the position of master of the Prince of Wales Lodge (No. 671) of Freemasons. Unlike many of the men of the new wealth of Llanelli, he was a keen agriculturalist, a breeder of Jersey cattle and a former president of the Carmarthenshire Agricultural Society.[148] Another past master of the Prince of Wales Lodge was Thomas Jones of Bradbury House, Llanelli, the land and minerals agent to the Stepney estate.[149]

In the town of Carmarthen the same type of person had risen to positions of authority and status by the 1880s. For instance, after an education at the Queen Elizabeth Grammar School and the University College of Wales, Aberystwyth, Henry Evan Blagdon Richards pursued a career as a merchant, importer and manufacturer of various products. In 1907 he retired as Carmarthen's mayor, and began to concentrate on his duties as the Chairman of Ferro-Cocoa Manufacturing Co. Ltd. of Carmarthen and London, the Carmarthen Steam Laundry Co. Ltd. and the Carmarthen Attractions Committee.[150] The rewards of self-help, diligence and thrift were also seen in the careers of the social leaders of the new urban communities. William Thomas Michael of the Croft, Ammanford, laboured his way to the position of manager of the Abertillery Tinplate Works, rising to be manager of the Aberlash Tinplate Works at Ammanford. He also continued with his responsibilities as chairman of the Abertillery and Talywain Collieries Co. Ltd. His increased social prestige and importance were confirmed by his membership of the Homfray Lodge of Freemasons.[151]

Scrupulous care of money was also a feature of the ideal of self-help and the secret of the success of many men of the Victorian age, so it is no surprise to find that bank managers were valued and respected members of the community. John Bevan Phillips, JP, of Llwynarthen, the manager of Lloyds Bank, Llanelli, was also a county JP, a senior acting magistrate of the Petty Sessional Division of Llanelli, an ex-chairman of the Llanelli Local Board of Health and Harbour Board, and a past master of the ubiquitous Prince of Wales Lodge (No. 671) of Freemasons.[152]

Proud of their town, proud of its achievements and its advancement, and particularly proud of the men, and a few women, who made it the model for all other towns to aspire to, Llanelli published its own *Who's Who* in 1910.[153] The book is a catalogue of the great and the good, the best and the brightest in the town, providing pen portraits of more than 180 local notables. It is an invaluable source for details of the people of Llanelli who were considered by their contemporaries to be leaders of society. In their ranks are bank managers, teachers, managers of tinplate works, foundries, collieries, shops, gas lighting companies, company managers, insurance and ship-brokers, electrical and mechanical engineers, choirmasters and organists, technical lecturers, surveyors, drapers, grocers, jewellers, works chemists, mineral water manufacturers, surveyors, publishers, pottery works owners, librarians, solicitors, harbour masters, railway engineers and directors, and of course, preachers. And what a multitalented, creative, determined, inventive, lucky and magical group they were. Talent there certainly was in abundance. Thomas Barker, of Bishop Auckland, after initial training in the metallurgical laboratory of Messrs. John Rogerson and Co. Ltd., Steel Works, Durham, proceeded to Durham and Sheffield universities, where he obtained his B.Sc. and M.Sc. degrees, and was awarded several distinguished prizes. He subsequently obtained the Fellowship of the Institute of Chemistry, the M.Met. of Sheffield University, and the D.Sc. of Durham University, and was awarded a Carnegie Research Scholarship by the Iron and Steel Institute in 1908. From 1904 he had held the positions of works manager and chemist to Messrs New Vanadium Alloys Ltd., Llanelli.[154] Forcefulness and determination marked the career of a man such as Clifford A. Bowen. Originally from Morriston, he passed through a variety of engineering jobs across Britain to reach management status at the Brickfield Chemical Works in Llanelli. In his case, the industry and dynamism were not confined to his works. In 1896–8 he captained Llanelli in rugby football, was a Welsh international against England, Scotland and Ireland, and played county cricket with Carmarthenshire and Glamorgan.[155] Inventiveness marked the career of Walter Davies, originally of Spittal, Pembrokeshire. A junior partner in the ironmongery firm of Davies Bros., his career flourished when a motor department was added in 1902 and production of the 'Stepney Spare Motor Wheel' commenced in 1904. Such was the demand that the ironmongery business was disposed of, and a large works was opened capable of producing 2,000 wheels per month. From its London distributing depot the company exported world-wide. In 1910, Walter Davies was chairman of the directors of the Stepney Spare Motor Wheel Ltd., Llanelli, the Stepney Motor Wheel Co. of Canada Ltd., the Stepney Auto Reserve Rad. GmbH of Berlin, and the Oesterreichische Stepney Auto Reserve Rad. GmbH of Vienna, and a half-owner in the firm of Davies Bros., Paris and Brussels. Here is evidence that shows the Welsh were an entrepreneurial people, that Welsh capitalism was international in its influence. When he could, Walter Davies found recreation in shooting and motoring.[156] Luck marked the career of Albert

Harding, who commenced work underground at a Swansea Valley colliery, where he 'miraculously' escaped death in the Birchgrove inundation of water which killed four men in 1888. By working late into the night, he achieved the status of a director of the Dyffryn Amman Colliery, Glanaman.[157] Creativity was represented in the person of 'Meudwy' – C. Meudwy Davies – choirmaster and organist at the Tabernacl Congregational Church, a former pupil of Joseph Parry at Aberystwyth, conductor of the Llanelli Harmonic Society, the Llanelli Temperance Choir and the Llanelli and District Band of Hope Union Choir. In 1903 he became the first Welshman to conduct the National Temperance Choral Union of 5,000 voices at the Crystal Palace, when his own composition 'The Fall of Bacchus' was performed. In 1910 he returned from his duties as the musical adjudicator at the Grand National Eisteddfod of Australia.[158] Welsh culture, like Welsh capitalism, was international. Magic was represented by David Williams. An ex-steel smelter, a Nonconformist and supporter of the Independent Labour Party, David Williams was by calling a phrenologist. Having obtained his diploma in phrenology at the Fowler Institute in London, David Williams began to give

> magnetic massage privately and free of charge, but as time passed his treatment and its effect became widely known and finally he gave up his employment and devoted the whole of his time to the work of healing, and as a result has had the great pleasure through his treatment of knowing the blind to see, the deaf to hear, the paralysed to walk and work and the insane to be restored to normal condition.[159]

Only a few women were allowed to enter this charmed circle. Miss Catherine Davies, a graduate of Girton College, Cambridge, was the headmistress of the girls' school, whilst Miss Catherine Muriel Cowell Stepney was the largest landowner in Llanelli.[160] The public image presents these people as stern, strong, indefatigable, industrious, relentless, remorseless, devoted to their various and curious careers. But in their zealously and jealously guarded private lives they were undoubtedly warm-hearted, charming and generous. These were the people who used the resources of John Bevan Phillips's bank to invest the rewards of their industriousness as provision for their old age and to ensure the continued prosperity and security of their families. The deaths of these men were occasions of massive public expressions of sorrow and the disclosure of the extent of their thrift. In 1909, J. S. Tregonning, 'one of nature's gentlemen . . . whose honesty was as clear as Noonday . . . suave . . . and idolised in the New Dock District', left an estate of £272,268 – 'the best monument to his memory'.[161]

Their domestic comfort was ensured by an army of domestic servants 'of good character and habits', who were often summarily dismissed if those characters and habits were tarnished – for the morality of these men did not deal in shades of grey. It was that strange creature the domestic servant, cradling other people's children, wearing hand-me-down clothing, eating leftovers, living on borrowed happiness and grief, growing old beneath other people's roofs, dying one day in their own miserable little room, and buried in a common grave in the local cemetery, who maintained the quality of life which these men enjoyed and others aspired to.

The rites of passage of these families, like those of the gentry, were public occasions which reinforced their social status and standing. 'Society' weddings were enthusiastically reported in the press, and, following descriptions of sumptuous menus, reports of the presents received by the young couple reflected their wealth and status. Amongst the gifts received by E. J. Powell and Miss E. Rees, daughter of the respected Captain Henry Rees of Mina Street, Llanelli, were an umbrella stand, several oil paintings, solid silver salt cellars, a drawing-room clock and bracket, an afternoon tea table, a Broadwood piano, a claret jug, several cheques, and doyleys.[162] No wonder that Madame Rose in an article on 'Christmas in Our House' could lament that for 'young married people who had received everything in marriage presents, I hardly know what to suggest except that the pride of the young housewife is amazing, and she is, I notice, always delighted with any gift for her drawing room'.[163]

Men in this social group set the tone of local government, politics and morality. They held respected positions, and were respected because they served the community diligently in all walks of life, from harbour commissioners, parish councillors, members of Parliament, to justices of the peace.

The habits, mannerisms and fashions of the middle classes were emulated throughout the county. But not all could afford the purchase of the social 'totem poles' of middle-class status and

Generally the children of the gentry enjoyed easier childhoods. Here the children at Glanbrydan take the dog out boating (By permission of Llyfrgell Genedlaethol Cymru/The National Library of Wales)

respectability. The most obvious of these perhaps were organs and pianos. To cater for their needs, local retailers, and the large mail order companies whose advertisements begin to enter the pages of local newspapers around the turn of the century, offered on hire purchase organs at 6*d*. a month and pianos at 10*s*.6*d*. a month.[164] There were, in Carmarthenshire, several worlds outside the 'bay-windowed respectablity' of the prosperous classes.[165] A silent social group struggled bravely between genteel poverty and the insatiable desire of emulating the 'better sort of people'.[166] Brave women fought heroically in long, private and bitter battles to keep the family's poverty from being noticed.

'To a large mass of the people, life's promise is but a promise of one great struggle, literally from cradle to the grave, to keep body and soul together.' So wrote the Llanelli socialist, Sidney J. Phillips, in an article on the 'Abolition of Poverty' in the *South Wales Press* in 1914.[167] The development of industry in Victorian Britain and the improvements that increased wages brought to the material life of the people give the impression that the period 1870 to 1922 was characterized by continuous advance. In Carmarthenshire wages did rise over the period 1876–1920. In agriculture, for example, the weekly wages of married labourers, not lodged at the farmhouse, rose from 11*s*.6*d*. in 1870 to 16*s*.7*d*. in 1898, to 17*s*.9*d*. in 1902, and to 18*s*.1*d*. in 1907. Wages declined during the opening year of the First World War, but rose rapidly to 23*s*.6*d*. in 1917.[168] Though wage rates in the 1870s were similar to those given by farmers in Cardiganshire and Pembrokeshire, wages for married labourers in Carmarthenshire rose more rapidly as the century progressed. At the turn of the twentieth century, wages were almost 2*s*. a week higher than those paid in Cardiganshire and a shilling higher than those paid in Pembrokeshire. The reason for the difference was the existence of rural trades and industries in Carmarthenshire which offered greater financial rewards to their workers. Agricultural wages in Carmarthenshire were tied closely to the advances which took place in the wages paid by Glamorgan farmers. The wages of colliers advanced substantially in the period 1874 to 1891; by 1891 the average wages of south Wales miners were 55.83 per cent higher than they had been in 1879 when the standard rate was set.[169] By 1901 average wages had climbed to 73.33 per cent above the rate in 1879 and to 58.95 per cent above that rate by 1913.[170] In the tinplate industry, the wages paid in 1920 to rollermen, doublers, furnacemen, behinders, first and second helpers, shearers and openers, had risen over 20 per cent on average, since 1874, when the '1874 List' set the wage rates per dozen boxes.[171]

Economic advance, however, is not uniform. In outlining the general experience of an industry, the particular experience of periodic decline and depression which deeply affected individuals are often forgotten. Moreover, average wage rates conceal as much as they reveal. Prices rose in tandem with wage increases, and, at times of economic stagnation, the response of owners was to cut wages. This happened in the period November 1891 to March 1893, when the average wages of south Wales miners fell from 55.83 per cent above their 1879 standard rate to just 15 per cent above the 1879 level. It also happened between April 1901 and August 1902, when rates fell by 20 per cent of their 1879 value.[172] But the average is deceptive, as the editor of the *Carmarthen Weekly Reporter* explained in 1915:

> What is the average income of the working man? It does not matter what the mathematical average is. It is no help to the man who gets £1 a week to be told that the average is 27s.6d. a week because skilled workmen earn £3 a week or thereabouts. Millions of men in regular employment earn 21s. or less. One does not need to look far to find these cases. It would be taking a generous estimate to assume that the average wage of the unskilled man was 22s. a week. After paying 6s. a week for rent and rates there is 16s a week for food, clothing, light, fireing, medical attendance, and amusements.'[173]

The editor calculated that the expenditure per person on food in such households was just 2*s*.6*d*. a week, and that they would 'be better off in workhouse and prison.'[174] He also complained that it was a myth that people could live more cheaply in country areas than in towns. Most agricultural produce, as several witnesses to the Royal Commission on Land in the 1890s stressed, had to be sold at market rather than consumed at home.[175] In November 1916, William Pugh of the Dockers' Union drew the attention of the county council's Roads Committee to the state of hauliers in the county. In order to 'live fairly and decently', their wages needed to be raised from £1.8*s*.0*d*. to £2.4*s*.6*d*. Pugh presented the committee with a weekly shopping list of a typical family which indicated that, in purchasing only the bare essentials, they would have to overspend by 7*s*. a week.[176] Miracles of thrift had to be performed, and heroic sacrifices endured by women in order to keep their families together.[177]

It is impossible to state categorically how many people had to endure such privations. In 1889, in a survey into the condition of the poor in east London, Charles Booth found that the poor comprised some 30 per cent of the population. Confirmation of these grim statistics were provided by Seebohm Rowntree who, to his own astonishment, found that almost three in ten of the population of York were poor, 'underfed, ill-clothed, and badly-housed'.[178] In Llanelli, as in the rest of urban Britain, the treasures of the poor were taken under the cover of darkness, and displayed not on homely shelves and dressers, but on the premises of Mr W. Bowen, in Station Road, Mr Puik in Murray Street and Mr Wherle in Park Street – the pawnbrokers, otherwise known as the 'poor woman's friend'.[179] Other women, how many is impossible to calculate or to discover from official sources, 'stole to survive'. One such was Ellen Clarke, who was fined 30*s*. for stealing three chairs from a furniture dealer in Thomas Street and apprehended trying to pawn them at Wherle's shops.[180] Others chose various means of offsetting their poverty. They took in lodgers to supplement the family's income, took in washing, acted as childminders, used and reused clothing, knitted, sewed, told fortunes, became amateur midwives, or gathered coal and rubbish from tips. In 1900 the *Carmarthen Weekly Reporter* noted that 'when the ash buckets are put out in the morning you will see gaunt, famished looking women upsetting them in the street and rummaging them for . . . second class fuel'.[181] Despite the hardened resolve of their stubborn pride, some of these women relaxed their respectability and entered the previously unacceptable trade of prostitution.

The human side of economics is suffering and depression. In 1891, in view of the difficulties of overproduction, the tinplate owners of south Wales agreed on a 'stop-month', so that trade could have an opportunity to recover. The decision had catastrophic effects on local communities. During the stop-month of June, fifty-two mills in Llanelli, five in Dafen, eleven in Kidwelly, four in Burry Port, three in Gowerton, seven in Grovesend, four in Pen-clawdd, four in Spitty, nine in Llangennech, nineteen in Pontarddulais, and twenty in the Aman Valley became idle. In Llanelli 3,753 people were out of work, in Dafen 300, in Kidwelly 700, in Burry Port 250, in Gowerton 150, in Grovesend 500, in Pen-clawdd 250, in Spitty 200, in Llangennech 950, in Pontarddulais 1,050 and in the Aman Valley 1,200. The loss of earnings ranged from £4,550 in Llanelli to £250 in Gowerton.[182] Without warning, workers could find themselves redundant and though many attempted to offset the severity of this misfortune through savings and insurance, the sums they had managed to save could not withstand a prolonged period of unemployment. Such a period was the mid 1890s in the tinplate industry. Following the passage of the McKinley Tariff by the US Congress, the local tinplate industry collapsed. Distress and suffering in the tinplate towns and villages was acute as thousands of tinplate workers were forced into idleness. Many left the area for good for the brave new world of the USA. Evidence of the severity of the depression was shown in the fact that employers were leaving as well as workers. J. H. Rodgers, a local tinplate manufacturer, severely hit by the tariffs on foreign tinplate imports into the United States, founded his own company in Gas City, Indiana, taking with him the cream of the Moorewood's labour force.[183] In 1897, Kidwelly tinplate workers, emasculated after six years of depression, followed Alfred Bright, the former manager of the Gwendraeth Tinplate Works, to Tuscany.[184] The local papers expressed sorrow at their departure, but others were less tender to the troubles of the worker. At the Llanelly County Court in 1895, David Jones, a Swansea debt collector, had several cases of small debts to recover from local tinplate workers and other labouring men. Having demanded that they speak in English, Judge Bishop ignored their explanation that their debts had been caused by the twelve months they had been unemployed, and informed them that they should leave Llanelli to look for work.[185]

Hard times were not confined to tinplate workers. In 1898 following a period of reductions in their wages, the south Wales miners embarked on a strike that lasted for six bitter months.[186] In gambling on a successful outcome the miners and their families, underwent considerable sacrifices in their daily lives. Debts built up with local tradesmen and shopkeepers took several years to repay. However, it is important to remember that the effects of depression and stoppages in the tinplate and coalmining industries were not confined to the workers of these industries and their families. Any downturn would have repercussions for whole communities. In the 1890s, the shipping industry, heavily dependent upon a buoyant export market for coal and tinplate, followed these industries into a period of depression.[187] The yellow metal and lead workers of W. H. Nevill also experienced difficult times as a consequence of the tinplate stoppage, as did the copper works at Dafen and Llanelli and several companies that serviced the tinplate works.[188] Shopkeepers, drapers, grocers and the myriad small retailers whose wares littered the street outside their shops to entice if not trip the customer into the shop also suffered hardship through the loss of trade. Hence, perhaps, the conservatism of tradespeople during industrial disputes. Even publicans in Carmarthen town complained of dry days in 1902, not because of the success of temperance campaigners but because a trade depression coincided with the absence of the militia from the town.[189]

Through their friendly societies, trades unions and insurance agencies, working men sought to stave off some of the ill effects of prolonged unemployment and ill health.[190] But the relative comfort and security of respectable working men could be swept away by any of life's contingencies – the death of the breadwinner, large numbers of children, old age and unemployment. During periods of trade depression the same patterns of deference, paternalism and loyalty which operated in the rural estate were evident in the industrial communities of Carmarthenshire. Just as landowners were expected to contribute to distress funds and to give rent abatements during times of agricultural depression,[191] so were wealthy townspeople expected to contribute financially towards their less-fortunate neighbours.[192] Candidates in elections were expected to be open-handed, and this proved to be a crippling burden for men such as Gwilym Evans.[193] At times of distress the Victorians applied themselves with characteristic diligence to the organization of soup-kitchens and distress committees. In 1877 Burry Port experienced deep depression when over 300 men became unemployed as a result of the closure of the lead works; many left the area to look for work in Glamorgan. The depression continued until Christmas when it was reported that 'some gentlemen are relieving the poorest families by giving them bread and meat as a Christmas box. A fund, raised by subscription has raised £25 for this purpose'.[194]

At Ammanford in March 1912, following the stoppage of local collieries because of a dispute, the Ammanford District Committee provided relief to forty-one families with 173 children. The principal contributors were E. Hewlett, the managing director of Ammanford Collieries, and Alderman W. N. Jones, JP, both of whom gave £10.[195] By April it was reported that the colliers of Ammanford were becoming 'hand-soft' and over 350 children were now receiving their food from the soup-kitchens of the Distress Committee.[196] Local chapels throughout the county donated their collections to the victims of the strike, and local publicans 'undertook excellent work' in helping to provide 3,000 meals in Prospect Place, Llanelli.[197] In Llanelli prosperous people were generous in their help towards those affected by the tinplate depression during the hard winter of 1895. Of the total of £192.7*s*.6*d*. raised by the Town Distress Fund, £3.3*s*.0*d*. was contributed by Richard Nevill & Co., £5.5*s*.0*d*. by William Howell, £5.5*s*.0*d*. by Gwilym Evans, £5 by Holmes Stead, £5 by Myron Jones, £1.10*s*.0*d*. each by the fifteen Nonconformist ministers of the town, and £10 by William Bytheway the brewer – charity, it seemed, took no heed of moral sensibilities.[198] The generosity of these people was not the result of the guilty conscience of a successful capitalist. It was part of the natural co-operation which had to exist between the classes if their society were to survive.[199] Charitable work was among the nobler and most praiseworthy virtues of Victorian and Edwardian Britain.[200] But some people were more cynical. The joy which greeted a telegram carrying news that the Gwendraeth Tinplate Works at Kidwelly was to restart after a long stoppage turned to tears and rage when it was disclosed that it was a hoax.[201]

The Victorians had classified the poor into two categories. There were the 'deserving poor'[202] who, through no fault of their own, were overcome by misfortune. In contrast were the 'undeserving' poor who, as Colonel Morris complained to the Llandeilo board of guardians (referring to an Ammanford out-door pauper), were 'a disgrace to civilisation . . . not fit to be amongst decent people'.[203]

The problem of the undeserving poor had exercised the minds of many people since Elizabethan times. The Victorians pondered their fate long and hard. Since 1834, the poor had been subjected to the workhouses.[204] The workhouse was detested by the poor from its inception. With its enforced discipline, the reduction of individuality, and its punishment by stone-breaking, the work-house, like the lunatic asylum, was a 'total institution.'[205] However desperate their circumstances, the poor sought to avoid internment in the workhouse. In February 1895, for example, Esther Evans explained to the Llanelli board of guardians that she did not want relief for fear of having to enter the workhouse. She preferred to live with her two daughters and their three illegitimate children in Pwll.[206] Others, however, had no choice.

On 1 January 1906 we find that the number of paupers relieved in the registration county of Carmarthen had increased by fifty-two compared with the number relieved on 1 January 1905.[207] On that day 145 people had been present in Llanelli workhouse, with an additional 1,563 receiving outdoor relief from the Llanelli guardians. At Llandovery thirty-seven received indoor relief, 324 outdoor relief, in Llandeilo fifty-nine were in receipt of indoor relief, 757 outdoor relief, while in Carmarthen 121 were in receipt of indoor relief and 1,144 outdoor relief.[208]

The concern of the official statistics with the people who fell into the category of 'able-bodied' makes it difficult to establish the type of person who was consigned to the workhouse. Primarily these were the very young, the unmarried mother, the abandoned wife, the old, and the tramping labourer. All, in their different but equally tragic ways, were victims of society. In the sense that it provided facilities and shelter for these people, the workhouse was a nascent institution of social welfare. These are the characters who appear in the sentimental, romanticized literature of Victorian Britain. An important Welsh example of this genre was the popular poem 'Tloty'r Undeb' by Trebor Mai.[209] Young girls, spurned by their lovers and families, turned to the workhouse staff for help during confinement. At the Penlan Workhouse in Carmarthen, the number of births between 1882 and 1904 averaged four per annum.[210] In the Abercennen Workhouse at Llandeilo, every mother who gave birth had a local address, suggesting that perhaps the workhouse formed an unofficial midwifery service for the area.[211]

The treatment of some elderly people was especially distressing. After a lifetime of work, unwanted by their families, they drifted to the workhouse to await death.[212] The jubilation which greeted the introduction of Old Age Pensions in 1909, is partly explained by the harrowing experiences of many old people in the workhouse. No longer did they have to slave and beg for their keep. People accepted that it was right for an old person to receive aid from the state. As the *South Wales Press* stated:

> Thousands of people now have a sense of security and comfort they have not enjoyed for many a long day . . . Many of them have been bearing up bravely against fate, snatching an hour's work here or there, and contriving to live by those miracles of management known only to the very poor. The help of the state is no longer a humiliation, it is a right, and the aged people therefore rejoice.[213]

Many orphans in the workhouse found themselves marked off from their contemporaries in a pauper's uniform and stigmatized with a pauper's haircut.[214] Many of the popular poems of Victorian and Edwardian Wales indicate that these unfortunates were a familiar section of society.[215] Official statistics confirm romanticized literary perceptions. Of the child population in Carmarthen in 1921, 4,385 children had lost one parent and 231 had lost both.[216]

The vagrant and the tramping labourer constituted a threat to discipline, respectability and stability, which were based on a secure home, work, cleanliness and order.[217] The boards of Poor Law guardians in Carmarthenshire, as in the rest of Britain, appeared to have been appalled, and at the same time fascinated, by the vagrant.[218] The fluctuations in the number of outdoor relief paupers caused concern to ratepayers because of the costs involved. Increase in their numbers through the vicissitudes in local economic fortune were lamented.[219] Strikes and stoppages in the works, such as that of 1898 in Llanelli, created profound problems for the guardians in defining the destitute.[220] In times of real distress, when significant numbers of people crossed the county to look for work, the guardians did try to assist the 'genuinely' deserving. In Llandovery in 1913, for example, the guardians established bread and cheese stations on the main roads from Llandovery to Carmarthen, at Llangadog, Glanaman, Cross Hands and Pontargothi, for 'bona fides'.[221] The 'way ticket' system was also adopted in the opening decade of the twentieth century whereby a 'genuine worker' was given a ticket entitling him to a half pound of bread and two ounces of cheese.[222] Without the 'way ticket' a person would be subjected to the disciplinary code of the workhouse of chopping wood and breaking stones.[223]

The level of outdoor relief given by boards of guardians is a fairly accurate barometer of the economic health of an area. The early 1890s, and also the years 1898–9 and 1909–12, were periods of severe hardship for many people; the number of outdoor paupers in the county increased by over 10 per cent during these periods.[224] Because of the link with the fortunes of industry there was an element of predictability in the variations in the figures of outdoor paupers, but what amazed, angered and concerned contemporaries was the unpredictability of the numbers of vagrants who passed through the county. A substantial increase in the number of vagrants could occur as the result of the tiniest stimulus – the occurrence of a fair, markets, races, or similar events, alterations in the conditions at neighbouring workhouses, new masters, or the distribution of charitable resources. Perhaps the crucial determinant of the number of vagrants on the road was inclement weather.[225] These, together with the urge to wander, were the motives which explain the constant movement of tramps across south-west Wales. But the popular perceptions of the dangers which tramps and vagabonds represented to society were probably more important than their actual numbers. In 1904 Sir Marteine Lloyd revealed the panic, persecution and paranoia that were characteristic of the public utterances of the rich when confronted by the very poor. He complained to the *Carmarthen Weekly Reporter* that over 6,000 tramps were passing through the county. 'On going to the fox hounds', he stated, '[he] saw seven in 200 yards, horrible-looking fellows that it would be a pity for any lady to meet on the road.'[226]

This restless, rootless army of the very poor was hounded and harried across Camarthenshire. Sensitivities apart, the actual numbers of vagrants present us with problems, for the same individual would be counted several times in any monthly or annual figures, because many moved from workhouse to workhouse across the county. Thus the figures of vagrants in workhouses for the year ending 31 March 1913 – 3,239 at Carmarthen, 5,000 at Llandeilo, 8,021 at Llanelli, 2,033 at Narberth, 2,999 at Newcastle Emlyn and 3,385 at Llandovery – must be treated with caution.[227] What is certain is that contemporaries were very conscious of the existence of the vagrants. In 1903 the *Carmarthen Weekly Reporter* complained of a plague of tramps in the town of Carmarthen which was 'as bad as the ten plagues of Egypt rolled into one' and advocated a 'campaign of terror against them'.[228] In 1905 Carmarthen was described as the 'Mecca' for tramps, and a 'plague of tramps' was reported as having descended upon Llandeilo.[229] At Carmarthen the casual wards were packed within a half-hour of opening, police turned more than forty people away during one evening. In desperation, to escape the terrible weather, vagrants committed obvious thefts and even broke police station windows to obtain shelter through being arrested.[230]

Mingled with the social fear and resentment of vagrants was a fascination with the romance of the open road. Carmarthenshire newspapers sent their 'social explorers' into the casual wards to discover the ways and wiles of the tramping fraternity. 'Amateur Casual', of the *Carmarthen Journal*, discovered the 'gager' and 'griddler', the 'grubbers', the 'moucher' and the 'door thumper'.[231] 'Amateur Casual', of the *Llanelly Mercury*, discovered the 'Mushfakir', the 'Welsh Prophet', the 'man with the Bible' and the 'tramp schoolmistress'.[232] Each tramp had his or her own ruse to obtain money. Begging was very common in the streets of Carmarthen. In 1896 the *Carmarthen Weekly Reporter* complained that begging was of an 'epidemic character'.[233] By 1907 Carmarthen bridge had become the main centre for begging, and a reporter described a 'typical scene':

> A man was looking about him and taking stock of the passers-by whilst he bore on his manly chest a board which stated that he had lost his sight in a colliery explosion! Feeling convinced there must be a mistake I asked the man how he was able to see so well after a total loss of sight in a colliery explosion. He could not read evidently and he asked in an agitated state what the board said. On it being read to him, he said 'Here's a pretty mess. I've taken out some other chap's board. I'm really deaf and dumb'.[234]

Faced with such an epidemic, the guardians of Llanelli and Carmarthen boarded vagrants and casual labourers out in common lodging houses.[235] It was in the lodging houses that vagrancy merged with the lower levels of the working classes in a raucous, rowdy, and violent sub-culture. Mill Street, Lammas Street, Water Street and Danybank, Carmarthen, and the ironically named Prospect Place, Llanelli, were the location of this underworld. Keepers of lodging houses were often intimidating and irresponsible people. Fired with malice and mischief many were notorious local characters. Ada Thompson of Mill Street appeared before the Carmarthen Borough Police Court at least sixty-five times on charges which included keeping an unmuzzled dog, theft, neglect of a child, four convictions for keeping an unlicensed guest house and at least seventeen charges of being drunk and disorderly.[236] George Rae of Mill Street made his fifty-first appearance in Court on a similar range of offences in November 1900.[237]

The links between the world of the casual labourer and the vagrant were complex. The person who symbolizes the robust vitality of this underworld most effectively is probably the navvy.[238] Scorned by society, yet the labour of his hands created engineering masterpieces – 'Si monumentum requiris, circumspice'. When those hands were not engaged in labour, they were frequently drinking and fighting. The pauses in the development of the waterworks in Felinfoel in 1900, in Cynwyl Elfed in 1902, and in Llanelli in 1914 are explained by the increased activity of the local police courts.[239] Large-scale constructions brought armies of navvies into Carmarthenshire. During the First World War, the construction of explosives factories at Pen-bre and Burry Port brought in large numbers of young unmarried workers.[240] So many arrived that local police despaired of prosecuting men for sleeping out, and concentrated on the more serious offences of gambling, drunkenness, assault and stabbing which were becoming common in the Pen-bre area.[241] Tensions were acute and fighting was widespread. One police constable described a typical Saturday night scene: 'There were hundreds lying about the ground at the time [10.15pm]. They were stretched out all about the street after the free fight between the crowd of Irishmen and Welshmen.'[242]

In 1908 Thomas Jones, a dispensing chemist, and the chief magistrate of Llanelli, expressed respectable society's view of the casual labourer in a decision involving John Donovan, a labourer at the tramway, who was caught sleeping in a stable: 'I have no sympathy with men of your class, and you will have to go to prison for seven days.'[243] In August 1911 during the Llanelli riots Thomas Jones's property was shown similar discourtesy.

Lack of money was not the only problem the poor had to contend with in their journey through 'life's great struggle'. They had to fight against dirt, disease, suffering, smells and squalour and a life marked by insanitary housing, ill health and an early grave.

4. *The Quality of Life*

The quality of life enjoyed or endured by people is one of the most difficult of all social areas to measure. Statistical information is notoriously misleading and confusing. Moreover, contemporary conceptualizations of society can give rise to dominant myths and images which become accepted as accurate reflections of social situations. One example of this tendency is the contrasting portrayals of rural and urban society in the late nineteenth century. Contemporary literature and the sentimental longing for the rural Arcadia of the past have created images of urban disease and degeneration, which are contrasted with rural health and vigour.[244] The abiding images of songs such as 'Cartref', 'Y Bwthyn ar y Bryn', 'Bwthyn Bach Melyn Fy Nain', and 'Y Bwthyn Bach Tô

Gwellt' are of cosy, whitewashed, rose-covered cottages set in a green and pleasant land.[245] But if we pause to look below the surface we discover that, for many in rural Carmarthenshire, living conditions were very different. In the opening of 'Y Bwthyn Bach Tô Gwellt', for example, the author loses his mother and father through illness: 'Fe Gollais fy nhad, Fe gollais fy mam Yn y Bwthyn Bach Tô Gwellt . . .'[246]

Clearly, the real condition of rural cottages was vastly different from the myth. In 1892 the indefatigable D. Lleufer Thomas drew attention, in his *Report on the Agricultural Labourer in the Poor Law Union of Narberth*, to two types of cottages in the region.[247] The first was constructed with:

> A mud walling of about 5 feet high, a hipped end, low roofing of straw with a wattle and daub chimney, kept together with hay rope bandages, and frequently from its inclined posture making a very obtuse angle with the gable end over which it hangs. This was a description of the exterior written in 1811 and it still applies to older cottages.[248]

The interior of these cottages were dark and cramped, comprising only two habitable rooms, so that 'the greatest economy has to be exercised as to space':

> Though these cottages are perhaps still in the majority throughout the rural parts of the Union, they are gradually being replaced by ordinary stone-walled two-storied cottages with a slate roof, and having two rooms downstairs, and two or three upstairs. All that can be said against these new cottages is that they are often left in an unfinished state, e.g. without a ceiling upstairs, so that they are scarcely wind and water tight. Seldom are there found any water shoots under the eves, or much pavement in front of the doors, with the result that when it rains and when slops are thrown out, pools of dirty water form in front of the house, causing in time, foul and dangerous exhalations to rise and enter the dwelling.[249]

In 1870 the Commissioners into the Employment of Women and Children in Agriculture were scathing in their condemnation of the cottages in western Carmarthenshire and the neighbouring counties. They found that:

> The state of cottages throughout the county is most disgraceful and cottages are too frequently built without any regard to the health, comfort, morality, or convenience of the occupants; generally badly

A typical Carmarthenshire cottage, c.1906 (By permission of Llyfrgell Genedlaethol Cymru/The National Library of Wales)

> ventilated and as badly lighted, damp and unhealthy walls and floors, the former of earth . . . overcrowding is the universal consequence and gross immorality the result. Privies are very unusual and oftener than not the piggery is attached to the dwelling. No attention is to be paid to the sewerage, which is constantly to be seen at the cottage door.[250]

In 1911 Edgar Chappell revealed that the view from the cottage door had not improved. In a series of articles in the *South Wales Daily News*, he drew attention to the cottages of Cardiganshire, Carmarthenshire and Pembrokeshire which had 'pretty exteriors of crawling ivy and bushes but inwardly were veritable death traps'.[251] The majority were built of local materials – clay and straw, mud and lime, and river stones – and the floors were often of mud and beaten clay. Without damp courses, the cottages were walled in on the sides by hills, trees and some even by a graveyard.[252] Though new materials such as corrugated iron were used, they did not represent advancement or improvement for:

> Usually . . . the iron is placed on top of the straw and the festering mass of rottenness allowed to send down its foetid and repulsive odours . . . Buckets are used to catch drippings and sacks and tarpaulins are placed over beds . . .[253]

The interiors of such cottages were dark and dismal: 'In fact it takes time for one's eyes to get used to the gloominess of the apartment and one's nostrils to adapt themselves to the often stagnant air'.[254] Many chimneys were little more than nine feet square, for large chimneys allowed the rain to come through in winter. Though the door was often open in the day, the good effect of this practice was lost at night when the family slept in close proximity to each other. Drainage was conspicuous by its absence in such houses:

> . . . It is a common sight to see festering messes of household refuse, animal manure, ill-smelling feathers etc. piled in close proximity to the dwelling, while often the pig sty is built against the end of the house just below the bedroom window. The yards are dirty and the sow and litter paid periodic visits to the kitchen.[255]

Surface water was used for drinking and a Tregaron doctor said that over 25 per cent of cottages were without any privies. The shocking conditions were such as to inspire one county councillor – 'normally', wrote Chappell, 'the most unsympathetic people to Sanitary reform' – to compose the following parody: 'The cottage homes of Gwalia, How dreadfully they smell, With phthisis in the thatched roof And sewage in the well.'[256] That many a true word is spoken in jest is endorsed by the reports of the medical officers of health. New medical officers, their enthusiasm as yet undaunted by the apathy of the health authorities, were often the most outspoken. In 1914, Dr Hughes, medical officer of health for the Carmarthenshire County Council, condemned nineteen farm houses in Llanfihangel-ar-arth, Llanllawddog and Llanpumsaint as 'a disgrace to our civilization'. Walls and floors were damp, and emanations from the cowhouse contaminated dairies which should be closed because they were 'not fit for man or beast'. Several years later, they were still inhabited.[257]

It is important to note that bad and insanitary housing was not confined to rural parts of the county. For it is not correct to offer a simplistic contrast between unhealthy rural areas and new cleaner, healthier urban areas. Conditions in the towns were often equally bad. In 1914 the Land Enquiry Committee stated that:

> There are some bad slums in Carmarthen, built in the early days, dilapidated and insanitary. They are built without through ventilation –

> crowded together in manner of yards where washing, etc, is done in front of the house. In some cases, the drains run under and through the houses in a most insanitary manner. The Medical Officer has cited cases where as many as six and eight have crowded into one room. I would estimate that a matter of 800 people dwell in Carmarthen slums . . .[258]

In his report for the same year, Dr Arthur Hughes, medical officer for Carmarthen, described the workers' houses in the town as 'squalid hovels' and 'hot beds of disease'.[259] In a prosecution for cruelty to and neglect of children, at the Carmarthen County Petty Session in 1911, the jury heard of Bancycapel Cottage, Llandyfaelog. The sky could be seen through the thatch at the northern pine end, the kitchen floor was of mortar and the parlour floor of mud. However, it was home for five adults and three children.[260] In 1911, in a series of articles and photographs, the *South Wales Sentinel*[261] exposed the 'fallacy that there were no slums in Llanelli':

> This we emphatically repudiate . . . Indeed we are more than acquainted with the recognised worst slum in Britain – Ancoates in Manchester – and we have no hesitation in declaring that these we show photographs of are worse in everyway than anything we ever saw in the vilest little hole in even Ancoates. Although we will remember the dirty, squalid poverty-strewn conditions that prevail in the slums of the finest business city in the world, we never saw anything like the awful, evil-stinking and devitalising conditions of Llanelli's little 'hell-holes'.[262]

Attention was drawn to the parlous condition of the houses in Foundry Row, Custom House Bank, Raby Street and Cawdor Row. The *South Wales Sentinel and Labour News* commented that the 'dark dungeons of disease and spacelessness . . . near the very heart of our little Bethel town are a scandalous reflection on all our boasted religiosity.[263]

Bad cottages were just one symptom of a larger malaise that affected both rural and urban communities. Water supplies and sewage disposal were non-existent or, at best, basic. In 1896 the editor of the *Carmarthen Journal* in an editorial on the 'condition of water' stated:

> What the town [Carmarthen] wants is a plentiful supply of water from a much less contaminated source than the river Towy into which the

> town drains empty themselves with the rising tides carrying their outflow backwards and forwards daily in front of the wells to mellow their brackishness.[264]

The medical authorities of the county were in agreement with the assessment of the condition of the county's rivers. In 1913 Dr E. Cambrian Thomas in his *Annual Report*, noted that at Llandovery, the aptly named 'River Bawddwr, which runs through the main Borough, acts as a main sewer. The stench arising from this during the summer months is abominable.'[265]

In 1921 the medical officer of health condemned the condition of the water supply at Llangadog, Brynaman, Llanybydder, and Pen-y-groes and their neighbourhoods, commenting: 'We denounce "drink" and rightly so, but I submit that by not providing a wholesome supply of drinking water we put a premium on drink . . . It is scandalous to think that in a civilised society one cannot be sure the water is fit to drink.'[266] The medical officer received a surprise at Llangadog, where

> I noted a midden privy in the twentieth century! And this is the method of disposal of excreta in vogue, that is, the excreta are deposited into rough pits in the ground, their contents allowed to overflow, saturating the air with effluvia, and to percolate into the soil . . . The drinking water is drawn from ill-constructed shallow wells sunk into this soil . . . [sampling proved that] . . . this water contained bacilli of the bowels of warm blooded animals, including man.'[267]

The conditions he encountered at Llandovery led him to the conclusion that: 'From a sanitary point of view the condition of things in this small town is a living reproach to our civilisation and an open scandal to our comfortable Christianity.'[268] He also condemned the disposal of excreta in the urban districts of Newcastle Emlyn, Kidwelly, Burry Port and Cwmaman, and the rural districts of Carmarthen, Llanelli, Llandeilo, Llandovery, Whitland and Llanybydder. In the latter district the disposal was 'sadly defective'. In all these areas, pails were emptied and collected at night by the 'night chariot' or, in Welsh, 'y cart cachu'. Commentators complained that these 'dripped [and that] the germs of disease escape into the air we breathe, and the atmosphere is charged with the poison for hours afterwards.'[269] The 'night chariot' was an additional obstacle for late-night drunks on their way home, many of whom, such as Thomas Davies of Tumble, crashed into it, spilling its offensive contents over the pavements.[270]

The sanitary improvements of the period 1840 to 1870 generally had a beneficial effect in the county. Motivated by the fear of cholera, many local health authorities had improved the quality of the rudimentary services of sewage and water.[271] But these improvements were not universal and several areas were largely unaffected by them. It is difficult to ascertain the precise impact of pestilential houses and poor sanitary conditions, but it is probable, as Ieuan Gwynedd Jones has argued, that their existence 'in all the growing centres of population, large and small, constituted a kind of reality which exerted a profound influence on people as a whole'.[272]

That influence was seen in the tone of local politics in the period up to the First World War. Underlying the growth at a local level of Labour politics and working-class movements was the same pungent whiff of sewage which had spurred on the social reformers of the mid-nineteenth century.[273] These conditions symbolized social inequalities and spawned political action.[274] Nowhere was this more true than of the new towns such as Ammanford, Cwmaman, Pen-y-groes, Pontyberem, and Tumble, where population growth consequent upon the expansion of coalmining and other industrial activity had placed considerable strain upon already insufficient sanitary facilities. In 1918 S. O. Davies and E. R. R. Lewis wrote to the *Llanelly Mercury* to complain about the insanitary condition of Tumble and in particular Carway village. They stated that:

> Ditches and gutters [are] blocked with offensive and obnoxious slime . . . Even in March the cesspools stank, and stagnant ditches abound all of which justify us in characterising the whole area covered by Carway Village as one accumulated mass of grossly foul and unhealthy matter . . . The worst is Pwll Newydd – an old shaft full of water, pigs and cows had fallen in and allowed to rot, when we visited dead dogs and cats floated on the surface . . . In a small house standing on the left side of the ditch, there laid at the moment of our visit the dead body of a child, one of the young victims callously sacrificed to that administrative incompetence reflected by such vile conditions.[275]

Given the conditions they graphically described, it is not surprising that their letter coincided with an outbreak of diphtheria

Pantglas, home of Gerwyn Jones, High Sheriff of Carmarthenshire in 1887 (By permission of Llyfrgell Genedlaethol Cymru/The National Library of Wales)

and scarlet fever. Outbreaks of diseases related to poor sanitation were frequent. Typhoid was an unwelcome but frequent visitor. In July 1917, out of fifty cases in the Tumble district, there were eight deaths, which brought 800 colliers, led by the local MP the Revd Towyn Jones, on to the streets to protest against the inactivity of the rural district council.[276] By August one family in Llangyndeyrn had lost four children to the disease.[277] In 1907 at Carmarthen, the editor of the *Carmarthen Weekly Reporter* noted that 'several cases of typhoid fever have been notified at Carmarthen particularly in the poorer quarters.'[278]

Diphtheria, enteric fever, scarlatina and whooping cough were other virulent diseases which created fear and tension in several areas during their visitations. In 1907, the medical officer of health for Llanelly Rural Sanitary District described Pen-bre as a 'hot-bed of pestilence' and reported that of 211 reported cases of infectious diseases in the district, eighty-eight had occurred in Pen-bre. Of these, twenty-six proved fatal.[279] In an attempt to combat such diseases, medical officers closed schools and urged the isolation of the afflicted.[280] But popular custom and behaviour reflected the human need to share grief and express compassion. In 1894, for example, in a diphtheria epidemic in Llanfynydd, twelve children died, four of whom were the children of Jonathan Evans, a carpenter. In a letter to *The Welshman*, 'Local Correspondent' expressed his profound shock:

> When a death has occurred from this malignant disease (diphtheria), the idea of allowing the corpse to be carried to a church or chapel is too awful to contemplate; and the holding of 'wyl nosau' and the like at the house where the corpse lies is still worse. It is no wonder that science is fast making a laughing stock of religion – if that can be called religion which tolerates such things.[281]

But communal expression of grief, compassion and sympathy outweighed risk to the individual. Because of the suddenness of the outbreak of such diseases, their visitations were, like industrial accidents, periods of profound anxiety for entire communities. Deaths at work, as the poet Gwenallt wrote, were like: '. . . y llewpart diwydiannol a naid yn sydyn slei O ganol d˘r a thân, ar wflr wrth eu gwaith.'[282]

The frailty of human life in the claws of industry is witnessed in the death of Myrddin Morris, a fourteen-year-old cold-roll-boy at the Burry Tinplate Works. When his clothes became caught in the rolls, he was whirled round by the machine with the result that 'fragments of the poor lad's remains were scattered around, and had to be collected and placed in a sack for conveyance to his home'.[283] Although the psychological impact of such events was profound their position in terms of comparative mortality rates was secondary.

The impact of diseases was more insidious, but took a greater toll of lives. In Gwenallt's poetic reconstructions of industrial south-west Wales, the ubiquitous background sound is cacophonous coughing:

> Ni freuddwydiais y cawn glywed am ddau o'r cyfoedion hyn
> Yn chwydu eu hysgyfaint i fwced yn fudur goch . . .
> . . .
> Saethai peswch pump ohonynt, yn eu tro dros berth yr ardd
> I dorri ar ein hysgwrs ac i dywyllu ein sbri.[284]

The differing impact of various diseases can be analysed from the sober tabulations of grim experience provided in the *Annual Reports of the Registrar General for Births, Marriages and Deaths*. In 1895 the Registrar General produced tabulations of the major causes of mortality during the decade 1881–91. It is possible from these tables to ascertain the major causes of death (from the twenty-four categories identified by the Registrar General) in the four main registration districts of Carmarthenshire – Carmarthen, Llanelli, Llandeilo Fawr and Llandovery.[285] In Llanelli the complaints of the sanitary authorities and the commissioners who examined the health tinplate workers and the conditions under which they worked,[286] appear to have been justified, as the major causes of death were from diseases of the respiratory system, with a crude death rate of 3.16 per 1,000 people.[287] Following this were 'Other Causes' (2.88), 'Diseases of the Nervous System' (2.74), 'Pthisis' (2.04), 'Diseases of the Circulating System' (1.07), 'Diseases of the Digestive System' (0.83) and 'Violence' (0.55). The latter included suicide and industrial accidents. In Llandeilo Fawr, which was primarily an agricultural community but also had significant numbers employed in quarrying and coalmining, the major causes of death were 'Other Causes' (3.76), 'Diseases of the Nervous System' (3.09), 'Pthisis' (2.74), 'Diseases of the Respiratory System' (1.28), 'Disease of Circulating System' (1.28), 'Diseases of the Digestive System' (0.79) and 'Violence' (0.55).

During the decade 1881–91 the crude death rate for the four registration districts were 16.84 per 1,000 in Llanelli, 16.76 in Llandeilo Fawr, 18.44 in Llandovery and 19.97 in Carmarthen.[288] These crude death rates represent only marginal improvement on the rates recorded in the decade 1841–51, when the rates were eighteen per 1,000 in Llanelli, nineteen in Llandeilo Fawr, twenty in Llandovery, and twenty in Carmarthen.[289] This evidence seems to suggest that within Carmarthenshire the mortality rates of rural areas exceeded those of the most intensely industrialized and urbanized areas. In the United Kingdom as a whole, the general pattern is that high death rates were generally found in the heavily industrialized areas.[290] In 1908 the crude death rate for England and Wales stood at 14.7 (corrected to 14.7), that for south Wales was 16.7 (corrected to 16.9), that for Glamorgan was 16.7 (corrected to 17.8), and that of Cardiganshire was 17.8 (corrected to 17.1).[291] By 1908, the county with the highest corrected death rate was Lancashire at 18.7. In second place came Glamorgan with 17.8 followed by Durham and Monmouthshire with a rate of 17.5. In joint fifth position alongside Northumberland was Carmarthenshire with a corrected death rate of 17.1.[292]

5. *The 'Massacre of the Innocents'*

These general mortality rates conceal the grim fact that the most vulnerable period in a person's life at the turn of the twentieth century was the first year. Concomitant upon their unenvied position as leaders in mortality, the same counties (though in a different order) provided the highest rates for the deaths of children under one year for every 1,000 births. In first place was Glamorgan with 151, followed by Durham with 147, Lancashire with 144, Northumberland with 143, Carmarthenshire with 139 and Monmouthshire with 136.[293] Moreover, these rates, high as they were, are not an accurate reflection of the actual infant mortality of an area. As late as 1904, the Inter-Departmental Committee on Physical Deterioration could lament the fact that still-births were still not being recorded.[294] In 1915, at a time of prolific waste of human life, the bishop of London brought out the terrible tragedy of these cold statistics when he remarked that: 'While nine soldiers died every hour in 1915, twelve babies died every hour so that it was more dangerous to be a baby than a soldier.'[295]

But Victorian and Edwardian social reformers had been aware of this tragedy. They acknowledged infant mortality as 'the most sensitive hygienic barometer'[296] and referred to it in graphic and typically melodramatic phrases as 'the slaughter' or 'the massacre of the innocents'.[297] Contemporaries and subsequent historians have considered that one of the primary causes of infant mortality was that an increasing number of people were being born in large towns with, in Sir John Simon's memorable phrase, their 'Herodian Districts'.[298] To contemporaries, the presence of Carmarthenshire among the list of counties with the highest infant mortality was inexplicable.[299] In 1909 the 'Herodian Districts' of Carmarthenshire were the urban districts of Kidwelly, with an infant mortality rate of 143 per 1,000 births, and Llanelli, with a rate of 133, the rural districts of Llandeilo Fawr with a rate of 155, Llanelli, at 157 per 1,000 births, and Newcastle Emlyn with a staggering infant mortality rate of 246 per 1,000 births.[300] What then were the environmental and physiological conditions which were reflected by this most sensitive of hygienic barometers?

In 1914, of 440 infant deaths in the registration county, 95 were caused by convulsions, 59 by premature birth, 50 by pneumonia, 48 by diarrhoea and enteritis, and 36 by bronchitis.[301]

In 1909 the medical officer of the Local Government Board had expressed concern at the abnormally high levels of deaths caused by convulsions in Carmarthenshire and considered that many of these deaths should have been returned as caused by developmental and wasting diseases.[302] However, the crucial point is that each of the causes of death noted above reflected on that most crucial determinant of infant health – the health and welfare of the mother. In Victorian and Edwardian Britain a great gulf existed between the ideal of 'motherhood' and the stark feminine reality. In both rural and urban areas, working conditions for women were physically hard and physiologically debilitating. In 1870, the *Report on the Employment of Women and Children in Agriculture* revealed that Carmarthenshire girls went out to service:

> at about the same age as boys, i.e. from 12–13 years of age. On dairy farms, besides the ordinary duties of domestic servants, they are expected to help the dairy-maid and look after cows, calves and pigs. On arable farms they are also employed in setting potatoes, hoeing turnips, and assisting in harvest work . . . The hours of work of the female servants are long . . . women get up at 5 a.m. to milk etc, and continue till bedtime to serve in the general duties expected on a small farm.[303]

In 1912, Edgar Collins and J. Hilditch, in the *Report on the Conditions of Employment in the Manufacture of Tinplate*, noted that in the sorting and packing process 'heavy weights are often carried by young girls' and that the work exposed them to noxious fumes and dust.[304]

The physiological effects of these arduous conditions were compounded by the poor nutritional value of the diet of women in south-west Wales. In the early 1890s W. O. Brigstocke, chairman of Carmarthenshire County Council, in his evidence to the Royal Commission on Land declared that:

> The Welsh tenant farmer is most thrifty and frugal; and his diet, . . . consists of tea, bread, butter, milk, bacon and vegetables, fresh meat is rarely seen at table, and the diet of the ordinary farmer differs but little from that of the labourer.'[305]

Scores of other witnesses emphasized that frugality and poverty forced Welsh farmers to sell their best produce at market and subsist on inferior goods.[306] When, as was often the case in a society where seasonal unemployment prevailed, there was not enough food to go around it was the women who took the least. Even in relatively good times it was customary for the men to get the meat and larger helpings whilst

> the wife makes shift with tea and other slops all through the day and everyday. This is also the children's fare, except when they have to take their dinner with them to school, in which case they dine on bread and butter or bread and jam . . . Much of the indigestion from which women in this position suffer is attributable to the pernicious habit of drinking tea for every meal of the day, while as to its effects upon the health and physique of the coming race one prefers not to think.[307]

In the late 1920s an investigation by the minister of health into the health of the population of the south Wales coalfield found that:

> The diet lacks a sufficient proportion of protein, mineral salt and vitamins . . . The inevitable sequel of the prolongation of such conditions must be a deterioration of physique . . . and the prevalence of rickets which we have mentioned is in our opinion the first manifestation of such a deterioration.[308]

The effect of dietary deprivation was clearly seen in the medical examinations of the county's schoolchildren. In 1911 the county's medical officer of health, Dr Arthur Hughes, reported that 'speaking generally, the state of nutrition is very poor. This applies to Rural and Urban Districts alike'.[309] Of the children he examined, only 10 per cent were described as well nourished. In 1909, in his report, Dr E. Evans stated:

> It is worthy to note that in the Medical Examination of 3,945 children in the county of Carmarthen, no less than 1,918 (or nearly 50%) were found to suffer from diseases, or physical defects that would interfere, to a more or less degree, with their educational progress.[310]

In 1910, when the age-standard height for children of fourteen and fifteen years old was 4 ft. 11.2 ins., Dr D. J. Morgan reported that in Carmarthenshire the average height was 4 ft. 9.2 ins.[311] Carmarthen children weighed 5 st. 13.5 lb., as against a national standard of 6 st. 6 lb.[312] Two years later, Edgar Collins and J. Hilditch concluded that tinplate workers aged fourteen to sixteen and seventeen to nineteen (the age at which most girls would have been employed in the works) were shorter and lighter than most other categories of workers except Sheffield grinders and cutlers.[313]

The World Health Organization has analysed the detrimental impact of malnutrition upon maternal and infant health.[314] But when poor nutrition, as was the case in Victorian Carmarthenshire, is added to the other aspects of daily life – arduous labour, damp, cold and overcrowded dwellings, and inadequate sanitary conditions – we can begin to understand the causes of the county's appalling high infant mortality rates. This was the backcloth against which the drama of a mother's delivery was enacted. During this crucial event the technical incompetence of midwives,[315] compounded by the insanitary environment, made it remarkable that any mother and child survived. Tradition and custom frequently added to the difficulties. In 1902, in an inquest into the death of Margaret James of Pen-bre following the delivery of a still-born child, the local doctor 'condemned the practice of the area to allow women to be confined on the floor'.[316]

Margaret James's tragic experience was common throughout the county. In Carmarthenshire, as in the rest of Britain, the majority of women were assisted in labour by friends, neighbours and local women who had learnt in the harsh school of experience. However caring, careful and sympathetic these women were, their efforts were undermined by their lack of training and the insanitary physical conditions in which women gave birth. Custom was also a powerful obstacle. In 1915 the county medical officer of health, Dr Cambrian Thomas, complained that:

> Even in populous areas like Llanelli, Carmarthen and the Amman Valley, where trained midwives are provided, the old type of midwife, with her gifted and honeyed tongue which glosses her ignorance, has a great pull over the trained and disciplined young midwife who wished to perform her duties in the light of recent knowledge . . .[317]

Insanitary conditions at births were reflected in the high incidence of puerperal fever and other dirt-related diseases. In 1916, when unqualified practice was said to be 'rampant', there were fifteen cases of puerperal fever in the county. The majority occurred in Llanelli and public meetings were held throughout the county to advocate the importance of cleanliness at childbirth.[318] The tragic consequences of unqualified midwives was often revealed at local inquests. In 1904 the inquest into the death of Elizabeth Davies of Llangennech heard that she felt cold after delivering a still-born child and fainted. A doctor called to examine her discovered that she had not been delivered of the after-birth.[319]

Historians have discerned class tensions in the relationships between doctors who advocated the adoption of new techniques and working-class women who preferred to adhere to time-honoured customs and practice.[320] To perceive this as a conflict between progress and the unenlightened is misleading. In Carmarthenshire, even in the 1900s, long after the pioneering work of Pasteur, Lister and Koch, the use of antiseptics by doctors and midwives was the exception rather than the rule. In 1904 an inquest into the death of Ann Morgan of Gors-las, who died from 'fits and palpitations' in childbirth, was informed that chloroform had been administered correctly by the doctor who attended her.[321] With such well-publicized failures of modern techniques, the cynicism of some women towards doctors was perhaps not surprising.

In other respects, too, the medical profession in the county faced severe difficulties. The provision of hospital beds was grossly inadequate to meet the requirements of the population. There were only two small hospitals, one at Llanelli with forty-five beds and the other at Carmarthen with thirty-five beds.[322] In 1920 the *First Report of the Welsh Consultative Council on Medical and Allied Services in Wales* drew attention to the need for the appointment of more doctors, dentists, midwives, trained nurses and health visitors in the county, the need to link these new officers by telephone and by road, and the urgent necessity of providing a maternity hospital in the county.[323] Fifteen years later, in 1935, Lady Dynevor made a radio appeal to attempt to raise funds for the construction of the long-awaited maternity hospital.[324] The difficulties of the medical profession can be seen from the fact that in 1920, only forty-four general practitioners, sixty-seven trained midwives and twenty-three trained nurses were qualified to serve the population of over 160,000.[325]

In these circumstances it is understandable that women would turn to any quarter for advice and help. The plethora of 'medical' advertisements in the newspapers which circulated in the county reveals one source to which women turned. Many adhered to folk remedies such as swallowing live slugs to cure consumption, or carrying a potato to cure rheumatism, using raw liver on the feet to cure pneumonia, or swallowing the earth from a molehill before daybreak to cure asthma. Such 'cures' were widely used in the county at the turn of the twentieth century.[326] In 1921, while examining erysipelatious infections in two Brynaman children, Dr Arthur Hughes discovered that the practice of 'torri y llech' was still prevalent in the area. This involved an incision in a certain part of a child's ear which was believed to cure all cases of backwardness of whatever degree.[327] To be effective the incision had to be made during the waxing of the moon. During this time it was claimed that:

> up to 250 babies per day were treated [and] . . . the valley train on certain days is full of whining children with bleeding ears. On these occasions, when the moon is waxing the streets in the neighbourhood of the house where the operation is performed are lined up with motor cars, and on some occasions even wagonette loads of women with babies waiting their turn to be treated . . . In fact the point duty of the local police officers on certain days consists of answering questions as to the address of the person engaged in Torri y llech.[328]

The medical profession, given the disadvantages under which it worked, could do little to combat effectively these practices and beliefs. Neither could it combat the respiratory ailments and hypothermia which were endemic because the poor could not afford sufficient fuel and clothing during winter months. These problems were clearly seen in an inquest in January 1911 into the death of Blanche, the infant daughter of John Andrew Davies of Llanelli. An unemployed mason, he was unable to afford a crib for his daughter. The family slept four to a bed and in winter got up late in order to save wood and fuel. The inquest was told that, on 20 January, Blanche had died during the night of suffocation not convulsions. The coroner remarked that no poverty could justify such behaviour, and urged local families to use cribs, even if they were 'orange-boxes'.[329] But his advice and admonitions could do little to combat infant mortality.

Given the strained budgets and traditional eating habits of the poor, the medical profession was equally unable to combat another cause of infant mortality, the feeding of infants. A vicious circle operated where undernourishment weakened the child's resistance to infection and infectious disease often resulted in a weakened digestive system, leading to further malnutrition at a time when protein was being destroyed during the illness. In Victorian and Edwardian Britain, poverty was the hand-maiden of infection and was the real cause of infant mortality.[330] The majority of people could not afford to purchase specialist baby food mixtures which had been produced since the 1860s. Infants in many families were given the same food as their parents, which often resulted in deaths by 'projectile vomiting' and 'convulsions'. More generally, the practice led to serious malnutrition. In 1910 the investigation of the Local Government Board into the high levels of infant mortality found that Carmarthenshire returned the highest infant death rate from 'convulsions' in Britain at 29.2 per 1,000 births. In second place in this grim table of the causes of infant death in the county was 'atrophy and debility', with a mortality rate of 26.2 per 1,000 births.[331] The harm inflicted on infants by being fed solid food at too early an age is obvious. But liquid food also had its perils. Palliatives, such as cordials, which were given to infants to pacify them at night were prepared from opium.[332] In 1883, an inquest into the death of the daughter of Thomas Evans, a tailor from Llanelli, heard that having run out of 'cordial' for his daughter, he had borrowed some from a neighbour. The normal mixture was prepared by a Mr Richards from half a drachm of laudanum, in one fluid ounce of treacle and water. The mixture borrowed from the neighbour was opium. The baby died before dawn.[333]

However, the most immediately accessible palliative in Victorian and Edwardian Wales was alcohol.[334] The press abounds with medical and middle-class complaints that the poor gave alcohol almost indiscriminately to infants.[335] In 1909, the editor of the *Carmarthen Weekly Reporter* revealed the philosophy behind the practice, stating that:

> The giving of alcohol to children is a common practice in the town of Carmarthen. In some localities mothers have great faith in a 'little drop of gin' for the baby. The baby cries and some experienced dame explains that it wants a little drop of gin to 'warm it up inside'. The baby gets the little drop of gin – sometimes in its feeding bottle. It soon stops crying and goes to sleep. The fact of the matter is that the poor baby has got 'blind drunk' and will be quiet enough until it has slept off the debauch. Then it wakes with a 'bad head' and is very cantankerous until it gets a 'pick me up'. Infant mortality will remain high so long as this idiotic practice prevails.[336]

In 1910 Evan and Elizabeth Evans of Llangennech were imprisoned for fourteen days for giving a four-month-old baby whisky in its milk because it was crying.[337] In July 1899, Dr E. Evans, medical officer of health of Llanelli Rural District Council, considered that the heavy infant mortality of 'the previous few months [was] due to the unnatural methods of feeding now in vogue'. He noted that beef, mutton, cheese and meat were given to children. He commented:

> Whisky and gin are sometimes given to the children for different complaints which exist in the parents mind. As you know, many women are fond of gin and it is an easy matter for them to let the child have a little as well. All these things are against the child's constitution, which is upset most seriously, with the result that convulsions set in and bring about the child's death.[338]

Dr Evans also complained about the extensive use of condensed milk. How effective the alternative was is questionable, because one of the most adulterated and contaminated substances in Victorian and Edwardian Britain was cow's milk.[339] Conditions in Carmarthenshire's dairies were virtually uniformly bad, and although medical officers of health had powers to condemn insanitary buildings, in practice lack of staff made it easy for people to ignore sanitary requirements and warnings.[340] Milk churns were frequently left uncovered and exposed to flies from stables and the milk inside was often three or four days old before it reached the customer. As a result of such conditions diarrhoea and other gastro-intestinal diseases were rife.[341] As they lacked running water in their homes, many of the county's poor could not combat the ill effects of these circumstances. Teats and bottles were left unwashed for long periods, or washed in water that had been used for other purposes, so that harmful micro-organisms thrived. Thus, when eventually given to the baby, cow's milk was frequently a potentially lethal cocktail.[342]

It was the interrelationships between all these adverse factors which gave Carmarthenshire its unenviable infant mortality rate. Shortly before and during the First World War the attitude towards infant mortality rates hardened into a determination that something had to be done. Ironically, the drive by many diverse organizations to stop the 'massacre of the innocents' coincided with horrific, unprecedented mass slaughter on the killing fields of Europe. In Llanelli and Swansea, the National Association for the Prevention of Infant Mortality was active in organizing lectures and child-feeding classes.[343] In Llanelli, Lady Stafford Howard was a generous and unfailing patron of these classes and a pioneer of better feeding and childcare. She established the 'Marged Fach Welcome', which organized childcare classes for local schoolgirls and distributed free feeding bottles and dinners to expectant mothers and children.[344] Through the efforts of such well-intentioned and noble women at the local level, and social welfare legislation such as the Children's Act and the Midwives Act of 1908 at the national level, a new attitude can be discerned in Carmarthenshire by the outbreak of the First World War.[345] Coinciding as this did with a gradual improvement in the general standard of living and domestic sanitation, the adoption of birth control techniques,[346] and other general social improvements,[347] the infant mortality rate of the county fell below 100 per 1,000 births for the first time in 1915.[348]

The stoicism of parents in the face of terrible personal losses has been interpreted by some historians as callous disregard toward infant life. Male-dominated communities such as the mining valleys are believed to have placed a low premium on infant life.[349] The presence of infanticide is considered to be proof of the callousness of parents. But many people did care passionately and mourned their losses with sincerity. The death of the first two children of David and Eunice Davies in the early 1920s haunted David Davies at the birth of each of his grandchildren in the 1950s. His feelings of loss were not unique.[350]

6. *Education and Change*

It has long been assumed that the pursuit of education represented one of the central features of the Welsh national character. In emphasizing the success of the educational movement in Wales the harsh conditions which pupils endured in Welsh schools and the apathy which parents exhibited towards education have been forgotten. These facts have been sanitized from a historiography anxious to emphasize the achievements of the pioneers of Welsh education. But it should come as no surprise to us to learn that the harsh conditions of agricultural life were reflected within the schoolrooms of rural Carmarthenshire. This is the clearest message which comes through to the historian in reading the log books of the county's schools for the period 1870–1920.

In his log book, the master of Esgardawe School in the parish of Pencarreg complained in 1890 of the dampness of the walls and declared that it was impossible to work in the school during windy weather as smoke was blown back down the chimney.[351] In 1897 the master of Nantcwmrhys School arrived at the school to find that the ceiling had collapsed.[352] In 1894 the headmaster of Caeo School noted that 'the school had been exceedingly cold all this winter. The windows ought to be mended as the children are too cold to write'.[353]

Given such conditions, it is not surprising that the historian, in reading the log books of the county's primary schools, encounters a catalogue of sickness and early death. In 1903 the headmaster of Coedmor School recorded that 'it was impossible to go on with the work owing to the children's coughing'.[354] The condition of the children was further affected by the adverse conditions which confronted many of them on their long journey to school. In 1919 the master of Berrisbroke School, Cil-y-cwm observed:

> The attendance this morning is thirty per cent of the total there being only three girls and five boys present altogether. The roads are covered with water and the majority of the children had to wade through it last night to go home, some failing to do even that. This morning it is the same and the children who have arrived are wet. It was thought better to send those children home and close the school for today.[355]

This problem of travelling long distances over bad roads was common to all children in the rural schools of Carmarthenshire. The words of the master of Pen-waun School in Capel Iwan can stand for many: 'The situation of the school is such that during very wet and stormy weather it is impossible for the children to attend.'[356]

Nancwmrhys School in Cynwyl Elfed was particularly badly situated. In 1890 the master asked the local council to:

> fix on a suitable footpath for the children of the south western division of the parish. Hitherto they have to travel over marshy soil, covered with stagnant water augmented in winter times by heavy rain, so that the nominal pathways become almost impassable. The parents in consequence naturally feel reluctant to send their children to school

> because they know that their feet would be wet before they reached halfway and to remain in such conditions for several hours would be detrimental to their health.[357]

On 1 August 1890, such were the conditions following a rain storm that not a single pupil turned up for school.[358] The master had complained since 1881 of the dangerous state of the footbridge which crossed the stream. In October 1907, the bridge was washed away in a storm, thereby isolating the school.[359] In 1908, in desperation, the master decided to remake the path himself.[360]

Yet, the reasons for non-attendance at school were not confined to the vagaries of the weather. The Forster Education Act of 1870 and the establishment of schools across the county did not of themselves create a new attitude towards education. Profound changes had to take place in the nature of society before the education imparted by the school could be considered to be useful. The timing of this transformation varies from parish to parish, as local factors, influences and idiosyncracies affected the timing of change. Yet in virtually all the rural parishes, it is a fairly accurate generalization to state that school was, for most pupils, a peripheral and ephemeral experience. Even when the politicians decreed that schooling was compulsory, people in rural and urban society viewed schooling as secondary to the dictates of economics or the agricultural calendar. In urban areas, the pattern of apprenticeship at an early age, whether to a miner, shopkeeper, chemist or another trade, necessitated that a person sought employment as soon as possible. This is one of the factors which helps to explain the fact that, as the authors of the Aberdare report on intermediate education found to their surprise, only fifteen boys in a population of over 10,000 in Carmarthen town received a grammar school education.[361] In the rural areas the proportion was even lower. Between 1870 and 1910 only one person from Cefnarthen undertook the fourteen-mile journey to Llandeilo Grammar School[362] whilst in Tre-lech a'r Betws only a tiny minority went to the Queen Elizabeth Grammar School in Carmarthen.[363]

In rural areas the elementary school was of secondary importance to the requirements of farming. School attendance was cyclical, following the demands of working the land. In June 1895 the master of Nantcwmrhys noted:

> The attendance for this week again is very low. Several of the scholars are employed in helping their parents to cut turf (which is used as fuel) on the surrounding moors. A country schoolmaster has many difficulties to contend with which the town master knows nothing of.[364]

Two weeks later he added: 'The farmers have commenced mowing and attendance is very low in consequence.'[365] At the end of July he reluctantly declared a holiday for the duration of the hay harvest. The next month, the following observation shows that the agricultural calendar was still affecting the school: 'Attendance very low today and yesterday owing to the corn harvest, deem it advisable under the circumstances to give a week's holiday'.[366]

Following the resumption of school in September, the slowness of the corn harvest meant that attendance was still low. October saw further disruption, for the potato harvest was a crucial element for the economic surval of cottagers. On many farms payment of wages was in the form of rows of potatoes, and for this privilege the entire family was expected to help with harvest work. By April a new agricultural cycle had commenced: 'Several of the children kept at home, the farmers have commenced sowing and harrowing.'[367] In May the children were gathering stones in the fields.[368]

The timing of the harvest varied according to local climatic factors and the organization of agriculture. The fact that a cottager could owe a debt of labour to more than one farm meant that a particular child was absent for a long period. This made it difficult for the school boards to regulate holidays, but it is doubtful whether many board members, themselves being farmers, wished to interfere.

The records of other schools show that the experience of the master at Nantcwmrhys was typical. In 1891, the master at Berrisbroke noted that: 'most of the bigger children attend fairly well now, having nothing else to do at present.'[369]

Similarly the log book at Cefnarthen noted in August 1882 that since the weather was bad for hay there was a good attendance. Across the county other elementary schoolmasters also recorded the ebb and flow of the agricultural season in their log books. At Rhydcymerau in 1874, the hay was harvested in the third week of June and the land was harrowed in the third week of April.[370] The agricultural character of various parishes differed. In Cefnarthen the sheep-shearing season was particularly disruptive to attendance in 1905[371] whilst in Cwm-dwr the master noted in May 1890: 'as the barking season has now commenced I find that several of the scholars are engaged in the woods carrying bark.'[372]

Reading these school log books provides the historian with valuable insights into the importance of children's work and labour in rural society at the turn of the twentieth century. But it was not only the duties of working the land which kept children away from school. The events and activities of the rural community also lowered the number in school and forced many to close for the day. For example, the school at Llanfihangel-ar-arth closed for the celebrations of Calan Hen in Llandysul, for the meets of the local pack of otterhounds and for the local horse races.[373] Other examples show the diversity of social events at this time: Rhydcymerau School closed for religious services in 1907,[374] Coedmor School for the Hiring fair ar Llanybydder,[375] and Caeo School closed in September 1882 to celebrate the marriage of Sir James Hills and Miss Johnes of Dolau Cothi.[376] Seven years later the children marched behind the Caeo Fife Band to celebrate the wedding of Sir James Drummond and enjoyed tea in the schoolroom.[377]

The problems which confronted schools were profound. Perhaps the major problem was that to the bulk of the population the teaching provided by the school was incomprehensible. The schoolmaster sought to impart knowledge in English whilst the monoglot Welsh children stared open-eyed. The master of Rhydcymerau School, on taking up his duties in 1874, 'Found the children very backward in everything. Not one was able to speak a word of English.'[378] Twenty years later the school inspectors found English still 'very poor' and 'could not recommend it for the grant'.[379] In 1895, on their visit to Berrisbroke, the inspectors reported that: 'The English subject seems to have been entirely neglected: the upper standards being unable to answer questions of the most elementary kind.'[380]

At Farmers School the results in English in the 1880s were particularly bad and in 1886 the inspectors noted that: 'The results in English this year did not satisfy the requirements of the code . . . children of six years of age should attempt something more than the alphabet in reading and counting up to twenty in numbers.'[381] At Gwernogle in 1877 a similar conclusion was reached by the teacher: 'An effort was made to teach the English language. I was very surprised to find that the knowledge of most of them in English was very limited. Found an English explanation, however simple, in many cases of no purpose.'[382]

In 1880 the same headmaster reached the inevitable conclusion that lack of knowledge of the English language was affecting the pupil's performance in other subjects: 'The great obstacle to the progress of the children in the extra subjects proves to be their ignorance of the English tongue.'[383]

At Caeo School the arrival of the five Evans children in 1892 added to the problems: '[They] have just arrived from Patagonia. Unable to speak English since their languages in Patagonia were Welsh and Spanish, both of which they speak and write.'[384] To offset this, many school teachers adopted the 'Welsh Not' to punish Welsh speakers for the use of the language inside the school grounds. To the torment of his own conscience, the young Beriah Gwynfe Evans, later one of the great champions of the language, punished small children in his classes for using their mother tongue.[385] A passage from the Esgairdawe log book of 1887 would have been echoed throughout the area: 'Today the teacher informed the scholars that no more Welsh is to be spoken in school hours within the school premises. The Regulation is to come into force on 1st November.'[386]

Others adopted the more practical and prudent approach of using the Welsh language as the medium for learning English. In 1891 the master at Pen-waun School noted that:

> In English the results were not so encouraging . . . I hope to advance by making every word understood in each of the lessons in their Readers . . . by using Welsh explanations . . . This is certain to be slow work at first, but the time spent will be amply repaid in the future.[387]

In 1908 His Majesty's Inspectors endorsed this approach, informing the master and the school board at Llanllawddog that:

> The scheme of work should be drawn up with a view of training the children to an intelligent and accurate observation of their surroundings rather than to aim at mechanical results. To this end, Welsh should be methodically taught and utilised to a greater extent than at present.[388]

But even in this there were difficulties. The observers who noted the reticence, shyness, and unresponsiveness of Welsh children in the rural areas of Carmarthenshire failed to appreciate that many of the concepts which they sought to teach were urban and therefore strange and alien to the children. The children's world was full of the rich and concrete idioms of local speech. A person who wavered was like a 'rhech mewn pot jam', a fat boy was like a 'llo yn sugno dwy fuwch' and a fat man 'fel pot llaeth cadw'.[389] These and countless other phrases coloured the speech of rural people. In contrast, the new knowledge, the new world that the children encountered in the schoolroom, was incomprehensible.

The schools set out to teach a number of things[390] many of which, when we consider the strength of religion in rural Carmarthenshire, might appear at first to be superfluous: amongst these were morality, honesty, decency, civility and basic Christian principles. In April 1872 the master of Llanllawddog recorded that he 'punished one of the boys for indecent conduct towards one of the girls'.[391] A similar approach was adopted at Cwmcothi School:

> The children in order to conduct and behave themselves properly were this afternoon duly cautioned in habits of punctuality, of good manners and language and cleanliness, of obedience to duty, of consideration and respect for others, and of honour and truthfulness in word and act.[392]

Such lectures were clearly needed. In 1874 and 1884 the master at Gwernogle warned the children about 'using improper words'.[393] In October 1884 he noted:

> [I have] censured the fourth standard girls severely for continued idleness and bad language used while in school. Deceitfulness is not a rare thing among them, and for this base habit, I had to make an example of Jane Davies and Sarah Jones before the whole school.[394]

The teaching of religion and morality by schoolmasters was another factor which, in the long run, would undermine the role of religion in rural society. But there were, at the close of the nineteenth century, deeper and more profound forces in Carmarthenshire society which worked to undermine the old certainties of rural society. These social and economic changes went further than any legislation passed by politicians. For although the national politicians decreed the laws which provided free and compulsory education throughout Britain, the context of school had to become meaningful before people would use the schools. When people began to appreciate the possibilities which schools opened up, they recognized that their material interests could be best served by sending their children to school regularly.[395] This profound change took place parish by parish in Carmarthenshire in the period leading up to the First World War.

During the nineteenth century the extension of the rail network opened up new possibilities and perspectives for people in the rural areas. They enabled the woollen producers of west Wales to send their products to the industrial areas of Glamorgan.[396] But to do this the industry had to change from a cottage-based industry to more efficient and effective methods of production. The factories which emerged along the banks of the Teifi produced too many goods for one woman to sell alone at market. Agents began to travel to the stores of industrial south Wales. To keep a track of their business, bills of sales, orders, invoices and accounts had to be kept both up-to-date and accurate. Literacy and numeracy, the tenets of education, were needed to enable people to do this work. Through commerce and trade new perspectives on and experiences of the business economy of south Wales entered rural areas. The railways had also introduced new opportunities for farmers. Milk, butter, cheese and meat could be shipped further afield and to do this they quickly appreciated the benefits and advantages of schooling as a mechanism of safeguarding their economic interests. The importance of the rail network was clearly appreciated in nineteenth-century Wales. But the network was static. In his evidence to the Committee on Agricultural Depression in 1876, D. W. Drummond, the agent of the Edwinsford estate, declared:

> The great difficulty of one estate which I manage is that it is very inaccessible to the railway, and with very hilly roads. That makes the price the of manures, lime and coal and all requirements very heavy. If there were railway facilities only for getting these up even, it would be a great improvement to the condition of the county generally.[397]

Light railways were regarded, by many as the most likely answer to transport problems at the turn of the twentieth century.[398] But the real solution was already apparent in the discussions of the road committee of the Carmarthenshire County Council. It was the road network which broke down the friction of space,[399] and linked the isolated rural hamlets with the wider world. Motor omnibuses and lorries were frequent sights on the roads of Carmarthenshire from 1903 onwards. In 1903 Llansteffan was linked by a bus service to Carmarthen[400] and by 1913 the relatively remote settlement of Tre-lech a'r Betws had passenger and goods services to St Clears station.[401] Soon such local services linked previously remote and isolated communities with the rest of Carmarthenshire, south Wales and the world.

Technological change was not confined to the roads. In the harvest fields and farmyards of the county new machinery was rapidly introduced in the opening decade of the twentieth century.[402] Reaping and binding machines had largely replaced the labour gangs that had previously performed these tasks. They also made redundant the old customs and festivities which had accompanied the work. As the Revd Daniel Parry-Jones recounted in his eloquent account of his early life in the county:

> I remember[ed] as a small boy the first mowing machine coming to our fields, a second hand Bamford, heavy and clumsy. The next stop to cut wheat . . . was to attach some extra tackle to the mower, just a rack behind the cutting plate to gather the wheat . . . it was soon followed by the reaper, . . . this dispensed with the extra gang of people, for the sheaves could be tied at leisure when the job of cutting was done . . . Then the binder appeared . . . the common people blamed the farmers for taking their work away from them.[403]

David Jenkins has observed that such was the effect of the introduction of the self-binder that 'it brought an end to the society that once existed'.[404] Gone now was the laughter and the banter of young and old in the harvest fields. The pace of such change is deceptive, for not all parishes experienced the same extent or pace of technological change and development. But to one contemporary observer the rapidity was bewildering. A correspondent to *The Welshman* in March 1910 must have voiced the feelings of many when writing that:

> Things are travelling dreadfully fast just now. New inventions and new scientific discoveries are chasing each other so quickly that to the man in the street they pass like pictures in a panorama, before he has had time to grasp half their significance.'[405]

Their significance was the profound changes in the social attitudes and outlook of Carmarthenshire people which followed them. Not only were there changes in work organization and the disappearance of harvest and other customs; there were also profound changes in the concept of time in the rural areas. As Richard Vaughan had perceived, people were 'Moulded in Earth'. To the farmer in the nineteenth century time was work, life was work bringing him subsistence and independence. The introduction of machinery provided farmers with time: time to think, time to contemplate. The opening up of Carmarthenshire's road network, linking through to the Welsh rail network, increased the farmer's commercial horizons. For the first time, surplus cash was brought in to the countryside making it both possible and desirable (because of the depopulation of rural areas) for investment to be made in new technology. Farmers were now no longer 'bond-slaves of the past'. The Welsh farmer has often been regarded as conservative, a reactionary clinging stubbornly to outmoded and old-fashioned ideas and practices. He has been portrayed as stubbornly clinging to outdated techniques and equipment rather than investing in new machinery.[406] But, in the short term, which is all farmers at the turn of the twentieth century in Wales could afford to contemplate, there was no clear or obvious reason to welcome new techniques. Self-sacrifice through ignoring established wisdom could have been disastrous. But when social and economic horizons began to change, the farmers of west Wales proved themselves capable of adopting and adapting new discoveries and techniques. Change and the willingness to change is relative to one's own experiences. When personal experiences indicate that change is possible, then change will occur. In the early 1900s, such perceptions of change became commonplace not because of political activity but because of profound economic and social changes which took place in several areas of the lives of individual people. To many, the First World War is seen to provide the death-blow to 'traditional' Welsh society, and in many ways, this is correct. When the lights were switched back on all over Europe in 1918, they lit up a world dramatically different from that which had existed when Sir Edward Grey watched them being extinguished in August 1914. Yet that pre-1914 world, too, was already changing substantially, for no society can ever avoid the experience of change. Carmarthenshire was no exception. William Llewelyn Williams, in his reminiscences of life in Llansadwrn, noted this phenomenon and considered that:

> cyn i'r Rhyfel dorri allan yr oedd Cymru wedi newid mwy mewn un genhedlaeth nad odid a wnaeth mewn un ganrif o'r blaen ar ei hyd . . . yr oedd dull yr hen fyd wedi mynd am byth.[407]

2

A Psychic Crisis? The Social Context of Mental Illness and Suicide

This awareness by individuals that they were living in an age of unprecedented rapid change and development, and the 'disenchantment of the world' that was perceived and articulated by many contemporaries, is clearly seen if we consider the mental health of Carmarthenshire's people at the turn of the twentieth century. To achieve this the historian needs to examine the tender and tortuous history of the county's mental health hospital. In the nineteenth century people were much harsher in their decription of this noble institution. A character in one of Caradoc Evans's short stories, the frightening and repulsive 'Shadrach the Large', described the Joint Counties Lunatic Asylum as 'The House of the Mad'.[1] This starkly unsympathetic description belies the view of mental hospitals which was current at their foundation in the mid-nineteenth century. Nineteenth-century writers, when they looked back at the establishment of the asylum system, conformed to the fashionable Whig interpretation of history, and saw it as the outcome of philanthropic and liberal concern for the welfare and well-being of the dependent poor. The association of the early history of the public Asylum with the mid-nineteenth century social reform movement, and the work of Shaftsbury and Lewis Llewelyn Dillwyn made it easy to view the asylum as a monument to the humanitarian concern of Victorian philanthropists with lesser, poorer, unfortunate souls, and to ignore the harsher aspects of asylum reality.[2] Andrew Wynter, in a panegyric written on the asylum – *The Borderlands of Insanity* (published in 1879) – declared that the 'county asylum is the most blessed manifestation of true civilisation that the world can present'.

Its specific purpose was the provision of an environment through which the insane could be cured. At the opening of the Joint Counties Lunatic Asylum at Carmarthen in 1865, Dr. Wilson claimed that 'patients will experience from the additional and superior comforts placed for them a permanent deliverance from their distressing affliction'.[3] But this optimism, these noble intentions, were not vindicated by the subsequent history of the Joint Counties Lunatic Asylum at Carmarthen, or by that of any other British asylum. Perhaps Caradoc Evans, for once, had accurately captured the spirit and attitude of the age.

In 1865, when the asylum, after seemingly interminable debates and arguments, finally opened, it was estimated that 40 per cent of the people admitted could be cured. It seemed as if the asylum could fulfil the hopes of its founders and restore the mentally ill to health and to society.[4] But by 1870 the estimated rate of cure had slumped to 7 per cent of admissions. The true and frightening nature of insanity in the area was realized. The majority of the patients brought to the asylum had hopeless, incurable illnesses. In 1877, of 77 patients admitted, 44 (57.2 per cent) were classified as having no hope of recovery, and 20 of the remaining 33 were described as having only a slight chance of recovery. The majority of these patients had been certified as insane for over one year.[5] In 1890, of the 78 admissions, only 7 were described as experiencing their first attack or as having been certified as insane for under three months, the only group for whom cure was regarded as a possibility. In this unfortunate year 91.1 per cent of the admissions were hopeless cases for whom no cure could be expected.[6] The asylum had become a dumping ground for the human refuse of society. In 1888 the frustrating situation is clear in the Medical Superintendent's report. 'Our first aim, our highest aim', he wrote 'is to promote recovery of mental health' but he added despondently 'sadly this can only be accomplished in a minority.'[7] For the majority of inmates the only escape from the confines of the asylum walls came when they were laid in the thin wooden boxes that served as paupers' coffins.

Given the situation in which only a tiny minority were discharged from the asylum annually, and that the death rate of mental patients declined as a result of the eradication of the grosser instances of physical neglect, the number of patients was bound to increase rapidly. Originally designed in 1863 to house 212 patients, at the opening of the asylum in 1865, 112 patients took up residence. By 1869 the number of patients had doubled to 220, by 1879 it had doubled again to 440; in 1889 it rose to 553 patients, and continued to rise annually until 1917 when there were 758 patients in residence.[8] To house the patients the local magistrates, alarmed at the rapid increase in the demand for places at the asylum, and motivated by the overwhelming desire to economize, adopted the general policy of British magistrates, adding wing after wing, storey onto storey, and purchasing the nearby houses, whose rateable value had plummeted because of their proximity to the asylum.[9] Indeed, there was a close link between the asylum's popularity in the local community and its cost to local ratepayers. On 16 May 1870, the *Carmarthen Journal* contained a report that condemned the 'sordid and improper economies of private Lunatic Asylums', but only a short time later it declared with pride that the maintenance costs at the Joint Counties Lunatic Asylum had been cut from 9*s*.4*d*. per head per week to 8*s*.9*d*.[10] The advertising columns of local newspapers contained invitations to tender to local businessmen to supply provisions to the asylum. The lowest-priced quotations invariably were successful.[11] In 1889 the responsibility for county government was transferred from the magistrates to elected county councils. In Cardiganshire, Carmarthenshire and Pembrokeshire, the new county councils were overwhelmingly Liberal and Nonconformist.[12] However, because of their greater accountability to public opinion, the pressure for economies in the expenditure of the Asylum increased. On 24 November 1899, the dispute which had continued since the opening became openly acrimonious, when C. M. Williams of Cardigan demanded that Carmarthen Borough, which was not included in the original agreement of the 1860s, should pay on its acceptance into the system, a 'full share of the original building costs of the Asylum'.[13] The meeting ended in uproar when it was suggested that the original plan for the counties' contributions be based on a rateable value should be changed to a percentage charge based on the number of patients each county had at the asylum. Cardiganshire and Pembrokeshire representatives, whose respective shares of resident patients had fallen from 27 per cent and 34 per cent of patients in 1865, to 22.99 per cent and 32.7 per cent in 1899, resented Carmarthenshire's refusal to accept the change, though its share had increased from 38 per cent to 44.29 per cent of patients. The meeting led to a deadlock that prevented any substantial improvements until 1917 when the Home Secretary, after annual threats to the local officers from the lunacy commissioners, was at last called in to force a settlement. The episode is one of the most unpraiseworthy in the history of public health in Wales.

The dispute between the three counties seriously affected conditions within the asylum. Living conditions for patients were depressing, overcrowded and uncomfortable. In 1910 the Lunacy Commissioners expressed profound concern and horror at the three counties' refusal to act responsibly and end the dispute, and noted its effect on the patients:

> There are 74 males and 36 females in excess of accommodation . . . all dormitories are improperly overcrowded . . . We would mention one in particular, the epileptic dormitory on the female side, where the bedsteads are much closer than they ought to be, whilst 18 patients are sleeping on the floor; and in the day rooms allocated to the more troublesome male patients, some of whom are of a very dangerous type, there are far too many for proper and effectual supervision, care or safety.[14]

In 1913 the editor of the *Journal of Mental Science*, a person well acquainted with atrocious conditions within British asylums, stated that he found it 'hard to believe that out of an average population of 700 over 100 are in excess of the number for which proper accommodation has been provided.'[15] During the First World War years, because of the use of the Cardiff City Asylum as a military hospital, the already atrocious conditions further deteriorated when forty-four patients were transferred to Carmarthen.[16] In order to accommodate these patients, rather than extend the building further and spend more, the authority transformed the sewing room, part of the laundry, the billiard room and the isolation hospital into dormitories.[17] The falsity of the authority's claims that this overcrowding had little effect on the health of the patients is revealed by the fact that, while the average mortality rate from respiratory diseases amongst the general public was 1.6 per 1,000 people, in the asylum the rate stood at 16.6 per 1,000.[18] Harsher condemnation of the authorities is provided in the complaints of the lunacy commissioners that they only infrequently visited the asylum.[19]

As the number of patients resident in the asylum grew, and as the physical discomfort of the patients increased, the authorities began to realize the hopeless nature of mental illness in the area and the function of the asylum changed. Ostensibly a centre established to 'cure' the mentally ill and restore them to a valued place in society, the asylum very soon came to be regarded as a detention centre. This internal function was given external confirmation in the asylum's architecture. The building was grim and Gothic and the strong wooden doors and sturdy iron locks were intended to confine the inmates.[20] The asylum was in actual fact a custodial centre concerned with the maintenance of order. As the number of patients resident in the asylum increased, the medical superintendent became an administrator more troubled by the routine of forms and memoranda than by attempts to solve the complex problems of the individuals in his care.

Life within the asylum was strait-jacketed into a regime of inflexible monotony, both for the patients and for the staff. Mrs M. M. Lewis, who commenced work at the asylum in 1903 in order to provide for her eight orphaned brothers and sisters, remembered with pain conditions at the asylum.[21] Patients were dressed uniformly in blue-black Welsh flannel smocks with yellow leg stockings and large awkward black boots. The chains and locks attached to the boots of the most troublesome patients added to their macabre appearance. The food consisted of a distressing monotony of two ounces of bread, butter, jam and coffee for breakfast, soup or stew for dinner, a repeat of breakfast for tea-time, and at supper a treat of a thin watery gruel. Meat made one of its rare appearances on the table when the lunacy commissioners or the committee of visitors called to inspect the asylum. The poor nutritional value of the food exacerbated the listlessness and apathy of the patient. Discipline, Mrs Lewis remembered, was severely maintained, especially under Dr Goodall. In his black frock coat, black shiny top hat, white gloves and stethoscope, he carried out continual spot checks to see if the patients were in the full prescribed uniform. If they were not, the attendant was fined a shilling. With the money the doctor bought Turkish rugs to beautify the building. Walking on these rugs merited a further punishment. Mrs Lewis observed that 'people were trained to walk around and not on the rugs.'[22]

The method of 'training' was to deprive troublesome and unco-operative patients of their privileges. Staff confiscated tobacco and other goods and ensured that the patient would be absent from the entertainments for a period regarded as sufficient punishment. Ervin Goffman has shown that people who live outside 'total institutions' – such as monasteries, prisons, and asylums, can have little perception of the terrible psychological implications caused to the individual by depriving him or her of seemingly trivial possessions.[23] From the patient's first encounter with the asylum – everything about the institution seemed to lessen the chances of cure.[24] On arrival, patients were deprived of all their personal belongings, including their clothes. All the mechanisms and tools with which the individual had defined himself to society – clothes, cigarettes, combs – were taken, the person was thrown naked and unprotected into a new and alien world. In place of the mechanisms that helped him to define himself, the new patient was given the standard uniform of the institution. Many patients actively resisted the imposition of the institutional uniform in the same way as tramps confined to the workhouse did, by tearing the uniform to pieces.[25] The insistence that the uniform should be worn on all occasions undermined any benefit that entertainments gave to patients. The authorities claimed that the work given to patients – helping on the asylum farm, in the laundry, in the making and repairing of uniforms – was useful employment. Yet it offered little in the way of self-respect for the patient, and was therefore depressing and degrading. In reality it was another cost-cutting device; cheap labour for the maintenance of the institution.[26]

The asylum was conceived of and regarded as a curative institution and staffed at the highest levels by men who had received medical training. Because of this, the problem of maintaining 'discipline' and order was subtly described in medical terminology. Where the Medical Superintendent wrote 'treatment' in his journal, the historian can substitute 'discipline', while 'medical care' was a term which, in the reality of asylum conditions, included the shower bath and the electric bath. The banning of mechanical restraint and its replacement by manual restraint, was, because of its reliance on human beings, probably more prone to abuse. In 1877 *The Lancet* commented that: 'Everywhere attendants, we are convinced, maltreat, abuse and terrify patients . . . Humanity is only to be secured by watching officials.'[27] Events in Carmarthen bore this out. In 1868 a matron was fined £10 for beating patients on their thighs with her keys.[28] On 4 January 1870, the *Carmarthen Journal* reported the death of Rees Price, a 69-year-old ex-labourer from Llandovery, in a padded isolated cell at the asylum. The cause of death was given as brain disease, but the inquest noted that four ribs on each side had been broken and that there was a massive lung infection.[29] On 28 January, a report in the *Carmarthen Journal* of a blind pauper lunatic, who died from pleurisy, recorded that 'there seems little doubt that this particular kind of injury is the consequence of the attendants kneeling on the chests of refractory patients in order to make them submit to discipline'.[30] A surgeon noted that several other similar deaths had gone unaccounted for. In 1874, William Lewis, an attendant at the asylum, was fined £15 or two months' imprisonment for a severe assault on David Thomas, a pauper lunatic. During the hearing it was remarked that attendants used chains to discipline patients.[31]

Worse than this physical violence was the indiscriminate use of powerful drugs by attendants unsupervised by the medical superintendent and administered irrespective of the age, sex, mental or physical condition of the patient. At night the temptation and compulsion to use the drugs in order to maintain peace was greater. Two such drugs, out of the large variety used, were viewed with particular apprehension by patients who saw them as punishment. These were the hyoscine injection and the use of croton oil. The former was described by a Dr Stoddart in *The Lancet* as a 'refined substitute for hitting (the patient) on the head with a club'.[32] The effect of croton oil was equally dramatic:

> The bowels after a strong croton purge may be opened 10 or even 20 times, often there is a severe griping, vomiting and fainting . . . strips of mucus membrane are found in the stools . . . (the bowels) are not only scoured out but flayed . . .[33]

Critics of mental hospitals, such as Kathleen Jones and Thomas Szasz,[34] have argued that custodialism should have been replaced by a policy of allowing the insane to remain at home. Such a policy could have had little success in south-west Wales in the nineteenth and early twentieth centuries. In 1881, David Jones, a sheep farmer from the lonely mountainous country to the north east of Llandovery, was let out on one month's probation from the asylum; on his arrival home, he brutally murdered his wife and committed suicide in the lane leading from his upland farm to Llandovery.[35] Several other melancholic suicide victims whose tragic stories litter the pages of local newspapers, had at one time or another been patients at the Asylum.[36] Some form of custodial care was clearly needed, not just to protect the insane and their families from their unpredictable and violent behaviour, but also to protect the mentally ill from the public's treatment of them. In his *Chapters in the History of the Insane in the British Isles,* published in 1882, D. H. Tuke refers to the case of a female 'AB' from near Brecon:

> She had been chained in a crouching position, her knees forced up to her chin, and she sat wholly upon her heels and her hips, and considerable excoriation had taken place where her knees pressed upon her stomach . . . When she died it required very considerable dissection to get her pressed into her coffin. This might be taken as a sample of Welsh Lunatics.[37]

In 1873, Dr Hearder, medical superintendent at Carmarthen, complained that the local populace were slow to send their patients to the asylum for 'treatment', and that the general belief that they were treated kindly at home was false. He wrote:

> The bodily condition of the patients admitted in very many cases gives evidence to the lamentable neglect and cruel treatment to which they had been subjected . . . Two cases suffering from acute mania had been tied down to their beds, and their excretions allowed to remain until extensive sores had formed on their backs . . . whilst a twenty-seven year old man was a mass of sores from the soles of his feet unto his mouth, he had been certified as insane for years . . . Now here is a picture of scenes which are to be found in a land proud of its Christianity and civilisation. Do they not fasten a stigma on both, and cry out for reform?[38]

In 1907 the head attendant at the asylum complained to the medical superintendent that he was continually being disturbed late at night by people bringing in their uncertified lunatic relatives.[39] These dark, depressing and sombre traits in the character of Welsh rural society are captured by Caradoc Evans with characteristic starkness. In the short story 'A Father in Sion', Sadrach Danyrefail replies to his children's persistent questioning as to the whereabouts of their mother: 'Dear me, have I not put her in the harness loft? It is not respectable to let her out. Twm

Tybach would have sent his wife to the madhouse of Carmarthen. But that is not Christian'.[40]

The mad woman locked in the attic is almost a separate genre of English literature, of which Charlotte Bronte's *Jane Eyre* and Wilkie Collins's *The Woman in White* are probably the most familiar examples. In both, the mad women are incidental to the story and are intended to stir fear and repugnance in the reader. The visits of tourists to Bethlehem Hospital, London, in the eighteenth century, the infamous 'Bedlam', is well known through Hogarth's prints. But one of the principal sights of the town of Carmarthen in the late nineteenth century was the asylum. After sampling the pleasures of the local taverns, work trips from Llanelli would journey to Johnstown to laugh, shout and gesticulate at the inmates of the asylum.[41] In his *Annual Report* for 1885, the medical superintendent noted that it was

> correctly stated that the female patients were not allowed to walk too far into the Asylum grounds because of the rude behaviour to which they were exposed by ill conditioned men . . . The annoyance was extended to the male patients and for this the assistance of the police was needed to overcome it.[42]

In south-west Wales there was little truth in John Dryden's celebrated remark about madness: 'There is a pleasure sure/In being mad which none but madmen know'.[43]

The increase in the number of certified insane in the nineteenth century caused deep concern. Several reasons were propounded to explain the increase in insanity. Amongst the most influential was the idea that insanity and suicidal behaviour, like all deviant behaviour, were closely related to the social dislocation consequent upon industrialization and urbanization.[44] The idea was based on very shallow empirical foundations which supported the simplistic interpretation of industrialization and urbanization as being unnatural and unhealthy intrusions into a previously natural and healthy rural Britain. It was argued that the pressures of life in modern civilization caused mental illness and suicide.[45] The theory was confirmed by the 'social explorers', who ventured bravely into the abyss of urban Britain and produced a mass of evidence of the unhealthy living conditions and the physical degeneracy of the urban poor.[46] The urban poor were portrayed as sickly, stunted in growth and mental development. They were portayed as a race apart, an inferior race compared with the healthy, robust inhabitants of rural Britain. In Wales, such notions were common. The countryside was regarded as superior to industrial and urban Wales in its morals, physical condition, health and honesty. Such notions formed an integral part of the concept of the noble peasantry – 'y werin' – and endured well into the twentieth century.[47] In a lecture on the subject of 'God and the Land' delivered in 1941 at Manchester College, Oxford, the vicar of Llannarth, Canon J. M. Lloyd Thomas argued that the creation of cities and urban life were unnatural and contrary to divine laws. He went on to argue that the bombing of Europe's cities was the punishment which 'Babel' deserved.[48]

The study of the home location of patients admitted to the Joint Counties Lunatic Asylum at Carmarthen from 1877 to 1897 reveals no evidence to support such a theory. For example, while the heavily industrialized and urbanized area of Llanelli recorded a rate of 2.33 certified insane per 1,000 of the population, the rural areas of Newcastle Emlyn, Llandovery and Narberth had rates in excess of 3.5 per 1,000.[49] The vast majority of patients resident at the Joint Counties Lunatic Asylum between 1865 and 1920 came from the agricultural districts of the county. Contrary to the arguments of Professor Andrew T. Scull, it was the rural and not the urban areas of the three counties that accounted for the growth in the number of patients resident at the asylum.[50] The statistics for 1900 provide further proof to support the conclusion that the confinement of the mentally ill to an institution was primarily a rural phenomenon. In this year the rate of confinement of the mentally ill of west Wales to the Joint Counties Lunatic Asylum was 73.3 for those patients living in rural areas, and 56.15 for urban districts. The year was not untypical.[51] These facts invalidate the arguments that the rural parts of west Wales had been spared the shattering blows to kinship ties that had occurred in the industrialized south. Charles Booth, in his survey into *The Condition of the Aged Poor* (1894), revealed that, whilst in the Merthyr Tydfil area children were willing to provide for aged parents without recourse to the poor law authorities, in west Wales, in places like Llandeilo and Aberaeron, children had a callous disregard of familial duties, and the poor law authorities were frequently forced to intervene.[52]

Part of the explanation for the disparity between rural and urban rates of the certified insane lies in the process of migration. It was the young, the healthy and the fit who left the rural areas in search of opportunities offered by urban life, leaving behind the old, the weak and the senile, thus increasing the percentage that could be admitted to the asylum. But the serious problems that had confronted rural communities for generations should not be ignored. Rural isolation and the lack of communication meant centuries of inbreeding. Medical officers of health noted with concern the effects of inbreeding in several different rural areas, but the problems are vividly brought to life by individual case histories. D. J. Williams, in his story 'Pwll yr Onen', highlighted the bad effects of these brooding tensions.[53] On 8 April 1881, Margaret Jones, aged thirteen, of Llandovery Union, was admitted to the asylum after continuous night wanderings, during which she tore her clothes and was 'dirty in her habits'. She was described as suffering from 'nervous debility', which was probably congenital. Margaret joined her three brothers in the asylum.[54] On 25 November 1882 James Davies, aged thirty-six, from Lampeter, an imbecile from birth who had two illegitimate children, and whose father and sister were imbeciles, was admitted and described as being violent and suicidal.[55] In the Medical Officer's Annual Report of 1889, Dr Goodall remarked that a male idiot admitted was one of the thirteen illegitimate children by the same mother. The mother and grandmother, he said, were both 'peculiar'.[56] In 1903, the medical superintendent in his *Annual Report* noted

> an interesting case of a father and two daughters recently admitted, suffering from 'communicated insanity', which was rarely seen, the circumstances predisposing to their development existed in this instance; neurotic degeneration in the family, lonely surroundings, unusual anxiety and a terrible suddeness of onset of the illness.[57]

Psychiatrists at the asylum, in common with British psychiatrists, were heavily influenced by Henry Maudsley's *Body and Mind* (1870) and readily accepted the idea that inherited physical constitution was often the major cause of insanity. Of the classifications of the cause of mental illness given in the *Annual Reports* of the medical officer, the groups 'hereditary disposition' and 'congenital defects' represent well over 80 per cent of patients. The lunacy commissioners continually expressed shock and distress at the abnormally high level of hereditary and suicidal patients housed in the Joint Counties Asylum. In 1910, they noted that the incidence of suicidal patients present at the asylum was second only to the massive Winson Green Asylum in the city of Birmingham.[58] In 1888 the medical superintendent reported that: 'insanity in this district presents an abnormally high proportion of cases with a suicidal intent.'[59]

While the average of cases with suicidal tendencies stood at 7 per cent of inmates for England and Wales, in the Carmarthenshire, Cardiganshire and Pembrokeshire Asylum the rate was 35 per cent. In the 1921 medical officer of health's report for the county of Carmarthen, suicides represented 6.66 per 1,000 deaths in the county in 1920. The rural parts of the county account for over three-quarters of the suicides.[60]

The preoccupation with the hereditary causes of insanity led to a therapeutic nihilism that helped doctors to accept that their role should be that of custodian rather than curer of the insane, but it also focused attention away from the other possible causes of insanity. Dr Charles Williams, in his *Religion and Insanity*, argued that religion is 'seldom a cause of insanity, but rather it is a preventative, its absence or loss is often a direct cause, while its restoration is sometimes the only cure.'[61]

At the Joint Counties Lunatic Asylum, as at the other asylums of Britain, attendance at church was frequently praised and urged by the lunacy commissioners, but its value in the recovery of patients is doubtful.[62] In 1884, in his Twentieth Annual Report to the committee of visitors, the medical superintendent declared that 'the prevailing feature of insanity in this area as in the other asylums of Wales seems to be morbid depression of spirits connected with religious views.'[63]

Ministers of religion provide a frequent occupational group of patients housed at the Joint Counties Lunatic Asylum and their suicides dot the pages of the newspapers of south-west Wales.[64] Throughout the night of 22 December 1883, David Williams, a patient in the asylum, was much depressed, sleepless and tearful as the result of his religious insecurities.[65] Renewal of religious allegiance and the intensification of religious beliefs in revivals were reflected in the issues which troubled patients in the asylum. Following that remarkable year 1904–5, the medical Superintendent noted, in his Forty First Annual Report of 8 January 1906:

> Sixteen cases were admitted as a result of emotional influences of, in this instance, a religious kind which their hereditary unstable natures were unable to withstand. Religious emotion, being more massive and more intense, and having so to say a wider striking area than other causes of emotion, is more apt to cause mental breakdown, and more apt to tinge mental disorder than other factors.[66]

But despite these facts, religion continued to be viewed as a beneficial influence on the insane, for people believed what they wished to believe and ignored any unpleasant realities. In a similar way, the effects of venereal disease, in particular the role of syphilis in the production of congenital defects, was not acknowleged, though its effects must have been more widespread than the one or two cases given official recognition annually as suffering from general paralysis of the insane. In 1898 the coroner for West Carmarthen noted that in examining the bodies of persons dying in asylums:

> one observes the comparative frequency of degeneration of the blood vessels (arteries) of the brain, and I quite subscribe to the view expressed by eminent authorities, that syphilis is the most frequent cause of organic brain disease in persons not much past middle life . . . A careful inquiry into the history of these cases often discloses the existence of hereditary or acquired syphilis to a surprising degree.[67]

The First World War drew attention to the serious deficiencies in British health standards and a number of schemes were introduced by the government to combat infant mortality and the ravages of venereal disease.[68] In Carmarthenshire, although local doctors and others denied the existence of the disease, and some argued that venereal disease was a punishment devised by God for the immoral and that treatment of the disease would cause an unprecedented sexual revolution in the county, 998 people from the county received treatment in 1917 for venereal diseases at Swansea General Hospital.[69] The causes of insanity were modelled to fit preconceived conceptualizations of society.

The study of mental illness and suicide allows the historian to penetrate beneath the common generalizations of economics and social sciences to capture the particular experience of the individual person. The historian is given privileged access to the neuroses, obsessions and phobias that were dominant forces in an individual's life. The Superintendent's Journal is one of the most remarkable historical documents available to the historian. It offers a window into a netherworld that existed in the reality of south-west Wales. It is a world in which jealousy, spite, envy, hatred, fear, resentment and malice were the main operating emotions – a world of forks being driven through eyeballs, of noses and ears bitten off. It is a savage, vicious world, a world in which fear ruled. But it is a world above all of the individual – the starting-point of all histories. Ann Praws, from the Cardigan Union, admitted to the asylum on 23 July 1881, imagined that she was to be boiled alive because of the enormity of her sins.[70] Margaret Morrels, a 34-year-old from Carmarthen, admitted to the asylum in February 1882, had been a gibbering wreck ever since her husband had deserted her two years previously.[71] Mary Rogers, aged thirty-six, admitted from Llanelli Union on 15 January 1884, was said to have been insane for six years as a result of injuries inflicted by a threshing machine.[72] The unsavoury atmosphere of jealous gossip and spite that permeated some neighbourhoods, that spilt over from the street corner into the police court, is also seen in the asylum. Fanny Thomas, a 54-year- old woman from the Llanelli Union, was convinced on 27 April 1887 that her neighbour had sent two men and a woman with loaded pistols and other weapons to destroy her. She joined her husband in the asylum. In another case, Mary Ann Jones, aged twenty-one from Carmarthen, certified as insane for one month, was admitted following accusations of immorality.[73] On 12 October 1881, John James, a blind man, was described as being very dangerous to those near him, as a result of his 'imagining that he can see his wife misbehaving herself'.[74] Henry Heeson was one of the many who chose escape from the pressures of nineteenth- century life through creating a dream world of his own. Henry's was the world of a seventeenth-century Tsar of Russia.[75] Particularly distressing to read about is the plight of the women suffering from puerperal mania. Victims of the insanitary incompetence of local midwives, these poor beings relived the horrors of their confinement and their screams rang shrill and sharp through the echoing corridors and out into the unresponsive, unsympathetic night. Condemned by contemporaries as irrational and irrelevant, ignored by the 'massive condescension of posterity',[76] the problems of these people, because of their common humanity and the insights which they

"The House of the Mad", or the Joint Counties Lunatic Asylum which opened in 1865 (Carmarthenshire Records Office)

shed into Carmarthenshire society, deserve the attention of the historian.

Suicide, even when publicly committed, is the most private and impenetrable of human acts. The historian is presented with the insurmountable problem that the participants usually leave behind them no written records, only a rippling pool of regrets and temporary sadness, gradually wiped away by time and forgetfulness, as if they had never existed, or perhaps lingering a little longer in the conscience of a friend or relative.[77] Statistics do not help the historian to penetrate these resonant silences. Throughout the nineteenth century death by suicide was recorded by the Registrar General in the general categories of 'Violent Death' and 'Uncertified Causes'.[78] The problem is compounded, for as P. E. Hair has argued, 'suicide cannot be subject to statistical calculation, since all too many suicides are not reported as such.'[79] From 1911, suicide was identified as a cause of death by the Registrar General, and analysis of these figures to 1919 enables us to discern general patterns in the suicide rate.[80]

The first conclusion to draw from the figures is that suicide was primarily a feature of the rural areas of the county. During the period 1911–19 rural districts of the county account for 66 per cent of the deaths recorded in the county. Of the suicides, 16.9 per cent occurred in Carmarthen Rural District, 15.1 per cent in Llandovery and 13.4 per cent in Llandeilo. The lowest rates occurred in Llandeilo Urban District, where 0.8 per cent was recorded and in Kidwelly Municipal Borough (1.7 per cent). The aggregate average for the urban districts of the county is 4.7 per cent, that of the rural districts 9.7 per cent of deaths by suicide. The second conclusion which we can draw is that suicide, despite the literary portrayal of the melancholic brooding female and the drowning Ophelia, was largely a male preserve.[81] Between 1911 and 1919, 69.6 per cent of deaths by suicide recorded in the rural districts and 66.7 per cent of suicides in the urban districts of Carmarthenshire were committed by males. In both the rural and urban districts, male suicides outnumber the female. In Carmarthen Rural District the rate of male suicide is 63.1 per cent of all suicides. In Llanelli Rural District the percentage of male suicides is 81.8 per cent and in Llanelli Urban District 71.4 per cent. Only in the municipal borough of Llandovery and the rural district of Llandeilo Fawr do female suicides outnumber male. The third conclusion which we can draw is that people in mid-life were more apt to commit suicide than any other age group. Suicides of people in the age group forty-five to sixty-four represent 48.5 per cent of deaths by suicide in the rural districts of the county and 47.2 per cent in the urban districts. The next age group, aged between twenty-five and forty-four, represent 25.7 per cent of suicide deaths in rural districts and 36.1 per cent in the urban districts. People aged under twenty-five represent 15.1 per cent of suicide deaths in rural districts and 8.3 per cent in urban areas. Finally, those aged between fifteen and twenty-five comprise 10.6 per cent of suicide deaths in rural districts and 11.1 per cent in the urban districts.

But these statistics can tell us little of the motives which enabled people to answer one of the fundamental question of theology and to 'go gently into that good night'.[82] As the coroner's records for the period under discussion are not open, the historian has to rely on the reports of suicide which appear in local newspapers in order to study the forces that drive an individual to desperate action. A survey of the newspapers has revealed over 260 reported cases of suicide committed in Carmarthenshire between 1900 and 1919. The survey reinforces the general conclusions which we have noted above regarding the age, sex and geographical distribution of suicide. It also reinforces P. E. Hair's assertion that suicide in the period was under-recorded. However, the main value of the survey lies in the details which it gives of the lives of the individuals involved. The reports give details of the proceedings at the coroner's court. The evidence, of course, is not that of the participants but that of friends, lovers, relatives and eyewitnesses, who pieced together the detritus of the last days of a truncated life. One often feels sympathy for those who were left behind. Many were very young and for them the discovery of the dead, mutilated or hanging body of a parent must have been a profound and enduring experience. The historian can only sympathize with the five-year-old who discovered his mother hanging in a toilet, and the ten-year-old who ran to tell his grandparents that his mother was attempting to drown herself and his younger brother.[83] Stunned, witnesses frequently did not know who to turn to, what to do or say. The bewilderment of the witnesses can be seen in February 1916 when a Tregaron inquest heard that, after discovering the body of Private David Davies of the Welsh Guards hanging in an outhouse, John Williams and his master 'sat by the fire for a while before cutting it down'.[84] Was their action based on a conscious desire to rest a little before the toil of the day and restore strength to the living, or was it the result of their bewilderment and revulsion at Private Davies' tragic act?

Love, rebuffed or scorned, the classic suicide motive of the girl in contemporary literature, had parallels in real life. In 1917, Maggie Morgan threw herself under a GWR express train after her boyfriend 'finished with her'.[85] Margaret Williams, a cook, poisoned herself and Muriel Morgan drowned herself in the Tywi following similar experiences.[86] David Davies, a farmer, found his daughter and her baby poisoned in their bedroom in November 1916. At the inquest he poignantly and painfully recalled that she normally spoke in her sleep, but that night she had been quiet and his suspicions had therefore been aroused. She had twice attempted to take out an Affiliation Order for the child's paternity at the Llanelli Police Court. Twice she failed. Strychnine ended her fears. At the inquest, the coroner, Dr Thomas Walters, remarked: 'Who ever the man is who led her astray, I doubt if he will have comfortable feelings hereafter.'[87]

But men too felt the wounds of love. James Evans, a farm servant, 'worried over a girl', hanged himself at Caer-bryn, Pen-y-groes in January 1905.[88] Henry Thomas, a collier, drowned himself in Pwll Du in the River Morlais when a paternity order was awarded against him.[89]

Those who survived the trials and tribulations of courtship found life no easier when married. Mary Lewis took carbolic poison when her husband left her.[90] Mary Davies, a farmer's wife, committed suicide when she and her husband separated in March 1905.[91] Thomas Rees Richards committed suicide rather than appear in court for arrears of £30 on a separation order awarded to his wife.[92] Having just lost a child, Mary Ellen Davies of Pen-clawdd murdered her three daughters, aged between two and four, and then committed suicide in an upstairs bedroom.[93] The inability to cope with adverse economic fortunes also features prominently in the reasons witnesses gave to inquests for the suicide of a friend or acquaintance. Charles Griffiths cut his throat with a razor because of his worries about his unemployment.[94] Arthur Williams, a bookmaker, committed suicide in July 1907 because of his financial problems.[95] George Blake, agent to the Stradey Estate, cut his throat in a greenhouse when his employer told him that his services were no longer required as the son would manage the estate.[96] David Bowen, a publican and timber merchant, a man, according to witnesses, with few problems, hanged himself with a horse's harness after he had failed to sell the animal.[97] John Jones of Llangynnwr, a coachman, committed suicide when he was sacked by his employer as the result of the purchase of a car.[98]

The First World War had a profound psychological impact on the home front as well as on the soldiers and this is reflected in suicide cases in Carmarthenshire. Soldiers suffering from 'shell-shock'[99] and hysteria – which had previously been considered peculiar to women – committed suicide with distressing regularity between August 1914 and November 1918.[100] Receipt of a letter confirming that the King required a person's service in the trenches was a frequent trigger to suicide. Henry Ridgen attempted to commit suicide at Llanarthne on receipt of such an invitation in August 1915.[101] Ernest Lloyd Morgan, a court registrar and nephew of the aspirant Poet Laureate, Sir Lewis Morris, was more successful. He 'shot his face off' after being passed fit to serve his King and Country.[102] But it was not only those directly involved in the fighting who found the pressures of the war too great to bear. Ruth Williams, worried about her sons in the colours, hanged herself in an outhouse, and Ann Williams, who had two sons on the Western Front, cut her throat.[103] When her husband Frank returned to the war in August 1917, Elizabeth Mundy drowned her youngest son and attempted to drown herself.[104]

Religion, as we have seen, sometimes intensified mental instability. The evidence of suicide cases confirms this. In 1919, the Revd John Crwys Evans committed suicide after prolonged depression following the death of his son.[105] The Revd John Thomas of Capel Isaac, suffering from indigestion but apparently no other problems, hanged himself in the garden shed.[106] But religion itself not only coloured the problems of an individual, it created new fears. Fears of God's revenge, of the fallen nature of man, of Hell, were real anxieties for a number of individuals. William Morgan, a forty-year-old collier from Llanarthne, advised to take a change of air by his doctor, walked to Dryslwyn Castle where he jumped into the River Tywi. Dragged out 500 yards downstream, he insisted that his sins were unpardonable. He was admitted to the asylum.[107]

In the majority of suicide cases the evidence which the historian has to consider is the recollections of witnesses. Only infrequently do we encounter the words of an individual who had wrestled with the 'Savage God' and resigned himself to death.[108] Despite the plots of melodramatic Victorian novels, suicide notes were infrequent. The note left by Thomas Hambury Powell tells us much about the motives that drove him to his death in Llanelli Dock and the forces which operated in his society:

> I did this rash thing because of drink. It forced me to do it, and I must make an end to myself in this way. The snares of death compressed me round about, and the pains of hell got hold upon me. O Thou Great and Merciful God, wilt thou forgive and pardon my sins that I have sinned against Thee, and for this wicked thing that I have done. – Dear Father, Mother and Sister, will you forgive me for this wicked thing I have done. Do not let it trouble you for I shall have forgiveness in the Lord. I hope all the young men of Llanelli will give up the evil drinking, and take a warning from me, dear friends.[109]

The motives that we have considered are but a few of the reasons which compelled individuals to end their lives. The plethora of motives are mirrored in the enormous variety of methods chosen – hanging from trees, bacon hooks, in toilets, outhouses, and bedrooms, drowning in rivers, streams, docks, baths and ponds, and surprisingly frequently the death of women in fresh water casks, taking strychnine, liquid ammonia, acid, other poisons, swallowing broken glass, shooting, cutting one's throat with a razor, or a blunt table knife, even decapitation underneath an express train.[110] Suicide is a random phenomenon that corresponds to the infinite variety of human motivations. Each individual's death had its own idiosyncracy, its own peculiarities.

Despite the evidence, the view that suicide and mental illness were, like all deviant behaviour, the product of life in unnatural and unhealthy urban and industrial environments continued, as we have seen, to have its advocates. The view fails to appreciate the realities of life in the rural communities of south-west Wales in the period 1870 to 1920. In the traditional view, rural Wales is seen as an idyllic Eden. The cottages are clean, whitewashed, with ivy growing on the walls, and latticed porches are overgrown with pink roses. The inhabitants of the houses are rosy cheeked, fit, healthy and sturdy. These notions are seen in the poetry and popular songs that romanticized the Welsh agricultural community. Works such as Crwys's *pryddest*, 'Gwerin Cymru', which was victorious in the Carmarthen National Eisteddfod in 1911 and the song 'Y Bwthyn Bach Tô Gwellt' abound with such images.[111] However, the reality of life was vastly different from the rural Wales of the imagination. The romantic view is based on insufficient analysis of the quality of rural life. The beauty of pastoral agricultural landscape is allowed to obscure the harshness of its living conditions. In 1864 Dr. Hunter, in a report to the Privy Council on the death-rate in south Wales, stated:

> The farmer in Wales as well as the labourer must be taken to mean a person generally badly lodged, and insufficiently fed and clothed. The property offers little attraction to persons of capital, and in which nothing but the sternest frugality can hope to find any gain . . . It may be truly said of the class that in many districts the farmer himself does not eat fresh meat once a month; that his only animal food is sparingly taken and consists of the leanest cheese, and lean beef or ham salted and dried to the texture of mahogany, and hardly worth the difficult

> process of assimilation . . . In Cardigan district a medical practitioner described the children as 'pining for want of food as soon as weaned', and thought that if the climate were colder the whole race would perish . . . Persons well able to judge believe that both men and women are going down to the lowest point of strength at which it is possible to live . . . (they are) . . . a debilitated and scorflous people.[112]

The evidence brought before the Royal Commission on Land in Wales and Monmouthshire from the three counties of Carmarthenshire, Cardiganshire and Pembrokeshire revealed that the quality of life had changed little by the 1890s.[113] In all aspects of health investigation in the late nineteenth century, it is found that the rural areas compared unfavourably with urban areas. Infant mortality tells its own sorry tale. In the report of the county medical officer of Carmarthenshire for 1922, the infant mortality rate of Llanelli stood at 79.3 per 1,000 deaths, that of newly industrialized and developed Ammanford and Burry Port stood at 66.6 and 49.6 per thousand respectively, while that of Llandovery was 161.2 and Newcastle Emlyn 166.6 per thousand.[114] Between 1905 and 1909, while the death rate per million from consumption for England and Wales stood at 1,125, that of London at 1,325, and that of Glamorgan at 1,134, the corresponding figures for Cardiganshire was 2,237, Carmarthenshire 1,525, and Pembrokeshire 1,393. Cardiganshire and Carmarthenshire came first and second in this sombre list.[115] In the 1930s the Report of the Ministry of Health's Inquiry into the Anti-Tuberculosis Service in Wales, re-emphasized the excessive mortality rates of rural Wales.

It was not only the living conditions which were harsh. The inhabitants of south-west Wales had to endure profound psychological pressures. Agricultural historians argue that the agricultural depression of the late nineteenth century was not as severe in Wales as in the cereal growing areas of England,[116] but it is irrefutable that Welsh farmers, as Dr Hunter noted, had to exercise severe frugality in order to exist. It was this frugality that enabled the Welsh farmer to survive the depression of the late nineteenth century. Essential to this survival was the contribution of the entire family. Condemned by historians for their lack of imagination and reluctance to invest in their land, the Welsh farming community took the only course of action open to them to enable them to survive – they saved and took no risks. All their collected wisdom and experience guided them to this option in their fight for survival.[117] But the pressures were not just financial. Farmers also laboured against profound psychological pressures. The demands of winning a living from the earth were crippling and incessant. Richard Vaughan of Llanddeusant wrote eloquently of this:

> And for all our sweat, for the resilience of our bones and the fibre of our muscles, for all that we gave it, the land only grudgingly returned us the fruit of our labour . . . The soil exacted its labour all right, dragging us downwards until one grew bent with work; flesh and bone returning with each step to its own element in earth. We were moulded in earth, soil-bound to the farm.[118]

Caradoc Evans expressed it with characteristic brevity: 'The Earth Gives all and Takes All.'[119]

The attachment of farmers to their farm and to their land stretched back for generations of the same family. Tradition and inheritance were unbreakable bonds which tied farming communities to the earth. It was tradition and pressures such as these, as John Davies has shown,[120] that explained the phenomenon of cheering crowds when a tenant purchased his farm at auction in the late nineteenth and early twentieth centuries. The attempt to safeguard and hold on to their inheritance through working land that could no longer provide an adequate living had profound mental and psychological repercussions for succeeding generations. Richard Jeffries expressed this vividly: 'The truth is we are murdered by our ancestors. Their dead lands stretch forth from the tomb and drag us down.'[121]

The poet R. S. Thomas has also noted the overbearing burden of history and inheritance in his poem 'Tenancies'.[122] Coupled with the profound psychological pressure that was caused by the determination of people to maintain, at all costs, their contact with the land were the peculiar pressures of village and hamlet society. The individual had to conform to pre-set, inflexible notions and expectations of behaviour.[123] Transgressions of these codes of conduct were punished by various defence mechanisms which society had devised, ranging from social ostracism to the 'rough music or Ceffyl Pren'.[124] People in rural society appear to have been obsessed by the activities of their neighbours. It was this morbid curiosity which fuelled the overpowering sense of claustrophobia to Caradoc Evans' writings. These pressures could, and did, become intolerable. The newspapers and court records of west Wales are littered with terrifying reports of lonely, melancholic, horrific, seemingly inexplicable suicides. But they were not inexplicable, for they stemmed from deep-seated social causes. The details of these brief, truncated lives illustrate in a hideous way the pressures that confronted and broke the individual in south-west Wales.

3

'Secret Sins': Crime and Protest

For many late nineteenth-century commentators, the most notable feature of crime in Wales was its absence. To Thomas Rees, writing in the 1860s, 'the inhabitants of Wales, under all their disadvantages, are more virtuous than their better conditioned neighbours in the adjoining English counties.'[1] In his memoirs of his early life in the parish of Cynwyl Gaeo, the Reverend David Davies identified the agent responsible for the Welsh people's superior virtues:

> it is the Protestant Nonconformity of the Welsh people, as lived and taught by their religious teachers during the last two centuries, that has preserved them from ignorance, lawlessness and irreligion, and made of them one of the most scripturally enlightened, loyal and religious nations upon the face of the earth.[2]

During the nineteenth century the custom developed of presenting judges at the Welsh assizes with a pair of white gloves when the Calendar before him contained no criminal business. From this custom there emerged the image of Wales as 'Hen Wlad y Menig Gwynion' – 'The Land of the White Gloves'. This imagined land was rural in its locale, intensely moral, free from crime and deferential to authority.[3] At the turn of the twentieth century the belief in the reality of this image was widespread.[4] In 1900, in his address as the new President of the Independents, the Reverend Thomas Johns of Capel Als, Llanelli, informed his mass audience that 'the Welsh rural areas are still the location of "Hen Wlad y Menyg Gwynion", only the southern industrial valleys have been corrupted by the influx of English people and their vicious habits.'[5]

But, despite the strength of the view of Wales as 'Hen Wlad y Menig Gwynion', dissenting voices were occasionally heard. Many of the judges on the assize circuits expressed concern at the lack of cases brought before them, as they were convinced that crime and protest were more common than their empty calendars indicated.[6] In the early 1880s, when Lord Justice Brett was presented with no business, he remarked to the local magistrates:

> Gentlemen, I would willingly congratulate you on the non-existence of crime in your several counties if it did not exist, but as I believe it does exist, though by some means it is not brought before me, my congratulations must assume a modified form.[7]

That acerbic critic of Welsh life and mores, Caradoc Evans, epitomized the judge's disquiet with characteristic brevity: 'Wales', he declared, 'is a land of secret sins'.[8]

Where then does the truth lie? Was west Wales a land of 'secret sins' or was it a paradisal land free of crime? Through analysing the criminal statistics of Carmarthenshire we can establish which of these diametrically opposed views most accurately reflect the reality of late nineteenth-century society in west Wales.

Historians of crime have drawn attention to the dark figure of unrecorded crime which exists in every society and consequently to the limitations of official statistics.[9] Comparisons of crime between societies are difficult because the criminal statistics have flaws in their local components – one police force will be more conscientious than another in recording offences, and would in certain areas of Wales where, for example, the temperance cause was very strong, concentrate on drunkenness and Sunday Closing offences rather than upon other crimes.[10] Such local features can be compensated for when a historian is using statistics for the whole country, since over-recording in one area can be balanced by under-recording in another. But it is only at the level of national figures and trends over time that criminal statistics can be used meaningfully. To use them on a smaller scale for a period of only four decades is to run a much greater risk of distortion, for, as David Phillips has argued, the smaller the scale, the greater the possibility that these distortions will significantly affect the figures.[11]

Yet all the historian can glean from large-scale analysis is an outline of national trends which may mask important and contradictory movements in the incidence of criminal activity, often of a very localized character. The national average lumps together agricultural and industrial, rural and urban, rich and poor areas, areas of active policing and areas poorly policed, areas badly affected by swings in the trade cycle and areas largely unaffected by them. To go beyond such generalizations the historian needs to attempt to study the criminal profile of towns, villages and hamlets within the administrative framework of a specific area. Only by sharpening the focus on particular communities can we establish the predominant features of crime in any society. The criminal statistics thus have to be treated with caution. To obtain information and detail on the pattern of offenders prosecuted and the working of the forces of law enforcement, the historian has to examine the original court records and supplement them with the newspaper reports of court proceedings.[12]

Having noted these difficulties, we will undertake a brief examination of the pattern which emerges from the official criminal statistics of Carmarthenshire. In his *Report* for 1887, the chief constable for Carmarthenshire reported that indictable and non-indictable offences within the county had increased from 2,653 in 1880 to 2,762 in 1881.[13] Of these 2,762 offences, 606 were under the Intoxicating Liquor Acts, 261 under Vagrancy Acts, 175 were for assaults, 130 were offences against the Excise Acts, 108 concerned various felonies, 78 were under the Game Acts, 55 were Weights and Measures offences, 38 were under the Salmon Fisheries Acts, and 26 were for cruelty to children.[14] The crime rate in Carmarthenshire remained relatively stable throughout the nineteenth century and the early decades of the twentieth century, despite the stated fears of contemporaries that crime was increasing.[15] In 1919 there were 2,603 offences in Carmarthenshire. The types of offences reflected social and technological changes which had taken place since 1881. In 1919 the most frequent offences were breaches of the Highway Acts with 539 prosecutions, and of the Education Acts with 396. These were followed by offences against the Licensing Laws and Drunkenness (422 offences), offences against the Sunday Trading Act (367), the Betting and Gaming Acts (95), cases of malicious damage (99 offences) and vagrancy (57 prosecutions).[16]

The majority of these indictable and non-indictable offences were dealt with in the police courts and petty sessions of the county. The more serious crimes were forwarded for hearing at the quarter sessions and the assizes.[17] In 1883 seventeen cases were sent for trial at the assizes.[18] These ranged from Ann Thomas of Llanelli, who was fined 10*s*.6*d*. for threatening behaviour towards Mary Thomas with a razor, to two assaults by husbands upon their wives. But the majority of offences were against the Game Acts, in particular salmon poaching.[19] By 1919 the number of crimes sent for trial at the assize courts had almost doubled to thirty-two.[20] This figure put Carmarthenshire a poor second to Glamorgan, where 232 cases were tried at assizes and quarter sessions. In comparison with its other neighbours, Carmarthenshire sent substantially more cases for trial. Cardiganshire and Pembrokeshire sent seven cases each whilst Brecknockshire sent only two cases to the assizes.[21]

The disparity between Glamorganshire, Monmouthshire, Carmarthenshire and the rest of Wales is partly explained by population and the existence of large urban centres where both the opportunities and the facilities available to criminals combined to increase the number of crimes.[22] But the chief constable of Carmarthenshire frequently argued that the correct measure of the criminality of a county was not linked to population but with the rate of crimes committed per police constable.[23] Using this yardstick in 1912, he argued that Carmarthenshire was not a 'quiet county with little crime, but in truth is one of the worst in the country.'[24] Per constable Carmarthenshire's record was worse than that of Glamorgan, ranking in the top six in Britain, whilst for crimes of violence the county was third, following Glamorgan and London.[25] There was, the chief constable argued, an urgent need for more police in the Aman Valley and in Llanelli town. But even after twelve extra constables were provided for these areas, the chief constable continued to complain that the county was underpoliced and unable to cope with the large crowds that gathered on Thursday and Saturday nights in Llanelli and in other urban areas.[26] The behaviour of youths, male and female, in town and in the countryside, was a continual problem that concerned the adult world.[27] The streetcorner culture of youth was vigorously condemned throughout the nineteenth and early twentieth centuries because many saw it as the start of the downward path to drunkenness, petty crime and moral degeneracy.

The historian has to be conscious of the problems which confront him if he accepts the chief constable's arguments at face value. The chief constable, with the laudable intent of the protection of the public, naturally emphasized the high level of criminal activity in his area of responsibility and the necessity for increasing the size of the police force.[28] However, his arguments did help to underpin the popular conceptions of crime and protest in south-west Wales. Many people in Carmarthenshire at the turn of the twentieth century regarded crime and protest as urban phenomena, committed by a small hereditary class of criminals, 'Strangers', and English people with their 'vicious habits'.[29] Many of the offences which appear in the chief constable's reports as criminal offences appear today to be relatively harmless. However, it is not the historian's role to draw distinctions in the degree of moral turpitude involved in different types of offences. Criminal behaviour in this study is taken to be behaviour which was in violation of the law as it was then defined. If an act was prohibited by law, and was treated as such by the agencies of law enforcement and the courts of law, then it is of relevance to this study.

If the historian considers the degree of opposition to an activity by the volume of complaints made against it then probably the most odious and reprehensible offence in the late nineteenth century was drunkenness. Drink was widely seen to be the root of all evil.[30] Temperance literature abounds with graphic examples of the deleterious effects of drinking and the stumbling, shambling, despicable deeds of the drunkard.[31] To many, drink was the cause of all social evil. This tendency to oversimplify was condemned by the editor of the *Carmarthen Weekly Reporter* in 1899:

> In the Middle Ages all misfortune was put down to his Satanic Majesty. In a later age everything from a Cholera epidemic to a big fire or a storm was looked upon as Divine Visitation . . . now crime, lunacy and poverty, and almost every evil are ascribed to alcohol . . .[32]

Temperance campaigners scoured the police courts for details of the activities of over-indulgent men in order to personalize their warnings of future retribution. Cases such as that of Henry Jenkins of Carmarthen who, in 1905, was arrested in King's Square for shouting indecencies at girls while drunk, provided the factual basis for moral tales of revivalists.[33]

Few areas of Victorian social life have attracted such a variety of conflicting statistical analyses as the consumption of alcoholic beverages. In Wales this usually meant beer drinking.[34] In

Carmarthenshire, as we have seen earlier, offences against the Licensing Laws and charges of drunkenness against individuals were amongst the most common offences in both 1883 and 1919. Temperance campaigners were keen to point out the high incidence of drunkenness which existed in the county, and the press of the county, both denominational and secular, is full of alarmist reports of increases in drunkenness. In 1916, for example, at a time when Lloyd George and the government expressed concern about the detrimental effects that drink was having on the war effort, Superintendent L. Jones informed the Llanelli Petty Sessional Division of an alarming increase in drunkenness in the town. Though orders to restrict the sale of alcohol were in force in Llanelli and Burry Port, to prevent munition workers from drinking during working hours, the number of people charged with drunkenness in the division increased from 340 in 1914 to 749 in 1915. In Burry Port the increase was from three to forty-six. Limited prohibition, it seems, was not working.[35] Prohibition was, for many temperance campaigners, the panacea which would cure the dependent of their addiction to drink.[36] But, as those responsible for the wartime orders found, popular behaviour was too entrenched to conform to the dictates of state legislation. Personal, social and physiological needs superseded the letter of the law.[37] There is probably no other area of Victorian legislation which was broken so frequently and by so many people as the laws relating to the sale and consumption of alcohol. In this respect Wales was no exception.

The passage of the Welsh Sunday Closing Act on 27 August 1881 marked both the commencement of separate parliamentary legislation for Wales and the zenith of the temperance movement in Wales.[38] The years following the passing of the Act witnessed an immense controversy over the efficacy of the Act, and detailed statistical warfare was waged as to whether the Act resulted in an increase or a decrease in Sunday drunkenness.[39] The unreliability of the statistics quoted in this debate and the impossibility of measuring objectively the actual volume of beer consumed on a Sunday and its effect on an individual's constitution renders much of this evidence of little value to the historian. What is indisputable is that there was a marked increase in the number of clubs in Wales following the introduction of the Act and in the production of flagons and off-licence sales. In addition, the bona fide traveller clause of the Act was frequently abused. Dr W. R. Lambert, the historian of the temperance movement in Wales, has suggested that: 'Generally speaking, the Act was successful in rural areas and in the towns of North Wales, where it was least needed, but met with a great amount of evasion in the urban communities of South Wales.'[40]

In Carmarthenshire the proceedings of the police courts suggest that evasion of the Act was probably as frequent in the rural areas as in the industrial districts of the county. That prosecutions were few should not blind us to the fact that the Act was ignored. The police admitted that they had difficulty in achieving any convictions in rural areas. They had to sneak up to public houses in rural areas where people watched out for them. Such behaviour, though initially exciting, must have been humiliating to both the drinkers and the police. But the police did have some notable success. In 1907, for example, James Norris, Ivor Laurie and Thomas Davies were fined 5*s*. and costs by the Llandeilo Police Court for being drunk at the Red Lion, Manordeilo. Each claimed to be resident at Llandybïe; as they were over seven miles away from their lodgings, they were bona fide travellers.[41] In 1912, Daniel Gravell, D. J. Hughes, William Hughes, William Richards, W. H. Jones and Oliver Jones were each fined £1 for wilful damage to gates at Ferryside. Superintendent Jones explained to the Carmarthen Police Court that 'They had been Sunday Beer Hunting at Llandefeilog and on their way home they had indulged in a game of throwing down the gates of fields . . .'[42]

At the Llanfihangel-ar-arth Petty Sessions in September 1904, fifteen people from Pencader and Llandysul were fined for offences against the Sunday Closing Act.[43] On 8 September 1892, the licensees of both the Pelican and the Chemical Hall in Kidwelly were fined for Sunday opening.[44] Licensees in Laugharne and Llanarthne were frequently brought before the courts.[45] In other villages the scale of Sunday drinking was even greater. In April 1892, the police raided premises in Cross Hands, 'an obscure little village about ten miles from Llanelli, where they found over fifty colliers drinking, and enjoying themselves to their hearts content, apparently entirely regardless of either the unlicensed premises, or the Sunday Closing Act.'[46]

In rural areas like the urban areas of Carmarthen 'the alcohol dripped through the dotted line'.[47] In contrast to rural areas, urban areas offered more opportunities to people intent on breaking the Sunday Closing Act. The towns and villages also had more police officers, so there was a greater chance that a person would be apprehended. In the town of Carmarthen, for example, it was widely acknowledged that the arrival of the militia usually coincided with an increase in Sunday drinking.[48] Such was the level of Sunday drinking at the turn of the century that the editor of the *Carmarthen Weekly Reporter* remarked:

> It is called the Lord's Day, but in Carmarthen it is par excellence the Devil's Day. Not only the Law of the Land, but the Ten Commandments are regarded as suspended for the time being by a very large proportion of the population.[49]

It is clear that in Llanelli the Sunday Closing Act was regularly breached.[50] A new twist was added to the pattern of Sunday drinking when the Catholics John Jay, William Ludcott and Thomas Prendeville admitted calling for a drink at the Castle Inn one Sunday morning before going to the service at the local Catholic Church.[51] But the main dispenser of beer on the Sabbath to the thirsty people of Llanelli were the clubs which had mushroomed with remarkable rapidity after the introduction of the Sunday Closing Act.[52] Many, such as that operated by the Cross Hands colliers, had the archaic administrative framework of the shebeen and the 'cwrw bach'. Others, such as the Ammanford Conservative Club, sought an aura of respectability.[53] When it was stated in court by the manager that the object of the club was 'to promote the interests of the Conservative Party' those present in the courtroom burst into open laughter. The local police alleged that there was 'no mention in meetings of any political issues' and that although £86.6*s*.10*d*. had been spent at the bar, only 17*s*.6*d*. had been spent on books and newspapers.[54] It attracted only three to four people on week nights, but on Sunday night the number rose dramatically to an average of between thirty-five and forty. Though it had a 'Library' of five books, the Club was exposed as a ploy to evade the Sunday Closing Act.[55] In 1887, William David, the Grand Worthy Chief Templar, expressed his relief when the police at last acted against the Central Club and Institute in Market Street, Llanelli, for he considered 'these dens of infamy and evil were a disgrace upon our civilization'.[56]

One remarkably consistent feature of contemporary views of Sunday Drinking is that it was primarily caused by people who had travelled to the area from elsewhere. The editor of the *Carmarthen Weekly Reporter* frequently asserted that drinking in the town on Sunday was predominantly undertaken by people from Llanelli.[57] To place the blame on outsiders for local anti-social behaviour was a frequent tendency in nineteenth-century Wales.[58] Given the varying interpretations and statistics which were amassed to support those interpretations, it is difficult to be precise about the level of involvement of outsiders in local activities such as drinking. In 1911, for example, it was noted that of 297 men arrested for drunkenness in 1909, 232 were local people and the remainder were of no fixed abode. By 1910, of 303 men arrested for drunkenness, only 186 were said to be local people.[59]

Outsiders and strangers were the people usually identified as being responsible for the sins of a community. When this could no longer be done with any degree of conviction or credibility, the hereditary criminal class which existed in many towns bore the burden of the paranoia of the respectable. To many contemporaries there was a clearly identifiable criminal sub-class, members of which were responsible for transgressions of both the legal and moral codes of society. An analysis of the police court records of Carmarthenshire reveals that, in terms of convictions for drunkenness, all sections of the county's occupational structure are represented. But the most common category, unsurprisingly perhaps, is labourer. In a sample of 780 cases, taken between 1896 and 1898, individuals turn up at random providing idiosyncrasy to virtually every arrest by the police.[60] Comparison with the newspaper reports enables the historian to flesh out the bare bones of the quarter session documents. These sources confirm the views of contemporaries that certain individuals were prone to appear before the police court.

In 1916, Margaret Owen, who used to be in service with Lloyd George at Cricieth, was charged with being drunk in charge of a child at Kidwelly. It was her twenty-ninth conviction.[61] Her case was not unique. Elizabeth Evans, Georgina Stagg, Harriet George, Mary Ann Evans, Alice Powell, Albina Dodd and the 'notorious' Ada Thompson all acquired over twenty convictions at the turn of the century for being in varying states of intoxication.[62] Drinking was clearly not just a prerogative of males. Many men, during the course of a life in which alcohol played a central role, also acquired several convictions. By 1906 Francis Donnio had acquired over twenty-six convictions.[63] Between 1906 and December 1908, William King received thirty-three convictions ranging from drunk and incapable and sleeping out, to performing an indecent act in public.[64] Daniel Price, a labourer of Glanaman, also amassed thirty-three convictions.[65] James Davies, a wool carder of Mill Street, Carmarthen was virtually in a league of his own, having established a total of seventy-three convictions by July 1914.[66] For the Rae family of Mill Street it was a case of like father, like sons. In December 1905 William, then aged twenty-five, was fined and blacklisted for one month because he had twelve previous convictions for drunkenness, his brother, Daniel, possessed twenty-five previous convictions for drink-related offences. By 22 February 1913 the family's notoriety was sealed by George, their father, when he was fined for the ninetieth time.[67]

The policy of the Carmarthen Borough Magistrates of blacklisting persistent offenders and of fining those found supplying drink to blacklisted persons proved to be of little benefit.[68] Many acquired considerable local notoriety from their blacklisting. The adventures of 'Tommy Mammy' became a regular feature of Aletha's column in the *Carmarthen Weekly Reporter* in the 1890s.[69] But undoubtedly the main celebrity was Daniel Jones, a shoemaker of Catherine Street, Carmarthen. In 1902, when he was asked his name by the magistrate who fined him for the sixty-ninth time, Daniel proudly informed the court that 'they call me "Danws" in the papers'.[70] By 1907, 'the Grand Old Drunkard' as he had become known, perhaps as a result of a resemblance to Gladstone, had amassed his ninetieth conviction despite the attempts of the Salvation Army and others to reform him.[71] His last appearance before the magistrate of Carmarthen was in January 1912 when, having been given an afternoon out by the master of the Workhouse on New Year's Day, he had gone on a debauch. At the age of seventy-four it was his ninety-seventh appearance. The editor of the *Carmarthen Weekly Reporter* suggested that, should he receive another three convictions, the magistrates should treat him to a centenary dinner.[72]

It is no surprise perhaps that the people who were most frequently convicted for drunkenness, indecent behaviour, theft and other offences lived in the less desirable quarters of towns. In Carmarthen, for example, it was the inhabitants of the Quay and

Mill Street – 'the name which savoured of everything bad'[73] – who provided most business for the police court.[74] It was here that the worlds of the lower working class merged imperceptibly into the floating world of casual labour, petty theft and crime.[75] The centre for this merger was the common lodging-house, in which the poor found shelter, companionship and a little comfort.

To many late nineteenth-century commentators, as we have seen, drink was the evil which underlay crime and other social evils such as theft, assault and battery. Persons who viewed Wales and the Welsh from across her borders were equally monocausual in their explanation of one of the country's apparent social evils. To them, the prejudiced saying 'Taffy was a Welshman, Taffy was a Thief' was axiomatic.[76] The quarter sessions records of Carmarthenshire enable the historian to test the accuracy of their assertions.[77] As we have seen, in both 1883 and 1919 the level of crime which was regarded as sufficiently serious to be forwarded to the assizes and quarter sessions, was relatively small in terms of its relationship to the total number of offences committed. But if we examine these statistics in terms of the volume of business conducted by the quarter sessions, it becomes clear that the authorities in Carmarthenshire viewed theft with great seriousness. Between 1878 and 1924, theft features as one of the most frequent crimes tried by the quarter sessions. In January 1909, for example, of forty-nine indictable offences which were sent for trial, eleven were for theft.[78] During the forty years after 1878 the number of crimes as a proportion of cases tried at the assizes and quarter sessions varied between 10 per cent in 1911 to 40 per cent in 1885.[79]

Given the nature of the statistics it is difficult to draw firm conclusions. But what is apparent is that the items stolen varied enormously. The range included dresses, chemises, trousers, stockings, shawls and other items of clothing, various items of money, bread, cheese, bottles of pickles and tins of food, cows, heifers, pigs, sheep, ferrets and other animals, trucks and coal.[80] The theft of coal reveals that there existed in Carmarthenshire complex communal interpretations of theft. Though the colliery and works owners viewed the poaching of coal from tips and stores as a crime, local communities regarded the taking of coal and other fuel as a social right. During prosecutions such as that of Adelina Dodd from New Dock Street, Llanelli, two opposing views of community rights were in irreconcilable conflict. In receipt of only 3*s*. a week relief from the parish, Adelina and her blind husband were described as 'very poor and starving'. To obtain fuel in the bitter winter of 1907, she stole coal from the overspill of the trucks of Nevill Druce and Co. Despite the condition of Adelina and her husband, the magistrates fined her 2*s*.6*d*.[81]

It is impossible to disassociate most thefts from the social position of the individual involved. Temptation existed at all levels. William Russell, a rural postman of Llan-non, was charged in 1909 with stealing £7.10*s*.6*d*. from a registered letter which had been given to him for safe delivery.[82] But despite the opportunities which came a person's way through occupational chance, the bulk of the theft committed in the county was of items of relatively little value. In 1903 Mary Vaughan and her daughter Mary Ann Forbes were both charged with the theft of a flannel and a petticoat from the home of Mary Francis in Wharf Lane, Llanelli. The items had been retrieved by the police from Mr Wherle's pawnshop.[83] Two years later in Carmarthen, Jane Lee of Mill Street was charged with the theft of a chemise and a woollen sheet from the clothes line of Mrs William Thomas. Until abandoned to raise two children by her husband, Jane Lee had been in respectable service in Cardiff. The magistrate took pity upon her in her 'hard struggle in the battle of life', rejected the charges and advised her to sign the pledge.[84] The Llanelli magistrates, however, showed little sympathy for John Dryden, a mate of a sailing vessel. Temporarily unemployed, he stole clothing to the value of 7s.6d. and was sentenced to a 17*s*.6*d*. fine or a term in prison.[85]

The story of several of those who found themselves before their betters in Carmarthenshire at the turn of the twentieth century is sad and pathetic. In 1908 in Llanpumsaint, William Smythe, a thirty-two-year-old labourer, was charged with breaking into and entering the home of Ellen Evans and stealing two plates of tart, one loaf of cake, a piece of bacon and a piece of cooked beef. In a statement to the police on 23 October he explained the reasons for his theft: 'Being without employment and frequently without food I called at the home of the complainant; knocked, saw no-one and took them.'[86] The judge had little sympathy, sentencing him to fourteen days hard labour.

To late nineteenth-century commentarors, the criminal 'under-world' was epitomized by the dirty, shambling figure of the tramp.

But it is worth noting that the quarter sessions records reveal that even in Carmarthenshire there appears to have been a professional criminal class. What its composition and number was, it is impossible to estimate. Events such as fairs, racing meetings, football matches and markets drew the criminal to them as moths to light. On his way home from market Josiah Williams, a butcher, was battered and robbed of £45 by thieves who had followed him to Waterloo Road, Pen-y-groes.[87] In January 1907, Patrick Murphy, a seventy-four-year-old optician, and John Jones, a tailor, were both imprisoned for fifteen and twelve months respectively with hard labour for attempting to pick pockets in Llanelli market.[88] A year earlier, a plain clothes police officer had arrested Thomas Jones for the same offence in the same place.[89] The goods and money obtained by the light-fingered fraternity were frequently passed on to pawnbrokers and jewellers. In June 1913, Jessie Riechaelieu, a Llanelli pawnbroker, was fined for receiving stolen property.[90] Charles Pritchard, of Coldstream Street, Llanelli, was similarly fined in 1903.[91] The locks fitted to the doors of the Farmers Arms in Pen-y-groes in 1904 offered little resistance to Charles and Margaret Currie. They used a set of skeleton keys to enter and steal £22.[92] The technique of John Lewis was less sophisticated. In 1897, he was caught in a yard in Thomas Street, Llanelli, between 12.00 p.m. and 1.00 p.m., 'having in his possession an implement of homebreaking, to wit a chisel'.[93]

The presence of professionals such as Charles and Margaret Currie should not be overemphasized. The majority of people convicted were local people like Henry Sutton, a goods porter on the GWR, who was fined £2 in 1913 for the theft of spoons from his place of work, and John Baccus who stole lead from the Penbre munitions works in 1917.[94] David Thomas, a fifty-three-year-old gardener, was imprisoned in 1902 for four months with hard labour for the theft in Kidwelly of garden seeds and potatoes valued at £3.10*s*.6*d*. The theft of property was always condemned.[95] However, the popular view remained that theft was the criminal preserve of vagrants and 'English travellers'. As early as 1848, Henry Leach asserted:

> By far the greater number of those who have been convicted of the highest class of crimes tried here, have not been natives of this county,

> but persons who, in familiar language, are called trampers; men who come to prey upon the fruits of your industry . . .[96]

This popular view satisfied a variety of prejudices and vested interests and was still firmly entrenched sixty years later. During times of social dislocation and crises which followed strikes and depressions, the fear of the illegal activities of the floating population intensified. It is probable that police supervision and observation of tramps and vagrants tightened accordingly.[97] Each theft by a person passing through an area intensified fears and confirmed prejudices. In April 1905 James Marriot, alias Saunders, was fined for breaking and entering in Llandeilo (Fawr), stealing a watch and several other items. He was sentenced to twelve months' hard labour. At the trial the court was informed of his criminal record which had commenced under the name of:

> George Bennett, Talybont Petty Sessions, 14 January 1897; theft of a pair of leggins; two months' hard labour (Carmarthen Prison);
>
> Tregaron Petty Sessions, 18 January 1898; theft of a ferret; two months' hard labour (Carmarthen Prison);
>
> Cardiganshire Quarter Sessions; 5 January 1899; burglary, twelve months' hard labour (Carmarthen Prison);
>
> Radnorshire Assizes, 8 March 1900; breaking and entering a warehouse; nine months' hard labour (Hereford Prison)

and continued under the name of

> James Saunders; Llansawel Petty Sessions; 28 February 1905; theft of a shirt, twelve months' hard labour (Carmarthen Prison).

Between 1898 and 1903, interspersing his periods of imprisonment, he had managed to acquire three summary convictions for drunkenness on his kleptomaniac journey across south Wales.[98] The severity of society's view of such men was expressed in the sentence of six months' hard labour for wandering abroad with no means of support, imposed on John Phillips, a sixty-one-year-old labourer, by the Carmarthenshire Quarter Sessions in April 1909. John had been previously convicted of the following offences:

> 'Llanelly Petty Sessions, 1 September 1889; theft of a pair of boots; one month hard labour;

> Llanelly Petty Sessions, 4 December 1899, theft of a cloth; two months' hard labour;
>
> Llanelly Petty Sessions, 7 December 1892, theft of a cardigan; three months' hard labour;
>
> Carmarthenshire Quarter Assizes, 10 April 1896, theft of three shirts; six months' hard labour.

Between October 1905 and January 1909 he received a further four sentences totalling nine months from these courts, and between 1889 and 1909, he received an additional forty-six summary convictions for vagrancy and other offences.[99] His shuttling to and fro between Llanelli and Carmarthen throws much light on the nature of vagrancy in Carmarthenshire. Such short-scale movement can hardly be interpreted as vagrancy. His almost immediate arrest upon release and imprisonment suggest that he yearned for the security, shelter and stability which Carmarthen Jail seemed to offer.[100] Though the more respectable members might not have agreed, having spent the best years of his decrepit life in the county, John had as much claim to be a part of Carmarthenshire society as anyone else.

The Vagrancy Laws had been formulated in Elizabethan times to keep this shambling, rugged and ragged army of the very poor under control.[101] By 1919 these laws included the prohibition of begging, sleeping out, gaming, being found in enclosed premises, possessing a picklock, living on a prostitute's earnings and a host of other offences.[102] The bulk of these offences were committed by people travelling through the county although, as the case of John Phillips shows, much of this movement was often only short distances across the county. One of the most common offences of vagrants was begging. As we have seen, during certain years, sections of the county became centres for frequent begging.[103] The period 1904 to 1912 appears to have been such a period[104] for much of the time of the police courts was taken up with continual complaints against the begging of vagrants.[105] In May 1904, for example, a correspondent to the *Carmarthen Weekly Reporter* complained about the beggars gathered at the entrance to Buffalo Bill's Wild West Circus during its visit to the town.[106] The majority of the cases were against individuals rather than gangs, and they were frequently told by local magistrates to leave the area. In 1910 Thomas Jones, one of the most prominent

Llanelli magistrates, warned Hiram Evans, a collier from Rhymni, to leave town or face imprisonment because he had been caught begging.[107] Though begging was primarily a solitary activity, some beggars worked together and sought to perpetuate the habit. In March 1891, Frederick Symms and Ann Randel were sentenced to one month's hard labour for training children to beg.[108]

The difficulty facing magistrates in dealing with vagrancy is highlighted if we consider the offence of 'sleeping out', probably the most common crime committed by vagrants. This offence also casts light upon the world of casual labour in early twentieth-century Carmarthenshire. New engineering, building and industrial projects attracted large numbers of unattached men, thereby causing severe housing problems. Between 1909 and 1912, there were over 200 convictions in Carmarthenshire courts for sleeping out.[109] Many, such as Hopkin John and John Phillips, who were convicted of twenty-two and sixty-four such offences respectively, were obviously 'professional' tramps[110] – the 'incorrigible rogues and vagabonds' who so upset Thomas Jones and his fellow magistrates.[111] But the vast majority were people who had come to Carmarthen and Llanelli to look for work. During 1909 and 1912, the lodging houses of the county were full and men were forced to sleep out in gasworks, lime kilns, brickworks, and other places.[112] The shortage of lodgings for casual labourers created problems for the police and the magistrates, for many vagrants and casual labourers deliberately committed offences in order to be sent to prison. In 1893, one labourer actually broke the windows of the Llanelli Police Station in order to obtain a bed.[113]

The involvement of casual labourers, tramps and vagrants in such offences, as we have seen, hardened opposition to them.[114] The involvement of tramps in cases of indecent assault on a seven-year-old girl at Cenarth in 1912 and on a sixteen-year-old girl in 1913 shocked contemporaries and reinforced their prejudices.[115] But the horror of these crimes should not blind the historian to the fact that the vast majority of assaults committed in the county were by people from the county. Brutal offences arising from domestic tensions were distressingly frequent.[116] In reality, all sections of Carmarthenshire society held conflicting and complex attitudes towards authority and the law.

The taking of another person's property was clearly regarded by society as a crime and, despite the financial difficulties involved, ordinary people in Carmarthenshire made considerable use of the legal system. It is clear from the police court and quarter sessions records that the people of Carmarthenshire accepted the legitimacy of the law, and the correctness of proceeding through legal channels to deal with offences of which they were the victims. But this willingness to use the legal system should not blind us to the fact that people's attitudes to the law were complex and contradictory.[117] This becomes clear when the historian examines the offences committed against the Game Acts and the Fishery and Salmon Laws.[118] Historians, such as Dr David Howell, using the evidence of landowners and the preservers of game, have stressed the harmony of the countryside and have underestimated the actual number of offences committed.[119] The late Professor D. J. V. Jones notes that 1,032 offences against the Game Acts were tried in Carmarthenshire's courts in the period 1875–91.[120] This gives an annual rate of 64.5 cases, far in excess of the two or three per annum which Dr Howell quotes.[121] The quarterly reports of the chief constable suggests that Professor Jones's findings probably underestimate the actual extent of poaching. In the quarter ending 30 September 1883, the chief constable reported sixty-six offences against the Game Acts and forty-four against the Fishery Laws.[122] Four years later, in the quarter leading up to 29 September 1887, eighty-four offences against the Game Acts and fifty-one against the Salmon Fisheries Acts were recorded.[123]

The quarter sessions papers offer the historian several insights into the character of poaching in Victorian and Edwardian Carmarthenshire.[124] Analysis of the court proceedings reveal that the persons involved were predominantly young, being aged from their early twenties to mid thirties, and that most social groups of the countryside – labourers, tenant farmers and farm servants – were involved in poaching. Farmers were particularly vociferous about the effects of game on their crops. This general discontent was articulated by several witnesses to the Royal Commission, who complained of the damage made to crops by ground game.[125]

In examining the court records, one is frequently struck by the remarkable and intelligent ingenuity of those charged with poaching and offences against the Salmon Fisheries Act. A bewildering variety of implements was used to catch elusive salmon. In 1881 David Pugh, William Davies and David Evans of Llansawel were fined £1 for fishing in the River Twrch with a light and spear.[126] In 1888 David Lewis, a labourer of Dan-y-banc, Carmarthen, was fined 11*s*. for fishing illegally, using a coracle and net.[127] Probably the most common piece of equipment used by Carmarthenshire poachers was the gaff. In 1884, John Richards of New Road, Llandeilo, was charged with aiding and abetting Rees Lewis in the use of a gaff to catch salmon and imprisoned for twenty-eight days.[128] Others were stealthier in their methods. Roger Rogers, a tailor of Llanfallteg, was fined four shillings in 1890 for unlawfully using 'certain fish roe' for the purpose of fishing for trout in the River Taf.[129] In November 1890 David Evans of Ffair-fach was fined £2.10*s*. and 15*s*. costs for having in his possession a 'certain wire with the intention to catch and kill salmon'.[130] In the same month Ebenezer Jones, a collier of Pantyffynnon, was fined £1.0*s*.5*d*. and 19*s*.7*d*. costs for using his 'hands to catch trout'.[131] In the coalmining regions, miners frequently appeared before the courts charged with poaching in local rivers. Not all had Ebenezer's dexterity and subtlety in obtaining free food for their families. In May 1890, David Rees of Llanddarog was fined 10*s*. for the 'unlawful use of dynamite or other explosive substance to catch and destroy fish in the waters of the river Gwendraeth Fach'.[132]

Thirteen years later, the fishing techniques of local colliers were no more sophisticated. In November 1903, the early morning peace of Pen-y-groes was shattered by the attempts of six colliers from Caer-bryn to dynamite fish in the River Lash.[133] Colliers obtained dynamite from their workplace. Poachers employed in other trades could also utilize items from their legal employment to assist their illegal work. Thomas Thomas, a railway worker from Pantyffynnon, for example, used his railway lamp and coat to catch trout in the Loughor.[134]

More ingenious were the excuses which persons caught poaching offered to bailiffs and police. These suggest that those involved in poaching offences were not the downcast members of a degenerate sub-culture, as editors of local newspapers claimed. Excuses given to Carmarthenshire courts range from 'I was collecting mushrooms', 'I was given the rabbits by a friend', 'It wasn't me', 'The police have mistaken me for someone else', to the rather uninspiring, 'I did not know I was there, I was so drunk',[135] while William James, Thomas Davies and Henry John of Llangennech, charged with being with dogs in pursuit of game on 11 November 1880, hired William Howell, a prominent Llanelli solicitor and Liberal, to defend them on the basis that: 'Tenants of the farm occupied by the defendant James had from time immemorial a right of way over Cilgwn to Bryn-tew, over which the defendant James had the right of shooting.'[136] Even though they had been shooting pheasants, the charges against them were dropped.

This appeal to immemorial natural rights was frequently resorted to by persons charged with poaching. It is clear from the evidence of the court records of Carmarthenshire that profound tensions were created by two different attitudes to game.[137] The owners of fishing and game rights viewed the nocturnal activities of poachers as illegal and sought to invoke the full power of the law in its prevention. The employment of gamekeepers on the estates of the county, many of whom were from England, added to these tensions.[138] George Luffman, the gamekeeper to C. W. M. Lewis, was of English origin, as were his successors, Thomas and William Toplis from Derbyshire.[139] Such was Luffman's conscientiousness that he brought two cases before the Llanelli magistrates in one month alone. In March 1881, he was the plaintiff in two cases involving eight persons.[140] In opposition to this view, poachers, drawn from almost all sections of rural and industrial society, considered that the taking of salmon, sewin, trout, rabbit, pheasant and hare was the God-given right of the freeborn Welshman. Allied to this belief in immemorial traditions and rights was the thrill of a nocturnal adventure fraught with danger.[141] These beliefs were enshrined in the comments of one observer of rural crime to the Revd H. Housley: 'There is a difference between poaching and stealing. I should not steal myself . . . Many people would be friends with a poacher, but would not like to be very great friends with a man convicted of a felony.'[142] In 1881 the *Cambrian News* confirmed this view, declaring that: 'The Workmen of this county do not recognise the divine rights of a game preserving class.'[143]

In 1907, in Llandeilo, Lord Dynevor sought to give concrete reality to his rights to the river by ordering a wall to be built across a path to the River Tywi. A group of at least ten people expressed the community's view by demolishing the wall.[144] In his

Confessions of a Welsh Salmon Poacher (1877), Griffith Evan Jones reinforced this view, declaring with pride: 'I never stole anything in my life; I would scorn to take anything that was not my own.'[145] Yet these noble sentiments did not prevent him from expounding at length on his success and adventures as a salmon poacher. Such was the community-wide involvement, claimed Jones, that two members of his gang were magistrates, for as he concluded: 'Laws grind the poor, yet Welshmen rule the Law.'[146]

Given these conflicting views on the legality of poaching and the existence of gamekeepers whose duty it was to 'stop and capture poachers',[147] it is inevitable that outbreaks of violence were frequent. In order to escape, many men used considerable violence towards gamekeepers and bailiffs. In February 1881, Llewelyn Williams and John Clement of Pontarddulais were charged with poaching offences and assaulting two water-bailiffs.[148] During the fight between the two defendants and the bailiffs, John Williams and John Darling, it was alleged that 'Clement picked up a stone and hurled it at Williams, smashing some of his ribs'.[149]

Undoubtedly aware of the dangers they faced, gamekeepers would leave well prepared for their unenvied duties. Thomas Toplis, the head gamekeeper on the Stradey estate of C. W. M. Lewis, informed a local court that: 'Our guns are always loaded when we go out. We take strong sticks also, and sometimes we carry handcuffs.'[150] On the night of 12 November, Toplis's preparations were proven to be justified. At around 2.00 a.m. he and his son William and another gamekeeper William Harries, encountered John Williams, Arthur Nurse, David Walters ('a man of dubious antecedents') and David John, or 'Dwt' as he was popularly known, poaching pheasants in the Dingle.[151] During a struggle between Nurse and Thomas Toplis, Nurse's gun discharged into his chest, killing him instantly. The other poachers also received rough treatment. At the inquest, Dr Sidney Roderick confirmed that he retrieved shotgun pellets from the legs of three defendants and also from the back of William Harris.[152] There were casualties on both sides in the poaching wars.

The use of physical violence against gamekeepers and bailiffs, if not actually condoned, was regarded by many as an occupational hazard. Given the different motives and attitudes of poachers and gamekeepers, some violent confrontations were unavoidable.[153]

In such cases one can discern two conflicting attitudes towards violence in Carmarthenshire society. Newspaper editors, ministers of religion, solicitors and other custodians of community morality were eloquent in their condemnation of all physical violence. But within Carmarthenshire society there were groups who regarded violence as the main method of arbitration in interpersonal disputes, whether over property or any other cause.[154] In 1902, the editor of the *Carmarthen Journal*, in reporting a fight, which led to charges of assault, between two colliers at the Colliers Arms in Garnant, stated that this was, 'Not the attitude that the Amman Valley, bad as it was, was accustomed to on a Saturday night.'[155]

Violence was endemic in Carmarthenshire society and even intruded into family life.[156] Certain towns, villages and areas of towns acquired unenviable reputations for violence during specific periods in their history. Mill Street, Jackson's Lane and Quayside in the town of Carmarthen in the 1880s and 1890s, Tumble in the 1890s, Seaside and New Dock in Llanelli in the 1890s and 1900s, Ammanford in the 1900s, and Pen-bre during the First World War all acquired reputations for violence and were scorned and despised.[157] But the historian should not allow the declarations of the literate to obscure the fact that recourse to violence was the common reaction of many contemporaries and that popular attitudes towards violence were complex.[158]

These conflicting attitudes become clear if we examine some of the more violent conflicts which occurred in Carmarthenshire in the period 1876 to 1920. In 1907 John Jones of Wern-fawr, Carmarthen, summoned John West and Henry Wilkins, two labourers from Llanarthne, for assault and threatening behaviour. West was bound over to keep the peace. On the completion of his sentence, the press reported that West had threatened Wilkins that: 'He would get him . . . he had no fear of the gallows . . . he would take out his intestines and cut them as small as matches.'[159] Fortunately the promise was never fulfilled. Despite the severity of his threats, provided they remained unfulfilled, West was not adjudged to have transgressed the bounds of popular morality. Issuing threats of violence was common in most cases of interpersonal disputes.[160] In many quarters the settling of disputes by fighting was the accepted solution and any agency which sought to intervene in the course of this natural justice, such as the police, fell foul of popular opinion.[161] The crowds which gathered to witness fights were fickle in the allocation of their sympathy and support. In 1900 three Llanelli men helped a local police constable 'against all odds, in the face of hostile mob' to arrest a man charged with assault.[162] In 1913, three police officers who attempted to arrest Patrick O'Brien were hindered and prevented from securing his arrest by a crowd of 'a few hundred'.[163] In 1915, Thomas James Davies, who had been wounded in the Dardanelles campaign with the South Wales Borderers, was helped in resisting arrest by a large crowd of soldiers and civilians.[164] When PS Lewis of Tumble arrested two men after 'a desperate struggle for assaulting him', the anger of the local inhabitants was such that a crowd of over 200 attacked PS Lewis' home with stones and broke every window. Having thrown stones weighing over 75 lb into the house, the crowd achieved their objective of securing the men's release.[165]

The sympathy and support of the crowd switched rapidly between the aggressor and the victim as the circumstances of each case became clear, and popular morality reacted accordingly. This was particularly so when interpersonal violence reached its inevitable climax – either manslaughter or murder. The quarter sessions and assize records, supplemented by newspapers, reveal that there were at least twenty-six murders in Carmarthenshire in the thirty-four years from 1884 to 1918.[166] Of these, three were changed to charges of manslaughter. There were also several cases of attempted murder.[167] Throughout this period, public opinion towards murder was relatively unanimous in its condemnation. In 1881, although the courts found them not guilty of both the murder and manslaughter of John Thomas, an eleven-year-old boy, local people 'hounded' Jane Maizey and her two sons David and Benjamin out of Kidwelly. They were, in the view of the local people, undoubtedly guilty.[168] Outraged by the circumstances of John Thomas's death, contemporaries were at pains to show that the Maizeys were not of their 'stock', but immigrants to the village.[169] Twenty years earlier, the citizens of Laugharne had shown similar hostility towards Betsi Gibbs. Though acquitted of two murders, local inhabitants burnt effigies of her nightly and forced her to flee the town in fear of her life.[170] Sentenced to death in 1871 for the brutal murder of his wife, William Brice of Llanelli was followed on his way to gaol 'by a very large crowd several of whom expressed a readiness to lynch him'.[171]

Probably the clearest example of community hostility to a murderer was the treatment meted out to William Tremble's body by the inhabitants of Caeo in 1879.[172] Having been refused the licence of the Dolau Cothi Arms in Pumsaint by Judge Sir John Johnes of Dolau Cothi, Tremble returned with a shotgun and shot the judge, his daughter Charlotte, the cook, Mrs Cookman, and finally turned the gun on the owner's dogs. Encircled by police at his cottage Tremble shot himself. In accordance with the coroner's warrant, Tremble's body was buried in Caeo churchyard in silence at about 11 o'clock at night. Sir John Johnes had also been buried in the churchyard and there was widespread concern that his murderer had been interred in the same consecrated ground. Later that night, the local inhabitants dug up Tremble's body and took it to Llandulas churchyard in Breconshire. When the inhabitants of Llandulas discovered this, they carried the body back to Caeo and unceremoniously dumped it back in Caeo churchyard.[173]

Popular reaction to murder was not, however, uniformly condemnatory. Though Esther Davies had been murdered in cold blood in November 1869, and strong suspicion attached to one man, police met a wall of silence in the locality of her farm, Blaenduad, above Llandysul.[174] The comparative rarity of murder, its savage finality and its theatricality, combined to give it a fascination which other crimes do not possess.[175] To many, a murder lit up the otherwise unremarkable years of their lives in a more graphic way than an election or many other public events.[176] Ballads were sung about the most ghastly murders, and Carmarthenshire seems to have had its share of brutal murders in lonely, peaceful, beautiful locations.[177] Such ballads frequently played upon the image of a peaceful, orderly Wales and the stains cast upon her by the dark deeds of her miscreants.[178] The ballad to the terrible murder which occurred at Llangadog in 1888 began:

> Hoffus wlad y Menyg Gwynion,
> Ydoedd enw Cymru gynt;
> Bellach gwlad y menyg duon,
> Geilw pawb hi ar ei hynt . . .[179]

When the Borth murderer was taken to Carmarthen jail, crowds gathered to jeer and threaten him. Hundreds of people collected outside the walls of the jail to view 'the dreaded symbol of justice', the black flag being lowered as he was hanged. The crowds are testimony both to the detestation and fascination people held for the crime of murder. Within the minds of the crowd there were complex and contradictory attitudes towards the use of violence and the extent of the power of authority. Communities collectively condemned the brutalities perpetrated by an individual. But communities also, without hesitation, resorted to violence when they perceived that their interests were in danger. Community protests such as the refusal to pay tithes, to continue to work under intolerable conditions, and to accept wage reductions, were frequently fringed with community-sanctioned violence. We shall examine these conflicting attitudes as they operated during the 'Tithe War' of the 1880s and 1890s, during the strikes and riots at Tumble in 1893 and 1906 and during the Llanelli riots of 1911.

Many social and public events in nineteenth-century Carmarthenshire were fringed with violent outbreaks. The county's electoral history is marred with violent outbreaks between the supporters of rival parties.[180] Though the intensity of these outbreaks had cooled by the end of the century, it had not entirely dissipated.[181] In 1885, for example, the Conservative offices in Carmarthen and Llanelli were attacked by large numbers of people.[182] Though political and religious views were also the ostensible motives for the Tithe Wars of the 1880s and 1890s, the resort to violence which was characteristic of Carmarthenshire society took ascendancy.[183]

Opposition to the payment of tithe towards the maintenance of the Established Church had rankled with Nonconformists since the early nineteenth century.[184] But in the late 1880s, the Liberal victories in the elections of 1885 and 1886 and the campaigns of Thomas Gee and the *Baner*, coinciding as they did with a depression in Welsh agriculture, turned the discontent into open rebellion.[185] The Revd W. Thomas of Whitland, a Liberal member of Carmarthenshire County Council and a prominent anti-tither, subsequently claimed that:

> The question of perfect religious equality has been already settled by the country at the hustings. An overwhelming majority of the population of Wales have declared at the polling booths their conviction that an Established Church is an anomaly and injustice.[186]

In August 1886, farmers in Dyffryn Clwyd in Denbighshire refused to pay the tithe.[187] Four months later, in January 1887, their action was emulated by Thomas Davies of Ffynnondafalog, Tre-lech a'r Betws.[188] By the end of the year, protests against the payment of tithe had spread throughout Carmarthenshire. The people who suffered most acutely through the suspension of tithe payments were the clergy, for most depended upon the tithe rent charge for a major part of their stipend. Many underwent the indignity of having to pawn treasured possessions such as books, and built up considerable debts at local shops.[189] One clergyman, due to receive £158.12*s*.9*d*. in tithe, only secured £19.14*s*.9*d*. and another, who was due to receive £200, secured only £8.[190] In order to protect their interests, clerics in west Wales formed the Clergy Defence Association with its headquarters in Cardigan. The Association took charge of all legal matters connected with the enforcement of the payment of tithes. One of the key figures in this association was the agent, Robert Lewis from Pendine, who, as a devout churchman, was convinced of the rectitude of the cause in which he was engaged. To assist him with his duties he recruited two young friends from Pendine, John Ebsworth and William Garrett.[191] While collecting tithe, the three ran a gauntlet of abuse and missile-throwing throughout south-west Wales.[192] At every farm and cottage where 'Robber Lewis',[193] as the Nonconformist press called him, visited to distrain property for non-payment of tithe, crowds gathered. When they attempted to sell the distrained goods at auction, the anger of the crowds intensified and often resulted in violence. 'Tithe Horns' were sounded to summon the scattered population to the farm where the sale was to be held. Vocal protests rendered the auctioneer inaudible, and rotten eggs, mud and dung were thrown. A greater hazard were bulls, which were frequently set loose on Lewis and his assistants as they attempted to distrain farmers' goods.[194]

Given the predominance of Nonconformity as a cultural, social, religious and political force in west Wales, the entire community was represented in the crowds who protested in the tithe wars.[195] In 1888, seventeen people from the neighbourhood of St Clears were charged with disorderly behaviour at the quarter sessions.[196] The disturbances occurred when over 600 people attempted to prevent Robert Lewis, his assistants and the police from distraining the goods of the farmers of Llwynhendy and Pen-coed for non-payment of tithe.[197] Twelve of the seventeen were subsequently fined £2 each for charges ranging from throwing missiles to disturbing the peace. Of the twelve, the majority were farmers; four were women, one of whom was over seventy years of age.[198] The presence of women further emphasizes the community-wide importance of the tithe riots. Such was the police presence that one woman at Newcastle Emlyn declared: 'Oh gracious they must have brought policemen from all over the world. I never saw so many policemen in all my life.'[199] A few months later, despite the presence of the world's police, the violent jostling of the agent and the bailiff, and the missile throwing which had become a traditional part of tithe sales, were accompanied by more sinister aspects. In September 1888, though police had been drawn from Carmarthen, Llanelli, Llandeilo, St Clears, Laugharne and Whitland, two hayricks at Blaen-y-waun farm, Llanwinio, were set on fire.[200] Church windows were also smashed[201] and effigies of priests were burnt.[202] Robert Lewis noted with disgust the 'Night terror' suffered by the Revd R. Hughes, the vicar of 'the remote, hidden parish of Llanfihangel Rhos-y-corn'. Night raids on the vicarage saw machinery broken, windows smashed, furniture damaged and 'his horses hacked in a revolting manner'.[203] For a brief moment the governing classes of Carmarthenshire were fearful that the granddaughters of Rebecca had realized their violent inheritance.

It is important to remember that, in the protest against tithe, all sections of society were involved. Naturally, as the leaders of rural society, Nonconformist ministers were prominent. The Revd W. Thomas of Whitland used his position on the county council's Standing Joint Committee to complain about the expense incurred by ratepayers because policemen were used to control tithe sales.[204] Other Nonconformist ministers assisted him in articulating the grievances of their communicants. At a public meeting in Pencader, in October 1888, the motion that people should refuse to pay the tithe was put by the Revd T. Phillips and seconded by the Revd W. Joseph of Llandysul. A newspaper report listed amongst those present the Revd R. P. Jones (Pencader), Revd Evans (Tynewydd), Revd P. Evans and Revd P .D. Jones (Llandysul), Revd P. Jeffreys (Saron Llangeler), and the Revd John Evans (Gwernogle).[205] Across the divide of tithe payer and tithe collector, two different worlds gazed at each other with bewildered hostility. In August 1893, for example, the warden of All Souls

College, Oxford, brought an action for non-payment of the college's tithe against Bethlehem Congregational Chapel of St Clears.[206] Robert Lewis and other churchmen protested against the involvement of chapel ministers, justices of the peace and other influential people in tithe protests. In his *Reminiscences of the Tithe War in West Wales,* he recalled that:

> Tithe Collecting in the Welsh Wild West is a dangerous business since the encouragement given to lawlessness and violence by those who ought to be the first to put it down has rendered the brutal treatment of a tithe bailiff a safe as well as a pleasurable diversion.[207]

There are numerous examples of widespread community support for people convicted of offences in connection with tithes. In January 1888, the Revd W. Thomas chaired a public meeting in Llanboidy to raise money to pay the fines of the people arrested for assaulting Mr Roblin, the local tithe bailiff. The meeting raised £12.[208] Many of those convicted, especially those imprisoned, became 'tithe martyrs'.[209] In August 1892, one such martyr, Evan Evans of Llandysul, was released from prison. Evans had been imprisoned for throwing eggs at the Revd D. Jones the Rector of Bangor Teifi). S. T. Evans, R. D. Burnie and Wynford Philipps spoke at a public meeting to welcome him home under the branches of the 'Reform Tree'. Dr Enoch Davies presented him with a purse of gold, a silver watch, and a chain and pendant on which was inscribed: 'Fel arwydd o barch ar ôl carchariad aberthol gan grefydd wladwriaethol 1892.'[210]

When John Davies of Pantyrholiad, Penbryn, Cardiganshire was met on his release by Lloyd George and two other MPs, the *Carmarthen Journal* noted sarcastically:

> A strange scene was witnessed in Llandysul last week . . . A young man deliberately breaks the law, and is prosecuted, is convicted, and sentenced to a fine or imprisonment, and elects for the latter. On leaving prison he is met by three members of Parliament and sundry Nonconformist ministers, is presented with an address 'on the occasion of his liberation as an imprisoned victim of tithe persecution', is given a purse, a watch and chain, is feted and patted on the back.[211]

With much glee the *Journal* reported the prosecution in November 1894 of Peggy Lewis, 'The Tithe Martyr', for cruelty to her cow.[212]

The passage of the Tithe Bill by Rosebery's government, through merging tithe-rent-charge with rent, made the payment of tithe easier to enforce, and the unpopularity of the tithe-owner declined rapidly.[213] Though the protests and violent scenes continued in the 1890s and surfaced again in 1913, they were not as bitter or as intense as they had been in the 1880s.[214] The 1891 Act was influential, but the decision of many tithe owners not to prosecute for non-payment was the major cause of the end of the riots.[215]

Industrial disputes which led to strikes frequently created tension which could not be contained. Violent attacks upon people and property were the result. In Carmarthenshire in the late nineteenth century, violence and threatening behaviour associated with industrial disputes was common. The differences between employers and employees, and particularly between employees who went on strike and those who continued to work, were articulated first in threats and then in violence. In July 1884, following a dispute at the Burry Port Docks, six men were charged with attempting to prevent Robert Lewis and James Davies from working on 31 March.[216] The hatred of 'blacklegs' and the sense of community betrayal which these men had perpetrated by returning to work is a consistent theme in assault cases brought before Carmarthenshire courts.[217] In 1905, for example, Thomas Lewis, Thomas Rees and George Elliott, all labourers at the local limeworks, who supplemented their income by farming, were charged with assault and disorderly conduct at the Golden Lion at Llandybïe. They had been intimidating 'blacklegs'.[218] Similar examples could be quoted extensively for the period from 1884 and 1920, but in order to see the community involvement in industrial unrest and the importance of locating a strike in its total social context we shall examine two specific outbreaks: the Tumble Riots of 1893 and the Llanelli riots of August 1911.[219]

On Saturday 4 March 1893 the cessation notices which John Waddel and Sons had issued to their employees at the Great Mountain Colliery expired.[220] The dispute had arisen over the decision of the owners to lower the wages for working the Big and Green Veins, their insistence that two men and a lad work together on all faces, and the replacement of the 'Pillar and Stall' method of mining by the 'long wall'.[221] In view of the uncertainty of the workers' reaction, the manager had issued instructions that horses should remain down the pit and that the water pump should continue to work. On the Saturday night a crowd of colliers travelled from Tumble to the pit to force the caretaker of the engines, a Scotsman by the name of Reith, to cease work. On hearing the news, the manager, Mr Beith, telephoned to Llanelli requesting police assistance. Superintendent Scott and seven officers arrived from Llanelli at 11.00 p.m., by which time the crowd had dispersed.[222] Following the confrontation at the pumping sheds, Rees Davies of Tumble Row was fined £7 for assaulting and intimidating workmen at the Great Mountain Colliery.[223]

The first day of the Tumble Strike set the tone for the following nine-month stoppage. There was open and bitter conflict between the strikers and those who remained in work. Given the policy of the owners of importing labour from the north of England and Scotland, the tensions assumed a racial character.[224] Before discussing the events of the 1893 riot, it is necessary to remind ourselves of their social context.

In 1893 Tumble bore many of the characteristics of a company town of the early nineteenth century. The town had grown rapidly with the foundation of the Great Mountain colliery in 1887.[225] This was the force that gave existence to the town. Before the opening of the pit, Tumble had been a small hamlet squatting on a bleak, inhospitable hillside. The rapidity of the town's growth created profound housing and health problems. The colliery company was the owner of a hundred cottages in Tumble Row and, in order to meet the demand for lodgings from the young unmarried men which it drew in, it built a 'model lodging house'.[226] In six years, the traffic to and from the colliery had transformed the village lane into a road, the complexion of which was as black as an oil slick. Sanitation was rudimentary. The village was built on a hill, and gravity was allowed to carry the effluent down to the valley floor. In August 1893, Dr Evans, inspector of the Llanelli Rural Sanitary Authority, watched in horrified amazement as human filth was dumped from the houses into the town's main source of drinking water.[227] Indeed, such was the physical and social deprivation that Tumble was described by one commentator as 'this gloomy, Heaven-forsaken valley' . . . this 'Hell on Earth'.[228] The only release from these depressing conditions were the chapels and the one public house – the infamous Tumble Inn. Poles apart in social tone and morality, chapels catered for people's social and spiritual needs, whilst the Tumble Inn offered a raucous camaraderie and a quick and fleeting escape from life's bitter realities.

These conditions provided the backcloth against which the events of the 1893 strike were enacted. The strikers received support from colliers throughout the area. Appeals in the Aman Valley, Cross Hands and Pen-y-groes raised money to support the Tumble men. On 8 April a mass meeting was held in Tumble and 'respectable' processions to the town were led by the brass bands of Cwm-mawr and Pen-y-groes.[229] At the end of the meeting, after listening to speeches from local miners' leaders, the crowd sang what was to become the revolutionary anthem of the anthracite miners, the hymn 'Aberystwyth', with its impassioned query: 'Beth sydd i mi yn y byd?' and its subsequent assertion that the collective fight was just.[230] On 4 May another mass meeting heard the Revd Morgan, of Tabor Baptist Chapel, declare that justice would triumph and the vicar of Llan-non, the Revd W. Jones, argued that the sliding scale should be reintroduced. The extent of community involvement was shown by the presence of a large number of women at the back of the meeting, many of whom were nursing babies.[231]

The main feature of the 1893 strike was the running fights between the strikers who were predominantly Welsh, and the English and Scots who were brought into the area by the colliery company. The policy of the company, together with its eviction of strikers from company-owned cottages, created profound tensions. In July, Robert Beith issued eviction orders to seventeen tenants of Tumble Row.[232] On 14 June, the *Western Mail* reported the eviction of a young pregnant mother and her children from her home, a sight which, the reporter said, was enough to make 'one's flesh creep'.[233] The Tumble Inn was frequently the scene of violent brawls and disputes for, as overindulgence led to confusion and to rows, oaths and fists were traded simultaneously. But in 1893 the traditional quarrels were augmented by the disputes of a race war. In April, John Rees, with the assistance of Arundel Davies, assaulted Thomas Banks, a bricklayer at the Great Mountain colliery. The provocation was Banks's conversation with William Currie, a Scot at the bar. Both were in a group of thirty recruited to the colliery since the strike had begun.[234] By July race relations in Tumble had deteriorated further. On the night of Saturday 1 July, a gang of Welsh colliers faced a gang of English workers across the bridge. Stones were thrown at the English and, as a result of the disturbances, three Welshmen, Daniel Evans, Enoch Clark, and David Williams, were fined at the Llanelli Petty Sessions for public order offences.[235]

When discussions between the colliery owners and the strikers' leaders broke down again in August, pride, frustration and anger could no longer be contained. On Monday 1 September, following another unsuccessful meeting with George Waddell and Mr Beith, a man was taken into police custody for threatening behaviour.[236] When the strikers realized what had happened, many of them marched towards the lodging house, where the Scots were lodged. Soon a crowd of over 500 had assembled outside and the six police officers present were powerless to prevent serious damage being done to the building. On their way to the lodging house, the men had proceeded through Tumble Row where they damaged many of the cottages owned by the company.[237] Despite the view of the *South Wales Press* that the violence in Tumble Row had been 'indiscriminate . . . more of a drunken brawl than anything else',[238] there was a distinct pattern to the destruction. As one eyewitness put it:

> Up this street after they had done their worst at the Lodging House the mob went pell-mell and picking up all the stones they could find en route, they landed them through the cottages as they proceeded. A good deal of discrimination and selection was exercised in this bombardment. The attention of the crowd were apparently extended only for their enemies. The cottages of turncoats and blacklegs unfailingly received their casual demonstrations of unpopularity whilst the others escaped without injury.[239]

The house of the resident police officer was also attacked, much to the fear of his family.[240] In panic the company representatives wired to Llanelli for extra police. Captain Scott and a force of officers arrived to discover apparent calm at 9.00 p.m.[241] However, at around 10.30 p.m., a crowd of men attacked Bryngwili, the home of the manager, Mr Beith.[242] Stones caused damage to the furniture and injured Mr Watson, Mrs Beith and her maid. Police arrived by train from Tumble and arrested three people.[243]

On Tuesday, to supplement local police, additional police were brought in and the Inniskillen Dragoons arrived from Swansea. By Wednesday there were sixty-two police officers (forty-four from the county, five from Carmarthen Borough and thirteen from Swansea) and twenty-four soldiers in the town. Tumble was virtually a town under siege.[244] The strike continued until 1 January 1894. Bitterness, hatred and suspicion continued and arguments were resolved by fighting, but the violence of the first Monday in September was not repeated.[245]

This level of violence was eclipsed by the events of August 1911 in Llanelli.[246] Winston Churchill, that acerbic commentator on the tendency of Welsh people to riot,[247] told the House of Commons that:

> The Llanelly rioters, left to themselves, with no intrusion from the police and no assistance from the military for some hours, in a few streets of the town during the evening, wrought in their drunken frenzy more havoc to life and limb, shed more blood, produced more serious injury among themselves, than all the 50,000 soldiers who have been employed on strike duty all over the country during the last few days.[248]

The Liberal home secretary's prejudiced analysis obscures the social context within which the violence was enacted in the stifling heat of August 1911.[249]

The backcloth of the events was the national rail strike which was declared at 5.00 p.m. on Thursday 17 August 1911. Twenty years of poor labour relations on the railways had made it certain that support amongst railwaymen for the strike would be solid.[250] The continued diplomatic tension between Britain and Germany and the spate of industrial disputes and strikes in 1910 and 1911 ensured that the government was particularly sensitive and responsive to the rail situation.[251] In Llanelli, throughout the strike, the railwaymen received the support of other groups of workers to boost the picket. This, coupled with the vulnerability of the town's railway station and its strategic importance on the south Wales rail network, heightened the sensitivity of both the rail authorities and the government.[252]

The first day of the strike, Thursday 17 August, passed relatively quietly. By 10.00 p.m., when the local police force arrived at the line, the picket was in command and held up the Cork express and two other trains. Despite several attempts by the police to dislodge it the picket held the line and tempers remained calm. On the morning of 18 August, 120 men under the command of Captain Burrows arrived at the request of the railway protection officer.[253] Though they temporarily dislodged the picket, this force was unable to retain control of the line.

Following the failure of negotiations between the railway leaders, local magistrates, the police, and the army, more troops were dispatched from Cardiff at the request of the local magistrates, Thomas Jones and Frank Nevill.[254] In all, 250 soldiers, under the command of Major Brownlow Stuart, and twenty-seven local police who had been away on picket duty in south Wales, were called into the town.[255] The police, with troops in support, were unable to force open the gates. With the worsening mood and increasing tension, the crowd rushed the gates and regained possession. In response, the main body of troops was called into action and quickly swept aside the picket. Though there were intermittent skirmishes and stone-throwing throughout the night, the situation was firmly under the control of the authorities until the afternoon of Saturday 19 August.[256]

In the early afternoon a train, unprotected by the authorities, left the copperworks crossing and proceeded westwards. When it was obliged to slow down at a cutting underneath the gardens of Bryn Road and High Street, a number of men ran up to the engine, extinguished the fire and immobilized the brake. When Major Stuart arrived at the stranded train, the crowd, who continued to swell in numbers, retreated up the embankment and began to hurl a fusillade of stones upon the troops.[257] Major Stuart climbed the embankment and tried to reason with the protesters. On his return to his troops, stones were again thrown and Henry Williams, a local magistrate, read the Riot Act.[258] Major Stuart warned that his troops would fire unless order was restored but the crowd, many of whom believed that the troops had only blanks, continued to taunt and throw stones. Suddenly a shot rang out, followed by another five rounds. Four men in the crowd were wounded, two of them, John John and Leonard Worsell, fatally.[259] The troops then returned to the station.

News of the deaths spread quickly through the town and a large and angry crowd gathered at the station throwing stones and other missiles at the soldiers. At about 5.00 p.m. a train carrying

Leonard Worsell and John John, the two Llanelli men shot by the military in 1911 (Llanelly and County Guardian)

provisions and kit for the Devon Regiment was stopped and raided by the crowd. The looting spread to a neighbouring warehouse and fires were started. The troops tried to stop the looting and extinguish the fire but, with a large area crowded with goods wagons, their task was difficult. When darkness fell on the torrid town, the looting intensified. At 10.00 p.m., two huge explosions rent the scene. In the frenzy of the looting, Joseph Platt of Trimsaran, whose mutilated body was later recovered, had set fire to a cylinder of detonators. The blast injured fourteen people, three fatally. Despite the loss of life, looting on the railway line continued until the early hours and other serious incidents occurred in the locality. At around 10.30 p.m., for example, a large crowd attacked the police station in New Dock and attempted to seize the driver of the first train that had stopped in the afternoon.[260]

Anarchy quickly spread throughout the town. At about 8.00 p.m. the windows of the grocery shop of D. C. Parry, in Stepney Street, a former chairman of the County Council, were smashed. Half an hour later the premises of Thomas Jones, JP, who was wrongly believed to have read the Riot Act in the afternoon, were ransacked. The crowd then moved to Jones's home, Bryn-mair, in Goring Street. They also attacked Henry Williams's premises in Hall Street and returned to loot the shop of Thomas Jones and other shops in Market Street. The police and the troops, hopelessly outnumbered and frequently arriving when the crowd had moved on, were powerless to stop the looting. Thomas Jones's premises were systematically ransacked. A roll-top desk was smashed open and ledgers and papers taken away. One man was injured as he left the shop when a box of sugar was thrown from upstairs onto his head by another looter.[261] At around 12.00 a.m., reinforcements from the Sussex Regiment arrived, and only now could the forces of authority begin to assert themselves. By 2.00 a.m., following several baton and bayonet charges by the police and troops, order was finally restored.[262]

Such then are the bare events of three of the most exciting days in Llanelli's history. In the wake of the riots, analyses and condemnation of the events of 19 August followed thick and fast. In particular, the looting was universally condemned. The *South Wales Press* could find no justification and offered no sympathy, describing with looting as 'a case of sheer wanton destruction'.[263] Others looked to the town's recent history to find an explanation. The *Llanelly and County Guardian* claimed that 'The construction of the traction system, filter beds, works and other things . . . has brought a large influx of nomadic labourers to this neighbourhood . . . the flotsam and jetsam of the highways and byways of the county.'[264]

Tarian y Gweithiwr echoed the *Guardian* in its social analysis, regretting that: 'O hyn ymlaen nis adwaenir y dref fel tref heddychlon ond fel trigfan terfysgwyr, lladron a meddwon. Y mae yn resyn fod y fath enw wedi ei ddwyn arni gan dorf o hwliganiaid diwaith a segurwyr ystwrllyd.'[265] The *Guardian* also attempted to remove responsibility for the worst outrages from the town to the neighbouring villages, where 'there were trouble makers . . . spoiling for a fight'. It claimed that: 'there are scores of khaki uniforms in Pontardulais, and large quantities of looted provisions in Gorseinon.'[266] This attempt to blame the riots on elements alien to the community and on 'strangers' is a common feature of riots.[267] But in outlying villages, the responsibility for the riots was clearly regarded as that of the town. A journalist staying at Llwynhendy was informed by his landlady: 'The people down that way [Llanelli] are not civilized.'[268]

Too late – police in Llanelli decide to guard a goods truck that has been ravaged by looters (Llanelly and County Guardian)

The *Carmarthen Weekly Reporter*, characteristically condemning Llanelli, saw the riots as stemming from the character of the town:

> Measured by police court business, Llanelly is twenty times as big a place as Carmarthen. There is undoubtedly a very unruly population in Llanelly. A highly respected magistrate – well-known in Llanelly – informed this writer . . . that the population of Llanelly is of a far rougher character than that to be found in the Rhondda . . . The majority of the people of Llanelly are responsible members of society but that does not alter the fact that there is a large rowdy element which is a public danger . . . It is undoubtedly a fact that there are enough hooligans in Llanelly to dominate the town.[269]

The paper also noted the prominent part played in the riots by women:

> There are women in Llanelly whose conduct bears a striking resemblance to that of the 'petroleuses' of the French Revolution . . . If the Germans occupied Llanelly in the course of a war, then the town would not suffer as much at their hands, as it has done at the hands of the Llanelly people . . .[270]

The prejudiced view of the editor of the *Reporter* does have the virtue of attempting to relate the events of 19 August back to the society in which they took place. For whereas the strike was the catalytic agent for the riots, the riots had other, deeper causes. These causes can only be discerned if we examine the social condition of Llanelli in 1911.

In 1911, Llanelli shared the expansive dynamism of the south Wales coalfield, whose economy, in contrast to that of the rest of Britain, was booming.[271] In the town, tinplate production benefited from the expansion in coalmining in the neighbouring parishes, as did the docks and its related activities. In 1904, the New Dock had been constructed.[272] In 1898 the Llanelly Steel Company had been founded by the Old Castle and Western Tinplate Works, to be joined later by an additional eight independent companies.[273] Shortly before the riots, Llanelli had rejoiced at the opening of the Pemberton Tinplate Works. Older firms added new mills to their works.[274] This activity led *The Economist* to remark in 1913: 'In the Swansea district more capital had been expended in the last seven years than in any corresponding period in the history of the trade.'[275] Industrial growth created a buoyant optimism in the town, embodied in the movement for the incorporation of the borough.[276] It also served as a magnet drawing people into the south-eastern section of Carmarthenshire. Between 1903 and 1912 the population of the registration county had increased from 125,000 to 163,727. In the six years between 1903 and 1909, the population had increased by only 4,456 to 129,456. Between 1909 and 1911 the pace of growth quickened, the population increasing to 148,914 in 1910 and rising again in 1911 to 161,067.[277]

The pace of change brought about widespread social tension. The growth in population and increased employment created a major consumer revolution in the town.[278] Almost every street had its grocer's shop, whose 'quality' varied according to its locality. The commercial heart of Llanelli was concentrated in a few streets; Bridge Street, Church Street, Cowell Street, Market Street, New Dock Road, Park Street, Station Road, Stepney Street, Thomas Street and Vaughan Street. The major centre of Llanelli's commercial life was Stepney Street. Along both sides of the street were crammed, shoulder to shoulder, dispensers of fashion, utilities and wonder. Fashion was obviously in the ascendancy, for along the street there were two watchmakers and jewellers, seven boot and shoe dealers, three gents mercers, twelve general drapers, a tailor and a hairdresser. The street also boasted a furniture dealer, an ironmonger, a saddler and harness maker. The wheels of commerce were kept turning by the branches of the Glamorgan Banking Co., Lloyds Bank and the Prudential chambers, while all possible bodily needs could be satisfied by four chemist shops, five grocers, one fishmarket and fruiterer, a butter and cheese dealer, two butchers, two confectioners, a tobacconist, a quinine bitters manufacturer, two temperance hotels, four public houses, the Ceylon Tea Shop and two other tea shops. The Central Pianoforte warehouse ensured that the population had access to an elevated culture. Tucked away in the arcade was a general merchant, an ironmongers, a jeweller, a hairdresser and tobacconist, an accountant, a lime and metals merchant, a stationers, a mercer and hatter, and that essential stop for the refined and tired shopper, The Chinese Tea Shop.

In 1911 Stepney Street had an unmistakable aura of prosperity.[279] The large and ornate windows of the shop façades displayed ithe social totems which were aspired to and longed for by the town's predominantly working-class population. The wanton destruction of these shop fronts, windows into other, better worlds on the night of 19 August, and the wholesale looting of goods, were a comment upon social status and a brief escape from social reality. For, as we have seen, living conditions for most were harsh and the standards of health low.[280] One of the streets where conditions were especially bad, Oxen Street, was closely linked with the riots. Ann Edwards and Frederick Williams, who were charged with looting, both lived in the street.[281] The inhabitants of Park Terrace, another deprived area, were also directly involved in the looting. Richard Nurse, Thomas Page and James Price, labourers who all lodged in Park Terrace, were imprisoned for looting the premises of Thomas Jones, JP.[282] With the development of industry came dirt and smoke. A visitor to the town in September 1907 noted that:

> Y peth cyntaf a'm trawodd ydoedd y ffyrdd budron, y mwg afiach a'r tram yn cael ei dynu gan un ceffyl . . . Am y mwg, wrth gwrs nis gellir osgoi hwn, cyhyd ag y bo'r holl weithiau alcam, dur . . . wedi eu planu yng nghanol y lle, a'r tai wedi eu codi yn grynswth direol o'u cwmpas. O rhyfedd anhrefn afiach . . .[83]

The *South Wales Press* dismissed claims that the town was not experiencing a social crisis, but the rapid demographic and economic development of the town suggests that an event such as a strike could ignite the town. Though religion was still a dominant social bond in Llanelli in 1911, other competing forces were increasing in number and diminishing the role of traditional leisure activities and forces of social control.[284] The success of the town's Rugby football team and the pages devoted to the Scarlets in the local newspapers reveals one alternative cultural force.[285] Religious leaders were conscious of the major threats to religion's dominance and produced a torrent of warnings, many of which graphically exposed the dangers inherent in these scurrilous activities. The streetcorner culture of youth, in which 'rowdyism' and gambling flourished, had long been condemned by the town's religious leaders.[286] But the technological advances of the early twentieth century brought new threats to religion. In particular, the cinema became the recipient of much criticism. In 1904 in Llanelli, crowds had packed out the cinemas to see each of the showings of *Dante's Inferno*. For all their gifted oratory and audio images, local preachers found it difficult to compete with the lurid cinematic depiction of the sufferings of the condemned. Haggar's and Buffalo Bill's circuses, the theatre, other travelling shows and the public house, with which Llanelli was amply provided, were other avenues of escape from the the restrictive confines of daily life.

At this time, the police court also offered entertainment to the amorphous society of Llanelli. Affiliation order and breach of promise cases and other details of the sexual misdemeanours of local inhabitants were particularly popular.[287] In some areas an alternative code of morality extended beyond the physical relationship of man and woman. Assault, theft and drunkenness were frequent occurrences. In the area around the dock, for example, epic pub crawls were often followed by frustration, anger and violence. In dispensing justice in the town's courts, Thomas Jones and Henry Wilkins built up a reservoir of resentment and bitterness against themselves which was increased by their involvement with the troops in August 1911.

To portray the society of Llanelli on the eve of the riots as placid, quiet and law-abiding is to misjudge the complex nature of the town's society. The 'Jerusalem of the Baptists' had several less laudable characteristics, and those who blamed 'strangers' and 'drunken hooligans' for the riots and looting on that dark, hot night of 19 August were capturing only a part of the reality of the moment. If we examine in detail those people committed for rioting and looting and those injured in the riots, what we find is that the Llanelli riots were clearly the creation and responsibility of Llanelli society.

Despite the extent of the rioting on 19 August, only nine people were brought to trial for riotous behaviour. The majority were from streets in the vicinity of the railway station. Despite the gravity of some of the charges, each defendant was dealt with summarily and fined 20*s*. The heaviest fine was one of 25*s*. against David Thomas Howells of Pont Tynon for being drunk, disorderly and assaulting a police constable.[288] This would suggest that the authorities in the aftermath of the riots did not wish to undertake wholesale reprisals, but rather preferred to make an example of a few.

The press reports of the looting are quite graphic in their depiction of the anarchic events of the night of 19 August. According to the reports, women were particularly active; the *South Wales Press* and the *South Wales Daily News* both wrote that at the railway goods yard:

> Women joined with boys, and men joined with both in this wholesale looting which continued for hours and hours without interruption. Women seized on articles of clothing, and to ensure getting into their homes with their newly acquired finery, took off some of the clothes they were wearing and attired themselves in the new ones on the spot.[289]

Their caution and confidence in changing their clothes in the riotous chaos of the moment were understandable. One woman, after repeated forays into Thomas Jones's shop, returned to her store of stolen goods in Mincing Lane only to find them all taken. Again, at the shops in Stepney Street, women were prominent in the looting. At Thomas Jones's shop it was reported that 'Women and children rushed in and out as fast as they could get, carrying away aprons full of eatables, boxes of cigarettes, tobacco, pots of jam, sugar, and everything of any value at all were carried out by the crowds . . .'[290]

If, in the excitement, women and children could parade with the theatricality of the cinematic images which filled their lives – boys dressed up in soldiers' uniforms and paraded in their finery – they were also conscious of the daily realities. Credit at the grocer's shop was one perennial humiliation. Perhaps here is the motive of the crowds in perpetrating the following: 'The roll-top desk [of Thomas Jones's shop] was smashed to bits, the papers in it destroyed and the books thrown out onto the street.'[291] Despite the prominence of women in the looting, both at Stepney Street and the railway goods yard, only one, Ann Edwards of Oxen Street, a thirty-two-year-old housewife, was subsequently charged and bound over.[292] Accompanying Ann before the Carmarthenshire Quarter Sessions were twenty men, eight of whom were charged with offences relating to the assault on properties in Stepney Street. Six of them were labourers and all were lodgers from adjoining streets, the only occupier being Thomas John Edwards of 12 Church Street, a thirty-year-old haulier.[293] The remaining twelve were charged with offences relating to the assault on the railway goods sidings. As a group, the twelve were spread across the town, six coming from Dafen, and were representative of more skilled trades – four were skilled metal workers, one was a mason, one was a bricklayer and two were miners.[294] Of the twenty-one charged with looting the average age of twenty-nine years and seven months would seem to refute the press assertions that the events of August 1911 were the work of the very young.

From the evidence given in their depositions to the court, the picture that emerges is of normal people caught up in bewildering events. Albert May claimed, 'I had the box from a man unknown. I was drunk'.[295] Inebriation and the receipt of goods from unknown donors were frequently used as excuses or justifications for a person's action. Others were more fortunate. One of the accused, William Trimming, stated: 'Myself and my wife were out shopping. When we were by the gates of the level crossing I found the ham close by the trucks and the boots as well which were lying there . . .'[296] David Davies was another upon whom fortune apparently smiled on the night of 19 August, for he too 'found ham'. This impression of bewilderment is confirmed in the details of the looted goods recovered by the police during their searches through various houses. Albert May was found by PC Tom Davies to have in his possession, 'a box of condensed milk, a box of candles, a box of Paisley flour, a box of jam, a box of cocoa, five pounds of sugar and a case of HP sauce'.[297] David Daniel John was charged with having in his possession a perambulator and a quantity of cheese.[298] In all, only a little over £42 out of a total loss of goods by the Great Western Railways and Thomas Jones amounting to £3,670, was recovered through the courts. This led the historian of the riots, Dr Deian Hopkin, to conclude that 'the police inquiries were brought to a speedier conclusion when the extent of community participation in the looting became clear'.[299] The authorities showed leniency in not bringing charges against the victims of the baton and bayonet charges of the police and soldiers.[300] The community also showed sympathy towards the victims. Large crowds gathered at the funerals of John John and Leonard Worsell, and petitions and appeals were organized to help their families.[301]

In the Llanelli riots, as in the Tumble and Tithe riots, precipitate action by the authorities offended popular opinion and served as a catalyst for community violence.[302] In the euphoria of release, the crowd, though unorganized, shared both special grievances and communal assumptions about the direction and legitimacy of its actions. Each crisis occurred within the framework of conventional social relations. In their actions the crowds at tithe sales, goods yards and colliery chose targets which were symbolic of their discontent at a community which was ostensibly of their creation.

What then does this study of crime and protest tell the historian about Carmarthenshire society at the turn of the twentieth century? It is certainly not a complete and rounded picture of daily life which emerges from the courts, but it is a vivid picture nonetheless. Most of the activities of the common people – at home, at work and in recreation – are reflected, albeit in a distorting mirror. The drinking habits of the working classes, the sexual and physical tensions within families, the role of violence in society, the position and the patterns of police operation, the difference between 'social crimes' and thefts and assault, these and several similar impressions can be built up by assembling the mass of fragmentary pieces of information and human experience which can be gleaned from court records. Such insights are naturally of profound importance to the social historian.

We have seen that there is much evidence to show that it could be a rough society and that recourse to violence was relatively frequent. But it is difficult to establish whether people feared for their lives or felt unable to use the roads at night. Some, such as

Mrs Sutton of Llanelli, undoubtedly did. Despite her husband's illness she informed the inquest into the cause of his death that she feared to go out after 10.00 p.m. even to get a doctor, or to her parents a hundred yards away.[303] Newspapers of this time are dotted with condemnatory reports of the streetcorner culture of youths. In 1894, 'Nishmi' complained that it was unsafe to be out on the streets of Ammanford at stop-tap[304] and the *Llanelly Mercury*, in an article on streetcorner loafers, considered that 'To enforce the Sunday Closing Act would probably lead to an armed insurrection and to attempt to put down local mendacity would in all likelihood end in the erection of barricades.'[305]

However, Llanelli was not alone in experiencing such tensions. Carmarthen also suffered from the anti-social behaviour of youths. In 1903 the *Carmarthen Weekly Reporter*, in an exposé of 'street blackguardism', spoke of:

> the wild stampede and the full throated roars of these hobbledehoys who seem as excited as so many buffaloes when the prairie is on fire, while the shrill laughter and terrible shrieks proclaim the females who wish it to be distinctly understood that they are not quite as responsible as they look. We have a lot to do before we get on our streets the model of decorum which one would expect in the Athens of Wales.[306]

But despite the vociferous condemnation by these model Athenians, and the undoubted roughness, fighting and casual violence which characterized street life, there was little lethal violence or serious injury. The paranoic protestations of shocked sensibilities of middle-class observers dot the pages of the county's newspapers. Yet these writings reflect concern for the moral well-being of youth rather than any real fear that the author was faced with personal physical danger.[307]

The collective violence of the 1885 election, the Great Mountain Colliery strike in 1892–3, the tithe war of the late 1880s and 1890s, the sporadic industrial disputes of the 1900s and the Llanelli riots of August 1911, considered together, these events did not present a serious threat to authority. Though they were exhibitions of rebellious and disorderly tendencies among some sections of the working people of the county, they never threatened to overthrow the existing system. The evidence shows that the majority of the population accepted the legitimacy of the criminal law as it affected them. Having broken the law, many people would attempt to the best of their ability to evade its consequences, but they did not (except in the case of poaching offences) openly deny its legitimacy. This held even at times of collective violence when strands of an alternative moral and social code came into operation. The working class of the county, as we have seen, had complex and contradictory attitudes towards the law and the operation of the police, as shown in the frequent assaults on police constables and even police stations. But these same groups of people were prepared to evoke the processes of the law in order to achieve redress of grievances, whether for physical assault or the theft of personal property, or the award of maintenance and separation orders.

Perhaps the most accurate conclusion to draw from a study of crime and protest in Carmarthenshire is the ambivalent one that it was not a particularly orderly society, but neither was it a markedly violent or disorderly one. Essentially, the picture which emerges of Carmarthenshire crime, despite the excitement and the characters involved, is an undramatic one. The great majority of offences were committed by normal individuals by chance as the opportunities arose in their normal daily lives. There did not exist in Carmarthenshire, as there did in the rookeries and flash-houses of London and other large cities and towns, an extensive professional criminal class.[308] However, the historian, and especially the social historian, should be aware of the differences in scale between different communities. To the contemporary observer, relativities were not important. It was no comfort to the victim of physical violence to learn that such events were more prevalent in larger urban centres. Contemporaries feared the threats offered to them by the low lodging-houses and the dingy, sabbath-black bars of Carmarthen and Llanelli. For danger, like beauty, is in the eye of the beholder.

4

Sexuality and Tension

The sexual behaviour of Victorian people has been more comprehensively misunderstood and misrepresented than probably any other aspect of Victorian life. Writers on Victorian sexuality have portrayed the Victorians as almost entirely repressive and repressed.[1] Despite the work of a number of historians who have dared to suggest that mutual pleasure was to be found in the Victorian marriage bed,[2] the word Victorian remains, like the word 'Puritan', synonymous with a set of morals and sexual values which are regarded as odd and even bizarre.[3] The dominant perceptions are those of a paranoid prudery which sought to protect statues with fig leaves, covered piano legs and bowdlerized Shakespeare and even the Bible. Victorian literature presents a tableau of pure women and passionless men, citizens of a solemn utopia where duty has routed desire and children are born but never made. As the editor of the *South Wales Press* asserted, 'the highest manhood and the noblest womanhood are not compatible with the pleasures of the senses'.[4]

In Wales these perceptions were reinforced through the strength of the religious affiliation of the Welsh in the nineteenth century. Following the unnecessary and unjust accusations by the education commissioners in 1847 that Welsh women were almost universally unchaste, a massive literary effort was undertaken to disprove these allegations.[5] In 1867 the Revd Thomas Rees prepared a reasoned defence of Welsh morality on the basis that the Welsh, like all other people, were not wholly bad or good.[6] But by the end of the century such reasoned arguments had become transformed into the belief that Wales was a land of absolutely pure and faultless morals: 'Cymru lân, Cymru bur'.[7]

The social institution which supported Evangelical Christianity in achieving the moral purity of the Welsh was the family. In the nineteenth century the family was believed to be sacrosanct and its beneficial influence was perceived throughout Welsh life. In 1898, in an article on the influence of the mother on the formation of the Welsh character, the editor of *Y Gymraes* declared:

> . . . Cartrefi Cymry i raddau helaeth sydd yn gyfrifol am yr hyn ydyw cymeriad y Cymru. [and added] A'r mammau i raddau mor helaeth a hyny, sydd yn gyfrifol am yr hyn yw y cartref.[8]

The family as a haven in a tempestuous world is one of the most powerful images of Victorian Wales. Works such as D. J. Williams's *Hen Dŷ Ffarm* and William Llewelyn Williams's *Gwilym a Beni Bach*[9] present images of peaceful, placid, orderly, happy families, in which children willingly respond to the requests of their parents. In their mind's eye, these authors walked again among the loved and loving people who gave warmth and beauty to the first years of their pilgrimage. The visual arts in Victorian Wales, in particular printing, painting and photography, abound with images of the 'Angel at the hearth' surrounded by her contented family. These visual images are confirmed by a wealth of prose and poetry which extolled the values of Christian family life. One of the most popular of the poems which dot the pages of late nineteenth-century newspapers and the transactions of local and national eisteddfodau was Samuel Roberts's 'Y Teulu Dedwydd'.[10] This commenced with the poet's discovery of the contented family:

> Mewn hyfryd fan ar ael y bryn
> Mi welwn fwthyn bychan,
> A'i furiau yn galchedig wyn
> Bob mymryn, mewn ac allan.
>
> Y Teulu Dedwydd yno sy
> Yn byw yn gu ac annwyl
> A phob un hefyd sydd o hyd
> Yn ddiwyd wrth ei orchwyl.

The whitewashed cottage is symbolic of the purity of the family and the poem is set firmly in the romantic pastoral tradition of

Welsh poetry which presents a cosy, picturesque, orderly peasantry happily toiling in a green and pleasant land. The secret of the happiness of the family is their religious beliefs:

> Pan ddêl yr hwyr, ac iddynt gwrdd,
>   Oddeutu'r bwrdd eisteddant,
> Ac am y bwyd, o hyd nes daw
>   Yn ddistaw y disgwyliant;
>
> Pan ddyg y fam y bwyd gerbron
>   Gwnânt gyson geisio bendith,
> Ac wedyn, pan eu porthi gânt.
>   Diolchwn yn ddiragrith.
>
> . . .
>
> Yn fore iawn, mewn nefol hwyl
> I gadw'r ŵyl cyfodant,
> Ac wedi ceisio Duw a'i wedd,
> I'w dŷ mewn hedd cydgerddant;

Their material earthly possessions are few, the family have greater rewards awaiting them:

> . . .
>
> Mor fwyn eu cân! Mor fwyn pob gair!
> Ac O! mor daer eu gweddi!
> A Duw yn siriol weni ar
> Y duwiol hawddgar deulu;
> Gwir nad oes ganddynt ddodrefn aur,
> Na disglair llestri arian,
> Na llawrlen ddrudfawr yn y tŷ!,
> Na gwely-lenni sidan.
>
> . . .
>
> Ond mae rhinweddol win a llaeth
> Yr Iechydwriaeth ganddynt,
> A Christ yn Frawd a Duw yn Dad
> A thirion Geidwad iddynt.

Fe'u ceidw'n ddiogel rhag pob braw,
Ac yn Ei law fe'u harwain,
Nes dwyn pob un i ben ei daith
Trwy hirfaith dir wylofain;
Pob un a gyrraedd yn ei dro
Hyfrydol fro paradwys,
Ac yno'n dawel berffaith rydd
Y cânt dragwyddol orffwys.

The family was central to the Christian cause and the religious household was the base from which to counter the evils of the world outside.

The punishment for those who sought to undermine the strength and cohesion of the family was clear. W. Edwards and E. Pryse, writing under the pen-name 'Ewyllyswyr Da', quoted the warning of the scriptures:

> Na thwyller chwi; ni chaiff na godinebwyr, nac eilyn-addolwyr, na thorwyr-priodas, na masweddwyr, na gwrw-gydwyr, na lladron, na chybyddion, na meddwon . . . etifeddu teyrnas Duw . . . bydd eu rhan yn y llyn sydd yn llosgi a thân a brwmstan, yr hwn yw yr ail farwolaeth . . . yn ddiau os na caiff y bygythion sobr a dychrynllyd hyn o lyfr Duw effaith arnat dos rhagot . . . Dos rhagot, ddyn aflan . . . Dos rhagot yn dy lwybrau aflan . . . Groesaw Uffern! Groesaw fflamiau! Groesaw gythreiliaid.[11]

The family was the haven, the nest within which to form and nurture young souls. In the Christian household, the organic relationships between husband and wife, mother, father and child, brother and sister flourished in tranquility; everyone knew his or her place and was content with it. The place of the woman was clear: 'Hi yw brenhines yr aelwyd'. She was the 'Queen of the hearth', and her duty was:

> . . . i drefnu y teulu, ac y mae llawer yn dibynnu ar hynny . . . Does ganddi hi ddim amser i chwedleua, ac i grwydro yma ac acw, yn ei thŷ y mae hi i fod, yng nghanol ei gofalon. Nid oes un esgys i'w gael yn erbyn hyn . . .[12]

Despite the moves to provide education for women, and the attempts to secure entry for women into the professions, the view in Wales continued to be that a woman's place was in the home.[13]

The only education a woman required was one which allowed her to acquire the requisite skills of needlework, cookery and general and moral cleanliness. A contributor to *Y Gymraes* expressed this view succinctly in 1909: 'Angen ein gwlad yw merched ieuainc a nôd uchel i'w bywyd sef cael cartrefi Cymru, a chartrefi y Deyrnas, yn esiampl i bob gwlad mewn trefnusrwydd, purdeb, a pharch i Dduw a dynion.'[14]

The Victorian marriage was based upon a clear understanding that there were separate spheres for wife and husband.[15] Hers was the private world of her family; his the public world of work. It was the husband's duty to provide an income for his family and the wife's to ensure that it was employed efficiently in providing a morally inspiring home for their children. Within the family unit the children, and in particular the daughters, were insulated from the dangers of the outside world. The virtues to cherish and aspire to were honesty, self-restraint, thrift and chastity. The authors of the prose and poems which extolled family life offered no practical advice as to how this ideal domestic happiness was to be achieved. They were reluctant to discuss aspects of domestic relations and particularly so the relationship between husband and wife. As late as 1900, in advising young girls, a writer under the pen-name 'Chwaer' advised that:

> Y mae rhyw bethau y dylai y rhyw fenywaidd eu dysgu, ac nid oes dim galw am i'r rhyw arall fod yn hysbys iddynt, ac yn wir byddai eu bod yn gwybod rhywbeth yn eu cylch nid yn ychwanegiad at eu gwybodaeth ond yn arwydd o wendid ynddynt. Dylai pob rhyw rhagori yn y wybodaeth fwyaf buddiol i'w sefyllfa.[16]

Similar attitudes hampered Rhys Gwesyn Jones during his lecture tour on the subject of 'Caru, Priodi a Byw' ('Love, Marriage and Life').[17] One deacon refused to announce the title of the lecture from the pulpit because it was Sunday. The lecture, which was delivered frequently in the 1860s, was one of the few attempts to provide sensible and practical advice to young couples on how to live contentedly together.[18] That there was a demand for the advice is shown by the fact that the lecture was reprinted five times before 1904.[19] The Revd M. Hopkins of Pen-bre was another minister who sought to provide advice on marriage in *Cyn, ac ar ôl Priodi; A'r Fodrwy Briodasol* ('Before and after marriage, and the Wedding Ring').[20] Though he ignored physical relationships, his criteria of the characteristics for a good wife – purity, sobriety, honesty, faithfulness, cleanliness and thrift – were admirable.

Historians who have examined the changes in popular morality during the nineteenth century have argued that the double standard which had operated for centuries became articulated in the Victorian years.[21] This double standard, whilst stressing the importance of sexual restraint for girls and young women, allowed young men the freedom of their senses. These contradictory aims were achieved through the existence of a class of fallen women who kept the rest of the world pure; as St Augustine remarked 'remove prostitutes from human affairs and you would pollute the world with lust'.[22] In his *History of European Morals,* Lecky wrote:

> But for her [the prostitute], the unchallenged purity of countless happy homes would be polluted, and not a few who, in the pride of their untempted chastity, think of her with an indignant shudder, would have known the agony of remorse and despair. On that one degraded and ignoble form are concentrated the passions that might have filled the world with shame. She remains, while creeds and civilizations rise and fall, the eternal priestess of humanity, blasted for the sins of the people.[23]

The extent of the operation of this double standard in Victorian Wales is difficult to perceive, but its existence enables us to penetrate beneath the generalizations and to capture some of the reality of Welsh Victorian and Edwardian sexual behaviour. In Wales there existed, as we have seen, a large body of opinion which regarded illicit sexual activity as equally unrespectable in both men and women. Yet its influence, as we shall see, was limited, in that its main attention was directed towards safeguarding the chastity of married women and the daughters of respectable families. Towards 'fallen' women it was less indulgent. Moreover, the emphasis on outward respectability resulted in the absence of any serious deterrent against successfully conducted clandestine activity. This was shown at the highest level in the activities of Lloyd George[24] and is expressed in Caradoc Evans' assertion, mentioned earlier, that 'Wales is a country of secret sin'.[25]

It is difficult to gauge the extent of prostitution in Victorian and Edwardian Carmarthenshire. Studying the period from 1870 to 1920, one gets the impression that prostitution was most prevalent in the 1890s and the first decade of the twentieth century. It is impossible to quantify the number of women involved but one cannot deny that prostitution did exist, and that it existed not only in the larger urban areas of the county but also in rural hamlets. Although it never approached the level of activity which occurred in Cardiff and Swansea, prostitution was recognized as a social problem in Carmarthenshire.[26] In June 1906, Canon Camber Williams, at a meeting in Swansea to raise funds for the Diocesan House of Mercy in East Moors, voiced concern at the increase of sexual immorality in Carmarthenshire, and claimed that 'prostitution is on the increase in the town of Carmarthen and . . . there has been an immense and terrible increase in the sin of impurity . . . Hundreds of little girls are going down the road to sin and ruin in our town.'[27]

Many motives compelled women to resort to prostitution, but the majority, like Grace Bell of New Dock, were forced into it by economic necessity. In 1915 she told the Llanelli Police Court that it was impossible for her to be 'respectable' on 10*s*. a week when the rent alone was 8*s*.[28] As prostitution was conducted on a semi-professional basis in Carmarthenshire in the nineteenth century, it is perhaps not surprising to find a large number of prosecutions for indecent behaviour in public places. In July 1884, Thomas Thomas of Merthyr Tydfil was fined for having intercourse with a woman of 'low character' in a Carmarthen churchyard.[29] In October 1902, Ellen Evans, a married woman, and James Protheroe, an unmarried collier from Llwynhendy, were fined 40*s*. each for indecent behaviour in the Llanelli Parish Church cemetery.[30] It would appear that once a deal was made, then back-streets, back gardens, public shelters, doorways, public house cellars, public parks – indeed anywhere – irrespective of the prominence of the location, would serve for some couples.

Some people did attempt to establish the business of prostitution on more profitable and comfortable lines. In February 1913, the police raided the premises of the Bird in Hand in Carmarthen after receiving complaints from a mother that her daughter and other girls were entertaining men in the upstairs rooms. The police found a couple in one bed and two men and a woman in another bed. Following an admission by one of the girls that 'there were tremendous numbers of fellows who went upstairs' at a fee of '1 shilling each time', the Carmarthen Borough Police court fined the publican William Evans £20 and sentenced him to two months' hard labour.[31] In drab and damp Carmarthen back streets, these girls, with their cheap perfume, exuded a whiff of Parisian sensuality. Common lodging houses located in the Mill Street area of Carmarthen and in the dock district of Llanelli doubled as brothels. The number of prostitutes in Carmarthen town increased whenever the militia were stationed in the town. In June 1907 the editor of the *Carmarthen Weekly Reporter* reported that: 'The Carmarthen Police have been greatly troubled by a number of undesirable females who have come to Carmarthen since the Militia's training started.' The ability of some of these ladies to entertain the militia is questionable. Mary Ann Davies, from Cardiff, was so inebriated that she had to be taken to the police station in a wheelbarrow.[32] Several other women also faced charges of being drunk and disorderly.

The response of local people to prostitutes and prostitution is complex. Acceptance was often dependent on the locality in which the person lived. Many women considered prostitution not only as a fall from grace but as a betrayal of the woman's duty to struggle to maintain a home on what she possessed, however little that might be. In December 1909, Sarah Jane Thomas of Pont-henri was charged with shooting and injuring James Jones because he had accused her of immoral relations with a John Smith. Local people had expressed their displeasure by assembling outside her house, smashing windows and burning an effigy of her.[33] People were clearly aware of the dangers which confronted young girls who failed to resist temptation. In a remarkable novel, *Martyrs of Hell's Highway*, published in 1896, H. Elwyn Thomas of Llandybïe portrayed the horrendous experiences of little Bell. Sold by her drunken father, Bell found herself in a brothel in London which specialized in child prostitution. Humiliated and shamed at the hands of a member of Parliament, Bell committed suicide. In fact reality was harsher than fiction.[34] In April 1913 Margaret Jones was charged at the Swansea Police Court with procuring fifteen-year-old Bridget Williams for an immoral purpose.[35] In May 1914, Hodge Lewis was committed on bail of £100 to the Assizes by the Llanelli Police Court on a charge of attempting 'to procure a girl named Una Gertrude Jarman of Llanelli to leave the country to become an inmate of, or frequent, a brothel elsewhere'.[36] Given the importance of maintaining respectability in public, local attitudes were a curious mixture of sympathy and self-righteousness when the news was received that Carie Gilmore, a Llanelli prostitute, had been found murdered on waste ground in Cardiff.[37]

If sex was an obsession which the Victorians sought to keep quiet, their obsession with statistics was made public. Following the 1847 Education Report, many writers raided the Reports of the Registrar General for Births, Marriages and Deaths to prove indisputably that Wales was more pure and moral than England. In his defence of the Welsh against their alleged unchastity, Thomas Rees produced figures for 1861 which proved that both south and north Wales were more moral than 'those English counties whose inhabitants most resemble the Welsh in social position and occupations', in terms of illegitimate births to every hundred births.[38] Yet, in 1909, when Gwilym Davies of Carmarthen compared the immorality of the Welsh with a different set of English counties, he discovered a rather different picture.[39] There had not been a revolution in Welsh morals between 1861 and 1909. The differences arise from the fact that Thomas Rees measured the illegitimacy of all sections of society, while Gwilym Davies used a more scientific measurement of illegitimate births against the number of women aged between fifteen and forty-five. But the Victorian proclivity to throw the first stone obscures one important fact which is apparent in the statistics of both Thomas Rees and Gwilym Davies. It was the rural areas of Wales which experienced the highest levels of illegitimacy.

This fact is graphically illustrated if we examine the illegitimacy rates of Carmarthenshire parishes and registration districts. Llanelli was the most heavily industrialized parish in the county. In the decennial periods of 1885–94 and 1895–1904, the illegitimacy rates for Llanelli averaged at 3.37 and 2.91 per 1,000 births respectively.[40] In the same periods the rate for Llan-non, which was predominantly a mining parish, was 3.50 and 3.21. Llandeilo (Fawr) contained substantial mining, quarrying and agricultural sections and this duality is reflected in average rates of 5.36 in the period 1884–94 and 3.87 in the period 1895–1904. Those registration districts which were purely agricultural had higher illegitimacy ratios. Llanddeusant had a rate of 8.13 in 1885–94, 7.53 in 1895–1904 and 7.15 in 1905–09; Talyllychau had rates of 7.61 in 1885–94 and 5.48 in 1894–1904, whilst Cynwyl Gaeo had rates of 10.12 in 1885–94, 8.60 in 1894–1904 and 6.68 in 1905–09. It is clear from these statistics that the rates of illegitimacy were declining over this period 1885–1914. But if we pick out individual districts in particular years we find that the rural/urban disparities become greater. In 1885, for example, the illegitimacy rate of Llanddeusant stood at 25.00, while that of Llanelli was 3.38. Clearly each village had its idiosyncrasies, and often its own code of morality.

This pattern of higher rural illegitimacy is not a Welsh peculiarity. T. C. Smout and others have shown that it was a common feature of many British rural communities.[41] It is in marked contrast with the European pattern of higher urban illegitimacy, and in direct conflict with Edward Shorter's thesis in *The Making of the Modern Family*.[42] Grossly simplified, Shorter's argument maintains that as the economy modernized and more women left their rural communities and their kin to seek employment in the cities and towns, so they left behind 'traditional values' which stressed that pre-marital sex was wrong. In urban environments, they encountered the values of the market-place which stressed personal independence and self-gratification, and they consequently began to search for a sexual fulfilment which they found, Shorter claims, in illicit sexual encounters. From this stemmed the rise in illegitimacy.[43]

The male inhabitants of rural Britain, because of the long hours of work involved in farming, developed the habit of courting late at night in the kitchen or bedroom of the girl's house or lodgings. The agreement to meet would be made during working hours, perhaps by an intermediary, for the suitor to call at the girl's lodgings at night.[44] To attract her attention it was customary for the young man to throw sand or light gravel at her window – called 'cnoco lan' – and he would then be allowed into the kitchen – 'noswylio' – or into her bedroom – 'caru yn y gwely'. That the practice continued into the twentieth century and did not end in the 1890s, as David Jenkins suggested in his study of rural society in west Wales,[45] and that it might entail pitfalls other than that suggested by the Registrar General, is shown in some cases which were brought before Carmarthenshire courts. Daniel Rees and Evan Jones, farm servants from the St Clears district, were both fined for criminal damage to farmhouse windows in 1905 and

1906. Having failed to attract the attention of the servant girls through throwing sand and gravel, in their frustration they threw cockles and half a brick.[46] In July 1912, in an appeal against robbery charges, Sarah Williams of Maenordeilo, a woman of 'bad character', added a new twist to the traditional courtship custom of the Welsh countryside when she claimed that Fred Rodley 'slid down my chimney and seduced me'.[47] The nocturnal activities of some courting couples caused resentment among other servants. Eleanor Lloyd complained to the Llanelli Police Court in March 1907 that she and another servant had been awoken by noise to find Rees Rees with a female servant in the kitchen 'where he behaved like an old stallion'.[48]

But statistics, as Koestler reminds us, 'don't bleed'.[49] The historical study of illegitimacy has been quantified and patterns of behaviour have been analysed, but the actual people involved have been ignored and forgotten. They remain anonymous in a ghostly army of statistically summoned spirits. Perhaps the best source for the social historian intent on discovering the personal secrets of young couples, and on studying an act which takes place between two people in a confined place, and usually without witnesses, are the accusations of paternity made by mothers, unmarried and married, of illegitimate children in local police courts under the Poor Laws.[50] These affiliation orders, reports and transcripts, of which over 1,000 are available for the period 1881–1914 in Carmarthenshire,[51] lay bare the aspirations, desires, hopes, feelings and personal outlook on life of the men and women involved.

The majority of the girls involved in affiliation order transactions claimed that they had been seduced by the promise of marriage.[52] This is understandable and natural when we remember that the girls had been raised up in a society that placed great emphasis on the values and virtues of purity, self-restraint, chastity and marriage.[53] In order to win a case, society demanded that the girl prove she was the innocent victim of a calculating seducer. The majority of applicants stressed that it was the promise of marriage that led to their fall from virtue. It was as if the promise pulled back a curtain in the girl's mind and led to thoughts of marriage, of home, of a family, above all to thoughts of happiness and an end to loneliness. Indeed, many had kept their virtue intact through long courtships. Sara Jenkins of Pwll, near Llanelli, courted Evan Morgan, a local collier, for five years before she allowed herself to be seduced following a promise of marriage in June 1904. Margaret Jones of Mill Terrace, Pantyffynnon, Ammanford, a dressmaker, had the added advantage that her three-year courtship with John Bowen, a collier, had taken place under the supervision, obviously not over strict, of her parents. Surely, she argued, under such conditions she could have been reasonably assured that John would act honourably.[54] Mary Thomas of Cynwyl Elfed, although an orphan, had grounds to argue that her seducer, William Thomas Davies, a joiner of Nevill Street, Llanelli, would act honourably. As her uncle's best friend he had, by March 1907, and after two years together, bought a seven-guinea diamond ring and sent her 133 letters. When they were read out in court, these tender declarations of apparent affection and love were giggled, laughed and sneered at by people who packed courtrooms to hear the details of local cases and to find entertainment and comedy in the agony of others.[55]

Moral and class preconceptions were frequently the basis for deciding the outcome of affiliation cases. Barmaids, for example, the objects of lust, of coarse comments, sometimes of actual body handling during their long working hours, and the epitome of all that was detestable and abhorrent to moralists, found affiliation proceedings emotionally trying, even where they appeared to have solid evidence. Often their only comfort would be the friendship of the girls they brought along as character witnesses. Edith Mary Williams, a nineteen-year-old barmaid at the Plough and Harrow, Glanaman, applied in February 1905 for an affiliation order against John Llewelyn, a local collier. Although her five witnesses testified to having seen the couple during happier times walking together along the area's known lovers' lanes, and that one had seen them having 'acts of familiarity' on the local common, her case was refused.[56] Sarah Jenkins, a thirty-year-old servant of Heol y Mynydd, Bryn, Llanelli, ran into the cruel face of class prejudice in the Llanelli Police Court in May 1905 during her paternity case against Edgar Thomas, the twenty-two-year-old son of her employer at Gwalia House, Llanelli. Throughout she was portrayed as the knowledgeable and scheming corruptor of youth. Thomas's lawyer, Thomas R. Ludford, the editor of the *Llanelly and County Guardian*, declared that:

> however much of a hardship is imposed upon the plaintiff by having lost her character and post it would be more of a hardship on the young man who has been to college for two years, where he distinguished himself, and is now respectably teaching. Besides she can produce no witnesses to 'the acts of familiarity.

Sarah's bitterly cruel position was callously scorned.[57]

Ministers, newpaper editors and other commentators inferred that affiliation order proceedings were the consequences of the behaviour of intemperate, wasteful people who submerged themselves in the impure and immoral atmosphere of public house and streetcorner gangs. But temptation existed even in the most exalted places. In January 1906, two months before the religious revival abated, David Henry Thomas, a draper of Capel Hendre who had provided a Bible, a £5 donation and the carpet for the stairs and the pulpit of Moriah Chapel, found his respectability and his character besmirched when he was summoned by Mary Williams for the paternity of her child. He was ordered to pay 3*s*.6*d*. until the child was fourteen, together with the costs of obtaining the order and the costs of the midwife.[58] In June 1905, Elizabeth Ann Rees, aged nineteen, of Pwll, Llanelli, summoned Joseph Morse, a tinplate worker at the Old Castle Tinplate Works to answer charges of fathering her illegitimate son. The authorities at Bethlehem Chapel, the place where the relationship germinated and grew, responded in a manner sadly too common amongst Nonconformists by expelling him.[59] Lydia Lewis, of Llangennech, was seduced by Morlais Harry, a fellow member at Saron Chapel, on a Sunday School trip in August 1907.[60] These episodes show that no matter how stern the sermon, the twinkling, inviting eyes in a young face could conjure away the wages of sin.[61] The Revd Gwilym Nicholas, a Congregationalist Minister of Gowerton, was summoned by Emily Maria Richards of Carmarthen for the paternity of her child in October 1918. Their courtship occurred when he lodged with Emily's mother while he was a student at the Carmarthen Theological College. Despite his claim that 'I cannot think how it happened', he was ordered to pay 5*s*. a week plus costs.

Perhaps the most calculating of seducers was William Thomas, a collier, of Pontyberem, described as a real 'Bond Street Swell' by the *South Wales Press*. He spent the summer months dossing as a tramp amongst hayricks and common lodging houses, although throughout the period he was in receipt of good wages. But in matters of seduction he had the aristocratic notions of soft lights, good food, and plenty of time. In June 1906 he spent the sum of £20 in creating the milieu for the weekend seduction of Catherine Rees of Trimsaran at the Hotel Metropole, Swansea. The details included several meals, and the classic procedure of unmarried couples seeking entrance to a hotel bedroom – the purchase of a ring to cover their intentions with the emblem of respectability.[62]

For many girls the attempt to portray themselves as innocents corrupted by the man's deftness in covering his foul intentions could fail in a torrent of character assassination from the defendant, the defence lawyer and witnesses. In May 1907 the case of Rachel Jenkins, of Vauxhall, Llanelli, against Samuel Jones, a servant at the Cleveland Hotel, was rejected when he and his witnesses claimed that she had kept frequent company with local soldiers and that she had been seen by one voyeuristic witness having intercourse with a soldier in Stradey Woods.[63] From the beginning of her affiliation order proceeding against David Thomas, Maria Bowen of Bryn Terrace, Llanelli, was put on the defensive. It was no great shock, for it was her second appearance.[64] She had strenuously to deny that her mother kept an immoral house, and that on the weekend of Buffalo Bill's Wild West Circus's visit to the town, she proved to be more of an attraction with the cast than the preparations for the show.[65] Esther Davies was rumoured to have had many suitors. In court Esther had to deny that she had to consult a fortune-teller to help her identify the father of her child.[66] It was cases such as these that drew crowds of people to the police court. Often the atmosphere in the courthouse resembled that of a burlesque comedy in the music hall. Magistrates had to struggle to keep order. Gales of laughter burst through the Llanelli Police Court when Christopher Theopolis, a collier, accused of paternity by Rachael Griffiths of Dafen, declared 'I would not kiss her for a fortune.'[67] Laughter was also the response in court when a witness in the case of May Jenkins against Ernest Treharne declared, 'You cannot deny that Ernest Treharne is the father of the child for it is the very picture of him.'[68]

Laughter is often the natural response of people, however adverse the situation may be. But within the laughter in the courtroom there is often a hardened cynicism, stemming from self-righteousness. These are the feelings one discerns in the attitudes of magistrates and the barristers. The case of Agnes Roberts of Tumble clearly illustrates such hard-faced attitudes to a tragi-comic attempts of a young gullible, girl to adhere to the notions of a delicate, insipid femininity which was implicit in the double standard.[69] Agnes insisted in court that intercourse followed a promise of marriage. When she confronted the father she fainted. Abandoned and distraught, she then attempted to take her life by hanging herself on the pine end of her home. When that failed she attempted to drown herself in the Llanelli dock. The response of the defence lawyer Thomas Ludford to this disclosure was to ask whether it was 'The New Dock?', adding 'There is no water in it yet.'[70] Amidst raucous laughter, her case failed.

The peculiar experiences of the First World War imposed such pressures upon local people that profound changes in social attitudes were brought about. It is a terrible irony that the profligate waste of human life in the trenches of the war led to a greater value being placed on infant life.[71] This change of attitude in the Empire's darkest hour was extended to the illegitimate child. Though illegitimacy rates had been declining, the departure of men to the war led to fears of an increase in illegitimacy. As the editor of the *Carmarthen Weekly Reporter* wrote:

> A proportion of our girls have simply flung themselves at the soldiers and many of them will be called upon to pay the bitter price. Such warnings as were given have been, in certain cases, of no avail, and now we have to face the grim question of the sad undesirable harvest. We shall be hearing of the slaughtered innocents and the unwanted baby will be the subject of many an inquest.[72]

The editor called for an active campaign by the chapels, churches and welfare agencies to ensure that there was no slaughter of the innocents. In the event Carmarthenshire, like the rest of Britain, did not witness a proliferation of war babies. The rates of illegitimacy in the period 1914–20 continued to decline as they had from the 1880s. What did change were people's attitudes. The set of moral perceptions which had operated since the mid-nineteenth century and which underpinned the double standard was effectively shattered.[73]

It is perhaps in the cases of indecent assaults on women that we can see the operation of a double standard at its worst. Not only did Victorians seek to deny publicly that lust – the dark engine of human biology – existed, but there were distinct attempts to keep such sexual transgressions quiet. The records of the quarter sessions and police courts of Carmarthenshire are littered with distressing histories of young girls being raped and indecently assaulted. Little sympathy was shown to many following their harrowing experiences. In the case of indecent assault brought by Jane Lewis, aged fifteen, of Llanfihangel Aberbythych, against John Nicholas, T. G. Williams, the defending solicitor, in a discussion as to whether the case should go from Llandeilo Petty Sessions to the quarter sessions, or to the next assizes, declared:

> The Grand Jury in the Quarter Sessions are tampered with in all these cases. Every man is seen before the trial comes on. I don't complain without reason, but within my own knowledge and experience; I am supported by the police, who will corroborate what I say. Every man of the Grand Jury is seen before it comes on.[74]

The Llandeilo magistrates however sent Jane's case to the quarter sessions, where the case was dismissed. In a decision upon the case of John Lewis of Wind Street, Llanelli, charged in November 1900 with having had, on three occasions, carnal knowledge of a fourteen-year-old girl – a practice a local newspaper editor described as being 'sadly an almost daily occurrence in Llanelli, especially in the dock district' – Judge Bingham delivered this astonishing verdict:

> 'I call it a most trumpery case. According to this girl all that happened is what is called a somewhat indecent assault. These cases are scandalous. They get a reputation for this part of the world that this part of the world does not deserve.' He then added to the jury, 'Do you want anymore of it gentlemen? I think this is a most trumpery case. If her story is true he is only guilty, as I have said, of a somewhat indecent assault.'[75]

Despite the protestations of the prosecuting barrister, John Lloyd Morgan, KC, MP, that there were two further charges of rape, the case, on the Judge's urging, was dismissed.

The frequency with which some couples had intercourse – every Saturday in the summer of 1904–5 in the case of May Lewis and John Johns of Llanfihangel-ar-arth, every Tuesday and Thursday in May 1905 in the case of John Jones and Ann Evans of Cynwyl

Gaeo – and the number of men named as having had intercourse with Agnes Roberts of Tumble in 1903 and 1904, implies that knowledge of and use of birth control methods were widespread. Mary Williams, a servant in the employ of William Scott, a farmer of Five Roads, claimed that he had offered, on hearing of her pregnancy, money if she kept quiet. When she refused he had locked her in a shed and attempted to force her to take saltpetres.[76] Owen Davies, a shop assistant at St Clears, denied in August 1906 that he had purchased drugs for Esther Ann Evans of Tre-lech a'r Betws to take in order to induce an abortion.[77]

It is impossible to gauge the extent of birth control methods in the nineteenth and early twentieth centuries,[78] but there are indications that knowledge of and use of birth control methods were widespread even in the rural parishes of Carmarthenshire. In the *Llanelly Mercury* of 7 February 1901, Professor Deaking, a herbalist of Alexandra Road, Swansea, published advertisements which were to continue until 1907. He offered for sale 'French novelties: 6d. each, 3 for 1s., or a dozen for 3s.6d.; postage extra. On sale weekly at the Saddler's Shop at the back of Llanelly market every Thursday.' He also offered 'confidential Cures by Herbal Treatment'.[79] The location of their sale, and the occasion – market day – must have offered frequent occasion for nods, witticisms and jocularity.

The most common form of birth control in the late nineteenth and early twentieth centuries appears to have been the widespread use of abortificants by women. In November 1898, after the trial of the Chrimes Brothers for blackmailing 3,000 mothers who had bought their tablets intending to procure abortion, *Reynold's Newspaper* found it astounding that apparently respectable newspapers still carried such 'hideous' advertisements.[80] Of the newspapers circulating in Carmarthenshire in the 1900s, the *South Wales Daily News*, the *Western Mail*, *The Cambrian*, *Llais Llafur*, *Tarian y Gweithiwr*, the *South Wales Press*, the *Llanelly Mercury*,, *The Sentinel*, the *Llanelly and County Guardian*, the *Carmarthen Journal*, the *Carmarthen Weekly Reporter* and *The Welshman* all carried such advertisements. More surprising is that the Independents' weekly, *Y Tyst*, the Baptists' *Seren Cymru* and the Methodists' *Y Goleuad*, even in the revival years, carried such advertisements. Several companies advertised, but characteristic of the majority is the following:

> Towle's Pennyroyal and Steel Tablets, Woman's Unfailing Friend. Guaranteed to correct all irregularities, remove all obstructions, and relieve the distressing symptoms so prevalent with the sex.

The advertisement is just as cold in the Welsh translations in the Nonconformist press.[81]

What makes this much more surprising is that these advertisement continued, not only after a well-publicized London trial, but after the inquest into the death of Ann Walker a twenty-eight-year-old haulier's wife, at the Swansea Castle Inn, Llanelli, in October 1898. The official cause of death was peritonitis but, in the course of the inquest, it became clear that Ann, terrified by the agonizing ordeal of her first confinement had taken a mixture of

> 6 pennyworth of Holland's gin, two pennyworth of essence of Pennyroyal and a handful of Lad's Love [the local name for the plant clematis that grew in profusion in gardens and on porches in south-west Wales] and stewing them until there was only a wineglass-full left.

The materials, except the Lad's Love, had been obtained from a local chemist, T. Davies, who claimed no knowledge of the properties of Pennyroyal. In preparing the mixture, Ann had been advised by neighbours. She died in agony. Although the Coroner, Dr J. S. Roderick, and the editors of the local press were horrified and demanded a full enquiry by the police to bring an end to a practice that was described 'as more common than we would care to admit', nothing in fact was done. The case was not unique. The editor of the *South Wales Press* warned that four cases involving the Llanelli and District Nursing Association, and a doctor, could be disclosed which 'are more deplorable because they are engendered among the upper form of the middle class'. Yet still nothing was done. The editor's sincerity was immediately called into question, for in the same issue there appeared advertisements for Towle's Pennyroyal and Steel Pills, A. Dasmail's Clovel's Women's Tonic, and the 'Pills for Females' of Mrs O. St Clair of Chancery Lane, London.[82]

It is impossible to ascertain the number of women who had to resort to abortion in Carmarthenshire at the turn of the twentieth century. What is certain is that many people with a medical training assisted women in getting rid of their unwanted burdens, often with fatal results. One of the most remarkable victims was Emily Cope, who died in Dr Hopkins's surgery in Carmarthen. At the inquest, the doctor claimed that she had died from a lung infection. Subsequently, her lungs were found to be in perfect health but the evidence indicated that she had given birth recently, and it became clear that she had come from Bristol to Carmarthen to procure an abortion. The inquest declared that Dr Hopkins was guilty of the crime and he was sent for trial, at which he was surprisingly found not guilty. One of the problems the jury encountered was the whereabouts of the infant's body. Speculation was wild, when the following incident occurred:

> When her almost putrid body was placed in the hearse, one of the four large dogs which Doctor Hopkins keeps at home, flew into a fit. It rolled on its back on the ground in front of the hearse, foamed at the mouth, howled in most pitiful manner, writhed as if in great agony and twisted itself almost into a ball. P.C. Hopkins had great difficulty in keeping back the crowd.

Concealment of birth, infanticide or suicide were often the only choices that offered themselves to a girl abandoned by her seducer and condemned by her family and by society. The local press is pockmarked with reports of the ghoulish discoveries of months-old rotting infant corpses in mines, drains, quarries and woods, of unskilful bloody door-step, back-garden and back-toilet abortions, and of the solitary, savage, suicide of young, unmarried pregnant girls. Despite the sensations aroused in the press, there was a distinct refusal to confront this dark, grisly, unpleasant reality.[83] Such an example is the acquittal of Mary Ann Ledster, a farm servant of Llwynhendy. In March 1901 she was charged at Llanelli Police Court with having concealed the birth of her child, by placing it in a parcel and depositing it between two hayricks, where pigs found it and commenced to devour it, until they were prevented by the farmer. The evidence against her was strong, but the bench showed its dissatisfaction and distaste that the case had been brought before them by quickly dismissing it.

Those who did not want to dispose of children often hired others to do so on their behalf. Baby-farming was common in Victorian Britain, particularly in the large cities.[84] But rural Carmarthenshire also had practitioners of this nefarious practice. In November 1905 Ellen Johnston, formerly of Llanelli, was sentenced to five years' imprisonment for cruelty and neglect of children entrusted to her care.[85] In June 1917 Walter and Lydia

Elms were sentenced for the murder of an unknown female child between 1 and 31 January at Pen-bre. Following the complaints of neighbours, the police and the NSPCC began to investigate. The body of a baby was discovered by a police sergeant using grappling hooks in a lonely spot near the mouth of the River Gwendraeth.

> The body was dressed in a merino night gown stitched up in three pieces of a woman's skirt and wrapped up in brown paper. A stone 19lbs in weight was attached to the body. A postmortem examination was made by Dr. Owen Williams who gave evidence that the child died of starvation . . . Walter Elms showed him [the sergeant] the place where he threw the child. Elms added that the child was no bigger than a rabbit.[86]

The couple were also charged with cruelty and neglect of two other children and sentenced to five years hard labour.[87]

These practices, horrendous as they are, were often the only option available to a woman. Hidden amongst the images of happy contented families were grotesque brutalities. The harsh reality for many people in nineteenth-century Wales was that happiness was an elusive and ephemeral ideal. Profound pressures and tensions existed in every family. There were tensions in the way parents, in particular fathers, sought to reconcile their authority and the instillation of discipline with the expression of love and more tender feelings. Tensions were created by the differing aspirations, ambitions and requirements of husband and wife, and, above all, profound tensions were created by financial stringencies. These tensions, and others, were normally contained and suppressed by an arsenal of defence mechanisms which individuals created around themselves. Husband and wife created distinct, separate spheres of influence in which one partner was acknowledged as the superior. Many sought solace in palliatives such as drugs and alcohol. Not least amongst these defence mechanisms was humour, a humour often self-mocking but born of a resignation to one's fate. Yet the tensions and frustrations could, and did, become unbearable. The proceedings of the police courts contain many terrifying accounts of vicious assaults and violent behaviour that took place within the family unit. Wives were abused and beaten, children were abused, assaulted, abandoned, battered. Brutality, chauvinism and malice were the dark trinity that ruled in many families in south-west Wales at the turn of the twentieth century.

The ending of the legal ties in the divorce court was one avenue of escape for women entrapped in such a tortuous enslavement. The ruin of the political careers of Parnell and Sir Charles Dilke as a result of their involvement in divorce proceedings reveals the power of an outraged moral conscience and the public opprobrium and stigma which were attached to divorce cases in the late nineteenth century. However, in considering the divorce proceedings which were brought before Welsh courts, one becomes aware that, as well as the sense of moral outrage, there was another popular attitude which derived considerable entertainment and fun from the salacious details of the clandestine comings-and-goings of the defendants. In the case of *Berry* v. *Berry and Carpenter* in 1893, Thomas Isaacs, a tinplate worker of Swansea Road, Llanelli, achieved considerable popularity amongst the crowds who packed the court or eagerly awaited the arrival of the newspapers reporting the case. To them Isaacs's accounts of his voyeuristic athleticism in clambering on top of outbuildings to witness the couple's romantic activities were highly enjoyable.[88] During the case of *Blake* v. *Blake and Wadell*, despite the moralistic outbursts of the *South Wales Press* (which rivalled *The Times* at its most self-righteous in the Parnell case),[89] popular behaviour in south Wales revealed far more complex attitudes. The 8 o'clock train from Llanelli to London was packed with people called upon to serve as witnesses and others seeking entertainment. The proceedings revealed the claustrophobic environment of gossip and spite that existed in the mining town of Tumble. During the case, details of the love letters sent from 'your sweet curly boy' aroused uncontrollable waves of laughter throughout the crowded courtroom.[90]

But such cases were exceptional. Divorce was expensive and consequently not an option available to many people. Historians have been mistaken in assuming that the low number of divorce cases brought from Wales before courts in the nineteenth century is evidence of the cohesion of the Welsh family unit. It is more likely to be evidence of the inability of people to pay the expensive legal costs involved and suffer the social ostracism that accompanied divorce proceedings. The only option for many people who discovered they could no longer continue to exist in an environment in which two sets of furious spites continually clashed was to apply for separation and maintenance orders under

The boisterous life of the Victorian public house

the Matrimonial Clauses Act (1898), the Married Women's Maintenance Desertion Act (1886) and the Summary Jurisdiction (Married Women's) Act (1895). That such actions were frequent occurrences in Welsh society at the turn of the twentieth century is revealed by the fact that the reports of almost 2,000 individual cases are available for the administrative county of Carmarthen between 1887 and 1914. Cases brought before local police courts under these Acts provide the historian with detailed information about the issues and actions which provoked people to the most extreme resolution of conflict. The details of such cases provide a plangent, mournful catalogue of the private stresses and sorrows of ordinary lives.

Several cases which were brought before the police courts of south-west Wales seemed to confirm the view of contemporaries that the people involved in such proceedings were members of a degenerate, immoral, drink-sodden underworld whose worthless, misspent lives revolved around the pub, the lowlier type of lodging houses and the workhouse. Ruth Jones of New Street, Llanelli, had to deny her husband's allegations that she 'drank gin at night, heard bells and saw the gates of Heaven'.[91] Susannah Davies, of Ropewalk Road, alleged that drink was the cause of Benjamin's violent behaviour. After drinking sessions, he frequently laid out the table for 'my corpse', sharpened knives in preparation, and wrapped towels around the children's throats and threatened to strangle them. Amongst his threats to his wife was the promise: 'I will rip you up and bottle your blood which I will send to your mother.'[92]

Yet to blame domestic violence solely on one cause is naïve and simplistic. Drink undoubtedly played an important part in the breakdown of family life, but it was as much a symptom as a cause of breakdowns. Drink served to exaggerate responses to normal disputes and bickerings. A large number of families from all social groups were split asunder by tensions which were neither caused nor intensified by one partner's addiction to alcohol. In July 1913 Gwenllian Lewis of Glanaman took out an order against her husband for his refusal to pay a maintenance order, awarded to her by a local court, which was £10.16*s*.6*d*. in arrears. The difficulty of their marriage was caused by the fact that, as a Pentecostal dancer, he believed that 'he could not be a disciple of Christ and serve his wife and children. If he could not worship as he liked he must give up his religion for the sake of his wife, and he was not prepared to do that.'[93]

David Lewis, a butcher from Bryn-teg, Carmarthen, was summoned by his wife, Catherine, on a charge of grievous bodily assault at Carmarthen Borough Court. She appeared in Court with black eyes and a 'mutilated face', alleging that although she had returned with over £25 from Neath and Aberavon markets, he beat her with a horsewhip because she was late. During the case, large crowds from their neighbourhood gathered at the court room to hear the saga of their marital purgatory, and many failed to gain admission. Her statement – 'I was struck senseless, and fell to the ground. I received several blows after I became senseless . . . He had kicked me upstairs' – was interspersed with bursts of laughter from the crowds. The judge was more sympathetic; David was fined £5 for assault and bound over for six months. The judge also advised the couple to separate.[94]

It is difficult to capture the exact nature of popular attitudes towards wife-beating and inter-family violence. The laughter of those present at the case of David and Catherine Lewis suggests that people derived considerable amusement from the marital unhappiness of others. In some social circles it would appear that wife-beating was an accepted part of married life. In December 1898 two police officers were seriously assaulted by a crowd when they attempted to intervene in a fight between a husband and his wife outside a Llanelli public house. Although some quarrels spilt out from the home to public arenas, most domestic violence was kept within the bounds of the home and there was both a public refusal to acknowledge that the problem existed and a personal refusal to admit to the realities of the abuse. Both attitudes are encapsulated in the warning 'scream quietly or the neighbours will hear'. It was claimed that John Parker, a signalman with the Great Western Railway, refused to let his wife Blodwen out because 'her black-eyes were showing him up'. Evidence of popular attitudes are both fragmentary and contradictory. The popular condemnation of wife-beaters which found focus in the activities of the 'ceffyl pren' continued, even in industrial society, well into the twentieth century. During the case which Mary Edwards brought against her husband, Thomas Charles, at the Llanelli Police Court in April 1895, it was stated that 'effigies of her husband were burnt by people in Pemberton Street'. In addition, neighbours had also physically prevented Thomas from selling the family's furniture.[95] It was clear that his action had gone beyond the bounds of acceptable behaviour. But, if the wife-beater was unpopular in nineteenth-century Wales, so, too, was the nagging wife. In a culture in which the oral tradition was still the predominant mode of communication, proverbs can be seen as representing the distillation of the collected wisdom of society. Many proverbs gave stark warning against the vituperative loquacity of the female tongue: 'Pwy bynnag sy heb wraig, sy heb ymryson', 'Goreu gwraig, gwraig heb dafawd'. It was even said that dry water and wet fire were as common as a silent wife: 'Tri peth anhawdd eu chael: dwfr sych, tân gwlyb, a gwraig dawgar.'[96]

The level of violence which existed within many marriages is shocking and the tolerance of some women to years of gross physical abuse is surprising. In analysing the details of separation and maintenance order proceedings, the historian is frequently confronted by the base elemental beast in man. John Emmanuel of Nevill Street, Llanelli, tried to put his wife on the fire.[97] William

Jones, a farmer from Carreg Cennen, was committed by Llandeilo Police Court for attempting to dynamite the villa in which his wife lived.[98] Margaret Evans stated that her husband, Benjamin, had 'a peculiar little habit of leaving dynamite caps about the house near the fire from choice'.[99] Mary Ann Lloyd of Water Street, Carmarthen, claimed that her husband Fred held a lighted lamp above her and her baby's head and threatened to put them on the fire.[100] It was inevitable that violence of this kind would lead to murder. David Jones, a sheep farmer of Llandovery and the son of the Revd John Jones, murdered his wife in 1883, after years of violent and threatening behaviour.[101] It is understandable that some women, subjected to such brutalities, followed biblical advice and returned wound for wound, stripe for stripe. Mary Ann Davies of Trostre Road, Llanelli, hit her husband with a poker, and it was a standing joke among Anne Rees's neighbours that, after a quarrel, they would 'look over the garden wall to see how much crockery was broken'.[102]

The tolerance by married women of the violence inflicted upon them by their husbands is perhaps not so surprising when we realise the profound economic and social disadvantages of women in Welsh society at the turn of the twentieth century. The overwhelming ideological importance of the marriage in all social groups led to the inability of women to admit that their marriage had failed. Beatings had a mental as well as a physical effect. The physical torture had the mental effect of debilitating a wife's capacity to take decisions. Often, the wife's contact with Poor Law authorities and the police served only to increase her feelings of guilt. Any refusal by the wife to carry out the dictates of her husband was interpreted as provocation, and her behaviour was perceived as a threat to the system of masculine and female prerogatives which underpinned the institution of marriage. The main factor which kept man and wife together was the lack of any realistic alternative for the wife. A wife had to care for her children. The only place she could turn to was the Poor Law workhouse. Even when compared with her hostile home environment, this was not an attractive alternative. The regimentation of workhouse discipline frequently meant that families were split up. In one instance, Mary Elizabeth Hope absconded from Llanelli Workhouse saying, 'I have been a prisoner in the workhouse for two years'. Marina Davies of Pleasant Row, Llanelli, suffered nine years of abuse before she was finally driven to confront the alternative.[103] 'Pleasant Row', Bryntirion, Bryn-hyfryd, Hyfrydle: one continually notices the obscene contradiction between the name of the house and the horrendous, secret brutalities inflicted on the innocent within its walls.

There was a multitude of causes of marital discord, but the most persistent and profound were those caused by financial stringencies. Interpersonal bonds, which were often stretched taut by disagreement and discord, snapped under financial pressure. Wives deprived of money because of a husband's drink addiction, his personal intransigence, or his abandonment of the family, were forced to live on their wits in order to survive. They took on a multitude of tasks – washing, skivvying, dressmaking, labouring in brickworks, serving in public houses, indeed any available task that often was the preserve of the very poor. The experience of many women reveals the centrality of the pawnshop in the daily lives of the Welsh working class. Any item, irrespective of the personal sentiment attached to it, would be exchanged at local pawnshops. Annie Bourne of Bynea admitted in court that she had pawned her wedding ring and the family Bible.[104] Many wives took in lodgers to supplement meagre family earnings. However, the presence of a lodger in a house often served only to deepen tensions within the family unit. Many husbands were jealous of the domestic arrangements their wives had to make in order to provide for lodgers, and many resorted to violence as a result of their suspicions that sexual services were offered clandestinely to lodgers.[105] Some men, however, were keen that their wives should obtain additional income in this manner. Mary Cottrell of Carmarthen alleged that her husband threatened her at knife-point and urged her to go with other men, something which she steadfastly refused to do.[106] Indeed many cases reveal that prostitution and venereal disease were widespread problems in south-west Wales at the turn of the twentieth century. Louise Williams stated that her husband, Henry, a farmer of Dolau Fawr, had brought a common prostitute into their home, kept her there for several months, and frequently forced his wife to share their bed. He also introduced several 'filthy diseases into the house'.[107] Similar accusations were also levelled against David Edwin Sheridan Phillips and Frederick Carter.[108] Historians have devoted considerable effort to studying the social impact of dramatic major diseases such as cholera, but little work has been done on the impact of diseases and infections, whose effects on family life have been less dramatic but probably more pernicious.

It was not only wives who suffered. There is, sadly, abundant evidence of the neglect and physical and sexual abuse of children in south-west Wales during this period.[109] In May 1913 the Carmarthen District Branch of the NSPCC reported that during the course of the previous year it had investigated 210 cases of cruelty to children, 205 of which were found to be true, affecting 268 offenders and 624 children. The inspector reported that 168 cases had led to warnings, nineteen had been otherwise dealt with, seven had been dropped, whilst sixteen had led to prosecutions and convictions, which showed 'we [the NSPCC] are not out to prosecute but to help'.[110] At the Annual Meeting of the Llanelli District of the NSPCC in April 1910, it was stated that the policy of the Society was not to prosecute but to warn offenders. These warnings, it was reported, frequently had beneficial effects.[111] However, there is evidence from Llanelli that, despite the warnings of the courts and the NSPCC officers, violence towards, and neglect of, children continued. William Morris, a former Llanelli and Wales international Rugby player, and his wife Elisabeth were warned in 1910 about cruelty to their children and were prosecuted two years later for their persistent neglect.[112]

Abuse and neglect of children were not masculine preserves. Mary Evans, a thirty-five-year-old widow from Llansawel, was censured by Sir James Drummond at Llansawel Petty Sessions for her treatment of her three children. It was, he said, inconceivable 'that any beast would treat their offspring so . . . [you are] unworthy of the name woman'. For similar offences, Margaret Mary Phillpot was described as 'a disgrace to humanity'.[113] Coroners' inquests frequently reveal evidence of the terrible physical neglect of children. Dr W. W. Brodie, deputy coroner for Carmarthenshire, at an inquest into the death of four-year-old Horace Lloyd at the Llanelli Workhouse, was told that on his admission to the Workhouse, 'Horace seemed to be in a dying condition and looked like a breathing corpse'. At the time of her death in 1913, Deborah Reed weighed only six pounds, although she was nine months old.[114] The tragic details of the truncated lives of such children are requiems to squalor and cynicism. The reports of the NSPCC inspectors at court proceedings tell of disgusting, verminous households and dirty, diseased, sickly, wild children. Inspector Idris Jones of the Llanelli NSPCC stated that he frequently found the children of Henry and Edith Evans on the doorstep of Holy Trinity Church and elsewhere late at night, and that in 1911 he had found them, 'living in a pig-sty, not in a house styled as a pig-sty, but in a proper pig-sty'. Although hardened to the grotesque physical conditions of the homes which he visited, an NSPCC Inspector vomited when he encountered an overpowering stench in an upstairs bedroom of the home of the Lloyds of Felin-foel.[115]

As with wives who suffered the indignities of beatings, mothers of the victims of child abuse were forced to take up degrading occupations in order to survive. Mary Ann Jones of Hawkers Lodging House, Carmarthen, obtained a living by calling upon householders and their maids and pretending to tell fortunes.[116] Mary Steward and several others turned to prostitution. When Inspector Jones of the Llanelli NSPCC called at her home to investigate allegations of cruelty, he found the father drunk, smashing crockery and frightening the children, one of whom was suffering from tuberculosis. Both parents were sentenced to four months' imprisonment with hard labour.[117]

Violence between the generations was not confined to the poor; as the editor of the *Carmarthen Weekly Reporter* pointed out that 'cases of cruelty do not come to light in country mansions as we all know'.[118] In 1913 William Rees Howells, a prosperous farmer of Whitland, was sued for a separation order by his wife. Although she braved his violence for twelve years, she could no longer tolerate the confines of marriage to William when he acted violently towards their six children. He was ordered by the judge to separate from his wife and to pay a maintenance order of 15*s*. It was to prove an expensive day. The next case in court was also against William Howells. Inspector Batten of the RSPCA charged him with cruelty to a pig, and for this offence he was fined 20*s*.[119] Some cases of child abuse ended tragically in homicide. It appears that many men had very low thresholds of tolerance; they took the most extreme action as a result of the slightest trigger to violence. Unable to cope with the stress and strain of an overcrowded, poverty-stricken existence, they simply exploded. In Carmarthen in 1887, and in Llanelli in 1908, three-year-old girls were murdered by their fathers with blunt knives.[120] 'Blind anger' was popularly considered to be the cause. If anger is of such importance to most forms of interpersonal violence, then historians need to analyse popular attitudes to loss of temper and examine the strategies which people evolved to cope with stressful situations.

Having considered the violence inflicted by parents on their children, it is not surprising to find that violence and neglect were reciprocated to parents in later life. The Poor Law authorities frequently brought the sons and daughters of elderly parents to court in order to compel them to pay the costs of maintaining their parents. But only a few authorities succeeded in enforcing the court order. In his survey, *The Condition of the Aged Poor* (1894), Charles Booth noted, as we have seen, that in west Wales, in places like Llandeilo and Aberaeron, children had a 'callous' disregard of familial duties. It is clear that the most relentless and persistent current of violence running through the nineteenth century was neither urban nor rural, but domestic.

The experiences which we have examined clearly show that not all people in Victorian and Edwardian Carmarthenshire conformed to the stereotypes of the sexually inert woman and the dutiful father. Once we examine sexual behaviour in Carmarthenshire in detail, we perceive that beneath the respectable façade the world of the senses thrived. Passion flourished amongst the prudery. In 1909, Gwilym Davies of Carmarthen complained:

> Nawr onid yw yr ysgrifen ar furiau ein urinals cyhoeddus yn ein lleoedd poblog, yn fynegiant o feddwl digon o'n pobl ieuangc yng Nghymru? Lle bynag yr ewch fe ganfyddwch y geiriau Saesneg am noethni y ddau ryw wedi eu hysgrifennu mewn sialc. Yr wyf, cyn hyn, wedi gweld darluniau o ddyn a dynes noeth ar lyfr emynau mewn capel yng Nghymru, ac ar Destamentau a ddefnyddir yn yr Ysgol Sul! – Y mae yn ymddangos fod yna nifer – pa wyr fawr y nifer, nis gwyddom – o'n bechgyn a'n merched ieuengc sudd â'u meddyliau wedi eu mwydro mewn syniadau o'r fath fwyaf cnawdol. Y mae ein heglwysi yn fud, y mae tadau a mamau yn rhy aml yn fud: goddefir i'r plant dyfu i fyny yn ysglyfaeth rhwydd i'r blys sydd yn dueddol i fod yn un o bechodau etifeddol y Cymro.[121]

If the graffiti left on hymn books is any evidence of the matters which occupied the minds of Welsh youths, there was also more public evidence of this preoccupation with the sensual. Some historians argued that the corset, and in particular the

Women at Work in Carmarthenshire market in c.1870
(Carmarthenshire Records Office)

controversy over tight lacing was another symbol of female oppression under the double standard.[122] But contemporaries regarded them more as erotic symbols. Their advertisements are scattered throughout the Welsh press. In 1898 Elwyn Thomas complained of:

> The unscrupulous fortune-hunters of every description [who] know in these days that, after failing in every attempt to make money, they can always succeed by devising some way to insert the semi-nude figure of a woman in their advertisements . . . the impetus to evil given by the too suggestive and unspeakably vulgar female sketches which accompany present day advertisements . . . are enough to weigh down the heart of the most cheerful optimist alive. Think again of the guilty silence of the pulpit in regard to this terrible sin.[123]

It is to the 'guilty silence' that we now turn.

5

Spiritual Skeletons: Religion, Superstition and Popular Culture

It was a truth universally acknowledged that nineteenth-century Welsh people were fervently religious. Moreover, they were Nonconformists. This message was ceaselessly propounded from the pulpits, the political platforms and the printing presses of nineteenth-century Wales. In 1866, Henry Richard, laid the foundations for the equation of Welshness and Nonconformity when he wrote: 'It may be stated that in general terms the Welsh are now a nation of Nonconformists.'[1] Probably no single statement from a nineteenth-century political leader caused as much joy and celebration in Wales as did Gladstone's assertion in 1891 that 'The Nonconformists of Wales are the people of Wales.'[2] The Grand Old Man had finally abandoned his ambiguity and a nation rejoiced.[3]

This assertion was frequently 'proven' by a large body of statistical analyses published in the nineteenth century. The most notable was the religious census of 1851 organised by Horace Mann, a senior officer at the Registrar General's census office.[4] The findings of the census confirmed the pre-eminence of Nonconformity amongst those who attended church or chapel in south Wales on Census Sunday in 1851. The Nonconformists accounted for 76.1 per cent of the presences at religious services on Census Sunday in 1851; 25.3 per cent were present at the services of Independents or Congregationalists, 22.3 per cent were at Baptist services, 18.0 per cent at Calvinistic Methodist services and 10.5 per cent at Wesleyan Methodist services. In comparison, the Church of England accounted for 20.5 per cent.[5] In terms of the provision of places of worship, 'Wales', to use Horace Mann's evocative phrase, was 'fortunately basking in an excess of spiritual privileges'.[6]

But the findings of the 1851 census are of little value to the historian who wishes to study the condition of religion at the turn of the twentieth century. There were other religious censuses organized during the nineteenth century, but none of them had either the administrative structure of the Registrar General to ensure statistical accuracy (in so far as such an emotive subject as religion could be quantified), or the impartiality of his officers. The historian must be aware of these deficiencies in considering the religious censuses of late nineteenth-century Wales. In 1891, for example, Thomas Gee published in *Moesoldeb Rhyfel y Degwm* his own census of attendance at Welsh chapels in 1887.[7] Designed to support Gee's arguments against Dean John Owen on the morality of the tithe war this census is undoubtedly partisan. But despite its limitations it is useful in offering an impression of the religious condition of Wales in 1887. Unsurprisingly, perhaps, the pre-eminence of Nonconformity is again illustrated. In the seven counties of south Wales a total of 468,731 people attended Nonconformist places of worship, while the total attending the Church was 89,047. In Carmarthenshire 38,756 attended Nonconformist services in the morning and 46,771 attended in the evening, giving a total of 85,527. Attendance at the Church of England was 9,172 in the morning and 10,619 in the evening, giving a total of 19,791.[8] It should be noted that the totals refer to attendances at morning and evening services and that no attempt was made to calculate the number of people who attended twice, which in nineteenth-century Wales would undoubtedly have been many.

The historian is doubly fortunate in that there was another attempt by the government to gather statistics of religious worship and that critical examination was made by official commissioners of the individuals and institutions presenting information. These statistics, for the year 1905, were published in the *Report of the Royal Commission on the Church of England and Other Religious Bodies in Wales* in 1910 and 1911.[9] The statistics presented are taken from denominational yearbooks and Church registers and provide details of the persons listed as communicants. They also provide estimates of the adherents of Nonconformist bodies and of the established Church. It is thus not a census of religious worship and should not be used as such by the historian. Its major value is to provide an impression of the relative strengths of Nonconformity and the Church at both national and local level. It should be remembered that serious efforts were made by the Commissioners to ascertain the accuracy and test the validity of the statistics presented to them. Thomas Johns of Capel Als, Llanelli, David James Davies, editor of the *South Wales Press*, and the Revd John Herbert, vicar of Llanllawddog, for example, were questioned intently for long periods by the Commissioners on the statistics which they presented.[10] The statistical evidence should not thus be dismissed out of hand by the historian in an over-pessimistic assumption that piety cannot be measured.

The figures reveal that the Church of England had since 1851 enjoyed a resurgence in its comparative position in relation to Nonconformity as the provider of the means of grace.[11] In 1905, 193,081 were communicants of the Church of England, which represented 25.9 per cent of the total of Welsh communicants. The Church had thus surpassed the Congregationalists and the Calvinistic Methodists, who respectively claimed 175,147 (23.5 per cent) and 170,617 (23 per cent) of communicants. The Baptists claimed 143,835 communicants (19.2 per cent) and the Wesleyan Methodists 40,811 (5.4 per cent).[12] In total there were 743,361 communicants of religious denominations in a total population of 2,420,921.[13] The publication of the statistics gave rise to a bitter debate. Some commentators argued that the figures provided irrefutable evidence for the erosion of religion as a force in Welsh life which had taken place in the half century since 1851. The fact that only 30.7 per cent of the Welsh people attended a place of worship was a fact which drew much attention. But other commentators and observers drew attention to the deficiencies which were concealed by the statistics. The Commissioners themselves in their report emphasized that the figures were of communicants, not the actual number of people who attended religious services. This was a factor of particular importance for in the nineteenth century many people attended chapels, but were not members of a particular chapel or denomination. They preferred to follow the 'big guns' of the Nonconformist ministry on their peripatetic pilgrimage through the pulpits of south Wales.[14] But the Commissioners were not satisfied with the accuracy or reliability of the statistics provided to them on the number of adherents, dismissing them as 'practically worthless'.[15] Nevertheless, after considering the numbers of communicants the Commissioners declared their belief that: 'from the evidence adduced before us . . . the people of Wales show a marked tendency to avail themselves of the provision made by the Churches of all denominations for their spiritual welfare'.[16]

If we examine the respective position of the denominations in Carmarthenshire, we find that the resurgence of the Church of England in Wales had not undermined the hold of the Congregationalists on the county. The Congregationalists were by far the strongest denomination in the county, with 28,813 (36.7 per cent) of a total of 78,556 communicants.[17] Following them was the Church of England with 19,191 (24.4 per cent),[18] the Baptists with 18,160 (23.1 per cent), the Calvinistic Methodists with 11,286 (14.3 per cent), and the Wesleyan Methodists and Evangelicals who together accounted for 1,106 (1.4 per cent) of the county's communicants.[19] Almost three in every five of the total population of 135,328 resident in Carmarthenshire were communicants of a religious denomination.[20]

Given the availability of the statistics, it is worth briefly considering the position at parish level. The historian should, however, be conscious of local factors before drawing any firm conclusions from the statistics. The location of a chapel and the lack of a return from a church could distort the actual position. The tiny parish of Llanfihangel Cilfargen, for example, had an estimated population of thirty-seven in 1905, while the number of communicants at the Congregational Chapel of Pen-heol was seventy, giving an attendance rate of 189.2. No information was given as to the number of communicants at the parish church, these being coupled with those of the sister church of Llangathen. If both parishes are taken together the percentage of communicants to population was 61.4, which, although high, is more consistent with the percentages of other Carmarthenshire parishes. Another problem is the fact that the statistics for parish population given in the Nonconformist statistics do not correspond with those given for the same parish in the Church of England statistics. The problem is the result of the differences between the civil and ecclesiastical parishes. This needs to be noted in calculating the percentage of the population who were communicants.

Having considered the limitations of the statistics, it is worth noting one surprising feature which emerges from the statistics in Carmarthenshire, a feature which the historian of modern Welsh religion, the Revd Professor R. Tudur Jones, has noted for Wales as a whole.[21] The traditional, established view is that industrialization and urbanization led to a decline in religious adherence. The view was eloquently expressed by D. Lleufer Thomas in 1915 when he wrote that: 'the ideal of . . . religion would seem in danger of being repudiated in some of the industrial districts in favour of an illusory ideal of a cosmopolitan, and perhaps to some extent materialistic brotherhood'.[22]

Yet, in fact, the process was slower and more complex than many contemporary commentators realized. Though industrialization contained elements that would develop to rival and undermine the position of religion in the long term, in the short term the development of industry actually helped religion in the same way as it did the survival of the Welsh language.[23]

If we examine the evidence of some Carmarthenshire parishes, it becomes clear that the urban and industrial parishes of south-west Wales were, unlike their larger English counterparts, areas of high religious adherence. A witness to the Commission commented upon this difference: 'In Ammanford and the Aman Valley . . . people who go nowhere [are] very few and of these hardly any were Welsh.'[24]

The percentage of communicants to population in Ammanford was 48.86; in nearby Betws it was 49.27, while in the mother parish of Llandybïe, the percentage, at 33.5, was the lowest proportion of communicants to population of all the county's parishes with a significant industrial population. In Llanelli Urban District the percentage was 52.8, in Pen-bre 57.18, in Llan-non 58.16, in Cwarter Bach 60.22 and in Llandeilo Urban 84.8. In marked contrast were parishes of a rural character, such as Newchurch, Llanfair-ar-y-bryn, Caeo and Pencarreg, which recorded percentages of 36.89, 37.4, 42.9 and 42.69 respectively. A comparison of eleven industrial parishes with eleven rural parishes reveals that while the average percentage of communicants to population in the former was 56.08 per cent, in the latter it was 52.48.[25]

The figures suggest that historians need to reconsider the established view of a highly religious countryside, contrasting with irreligious towns.[26] The scattered nature of the population in some Carmarthenshire parishes and the physical difficulties of reaching a place of worship to attend might account for the low incidence of religious affiliation in some parishes. But there is evidence to suggest that even where churches were located near centres of population, not all communicants attended. At St Clears for example, a Mr Wilkinson told the Commissioners that although the chapel was located near the majority of the population, 'barely half of the communicants and adherents attended on the average Sunday'. He added that, as discussed earlier in relation to education in Carmarthenshire, the pattern of attendance varied according to the time of year: 'In the winter months during the tied period of the horses and cows, they [farmers and labourers] have so much work to do with them that it is quite impossible unless you neglect your duties towards your stock.'[27] Farm duties, fatigue at the end of a hard day's harvesting, coupled perhaps with apathy and indifference, led to empty pews in village churches and chapels.

In almost all the county's parishes, Nonconformity was in the ascendant but, considering the denominations individually, interesting patterns emerge. The Congregationalists were numerically the strongest, but their domination of the county was not complete. In the Tywi Valley, in the towns of Carmarthen and Llandeilo, and in the west of the county, in the parishes of Laugharne, Pendine and Llan-dawg, the Church of England had the highest number of communicants. This fact, given the social composition and the influence of the gentry in a town like Llandeilo, and the historic eccentricities of a town like Laugharne, is perhaps not surprising. More surprising, perhaps, is that the church also had the highest number of communicants in the urban parishes of Llandybïe and Llanelli Urban. Another pattern to note is the dominance of the Calvinistic Methodists in the north-east of the county in the parishes of Cil-y-cwm, Caeo and Talyllychau and also in Llanfihangel Cilfargen and Llangathen. The weakest of the main denominations in Carmarthenshire were the Baptists, whose members represented the highest number of communicants in Newcastle Emlyn and the industrial parish of Llan-non.[28]

Such is the general picture which emerges of the distribution of religious communicants in Carmarthenshire at the turn of the twentieth century, according to the evidence of the Royal Commission. This pattern of religious adherence had developed during the nineteenth century because of the cultural, social and psychological functions which religious denominations performed for and offered to people.[29] We shall study each of these functions in turn, but initially it is worth noting briefly the cultural and social aspects before considering the others. The social and cultural importance of Nonconformity in nineteenth-century Wales cannot be over-emphasized. Churches and chapels were important institutions, whose services marked out the rites of passage of people's lives in both industrial and rural communities. As Gwenallt noted in his sonnet to the Chapel in Carmarthenshire . . .

> . . . Y Capel a roddai yn ddi-wahaniaeth,
> Yn y glesni a'r glaw gwledig, ac yn y mwstwr a'r mwrllwch,
> Y dŵr ar dalcen, y fodrwy ar fys a'r atgyfodiad uwch yr arch.[30]

The Revd Thomas Johns of Llanelli explained to the Royal Commissioners the social importance of chapels to the people of south-west Wales. He claimed that the Free Churches of Llanelli had

> branches of the following: International Bible Reading Association, Christian Endeavour, Young People's Guilds, Mothers Meetings, Bible Classes on weeknights, Band of Hope – in connection with all the churches there are adult temperance societies, Rechabites Tents, Good Templars, and so on . . . There are also women's temperance societies, among the Free Churches mostly, namely British Women's Temperance Society, and Undeb Dirwestol Merched y De . . . There is also an entertainment held every Saturday night during the winter months, mainly for temperance purposes . . . at the Atheneum Hall. There are literary societies, mutual improvement societies, savings banks, Dorcas societies, libraries, cricket clubs, bands for collecting towards Dr. Barnardo's Homes, Dr. Stevenson's Homes, the various missionary societies, . . . musical festivals, choral unions . . . and so forth.[31]

The Revd T. R. Walters, vicar of St David's Church in Carmarthen, testified to the cultural and social vitality of the Church of England; he provided the Commissioners with a calendar of daily meetings which showed that it too was not just a 'one day a week religion'.[32] In their insistence upon morality, temperance, sobriety, honesty, thrift and self-improvement, religious organizations offered disciplined attitudes to life that were welcomed by a large number of the Welsh people in the nineteenth century. There were also, of course, as one observer has noted, deeper forces which drew people towards religion:

> by its putative capacity for invoking supernatural support, consolation, and reconciliation in this world, and through the prospect of other-wordly salvation, religion can satisfy basic human aspirations for transcendental meaning, emotional security, or spiritual assurance.[33]

That there was a demand for these functions, and the other functions of religion in nineteenth-century Wales, is clearly shown in the large numbers of people who received communion. It is dramatically proven by the 1904–5 religious revival which had profound effects in Carmarthenshire. The revival constitutes one of the most important events in modern Welsh history and deserves more attention from historians. The events in Carmarthenshire were remarkable.

Ever since the publication of *Caniadau y rhai sydd ar y Môr o wydr* by Carmarthenshire's most famous son, William Williams of Pantycelyn, in 1762, the renewal of religious bodies by the acceleration of acute spiritual awareness had been a characteristic of Welsh religious life.[34] By 1904 there had been several revivals, some of which remained local in their extent and influence, whilst others, such as those of 1812 and 1859, spread quickly to affect the whole of Wales. The Revd Dr G. M. Roberts recorded sixteen revivals between 1785 and 1904.[35] They all had the common features of a heightened consciousness of sin, profound concern for personal salvation, intense, sustained, and passionate prayer, 'rejoicing' at the 'reception' of the 'spirit', and, especially from 1859 onwards, prolonged and enthusiastic singing. These periodic outbursts of intense religious enthusiasm characterize Welsh religious life in the nineteenth century.[36]

The spontaneity of the outbreak of the 1904–5 revival, and the rapidity of its expansion throughout Wales, led many commentators to assume that the 'Revival' began with Evan Roberts' experiences in Newcastle Emlyn.[37] This view separates the revival from its true origins which are enmeshed in the Welsh revivalist tradition. Ever since the waning of the enthusiasm connected with the 1859 revival Welsh Nonconformist opinion longed for another revival.[38] In the 1880s south Cardiganshire and parts of north-west Carmarthenshire experienced an outbreak of religious enthusiasm.[39] In 1897 the Llanelli newspaper, the *South Wales Press*, carried a report on the expectation of many people in the county that another revival was imminent.[40] A week earlier, its rival, the *Carmarthen Weekly Reporter*, had carried reports of the successful mission of the Wesleyans at Ferryside.[41] Two years later the same paper, perhaps influenced by Joseph Parry's celebrated prediction that the next revival would be 'a singing revival', carried the story of the visit of Raymond Preston ('the Singing Evangelist') to the town.[42] These and similar occurrences mark out the years between 1859 and 1904 as a period when yearning for another revival became acute.

The origins of the 1904 revival in Carmarthenshire lay thus in the people's desire for another revival and in the influence of the meetings of several evangelistic groups. In 1902 the Pentecostal League had been active in Carmarthen under the Presidency of Reader Harris, QC. In early 1903 the Revd R. B. Jones and Mrs Penn-Lewis led a convention at Heol Awst Congregational Chapel.[43] By May a group of ministers influenced by W. S. Jones's preaching began to meet regularly in Carmarthen to pray and discuss their religious experiences. After hearing Dr F. B. Meyer in Llandrindod Wells, one recalled that 'a new world had opened to them and they could not but lead others in'.[44] Seth Joshua recalled this ferment of activity and considered 1903 as the most dramatic year of his life.[45] It was from such meetings that the 1904 revival would burst forth and, as in 1859, Cardiganshire ministers were influential.

The experience of the Keswick mission of 1902 left a profound mark upon the Revds John Thickens and Joseph Jenkins. After listening to the Revd W. W. Lewis of Carmarthen address their 'seiat' in late October 1904, both became convinced that they should intensify their efforts to lead others into this 'new world'.[46] Their missions and meetings spread forth into neighbouring villages from their base at New Quay. As Seth Joshua led the congregation in worship at Blaenannerch, a twenty-six-year-old collier fell poleaxed to his knees, his face streaming with sweat, with great difficulty he uttered the words that hundreds of tortured souls would subsequently utter: 'Plyg Fi O Arglwydd' ('Bend me O Lord'). The collier, a student at the Revd John Phillips's private grammar school in Newcastle Emlyn, had prayed for over thirteen years for such a spiritual experience. His name was Evan Roberts.[47]

Though the attention of contemporaries and historians has focused upon what the *Western Mail* insisted was 'Evan Roberts's Revival', it should be remembered that he was not omnipresent. Others were also influential. Religious leaders such as John Thickens, Joseph Jenkins, Seth and Frank Joshua, Dan Roberts, D. M. Phillips, W. W. Lewis, Annie Davies, Elfet Lewis and Keri Evans were the people who brought the revival message and spirit to many hamlets, villages, parishes and towns. Following his experiences at Blaenannerch, Evan Roberts, on the Holy Spirit's instructions, returned home to work amongst young people of Loughor. But the revival continued in New Quay and south-west Cardiganshire and the spiritual ferment spread quickly to north Carmarthenshire.

Here, one of the most influential figures was Joseph Jenkins.[48] On 30 October 1904, he began a week's preaching mission at Bethany Calvinistic Methodist Chapel in Ammanford which was to have a considerable influence and effect on the revival. The following evening, according to the minister, W. Nantlais Williams, 'torrodd yr argae' ('the dam burst').[49] Meetings lasted for hours (some until dawn), and were characterized by public confession of sin, intense and impromptu praying and singing, and weeping. All the moon long they hymned and rumpused. It seemed as if no prayer was long enough to express all the congregation would like to say about the need for mercy for their souls. The following week Seth Joshua honoured a long-standing commitment to Nantlais Williams and arrived in Ammanford on 18 November to lead what was to have been a Forward Movement Venture. He was quite unprepared for his reception:

> At 7.30 I went to meet the workers in the chapel. To my surprise the chapel was filled with people. Seeing my opportunity I commenced at once, and at the close fully twenty confessed Christ. There is a wonderful fire burning here. The ground is very prepared, Thank God.[50]

That preparation had been undertaken by the minister W. Nantlais Williams. The eloquence of Joshua and his obvious experience of every step in spiritual life, from the lowest levels of life, as one commentator said 'from the sawdust of the tap room to the heavenly places in Christ Jesus'[51] was to have profound effects in Ammanford. Such was the intensity of the religious experience that Joshua described Sunday 20 November as:

> One of the most remarkable days of my life. Even in the morning a number were led to embrace the Saviour. In the afternoon the blessing fell upon scores of young people. The crush was very great to get into the Chapel. At 7 o'clock a surging mass filled the Christian Temple, with crowds unable to gain entrance. The Holy Spirit was indeed among the people. Numbers confessed Jesus, but it is impossible to count.[52]

Through the dedication of Nantlais to his own chapel and cause, the revival continued and prospered in Ammanford throughout 1905.[53]

Joseph Jenkins was also influential in revival meetings in Carmarthen. By June 1904, prayer meetings for young people in Water Street Chapel had been signally blessed following earlier mission work of Reader Harris and W. R. Lane.[54] In November and early December, Joseph Jenkins, J. M. Saunders and his wife, assisted by W. W. Lewis, ministered to a series of meetings with powerful effect.[55] On the last day of the conference:

> Hardly a quarter of an hour passed without a number of people, young and old, men and women, in one part or another of Water Street Chapel praying themselves or others from the bondage of sin to the liberty of the gospel.[56]

The same experiences were also witnessed in other chapels in the town, in Peniel, Ebeneser, Elim, Zion, Bethel, Tabernacl and St Peters for the 1904–5 revival was no respecter of denominational boundaries. The effects on social morals and behaviour was profound. Bookshops complained that they could not obtain a sufficient supply of Bibles. One man told a congregation that he used to hide his money in the Bible to prevent his wife finding it, but that he had abandoned the practice following the revival.[57] Prayer meetings and hymn singing at the start of shifts transformed life in coalmines and tinplate works.[58] Public houses became more orderly and an Ammanford licensee reported that it had become a pleasure to be in the trade. The manners of his customers were better, the lewd talk and blasphemy had disappeared. But others were to find the trade less pleasant. Henry Edmunds of the Railway Hotel, Burry Port, ended up at the Carmarthen Bankruptcy Court as a result, he said, of the colliers' strike and the revival.[59] In Gwauncaegurwen beer consumption had declined by an estimated third within a month of the start of the revival.[60]

The onslaught against the evils of drink was one of the most notable features of the revival in Llanelli, where the recently converted were most vociferous. In mid December 1904, Ebeneser Chapel was packed to overflowing, with ten people in pews designed for five. In the 'stifling heat' the enthusiasm of Miss Maggie Griffiths, 'an ex-reckless girl' of the Presbyterian Christian Endeavour Society who had done 'glorious work' at Laugharne, drew forth remarkable scenes.[61] Sidney Evans urged those present to go around the streets and gather in drunkards. Women missionaries visited pubs. On Saturday night, the main target of the revivalists was the dock district.[62] Miss Jones and the Revd Trevor Jones, on tour through Embankment Row, hearing a quarrel in a private house, entered, held a prayer meeting, and converted the entire family.[63] But such aggressive missions were not always so well received. A procession from Bethania Baptist Chapel to the Whitestable Inn converted a young man and a woman. But the publican and two customers proved more reluctant. A man and a woman drank 'mockingly' at the open door and then danced a jig 'pint in hand'. When offered a pint the revivalists threw it upon the floor, only to have the contents of a beer stein and water thrown over them by the landlord and another female customer. The revivalists' parting words, 'forgive them Lord, for they know not what they do', testifies to the gulf which still existed in Carmarthenshire society.[64] Despite the considerable success of the revival, unanimity in religious adherence would never be achieved. One revivalist subsequently admitted that '[ni] phrofodd Llanelli yn dir hawdd ei drin'.[65]

As 1904 slipped away, in W. Anthony Davies's wonderful phrase, 'yn sŵn Hosanna a Haleliwia', the main features of the revival were clear.[66] Evan Roberts informed the nation of the four conditions of the revival which the Holy Ghost had related to him: (i) confessing sins openly before God; (ii) the removal of all doubts from a person's life; (iii) immediate response to the dictates of the Holy Spirit; and (iv) public confession of Christ as Saviour.[67] These laid the foundations for the spontaneous enthusiasm and lack of formal order which characterized revival meetings. The expression of enthusiasm in revival services was primarily done by the young, and in particular women. While the preacher spoke, others would weep, collapse, beseech salvation, confess sins, or pray and the mention of a line in a hymn could bring forth an immediate rendition. This uncontrolled enthusiasm brought forth criticism from many people, who were concerned at both the 'quality' and 'sincerity' of some converts.[68] The following anecdote reveals some of the tensions which existed between the 'traditionalists and the revivalists':

> At one revival meeting, where there was a great noise and commotion, when the leader of the meeting . . . asked all those to stand up who were 'on their way to Glory' or wished to go. Up stood all the congregation, consisting of all types of people, who had been swept in from the public houses and the streets. There was one exception. An old deacon in the corner of the big pew, sat down persistently . . . At last the leader of the meeting, looking at him asked 'Don't you want to go to Glory, John Thomas?' The old man looked up and replied, while he remained seated, 'Oh yes, I want to go to Glory, but not with this excursion, thank you!'[69]

He, like Gildas Rees, believed 'that the fervour and excitement of those around him were unnecessary adjuncts to the simple communion between a man and his God.'[70]

Others were more kindly disposed towards the anarchic enthusiasm of the new found converts. The Revd Elvet Lewis, for example, considered that:

> We need scarcely refer to some of the extravagancies of excitement which have spasmodically broken out here and there they are local, they are temporary, they are confined to the few. They are part of any great movement; perhaps Flagellants and White Hoods in one age and country, Pentecostal Dancers and miracle-mongers in another age and country.[71]

In Carmarthenshire these phenomena proved remarkably resilient, lasting throughout the course of the revival and into 1906. Indeed, Carmarthenshire was to witness some of the most remarkable scenes of the 1904 Revival. It is not proposed to discuss them all in detail, but the following are representative of the anarchic spiritual ferment which characterized many Carmarthenshire towns.

The mission of Pastor Howton to Carmarthenshire drew considerable controversy and attention.[72] In November 1905 he undertook a mission to Carmarthen town and to the Aman Valley. At Priordy Chapel in Carmarthen, he claimed that only he was the authentic medium for the voice of God. The uproar which met this claim was nothing compared to the furore which greeted his boast that at his faith-healing establishment in Glossop he had raised a boy named Houghton from the dead. But the greatest outburst of public disapproval met the news that his supporters at Zion Presbyterian Chapel held ceremonies in which 'devils' were cast out. Part of the ceremony involved smearing women's heads with oil. The *Carmarthen Weekly Reporter* thundered against these 'corybantine orgies in the name of religion'. The Revd Fuller Mills urged that common sense and reason should be restored to Carmarthen town, but people flocked to Howton's meetings. At the end of his visit, Howton prophesied 'eternal doom for Carmarthen'. In Bethany Chapel, Ammanford, where Howton held his first meeting, sick children were brought to him in the pulpit.[73] In the heady, millenarian milieu of revivalist Carmarthenshire many – perhaps (they would claim later) against their better judgement – chose to believe that Howton possessed spiritual powers that healed the sick. This was, it would seem, particularly true of Peniel Chapel, Carmarthen. This chapel had been without a minister for five years and consequently the congregation was in need of spiritual leadership.[74] Indeed, a number of notable people, like the Revd E. Keri Evans, did defend Howton.[75]

A remarkable feature of the 1904 revival was the way in which previously obscure individuals rose to prominence and captured the attention not only of a single chapel but that of a whole county and even a whole nation. Such a person was Sarah Jones of Gorsfach Cottage, Carmel, 'a white washed and thatched-cottage which stands by itself . . . of the primitive type you see in country villages'.[76]

From such unlikely surroundings, Sarah Jones emerged in April 1906, was to lead what was described as 'The New Revival'.[77] The origin of Sarah Jones's spiritual strength is a matter of dispute. Some claimed that she received divine blessing following Pastor Howton's visit to Capel y Sgwâr, Pen-y-groes, when she was anointed with oil; others that it was as a result of Evan Roberts's laying on of hands in April 1906. But it would seem from other

The "Wonderful Woman of Carmel": Sarah Jones and her family at home in 1906 (South Wales Daily News)

accounts that there had been a deep spiritual awakening in the Cross Hands–Pen-y-groes area which predates the Loughor meetings of Evan Roberts.[78] For two weeks in April 1906, Sarah Jones's husband, Daniel, had been unable to attend his work as a collier in Cross Hands Colliery because she was, in the words of one follower, 'living almost completely in the spiritual world'.[79] In early April the Press Association correspondent covering the revival visited the Cross Hands area and interviewed several local people. In the report which appeared in the press it was claimed that 'the wonderful woman of Carmel':

> has supernatural powers and has cured several people of various diseases. The inhabitants of the village regard her with awe, and declare that she will raise the dead as a sign for unbelievers. One well-known Baptist minister who had a partially disabled arm was told by her to 'stretch the arm and it shall be whole'. He obeyed and the arm has been strong ever since.[80]

Though she was illiterate and could not even read her Bible, 'There are scores of good Christians in the District who thoroughly believe in her. They say that she has been born again and is with Christ.'[81] Her services, which commenced at 7.30 p.m., often did not finish until 11.00 a.m. the following day and were characterized by frenzied, uncontrolled worship. At Cross Hands 'men and women tore their hair, threw themselves on the floor and prayed with intense fervour'.[82] One observer in the congregation noted that: 'When she speaks there is a strange light in her eyes, her countenance beams, and she is as one transfigured.'[83]

During the mission organized by the Revd William Bowen at Pen-y-groes, in a packed afternoon session, she seized the seat in front 'without word and swayed to and fro in great agony of soul'.[84] When she recovered, holding up her Bible, she declared:

> I was washing the feet of Christ yesterday – yes and drying his feet with the hair of my head . . . They say I am not a scholar, but I have faith in Him. Here is my book, here is my light, here is His Word. I have been with Jesus, I have been in Heaven with Christ and His disciples. I have been crying to the Lord.[85]

At this point the congregation burst into the hymn 'Diolch Iddo, byth am gofio llwch y llawr'. Amidst the singing she continued:

> I have been speaking with Jesus himself. He is coming to the world again shortly, You don't think that I can cast out Devils but I can [cries of 'Yes, you can']. There are wonderful things at hand. Christ is coming to the world. He is going to do wonderful things through me. Do not fear me but fear the Lord . . . You must believe in Jesus . . . If you only have faith in Him, He will receive you . . . The second coming of Christ is coming near . . .[86]

Sarah then collapsed. The preacher, on his knees with his head in his hands, commanded the congregation to sing 'A welsoch Chwi Ef?' ('Did you see Him?'). Several people publicly confessed their sins while others saw the presence of Christ.[87] At Maesypica Farm, Cwm-twrch, when Sarah Jones saw 'a thousand angels', it was claimed that several 'spoke in tongues', that a portrait of Christ appeared on the ceiling and that the Devil had been cast out of a man.[88] A reporter noted that when the possessed man recovered consciousness:

> his first words were 'Diolch Iddo!' Periods of laughing, crying, praying, shouting and gesticulating continued in rapid succession, the scene going beyond anything yet witnessed even in connection with this so called mission of 'The Wonderful Woman of Carmel'.[89]

One witness, D. D. Griffiths, was sceptical. In a letter to the *South Wales Daily News*, he recalled that one man he sarcastically called 'the Prophet':

> now began to claim that he was the Holy Trinity, and that he could raise the dead, split the mountains as well as oceans in two . . . While he was talking all this nonsense someone in the corner began to kick and tumble about and here Mrs Jones declared that it was the Devil. The process of casting out this person then began . . . It was merely standing over him and mumbling something.[90]

At this point D. D. Griffiths left. But others, too, were sceptical of Mrs Jones's supernatural powers. One newspaper caused great offence to her followers by claiming that in a spate of spiritual excitement she had climbed the garden hedge to fly to heaven, only to land in the onion patch.[91] The Revd Evan R. Hughes of Taff's Well was also scathing in his condemnation of Mrs Jones. But Seth Joshua, speaking at Swansea's Central Hall, stated: 'I believe in the depths of my heart this woman is blessed by the Spirit of God. So you will kindly pass it on to our friends. Don't ask them to see Mrs Sarah Jones. Ask them to come and meet the Lord.'[92]

Miracles were not confined to the Nonconformist denominations. In June 1906, newspapers carried a story reported by Revd D. E. Hughes, curate of Llangeler, concerning Mrs Mary Jenkins, a resident of the parish. For eight years she had been confined to her bed. Following a service in her house, Glynderi, on a Sunday when there was no service in Capel Mair, Mary Jenkins had been unable to sleep. After a personal prayer on Monday she found that she had recovered from paralysis.[93] Given the intensity of millenarian belief in 1904, it is not surprising that some people became mentally unstable. A man from Llanelli was confined to the Lunatic Asylum in December 1904. At Capel Mair Baptist Chapel, he prayed for the minister and the deacons who, he insisted, were 'addicted to drink'; he refused to work at the tinplate mill and, on God's instructions, prayed for the manager, the company and 'the spiritual welfare of the clerical staff'. He then prayed until 4.00 a.m. for his wife to be saved.[94] In all, sixteen people had been confined in the Joint Counties Lunatic Asylum in Carmarthen by the early part of 1905 because of religious delusions.[95]

What were the forces that created the conditions in which such events could be credible to contemporaries? It would be impossible to offer a comprehensive answer to these questions in a discussion of the history of one county. All we can do is to provide an indication of the complex economic, social, historical, religious, psychological, personal, political and national forces which combined in 1904 to spark off the revival.[96]

The 1904 revival occurred, as we have seen, at a time of profound social change.[97] These were years of accelerating industrial development when south Wales became a focal point of the Atlantic economy. To fulfil the demand for colliers and other workers, the rural areas exported their most precious product – their people. The drift from the land, coupled with increasing mechanization on farms, led to the decline of traditional crafts and customs. This, argues one historian, led to a rootlessness in the rural population of west Wales, to the awareness of anomie, to a 'disenchantment of the world'.[98] These changes produced profound social and psychological pressures in rural and urban areas. The emergence of new class attitudes in the urban areas of Wales amongst an uprooted and newly transplanted rural populace, who continued to adhere to their religious denominations in industrial areas, was one of the reasons T. M. Bassett, the historian of the Welsh Baptists, singled out as a cause of the revival.[99] Thus the links between rural west Wales and the industrial area of Llanelli and Loughor, which were personified in Joseph Jenkins, John Thickens and of course Evan Roberts, are significant.[100] For both communities were in the throes of a social crisis. In Carmarthenshire the local economy in 1904 seems to have experienced a lull in its development. At the time of the revival the coal mines and works in the Pen-y-groes area – one of the areas most deeply moved by the revival – had been idle for a long time. At Tumble, the Great Mountain and other collieries had been on strike for over ten months.[101] This led to violence when colliers from Glynea Colliery broke windows in Cwmfelin and Llwynhendy and attempted to assault 'blacklegs' and stoned police reinforcements called in from Llanelli.[102]

Since the general election of 1868, the political life of Wales had centred on the grievances of Nonconformity.[103] So strong were the links between religion and politics that by the end of the nineteenth century they appeared inextricable. Biblical imagery punctuated the election campaigns: to *Y Tyst,* the ministers of Llanelli were like 'Samson's foxes destroying the lairs of Toryism.'[104] The chapels provided Liberalism with a focus and a forum for organization. The distinctions between political and religious meetings had, by the mid-nineteenth century, become nebulous. Thus the attention given to 'political' causes in the press and from the platform also drew attention to 'religious' issues. This was particularly so in 1904 while the disestablishment campaign continued to receive considerable attention.[105] But the force which gave sharper focus in 1904 to religious and political grievances was the campaign against the Education Act of 1902. The Act, which placed all schools – 'provided' and 'non-provided' alike – on the local rates, caused a massive revolt among Welsh Nonconformists and local authorities.[106] Liberals and Nonconformists had a clear majority on the Carmarthenshire County Council.[107] The Council was led by men of the calibre of the Revd William Thomas of Whitland, the Revd Thomas Johns of Capel Als, Llanelli, the Revd Professor D. E. Jones and the Revd David Eleazar Jones of Carmarthen.[108] Carmarthenshire was one of the first counties to oppose the Act and its recalcitrance, stemming from the fierce independence of its Nonconformist leaders, brought forth a full government enquiry.[109] The meetings in opposition to the Act continued well into 1905 and the sense of grievance and injustice lingered long after being aired at the public enquiry of 24 and 25 March 1904.[110] In meetings throughout the county, and in press reports and editorials, attention was focused upon a religious grievance at precisely the time when Wales was undergoing a religious reawakening.

These social, economic and political factors provide the backcloth against which the drama of the 1904 revival was enacted, but they cannot in themselves provide a complete and comprehensive explanation of its occurrence. Some historians have sought to do this by examining the condition of religious life in Wales at the turn of the twentieth century. C. R. Williams, in his study of the revival, emphasized the parlous condition of Nonconformity. He points out that there was a crisis at the heart of Welsh Nonconformity. The gulf in social attitudes between preachers and deacons and the members of the congregation, which had always existed, was perceived to be widening at the turn of the twentieth century, the number of members was declining and there was theological uncertainty.[111] Carmarthenshire provides evidence to support this thesis. As we have seen, the statistics for 1905 included in the *Report* of the Royal Commission of 1911 show that a substantial decline had taken place since the 1851 Religious Census in the numbers of chapel members. The qualitative evidence supports this quantitative evidence. In 1901 the *Carmarthen Weekly Reporter* noted that 'In Carmarthen, about 2,500 worship every Sunday in Welsh, about 1,000 in English, and 6,500 don't worship at all.'[112] Later, the same newspaper observed that: 'The fact remains that a very large proportion of the population is entirely outside the pale of any religious organisation . . . There are thousands of people even in Carmarthen who have no religious principles of any kind.'[113]

Within some chapels there would seem to be a correlation between social and religious prestige. In Carmarthen town in the late nineteenth century, deacons in the Baptist chapels were largely drawn from the farming and shopkeeping classes; very few were workers.[114] In 1896 the *Carmarthen Weekly Reporter* voiced the frustrations of many people who chose to stay away from chapels: 'Class division might not exist in Heaven, but if Christ went to some Carmarthen Chapels he would have to sit near the door whilst his "betters" sat higher up.'[115]

However, this sense of grievance and alienation was not articulated effectively until after the revival, when the Revd Iona Williams and others began to preach the doctrines of the 'New Theology'.[116] What worried the ministry in the county in the early years of this century was the plethora of counter-attractions which eventually undermined the social importance of religion. The public house was the old enemy, but now football, Rugby, cricket and other spectator sports flourished, as did the theatre, the music hall, and the cinema. The latter, in particular, was vehemently condemned from the pulpit. When Dante's 'Inferno' played at a local cinema, crowds of several hundred flocked to see the flickering images of the torments of the damned. The posters, in lurid colour, spoke of 'the realistic breathing effects, the agonies of the Lost Souls'. The fact that no one under sixteen was allowed in guaranteed a full house.[117] Such competition and aggressive marketing drew away the only people who could provide a long-term future for the chapels – the young. In response the chapels attempted to cater for this increasingly sophisticated audience. The Revd M. H. Jones toured the county to deliver his lecture 'How to make the Sunday Schools interesting to the Young',[118] but the evidence of decline became clearer and clearer.

There was, at the turn of the nineteenth century, a crisis in religion, a crisis that found expression in the writings and sermons of the leading theologians.[119] But there was also a crisis at the grass-roots level. The historian of religion in Carmarthenshire cannot fail to be struck by the large number of petty squabbles and disputes, both between individuals and between rival chapels, which marred the religious life of the county up to 1904.[120] Sectarianism continued to be a divisive element until well into the twentieth century. Pentecostalism and the Apostolic Church, which began in Pen-y-groes, were perhaps the most prominent forms.[121] But the old divisions between Independent and Baptist, Calvinistic Methodist and Wesleyan, continued to intrude into politics and religion.[122] In 1906, in his frustration, Seth Joshua remarked that 'probably there is no town in Wales where sectarian division and feeling is so strong as at Llanelli.'[123] It was so strong that the Llandeilo Board of Poor Law Guardians failed to appoint a missioner to the tramps in the county because they could not agree to which denomination he should belong.[124]

These and other forces were matters which created anxiety among the religious communities of Wales. Anxiety about the condition of religion in the county was one of the forces which led men like Gwili Jenkins and others to yearn for a revival to reawaken the spiritual life of the nation.[125] But this is only one factor amongst several which brought forth the 1904 revival. None of the forces we have examined so far can explain why people behaved as they did in 1904–6. To explain this we need to examine some of the personal and psychological aspects of the revival, and to examine how the people themselves perceived the causes of the 1904 revival.[126]

The work of two French investigators who visited Wales during 1905 to witness the revival provides valuable insights into the psychological condition of the Welsh people at this time.[127] J. Rogues de Fursac, a psychologist by calling, sought to apply personal and individual characteristics to the national character.

The Welsh, he noted, were a religious race, a race well used to periodic revivals. Welsh culture, permeated by the values and morals of Nonconformity, provided the individual with a clear model of the ideal to which one should aspire. Although this ideal could not be achieved, it remained in people's subconscious to be awakened by a sudden spark – a powerful sermon, a moving hymn. It was this dramatic realization of a person's inability to conform to the ideal which provided the suddenness of conversion during the revival services. De Frusac translated these features from the individual to the nation. He considered Wales probably the most religious nation in the civilized world. Its culture was intensely religious, with Biblical imagery and metaphors punctuating social and political discourse. At the turn of the century there was growing awareness of the drift away from religion and an anxiety that the national 'ideal' should be re-established. The missions of Joseph Jenkins, John Thickens, Evan Roberts, Sarah Jones and others provided the spark.

Henry Bois set out a similar psychological model to that of de Fursac, but placed more emphasis upon the peripatetic nature of the ministry. This forced preachers to bring the congregation to a quick state of spiritual excitement and anxiety as they had to move on to other places. Keri Evans's reminiscences of 'Cerbyd yr Efengylydd', which took him and fellow ministers on rapid tours of various districts to preach the gospel in the open air, is a graphic example of such instantaneous conversions. Here technology was at the service of religion, giving it speed and mobility.[128] Several centres could be visited during a day, giving urgency to the communication of the message and providing remote places with a kingfisher flash of importance to brighten otherwise uneventful lives. Bois also noted the importance of the campaign against the Education Act and the disestablishment cause, both of which focused attention on religious affairs, and the rapid social and economic changes of the period leading up to 1904. He also perceived a crisis of 'Welshness' at the time, which provoked a 'traditional response' – a revival.[129]

Valuable as these works are, the historian should also be aware that the most valuable source to explain why people behaved as they did during the revival is the public confessions of individuals and the hymns of the revival services. These lay bare the anxieties, concerns and fears of the individual at his moment of spiritual torment giving poignant details of their pious and platitudinous hopes. Evan Roberts and the other revival leaders adopted the methods of Charles Finney and the American evangelists concerning public confession of sin.[130] The reports of many revival services contain graphic accounts by individuals of their former aimless, reckless, sinful, wasteful lives. At an Ammanford meeting in November 1904, W. Nantlais Williams's confession of personal vanity – praying for Eisteddfod success with a *pryddest* – was followed by the confessions of a professional thief, who had been imprisoned for three years. The audience also heard what was to become the classic type of confession. A man aged between thirty-five and forty admitted in tears, with his child in his arms, to squandering his pay and robbing the child's money box for money to buy drink.[131] These confessions were all motivated by the belief, as Sarah Jones's testimony shows, that retribution for past sins would be severe and that the day of reckoning was nigh. Confessing sin and craving forgiveness was the only course open to save the individual's soul. As the Revd Elvet Lewis observed: 'There must be deep in the human heart an indestructable sense of sin, which may be awakened by a sound of thunder from Sinai, or by a whisper from Gethsemane; by a torrent or by a rain-drop from Calvary's clouds.'[132]

This fear was one of the underlying forces which compelled people to confess real and imaginary sins and to crave forgiveness. Once the sense of sin had been reawakened, noted Elvet, fear was replaced by love of the Redeemer. The hymns popular in the period show this. The two most popular which were repeated frequently in the services were 'Diolch Iddo byth am gofio llwch y llawr' and 'Dyma gariad fel y moroedd'. The latter Elvet described as the spiritual 'love-song' of the nation.[133] The hymns were often intensely personal: 'Fi fi I gofio amdanaf fi; O ryw anfeirol gariad I gofio amddanaf fi.'[134] The repeated singing and intense heat of the packed chapels created what James Williams recalled as a 'spiritual sauna' – he noted that 'it was sound which converted not sense'.[135]

These economic, social, political, religious, personal and psychological factors created the conditions from which the revival could stem. But the historian should remember that many people in 1904 believed that Wales was experiencing the work of God through the agency of the Holy Ghost. To them the intervention of a providential agency was the only explanation of the 1904 revival.

This belief was the dynamic force which motivated people in 1904. The contemporary statements are clear and unequivocal on this point. A correspondent to *Y Tyst* on the religious condition of Milo and Pen-y-groes was clear about the force that had over-filled both chapels so that they had to build a new chapel to accommodate the overspill: 'Y mae'r Arglwydd yn gwneud pethau mawrion yn ein plith'.[136]

Gwili Jenkins, in his sermon on 'Y Swn o'r Nef', 'the sound from Heaven', commenced: 'Wedi blynyddoedd o sŵn y ddaear, y mae'r sŵn o'r nef yn ein tir drachefn. Nid rhaid mwy ofyn ystyr 'y sŵn seraffaidd nefol' . . . canys ni a'i clywsom ef ein hunain . . . Yr Arglwydd a wnaeth i ni bethau mawrion, am hynny yr ydym yn llawen.'[137] More colloquially, a secretary of a football club remarked that he was now a secretary for Christ and a former member of a tug-of-war team declared that he was now 'pulling against the Evil one.'[138] D. P. Williams, one of the founders of the Apostolic Church in Pen-y-groes, remembered:

> During 1904–05, God's visitation in this village was like unto a moral earthquake shaking the neighbourhood to its foundation. Sinners trembled with fear at God's justice. . . . We witnessed the sublimest manifestations of the Holy Ghost with 'tongues of fire'. They were days of wonderment and amazement, bearing as they did, the impress of His Divinity.[139]

It is significant that this view was echoed by people one would not normally associate with religious enthusiasm or extremism. Gwenallt, in his fictionalised autobiography *Ffwrneisiau*, noted this power; James Griffiths was deeply influenced by it, and D. J. Williams believed that in the revival '. . . yn ddiamheuol, yr oedd 'Ysbryd Byw y Deffroadau 'yn disgyn yn ei Nerth i lawr ac yn gweithredu'n rymus ar y tyrfaoedd'.[140]

The conviction of sin was accompanied by the conviction that the forces of light and darkness, of good and evil, were waging a titanic battle in Wales.[141] The awareness of the Devil and his work in the period leading up to the revival was acute. *Pulpud Cymru* abounds with warnings against the subtleties of the Devil's evil and devious ways.[142] Evan Roberts saw his mocking face in a hedge at Newcastle Emlyn, and was persistently troubled by his torments and mockings throughout the revival.[143] Evans Roberts later, together with Mrs Penn Lewis, formulated these beliefs into the complex demonology of *War on the Saints*, a substantial work outlining the 'deceptions of the Devil and Evil Spirits in the modern times'.[144]

If the religious leaders of the period believed in the shadowy world of the spirits, then we should not be surprised that such beliefs were widespread throughout society in south-west Wales. Religion was not a complete world-view which replaced superstitions, as some nineteenth-century writers argued.[145] The religious realm extended beyond the chapels and the churches, indeed beyond Christianity, to encompass an abundance of pagan magic and superstition.[146] These, like religion, were responses to 'the sacred', to 'supernatural powers', and to the recurrent problems of human existence. Thus, in studying the religions of any community or society, one should also seek to consider its superstitions. They were not a counter-religion to Christianity, but rather the two co-existed and complemented each other. On the margins of religious ideas, where no solutions were offered to the perennial problems of life, magic and paganism flourished.[147]

It is important for the historian of popular beliefs and superstition to remember the characteristics of the pagan world view. As Obelkevich has noted:

> In its totality the pagan universe was a large, loose, pluralistic affair without any clear unifying principle. It encompassed superhuman beings and forces, witches and wise men, and a mass of low-grade magic and superstition. The whole was less than the sum of its parts, for it was not a cosmos to be contemplated or worshipped but a treasury of separate and specific resources to be used and applied in concrete situations.[148]

The major problem that confronts the historian in establishing the extent of belief in each of these individual strands in a given historical period is to differentiate, as John Rhys remarked, between 'story and history'.[149] Many of the stories relating to the Devil, to corpse candles, to wisemen and 'y tylwyth teg' can be traced back from the late nineteenth century to the start of the century and in some cases even earlier. For the sake of this study, the only examples that will be cited are ones which relate specifically to the period between 1870 to 1920.

Another difficulty for the historian is ascertaining from the contemporary evidence the true extent of superstitious beliefs and practices. Given the ridicule that was heaped upon various customs, people were understandably reluctant to admit to believing in practices which even such a sympathetic observer as Wirt Sikes considered 'ignorant and childlike'.[150] John Rhys noted this problem when recording folklore in Wales at the turn of the twentieth century:

> The chief initial difficulty, . . . meeting anyone who would collect folklore in Wales arises from the fact that various influences have conspired to laugh it out of court, so to say, so that those who are acquainted with superstitions and ancient fads become ashamed to own it; they have the fear of ridicule weighing on their minds, and that is a weight not easily removed.[151]

Despite these difficulties, there is a considerable body of evidence to prove that belief in a plethora of superstitious customs and practices was widespread in the period 1870 to 1920. Although the remarks of Edmund Jones', 'Yr Hen Broffwyd', were written almost a century earlier, they could also be applied to the end of the nineteenth century. He considered Carmarthenshire to be 'that part of Wales where we shall meet with the most numerous, and most notable account of Apparitions.'[152]

Certainly, belief in supernatural beings was widespread in the late nineteenth century. Mary Jones noted simply of the inhabitants of her childhood home: 'credent mewn ysbrydion'.[153] Ghosts and spirits, 'bwcis' as the inhabitants called them, were found throughout the county.[154] Several were found at the scenes of violent deaths, or where a fortune lay concealed.[155] In the 1870s the story was told by Revd Thomas Lewis of the Tywi Valley of how the ghost of the suicide, Ann Dewy, led a small boy to a fortune of over £200 in gold.[156] The story is interesting for it reveals some of the characteristics of a society without easy access to banks. Savings were hoarded and hidden in a place known only to an individual. It must thus have been a common dream and ambition for many people to find such a treasure.[157]

Other spirits were less kindly disposed towards the living. In 1902, at a house in College Road, Carmarthen, near to a spot where a murder had been committed nine years previously, the activities of a spirit were such as to cause a man and a boy to be confined to their beds and to render a woman hysterical.[158] Three years earlier, in March 1899, a ghost had troubled the inhabitants of Burry Port.[159] The First World War, which saw celebrated examples of supernatural phenomena on the Western Front, was a period of marked activity for Carmarthenshire spirits. Throughout January and March 1917, local newspapers reported the activities of the Kidwelly ghost. J. Arthur Hill, author of *Religion and Modern Psychology* and *New Evidences in Psychical Research*, visited the house on behalf of the Psychic Research Society and declared that the ghost was genuine. A week after his visit the ghost threw a chair.[160] In the same period, a ghost or poltergeist at Mrs Edwards's house in Campbell Road, Llandybïe, confined itself to throwing smaller items such as clothes and kitchen utensils. The Revd Gomer M. Roberts recalled that when the Revd Phylip Evans, Revd Davies and Revd Canon D. W. Thomas called to examine the house, the group were terrified when the spirit moved a vicar's hat and gloves.[161]

Belief in ghosts was not, as Wirt Sikes and other observers had believed, confined to the lower orders of society.[162] Those with a relatively high level of education also believed in their existence.[163] Spirits and ghosts also troubled the middle and upper classes at the close of the nineteenth century. Charlotte Hills-Johnes of Dolau Cothi noted in her correspondence the receipt of 'Communications from spirits fortelling [her daughter] Cha's future and predicting marriage to a sea captain.'[164] It is more difficult to establish whether or not the belief in the fairies – 'y tylwyth teg' – was widespread during the period between 1876 and 1920.[165] Wirt Sikes considered that 'Among the vulgar in Wales, the belief in fairies is less nearly extinct than casual observers would be likely to suppose.'[166] Thirty years later, vestiges of the belief remained. Jonathan Ceredig Davies noted that 'the belief in fairies in Wales has almost died out.'[167]

But it is difficult to locate specific stories in an actual historical period because of the mists of memory and the uncertainty as to dates in popular memory and the oral tradition of rural west Wales. Few witnesses venture beyond the generality of 'slawer dydd', which either take one back to childhood or even further to the youth of a grandparent or even great-grandparent. The fairies were regarded as an agency that could work for good and evil.[168] If a person strayed into a fairy ring, he would be drawn away for many years.[169] William Llewelyn Williams retold a story current in his youth of a man taken into a fairy ring who returned to his home several generations later, turning into dust when touched by his great-nephew.[170] A writer to *By-Gones* in 1897 noted: 'There are fairy-rings near Pantybeudy, and most beautiful singing is heard on moonlight nights. People [are] drawn to the rings, if drawn too close [they vanish].'[171] Significantly, the report uses the present tense, showing that the beliefs were still prevalent. Such beliefs could perhaps have evolved as an explanation for a person's sudden departure from a neighbourhood, for whatever reason. The fairies would also steal 'lovely children', often leaving obstreperous 'changelings' in their place. This could be a human explanation for the sudden change in a young child's temperament. When no child was substituted it is probable that the fairies became a convenient excuse for infanticide.[172] John Rhys refers to traditions, which he said were still current in the 1880s amongst sailors on the Carmarthen and Pembroke coast, of offshore fairy islands which would disappear when a sailor landed. The inhabitants of these islands were said to frequent markets at Milford Haven and Laugharne.[173]

W. Wentz, a student of John Rhys, undertook a journey in 1908 to gather information on the prevalence of fairy beliefs in west Wales and the Celtic countries generally. A female informant from north-west Carmarthenshire was insistent that:

> I firmly believe that there are fairies and other spirits like them both good and evil. I have heard a phantom dog howl before a death, and have seen more than one death candle. I saw a death-candle right here in this room where we are sitting and talking . . .[174]

In her belief in corpse candles this woman was representative of a large number of those in south-west Wales, for whom portents of death appear to have been the most common supernatural manifestation. T. Gwynn Jones traced the phenomenon to the tradition of St David who, seeing that the people were careless of the life to come, prayed that signs of the immortality of the soul and of life to come be given by presage of death. Following this, corpse candles and other phenomena were frequently seen, particularly in the diocese of St David's.[175] On his tour through 'Wild Wales', George Borrow received this graphic account of the nocturnal activities within the county from the gate-keeper at Llandeilo:

> We were in the habit of seeing plenty of passengers going through the gate without paying toll; I mean such things as are called phantoms or

> illusions – sometimes they were hearses and mourning coaches, sometimes a funeral procession on foot – the whole to be seen as distinctly as anything could be seen especially at night time. I saw myself on a certain night a hearse go through the gate while it was shut; I saw the horses and the hearses, the postilion, and the coachman, and the tufts of hair such as are seen on the tops of hearses, and I saw the wheels scattering the stones in the road, just as other wheels would have done, . . . once a traveller passing through the gate called out to me 'Look! yonder is a corpse candle coming through the fields beside the highway.'[176]

The gatekeeper and traveller who watched the candle's progress were not unique. The Revd Gomer Roberts, in an essay in 1977, recalled the experiences of: 'William Meles o Gae'r Bryn, gˇr y dywedid y câi ei wasgu'n dynn ar adegau i'r clawdd wrth gerdded ar hyd lonydd cul y wlad a hynny wrth gwrs gan wasgfa tyrfa anweledig y toili, sef rhith angladd.'[177]

Several witnesses report these portents of death were seen throughout Carmarthenshire and still occurred in the twentieth century.[178] Having examined the evidence from Laugharne for the existence of corpse candles, Mary Curtis noted in 1880 that: 'I have received many relations of these appearances from parties of great respectability and whose veracity and freedom from fanciful imagination I am sure of.'[179] Of another supernatural phenomenon, phantom funerals – 'y toili' – she reported: 'It seems from all I hear that they are seen as much as ever'.[180] Throughout her researches she maintained an open-minded and enlightened attitude towards her witnesses and declared: 'I give no opinion; but I am not going to tell a person whose veracity I have no reason to doubt, that he did not see what he tells me he did see.'[181]

Three-quarters of a century later, H. G. Davies, in her reminiscences of her rural village, stated:

> Rwyf yn cofio mam yn crynu'n ofnus os clywai geiliog yn canu, neu gi yn udo am hanner nos. Yr oedd pawb yn credu mewn canwyll gorff: os gwelid golau bach gwyn yn symud yn y tywyllwch, yr oedd yn arwydd fod plentyn i farw, ac yr oedd golau yn fwy ac yn gryfach pan fyddai'n rhybuddio marwolaeth rhai mewn oed.[182]

Other supernatural phenomena which inhabited the county's nights, causing terror and fear were phantom dogs,[183] corpse birds,[184] Mallt y Nos, Gwrach y Rhibyn[185] and 'Y Cyhyraeth'.[186]

The nature of the 'Cyhyraeth' was explained to Wirt Sikes by:

> the judicious Joshua Coslet, who lived near the river Towi in Carmarthenshire. [He] testified that the Cyhyraeth is often heard there, and that it is a doleful, disagreeable sound heard before the deaths of many, and most apt to be heard before foul weather. The voice resembles the groaning of a sick person about to die; heard at first at a distance, and then comes nearer, and the last near at hand, so that it is a threefold warning of death . . .[187]

There were a plethora of beliefs, practices and omens which sought to foretell the future.[188] These responded to the ingrained human desire to know the future and thus to face it with confidence and minimize the anxiety and uncertainty of particular projects or of one's life as a whole. Girls who wished to discover information relating to their future husbands had a variety of methods. If a girl sleeping in a new bed for the first time placed a sixpenny piece in a stocking, she would dream of her future intended.[189] If, on the Thursday night before a full moon, she went out to the leek patch in the garden and walked around it nine times reciting a rhyme, her future husband would come to her.[190] All Hallows Eve was also an important occasion for a young girl intent on discovering the future. If she parted her hair in the centre at 12 o'clock, her future husband would come and stand behind her and she could see his reflection in a mirror in front of her.[191] There are a multitude of such beliefs, but many sought to discover their future through an intermediary. In February 1908, Madame St. Leonard, of Coldstream Street, Llanelli, the 'well-known clairvoyant', was fined £5 by Llanelli magistrates. It was said that 'people were swarming to her after [her] prediction that there would be an explosion in Trimsaran pit at Waunhir'.[192]

The First World War, because of its disruptive influence on family life, seems to have increased the trade of clairvoyants, palmists, tea cup readers and other seers of the future. Drusilla Markham, Alice 'Gipsy' Smith and Professor and Madame Virago were busy throughout the war.[193] In 1917 Rose Barnes was charged with making 'statements likely to interfere with the success of His Majesty's Forces'. She had predicted an explosion at the West Wales Munitions Factory.[194] These people took over one of the roles which had been performed in the early nineteenth century by the wise man and the white witch.[195] The most celebrated in Carmarthenshire was John Harries of Cwrtycadno, whose powers of prophecy were renowned throughout Wales.[196] Though he had died in 1839, belief in Harries's power had not vanished by the start of the twentieth century. In 1904 the family of Rees Rees of Llan-giwg, Glamorgan, contested his will because they claimed he was not of sound mind when he wrote it, being prone to eat bloater and apple pie and believing himself bewitched by Dr Harries, Cwrtycadno. The judge, in refusing the family's complaints, remarked that

> That he had some belief in witchcraft would not [he thought] in the present state of the law have any possible effect in depriving him of the power of making a will . . . Lots of people believed in Dr Harries, and he was said to have effected marvellous cures of sick people. It was not strange therefore that the testator had that belief.[197]

One senses in the testimony of contemporaries and the folklorists who questioned them that belief in witches was declining but belief in witchcraft continued to be strong. In 1926, members of staff of the University College of Wales, Aberystwyth, who had collected stories of numerous superstitions in the counties of Cardigan, Carmarthen and Pembroke, recounted the tale of a dairy instructress in the college's Agriculture Department. Called to a farm where difficulty had been experienced in making butter:

> She discovered what was wrong with the milk, and her instructions being obeyed, the butter soon came. The farmer's wife however explained matters by saying that someone had laid a spell upon her churn, but that the witch from the College, being the more powerful sorceress of the two, had been able to take it away.[198]

Where religion failed to offer practical solutions to the problems of everyday life, magical practices and superstitious beliefs flourished. This was particularly true with regard to medicine. Dr Harries of Cwrtycadno offered cures for a wide variety of illnesses ranging from measles, to tetanus, pleurisy, diarrhoea, putrid fever, small pox, gout, diabetes, yellow fever, continued fever, irregular gout and venereal diseases.[199] Throughout the county people, in their desire to cure various ailments and illnesses, consulted 'wise men' and utilized everyday substances in numerous ways. Urine was considered to be a good cure for bruises and blisters. Cow dung was frequently used as a poultice. D. G. Williams reported that a certain cure for a child who wetted his bed was to make a soup from a well-boiled mouse and give it to the child. Corns on the feet could be easily cured by beating them with holly branches. The wedding ring offered a certain cure for 'llefelin' and a metal ring could cure temporary fits.[200] Water was one substance which was readily available. The belief in the medicinal powers of many fountains and wells in the county continued to hold sway until well into the twentieth century. Ffynnon Deilo was said to cure rheumatism, and Ffynnon y Pentre near Llandybïe was believed to cure sore eyes and was still in use in 1939.[201] Incredible as these beliefs may seem, the historian should not dismiss them out of hand.

Wise men and women were frequently the agencies through which such cures became known.[202] It is probable that some of the more outlandish cures originated from a person's misinterpretation of the wise man's instruction. When the traditional curses failed or a problem was too severe, people would turn to the wise man. In 1909 Marie Trevelyan remarked:

> The rubber . . . is still to be found in many parts of Wales, where also people called bone-setters live. It is strange to hear of people still going to the rubber and the bone-setter, in whom they have a great faith, when hospitals and surgeons are close at hand. The herbalist is another with potent influence among the peasantry and the colliery population of North and South Wales.[203]

In 1907 the *South Wales Press* reported the inquest into the death of sixteen-year-old William George Griffiths of New Dock Road, Llanelli. A door boy at the fixing department of Pembrey Copper Works, he had been scalded by molten iron. Though Dr J. H. Williams (later the first Labour MP for Llanelli) had been consulted, the family still sent for Mr Williams, 'the faith healer of Princess Street', to see to the suffering boy. Although poultices of bran, vinegar, and then bread and milk were applied, the boy died.[204] 'Torri lleche', as we have seen, was another folk custom which was common in the industrial areas of Carmarthenshire. It is clear from the evidence that there was not a clear divide between the superstitious rural areas and the enlightened urban areas. It should be no surprise that colliers, tinplate and ironworkers, confronting as they did, often in the dark, the elemental forces of nature, created their own distinct beliefs and superstitions.[205]

The historian of folk traditions and superstitions cannot help but note the pessimism which underlay the cosmology of Carmarthenshire people at the turn of the twentieth century. Though the concept of 'luck' was clearly established, portents and omens of bad luck far outnumbered those of good luck. Any of the following were considered unlucky: if crows stopped nesting near a house after a few years, if a cow was braying without obvious explanation, if a hare ran in front of one on a path; if mice flocked to a house; and if money was paid out on a Monday it was believed that terrible events would soon occur. Women were believed to be particularly unlucky. If a woman was seen first on New Year's Day or on a Monday and if a person met a woman on a journey – especially a cross-eyed woman – bad luck was certain to follow. In view of its importance in the cottage economy, it is understandable that the death of a pig should signal misfortune for the whole household.[206] This pessimism was so ingrained that suddenly to dress well was seen as tempting fate. As Caradoc Evans noted in the short story, 'The woman who sowed iniquity', this sort of behaviour drew immediate condemnation: 'Worshippers on their way to Capel Seion the preceding Sunday had shuddered at the sight of Betti Lancoch flaunting herself in fine garments.'[207]
D. J. Williams in his story 'Blwyddyn Llwyddiannus' pointed to similar lessons.[208] The pessimism implied by popular superstitions and beliefs was that whatever anyone did, he/she was likely to suffer, that life was at best a narrow path, with bad luck threatening on every side. As Obelkevich has shown:

> Superstitions gave indirect but faithful expression to the insecurity of the rural poor, their powerlessness in the face of adversity. Like Christianity, it assumed that life was a 'vale of tears', but was even more precise in its pessimism.[209]

The world-view of the characters in Caradoc Evans's short stories borrows freely from the practices and dictates of established religion, while at the same time drawing heavily upon superstitious beliefs.[210] The folklore collectors of the nineteenth century, in revealing that pagan beliefs and practices survived the Reformation, showed that these were general beliefs in south-west Wales. People drew on both Christianity and superstitions to provide explanation and meaning for death, illness, evil and all kinds of misfortune.[211] Christianity, in the short term, appeared to be the most pessimistic, for it could only refer people to God's will. Its optimism was long term, contained in its central doctrine of salvation. The short-term deficiencies of Christianity left room for superstitions which, through a myriad of practices and beliefs, provided explanations for everyday problems. Obelkevich again provides a useful summary: '. . . A hundred little misfortunes too trivial for God could travel along the networks of superstition to a hundred quirks of bad luck. But still they were explanations, better than meaningless and perhaps more comprehensible than the will of God.'[212]

In the same way that individuals borrowed freely from the ideas and doctrines of both Christian religion and superstition, they also responded in a complex manner to differing codes of morality in their daily lives. Popular belief is an amalgam of the normal doctrines of the church and Nonconformist chapels and a different code of moral behaviour. Individuals lived their lives in a more complex manner than historians have been willing to accept. Their moral outlook was fashioned by a variety of factors, such as temperament, religious, social and economic background, to suit the circumstances in which the individual found himself at any given moment. The same individual behaved differently at chapel, church, football match, political meeting and public house. Historians should guard against the simplistic view that there were two opposing polarities in the popular culture of south-west Wales.[213] Though there is truth in the view which presents the religious community on the one hand and 'the world' on the other, it obscures the very real interrelationship which existed between them. As the social environment changed, so did the temper, character and nuances of individual behaviour. Popular culture, like popular belief, was an amalgam of several different, often contradictory elements. The major characteristic of the community's cultural life was its plurality.

The religious denominations, as we have seen, provided a wealth of cultural services to their adherents in addition to their primary function of preaching the gospel. Pre-eminent amongst these were the temperance societies for men, women and children which offered instruction in social behaviour and morals. But the chapels served also as music halls and theatres. Members of various chapels in Carmarthenshire produced a variety of outstanding theatrical and musical performances, ranging from operas, cantatas and oratorios to short plays and dramas. Beriah Gwynfe Evans's dramas, ‘Llewelyn ein Llyw Olaf’, ‘Glynd˘r’ and ‘Ystori'r Streic’ were popular and performed in many chapels throughout the county.[214] The latter, published in 1904, was a humane attempt to understand the problems of families in a community during an industrial dispute.[215] Chapel performers toured the county to perform before the congregations of other chapels. In February 1898 a group from Felinfoel took its production of ‘Joseph and His Brothers’ to Calfaria Baptist Chapel in Pen-y-groes.[216] Performances were of varying standards. Some chapels had long traditions of public performances. T. J. Morgan found that the performance of ‘Elijah’ by the Tabernacl, Llanelli, in January 1912 was the chapel's thirty-fourth consecutive oratorio. In contrast the performance of ‘Acis and Galatea’ in neighbouring Moriah was only the fifth performance by that congregation.[217] While the piano became the status symbol of the period, with all the best homes proudly displaying one through the net curtains of the parlour, the organ assumed the same status for chapels. On 27 February 1913 *Llais Llafur* reported that a new organ had been installed in Carmel Chapel, Gwauncaegurwen, that a new organ was being installed at Tabernacl, Cwm-gors, and that Siloh had also ‘determined to go in for a new organ’.[218] The excitement, hair-raising drama, thrills and laughs, acting, storytelling, parable and illustration of such performances provided an escape from the drab and dreary realities of ordinary daily lives. When the competitive edge was added in the local and national eisteddfodau, loyalty to the chapel was intensified.

These secular aspects of religious life, which take the historian beyond the fringe of organized or popular religion into the realm of popular culture, served to remind Nonconformists that outside their father's house there were also many mansions. Eisteddfodau were found in virtually every hamlet, village and town in Carmarthenshire. So that they did not clash, the local eisteddfodau were organized on a set pattern. In the north-west, Pen-y-bont held its Eisteddfodau on Christmas and St David's Day, Cynwyl Elfed on Easter Monday, Bwlchnewydd on Christmas night, and Talog on New Year's night.[219] Winning the crown or the chair at the National Eisteddfod was viewed with great pride. For instance, the people of Llanelli packed the streets to welcome home the Revd R. Gwylfa Roberts after he won two crowns, at Blaenau Ffestiniog in 1898 and Cardiff in 1899.[220] Similar scenes of pride greeted Watcyn Wyn's homecoming after his victories in Merthyr in 1881, in Aberdare in 1885 and in Chicago in 1893.[221] Llanelli's preoccupation with the preparations for the 1895 National Eisteddfod was one reason why the Liberal Unionists surprisingly won the Carmarthen Boroughs seat in the general election. According to one newspaper correspondent, 'the national stage ranked higher than the political'.[222] The high standards of local choirs were jealously, indeed violently, guarded. In 1897 the adjudicator at the Llandybïe eisteddfod was followed to his train by a hostile mob who booed, jeered and threatened him with physical violence. His offence was that he had withheld the prize in the choral competition and dared to suggest that the quality of singing was poor. Tension was also high in rural eisteddfodau. In 1923 the *Celtic News* reported that: 'The Deputy Chief Constable is to be admired for his attitude in trying to stamp out the rowdyism in these competitive meetings and we are certain that all the Eisteddfodwyr wish him success in his campaign.'[223]

As Gwenallt shows in his chronicle of boyhood, the poetic and bardic tradition was strong in the industrial areas as well.[224] Watcyn Wyn was the most notable example of this tradition in Carmarthenshire but the young anthracite miners, Amanwy, Gomer Roberts, and David Mainwaring, and the other poets who produced *O Lwch y Lofa*, were notable poets in their own right.[225] Rough perhaps, but diamonds no less.

There was, of course, a separate theatrical and musical tradition which had no contact with the religious.[226] The theatre has a long tradition in Wales, a tradition which drew it into conflict with the religious denominations and moralists. Although most of the theatre groups performed as touring companies with portable theatres, palatial theatres were being established by the 1890s. In 1891 Noakes established a theatre in Llanelli, seating over 1,500 people,[227] and in 1910 the ambitious entertainer William Haggar purchased the Royalty Theatre, Llanelli, for 'variety entertainment and bioscope pictures.'[228] Arthur Mee recalled the pioneering early days of the portable theatres:

> The place was frowzy. The piece consisted of dancing, lovemaking and terrific broadsword combats – the last were always a great feature of the

The Llandeilo Literary Society (By permission of Llyfrgell Genedlaethol Cymru/The National Library of Wales)

> entertainments. Prior to the perfomance, the proprietor and the cast would parade on the stage outside the building, and there would be music and a bit of dialogue to entice the people within. I don't fancy these dramas were greatly patronised by the elite. Probably there were too many souvenirs to carry away in the shape of fleas and such things.

The custom-built theatres might have improved the standard of entertainment but not the conditions:

> Years later, when there was a wooden theatre in Cowell Street – Noakes or Rainbows or somebody else's – there was good acting to be seen, that is to say, when the stage could be seen at all, which was seldom on account of the tobacco smoked. Everybody smoked and perspired and was happy and so were the fleas![229]

Haggar, probably the first and certainly the most inventive, entertainment entrepreneur in Wales saw the possibilities that the bioscope and the camera provided and laid the foundations for the cinema industry in south Wales. His 'Maid of Cefnydfa' ran to rapturous audiences. But in culture, as in the economy, it was difficult to escape the influence of America. Just as the economy swung to the rhythm of the Atlantic economy, and Welsh revivalists sought salvation in the songs of Sankey and Moody, so too did local cinema audiences react and respond to the cinematic creations of Hollywood. By 1915, Llanelli, in common with several other towns in south Wales, was hosting its own Charlie Chaplin impersonation competitions. Splenetic chapel elders saw the cinematic presentations of the greatest story every told as evidence of the blasphemous nature of the new medium. They called for censorship and control, voicing concerns that would be all too familiar to a later age. In 1916 Sir Stafford Howard complained to the Carmarthenshire County Council that there was an urgent need to supervise and censor the cinemas, since the increase in juvenile crime was directly attributable to its pernicious effects.[230]

In a society where literacy was enjoyed by the majority of people, the printed word was of considerable importance. The social historian should remember that although the printing presses of Wales produced a phenomenal number of denominational newspapers and magazines, biblical commentaries and *cofiannau*, the presses also produced a plethora of publications upon which moralists would frown. The most popular 'railway novels' in the county in 1905 were said to be the works of Allen Raine and Gwendoline Price, author of *John Jones Curate*.[231] But much popular fiction went beyond their more genteel tone. In 1904 Sir Lewis Morris complained of the 'bloodthirstiness of current novels' and voiced his opinion that:

> It is a bloodthirsty literature this, with hardly a single redeeming moral trait . . . [However] this is a time of bloody war and wholesale massacre appeals for a while to a public never attracted by namby pamby romances in pseudo-Saxon English of an impossible medieval England.[232]

Sunday newspapers were also a cause for concern. The *Carmarthen Weekly Reporter* complained of the 'type of papers which give a full, true and particular account written by a bigamist and describing his adventures with his "32 wives". These newspapers are hawked during the time that churchgoers attend Divine worship.'[233]

This view fails to realize or understand that the newspapers served a complex plurality of cultures which had developed in Carmarthenshire by the turn of the twentieth century. Cultural activities of a bewildering diversity and differing respectability had been established which do not conform to simple monalistic condemnation or conceptualization. One of the features of these Sunday newspapers was the reporting of organized sport such as Rugby and football matches. In Wales the growth of Rugby football was one of the most notable leisure developments of the late nineteenth century.[234] Not all ministers of religion viewed Rugby as unfavourably as those who described the game as 'kicking the head of John the Baptist'. Many of the more 'muscular Christians' saw merit and virtue in the game. During the 1904 revival the Revd Iona Williams, in the face of considerable opposition, declared at Park Congregational Chapel, Llanelli: 'if you expect me to curse football . . . you will be disappointed, I owe too much to the game.'[235]

Others, too, felt the excitement that Rugby football could engender. For example, the match between Wales and New Zealand in 1905 attracted considerable excitement. The *Carmarthen Weekly Reporter* noted:

> Carmarthen people are sometimes moved by religious controversies, and sometimes by political conflicts. But in none of these matters of late years has there been anything like the interest which was taken in the football match between Wales and New Zealand. Business almost suspended to wait for the telegrams . . . The result . . . [produced] scenes only rivalled by the relief of Mafeking.[236]

Each of the towns in Carmarthenshire established Rugby teams. Many were untouched by success; the main characteristic of their history was the simple and noble human virtues of perseverance and persistence. Llanelli, however, enjoyed a glittering history of success and the knowledgeable but partisan supporters of the 'Scarlets' jealously guarded their team's honour and reputation.[237] The team's defeat by the 1907 'Springboks' was attributed to bad refereeing, which meant that a try had been disallowed to Llanelli whilst one was awarded to the Springboks in similar circumstances, and that the other Springbok try was from an unpunished knock-on. The crowd, said the *South Wales Press* reporter, were not biased, they had not used obscene language and the referee did not need police protection to leave the town.[238] Other teams might score more points but Llanelli would not lose.

Less popular sports were association football clubs, cricket and boxing. Large crowds could, however, be drawn to certain fights of local interest.[239] The twelve two-minute round fight between Joe White and Ted Jones on the fairground and the epic battle between Jack Jones of Llanelli and Willie Phillips of Garnant, over fifteen rounds, were celebrated contests which drew large crowds.[240] Tennis, because of the expense, remained the leisured pursuit of the gentry.[241] But other sports traditionally associated with aristocratic life, in particular the Prince of Wales's circle, had a more popular appeal because of the gambling that accompanied them.[242] The Lord Lieutenant's Plate, valued at over fifty sovereigns, was a particularly popular event in the local horse racing calendar.[243] The chance to win a small fortune on an outsider appealed to the sense of adventure of many Carmarthenshire people. Gambling also took other forms. In 1912 Alfred Cooper, a cripple and 'one of the gang who rushed the railway bridge in the Llanelli Riots', was imprisoned for ten days for playing a game of chance ('under 7 and over 7') with dice at the Sports Field in Ammanford. In pursuit of the elusive big win, he neglected his wife and family.[244] Gambling was surprisingly one of the main attractions of the temperance cause in Kidwelly for, as one outraged moralist complained in 1892, the coffee and temperance shops of the town were little more than 'Gambling Dens': 'Card playing, tippet, pedro and other gambling devices are used to draw our youth to frequent these places.'[245]

Popular gambling, imitating that pursued by the aristocracy, derived from the need for sociability, but above all it was part of an economy of expediency which characterized the life of the labouring classes. The horse races, the 'pitch and toss' matches under the bridge in Carmarthen on Sunday mornings, the card schools in public houses, the bet on a billiard match, all offered the hope that fortunes could be redistributed by Fortune. The social universality of gambling stemmed from the magical concepts of chance and luck. The poor fervently hoped that luck might cancel fate and transform their fortune. In a society which displayed consumer goods in increasing profusion in the growing retail centres of towns, and where the fortunes of the rich were ostentatiously displayed, gambling offered the hope that destinies might change.

That perceptive commentator on rural life, D. J. Williams, has shown how the demands of working the land created their own pastimes and cultural activities. In these, physical strength and the capacity to control heavy equipment and animals were skills which were prized. Ploughing matches, which were common in the rural parts of the county, provided opportunities for labourers to exhibit their prowess.[246] Agricultural shows were the theatres in which many rural skills, ranging from the domestic abilities of the farmer's wife and maid, to the craft of the blacksmith, turner and other rural craftsmen, to the athletic skills of the horsemen, could be displayed, admired and rewarded.[247] Many pastimes also served to cement social relationships within the Carmarthenshire countryside. The otter and fox hounds provided opportunities for farm servants and estate workers to pursue the glories of the chase in the company of landlords.[248] Here at least it was possible to cross class and cultural boundaries. Along the coast a similar co-operation took place in the regatta, when expert sailors combined with those members of more prosperous classes who sailed for leisure and pleasure.[249]

In addition to all these diversions there was one social activity which was of central importance – drinking. Alcohol was an essential social lubricant in Carmarthenshire society in the nineteenth and early twentieth centuries. In the words of Brian Harrison, alcohol was the 'thirst quencher, the reliever of physical and psychological strain, the symbol of human interdependence.'[250] It was a pain killer, a morale-booster, a sleeping draught and a medicine, it was an essential calorific food, it provided 'Dutch courage' and offered an escape to those who found the reality around them too harsh to bear.

Alcohol supplied much of the energy expended on hard arduous tasks. In the rural areas of the county, special, often very potent, brews were prepared by the farmers for harvest time. The Commissioners on Agricultural Labour noted the prevalence of this custom in western Carmarthenshire and the Cardiganshire and Pembrokeshire border.[251] Special brews were prepared at Christmas and to celebrate New Year's Day. The completion of important tasks such as the timbering of the roof of a building ('cwrw cwple') were celebrated with the tapping of a barrel. The farmer produced beer for blacksmith and carpenter ('cwrw bando') and to celebrate the arduous task of repairing a wheel at the local smithy. Beer and spirits were also provided on the day of the killing of a pig, and farm auctions and sales were characterized by a liberal distribution of 'cwrw ocshon'.[252]

The Regulars of the Cross Inn Hotel, Ammonford, begin their outing (By permission of Llyfrgell Genedlaethol Cymru/The National Library of Wales)

D. J. Williams recalled that, having struck a bargain at Llandeilo mart, farmers would retire to the White Hart Hotel to seal the deal over a pint of beer.[253] Social events such as weddings were often made more convivial and exciting through the distribution of beer. The 'cwrw bach' had its origins in the custom of parents or guardians of a betrothed couple brewing a barrel of beer and selling it to the guests, thus raising much needed finance for the young couple. In some areas it was not considered to be sinful to overindulge, as the indulgence was for a good cause.[254] W. Llewelyn Williams claimed that in the Llansawel district: 'Nid oedd neb yn cael ei geryddu gan y seiat am "fyn'd ar y criws" mewn . . . cwrw bach, – er yn gwneud drwg iddo'i hyn ['roedd] yn gwneud hynny er lles eraill.'[255] The attitude of the Nonconformists towards drinking clearly needs to be analysed with care. For those in industrial occupations, drinking was primarily to quench thirst. In 1910 it was claimed that the 'tinplaters shovel and roll and sweat and drink all day', a claim strenuously denied by the inhabitants of 'Tinopolis'.

Brewery workers, it was said, always helped themselves to a few pints from the casks to start the day.[256]

The tinplaters of Llanelli certainly had plenty of opportunities to drink. In 1896 Llanelli temperance campaigners produced a map to show that there were no fewer than forty-five public houses and eleven licensed premises within 225 yards of Llanelli Church.[257] In all, Llanelli had a ratio of one public house per 179 people; in Swansea the ratio was 1:224, in Newport 1:304, in Cardiff 1:477 and in Liverpool it was 1:319.[258] Temperance campaigners noted with concern that the number of public houses had risen from 143 in 1898 to 241 in 1915.[259] Carmarthen, Llandovery, Llangadog and Llandeilo were also amply endowed with palaces of drink.

The nineteenth century produced a massive literature outlining the evils of drink and the public house. So pervasive did the views of the temperance campaigners become that it is difficult to get a clear picture of the social importance of the public house. The views temperance campaigners, and those of the police, which we find in the court reports relating to drunkenness charges, were uniformly hostile. But it must be remembered that public houses were a perfectly ordinary part of everyday life, providing thousands of ordinary people with food and drink. The tavern provided people with a meeting place, where drinking was often an excuse for day-to-day companionship and conviviality. In the early history of the temperance movement in Carmarthenshire, meetings were actually held in the public houses.[260] Brian Harrison exaggerates when he claims that 'no respectable urban Englishman entered an ordinary public house'.[261] Certainly, many respectable Welshmen entered ordinary public houses without loss of face. Throughout Carmarthenshire the public house performed essential functions for men, respectable and unrespectable of all occupations. Contrary to another stereotype, the public house was not an exclusively male domain. In reports on police raids, it is not only the prostitutes that the historian encounters but also respectable housewives, the wives of shopkeepers, tinplate workers and colliers. They went to the pub alone, or in groups, with husbands, workmates, or lovers, to enjoy the conviviality, warmth and relative comfort of the public house. Some unashamedly took their children.

The pub was the setting for a wide range of activities, many operating in grey areas of the law: trafficking, theft and prostitution were the most obvious.[262] Gambling was also a prominent activity. In 1914, when the police raided the Spread Eagle Hotel in Queen Street, Carmarthen, they discovered details of seventy-five bets in the landlord's possession, together with copies of *Macaul's Racing Chronicle 1910, A Record of Sports* and a telegram reading 'Election 10/- each way'.[263] The Edwinsford Arms in Talyllychau, the Albion Inn in Murray Street and the New Inn, New Dock, both in Llanelli, and the Jubilee Hotel in Carmarthen were also raided because of their illegal gambling activities.[264] The pubs of Carmarthen were also frequently used for rabbit coursing and betting.[265] Even temperance establishments found themselves on the wrong end of the law. In 1917 the owner of the Tumble Temperance Hotel was fined £20 for allowing betting with a 'Clown' machine to take place on his premises.[266] In the poorer areas of Carmarthen and Llanelli, the dingy public houses merged into the world of the low lodging-house, the navvy, the casual labourer and the tramp. The idleness, drunkenness, wastefulness and evil habits of their frequenters haunted the minds of police, moralists and the respectable. The claustrophobia of many of the smaller public houses led to quarrels and violence. Arguments could be over virtually anything – the quality of the beer, the attentions of a young lady, Cronje's ability as a commander in the Boer War. Words led to blows, oaths led to fisticuffs and the fighting spilled into the street. For many, fighting was less a deliberate act of transgression than a manifestation of a code of behaviour which was physical. Husbands fought wives and lovers, and rivals fought with the violence of complete strangers. It is easy to understand the terror felt by the respectable people of Mill Street, Carmarthen, and the New Dock district of Llanelli at these regular weekly fights, but the noise, shouting and broken furniture resemble a cultural performance. As Daniel Roche observed of the Parisian poor:

> The element of display, provocative sexual abuse and exaggerated gestures made these brawls a charivari in popular mores, belonging to the sphere of gaming, fetes and physical exchanges. In the landscape of the popular classes, a rough-and-tumble or a hail of blows were like marking the end, almost deliberately, of a fine summer evening or autumn Sunday.[267]

But leading up to these violent outbursts there was the world of popular gaiety and its solidarity, honour and nobility. On the fringes of poverty there was an economic system of giving and taking which can never appear in historical statistics, and it was encouraged by the public house atmosphere of spontaneous conviviality and generosity. There was a good deal of give and take between the fortunate and the unfortunate, for poverty, like wealth, was shared.[268] These noble traditions were deeply ingrained in the popular culture, and the attempt of the government and the authorities in the First World War to stop them through making 'treating' illegal was actively and openly resisted.[269] In this rough, honest and dishonest, boisterous, sardonic and irreverent milieu, people found escape from the multitude of pressures that restricted their ordinary existence. They danced, they sang raucously and, for a few blissful hours, they forgot.[270]

Those who were too young to be able to enjoy the pleasures and perils of the public houses found excitement and entertainment on the streets. The moralists, as we have seen, were eloquent in their condemnation of the streetcorner culture of youth.[271] From the streetcorners of Pencader, Llandeilo, Llandovery, Llandysul, Llanelli, Ammanford and Carmarthen, youths watched people spilling out of the pubs, listened to drunks staggering home and offered uninvited and unwanted advice to the respectable people as they journeyed home from chapel and temperance meeting and Eisteddfod; they listened to the music of the passing bands and the Italian organ-grinders, watched the dancing Hungarian bears and ruminated on the insensibility and chaos of the adult world.[272] The mannerisms of the gang leaders, such as 'Jim Pais'[273] – the way he held and lit a cigarette, nonchalantly combed his hair, impressed and insulted the pert and pretty girls as they paraded the pavements, and irreverently addressed the more respectable and reverent members of Carmarthenshire society as they cantered home from chapel – were gestures taken from the stars of the local cinemas. These were mimicked by his cronies, until 'Jim Pais' too became respectable and therefore irrelevant to the next generation of 'corner boys'. For this streetcorner culture was also continually changing and evolving, just like every other Carmarthenshire culture.

Conclusion:

Carmarthenshire and Welsh Society

G. M. Trevelyan has been famously, and frequently, misquoted as stating that social history is history with the politics letf out.[1] Gwyn Alf Williams, somewhere, sometime, mischievously commented that for a long time Welsh history has been history with the Welsh left out.[2] Whatever words may be wasted in condemnation or praise of this book, it is hoped that no-one will describe this as a history of Carmarthenshire with the people left out. The individual case history, bristling with novelty, inconsistency and unpredictability, has been the building-block of this historical work and it is pertinent that before concluding we establish what type of edifice we have erected. It is perhaps too speculative, probably too sprawling and overcrowded, and undoubtedly contains too much jerrybuilding. But it has been conceived as an attempt to portray some of the tragic and triumphant variety and vibrancy of human experience. This celebration of the experience of individuals has brought us to the boundary between social history and antiquarianism – a subject despised by historians as being without explanation, devoid of analysis, and sterile in interpretation. To many purist historians, much of what has preceded this summary synopsis which passes as a conclusion will be seen as evidence of the deterioration which has taken place in scholarly history. Their view undoubtedly will be that this work is an inchoate amalgam of fashionable fads, trivial trends and prurient sensationalism a historical gallimaufry. How successful this has been in avoiding such a fate is a matter for others to decide. At this point it is appropriate to pause in orders to recall and reconsider the underlying arguments of this study, to ascertain whether they have been of value in the effort of establishing a new kind of social history for Carmarthenshire, and to decide what lessons, if any, can be learnt for the social history of Wales.

It would be simplistic to suggest, and pretentious to pretend, that this portrait of the social history of Carmarthenshire can present an accurate picture of Welsh social history at the the turn of the twentieth century. Such a conclusion would ignore the profound differences which exist between different communities and negate the special characteristics of specific societies. The experiences of the Welsh nation were naturally more complex and complicated than those witnessed within the compressed confines of Carmarthenshire. The microcosm is not wholly representative of the macrocosm. The historian has to remember that the experiences of a particular society differ and vary from thos of the general or national society. While accepting these reservations, we should also recall the intention of this work. Our aim has been to provide a portrait of Carmarthenshire society at the turn of the twentieth century. Our objective has been to use the particular experiences of individuals as a mechanism for testing the common-held generalizations of Welsh historiography. Individual experience varies enormously according to the influence of a number of different factors. If we look at the history of Carmarthenshire through the eyes of one of the well-to-do middle class we might conclude that the years up to 1920 wre characterized by prosperity, opportunity and enjoyment. But if we adopt instead the perspective of one of the inhabitants of the low lodging-houses of Mill Street, Carmarthen, or the ironically named Prospect Place, Llanelli, we could conclude that these were locust years of poverty, deprivation and misery. Through narrowing the focus onto the smallest constituent part of society – the individual – we have been able to change the configuration of the kaleidoscope and present a new image of Carmarthenshire society. That transformation in perception has important implications for Welsh social history.

The dominant images of rural Victorian and Edwardian Wales which abound in art, proliferate in literature and reverberate in music are wistful, elegiac descriptions of a green, pleasant, idyllic land in which a healthy, robust peasantry – 'gwerin' – live contented lives. Rhys Davies' description of Carmarthenshire as 'prosperously lactic' perfectly encapsulates this bucolic Eden. But prosperity was not often found in the insanitary buildings which housed the rural poor and conditions in the towns were often little better for the people who had tried to escape the cruel conditions in the countryside. The idyllic picturesque cottages, with their whitewashed walls blindingly bright in the summer sunshine, and with sweet smelling pink roses clambering around the door-frames, were often the breeding grounds for disease and death. To protray them as the healthy homes of a generous *gwerin* has little basis in fact; it was more a fiction, often perhaps it was fantasy. The towns have been portrayed as the places in which the traditional bonds of Welsh life, the family and religion, gave way under new and alien pressures. But in this study we have uncovered evidence which suggests that the mentally ill, the old, the infirm and the young pregnant mother were more likely to be cared for by their family in the towns than in rural areas where traditional community values were considered to hold sway. Cases of suicide and mental illness were more numberous in the countryside. In the late nineteenth century, the typical suicide was profiled as a young girl. Abandoned by her lover, she would take her own life by drowning in a river. But such Ophelian tales of the riverbank were the myths of a male-dominate society. The statistics actually suggest that the person most likely to take his own life was a middle-aged farmer who could no longer withstand the oppressive pressures of life in rural Carmarthenshire.

Morality was considered to be one area of life in which the Welsh excelled. The high levels of moral probity were the pride and passion of a legion of Welsh authors and polemicists. Whilst English authors struggled with the decadence and sensuality of the *fin de siäcle*, Welsh writers enjoyed the decency and sensibility of 'Hen Wlad y Menyg Gwynion'. This concept of a land of moral purity and perfect people was frequently proclaimed from pulpit and press. Yet the statistical information gathered and published annually by the registrar general provides evidence to suggest that it was in rural, not urban areas that chastity was most likely to go the way of all flesh. The rural areas of Carmarthenshire had the highest rates of illegitimate births. It was in the countryside that 'caru yn y gwely' and countless cheerful courting customs continued longest. Prostitution, back-street abortions and infanticide were far more frequent than historians have allowed. Drunkenness and petty theft were Carmarthenshire's most common crimes, but vicious assaults and murder were not absent and there were several outbreaks of serious disturbances and rioting. The link between the county's Nonconformist leaders and the violence associated with the Tithe disturbances in the late 1880s, and the self-help, but illegal, culture of the poachers, which was strong throughout rural Carmarthenshire, are indications that popular attitudes to the forces of law and order were complex, conflicting and contradictory.

The insistence upon an inflexible and unyielding moral code was one of the most depressing aspects of Nonconformity in nineteenth-century Wales. The casting out from chapel membership of those who had transgressed the dictates of this code contributed little to the finer qualities of the Christian spirit, and eventually proved detrimental to the popular image of religion. This acceptance of Wales as a land of Bible-black morality has coloured and distorted our perception of the Welsh people in Victorian and Edwardian times. The portrait of eminent Victorians that we retain is of sober, stern-faced men and solemn, straight-laced women. The Welsh Victorians are often depicted as a people devoid of humour, whose moral indignation often appears like jealousy ennobled with a halo. In the 1950s, Gwyn Thomas could still evoke this serious and sombre legacy when he claimed 'there are still parts of Wales where the only concession to gaiety is a striped shroud'.[3] But in reality Welsh society had its humour, many people approached life with levity and laughed in the face of adversity. Welsh people placed importance on the pursuit of purity and honour, but they also sought pleasure and happiness. Their pursuit of happiness is an important feature of life which has been forgotten from our history. Unlike the lady who gave her name to the age, Victorians were amused.

'Y Teulu Dedwydd', 'the contended family,' was another cornerstone of the popular imagery of Carmarthenshire society. Contemporaries portrayed the family as free of tension, happy and religious. 16 was seen as a haven, sheltering those within its cosy bonds from the tempests of the world outside, as private world of peace in a public world of pain. However, again the facts show that domestic violence was persistent and widespread. The reports of the NSPCC inspectors bear testimony to the terribly tragic lives endured by many wives and children in this community. Women braved raging torrents of abuse and children confronted cascades of cruelty. Carmarthenshire has proven itself to be one of the most fertile grounds in Wales for the development of religion, that most supreme and sublime of all efforts undertaken by the human spirit. In one of his great spiritual poems, 'Y Capel yn Sir Gaerfyrddin', Gwenallt noted that in rural Carmarthenshire only a thin wall separated the Saviour within the chapel and the Creator of the world outside. The poem contrasts the natural spirituality of the countryside, where religion was in gracteful harmony with the boundless fertility and creativity of nature, with the chapel in industrialized South Wales, where religious peace struggled against the bustle, noise and smog of collieries and industries.[4] The central message of the poem was that in industrial Wales it was difficult to give great truths a hearing amid the tumult of easy falsehoods. The eternal and the immutable were lost among the transient and disposable. But the evidence that we have considered from the 1911 Report on the Church in Wales indicates that attachment to religion was in fact strongest in the urban areas of the county. The remarkable events witnessed in Carmarthenshire during the 1904–5 Revival, when angels and devils walked the county's highways and byways, indicate how close the links were between established, formal religion and the shadowy world of superstitions. In Carmarthenshire, corpse candles, phantom dogs and spirit birds continued to be seen, and the beautiful singing of 'Y Tylwyth Teg' was still heard up until the First World War. Education played a part in the erosion and eventual eradication of such beliefs. Yet in rural Carmarthenshire throughout this period, the role of the school and schooling were secondary to the physical demands of the farming calendar. A transformation had to take place in the way people viewed their world, some would argue that a 'disenchantment of the world' had to take place before schools won their place in society.[5]

Politics has not intruded directly into this study. This is not to deny that politics does have an important role in every society. Many historians, and Welsh historians in particular, have attached great significance and importance to the role of politics as a means of studying society. But profound cultural, economic, psychological and social transformations took place in people's lives in a period of relative political quiescence and stability. A baffled bewilderment at the extent and rapidity of change in people's daily lives which had recently taken place is a consistent theme in the writings of many authors and the memoirs of many men at the century's turn. None of these authors, not even the MP William Llewelyn Williams in his tender tribute to his home county '*Slawer Dydd*, include politics as an agent of change. The level of attachment of politics and political causes is also problematic. In the corporate politics of Carmarthen town up until the First World War corruption continued to be the predominant feature of the borough's political character. This again would seem to indicate that the town's public morality was more fragile than contemporaries claimed.[6] In Llanelli in 1895, organizing a successful National Eisteddfod for the town took precedence over the preparations for the parliamentary election. To quote the editor of the *South Wales Press*:

> the general election is the latest hydra which has shown its hideous head against the Eisteddfod. All outside things to conspire against us at Llanelli. In spite of it all Llanelli people won't be the courageous people we have taken them to be useless they put their shoulders to the wheel and work for the success of the Eisteddfod notwithstanding all the forces which have arrayed themselves against it...[7]

The paranoia of the editor of the town's leading Liberal newspaper clearly indicates which event carried prestige and pre-eminence for the town. To many people in Carmarthenshire at the turn of the twentieth century, the problems which pre-occupied them were not political and public but private and personal. The basic facts of life, of birth, copulation and death and the battle to scratch, scrape and dig a living from unforgiving and infertile land, were the predominant concerns.

These contradictory conclusions make it difficult to reach any general conclusions about the nature of Carmarthenshire society. At first sight it seems that the only conclusion that can be ventured with any degree of safety is the negative one that no generalization is possible. But this view is perhaps too bleak and pessimistic. Though many of our conclusions are contradictory, there is a good and an obvious reason for this. These contradictory and conflicting conclusions reflect the central fact that human society itself is complex and contradictory. Their significance and importance for Welsh history is that they may provide us with a new approach to the wider context of Welsh social history. This work has unearthed a wealth of evidence which questions the accepted conceptualizations of Welsh society at the end of the nineteenth century. Perhaps the major contribution of this work is the number of different questions which it provides for further historical researchers. Amongst the plethora of questions that future historians of Welsh social history can consider are: What role did politics really play in the lives of the Welsh people? What was the actual role of education in Welsh life? What was the real contribution of education to Welsh society? What was the real significance of religion in the mental worlds of the Welsh people? What did the Welsh people really believe in? How were the yearning for a place in Heaven and the fear of eternal damnation in Hell reflected in the daily lives of the Welsh people? Was there a threat to the forces of law and order in Wales at the turn of the twentieth century? How did people respond to mental illness? What was the attitude of the Welsh people to sexuality? What defined Welsh men as masculine and Welsh women as feminine? What were the qualities that made a man a gentleman? What were the characteristics that marked people as respectable? How did people respond to the profound changes in the perception of time which took place in the period leading up to the First World War? Was Wales the idyllic, moralistic land that it was so often claimed to be? What forces really concerned Welsh people: were their concerns political and religious or were they personal and psychological? How did men and women learn to live together? Why did friendship between many men and women prove to be so fragile? Was this a happy society or did loneliness ensnare the Welsh people? How did children and youths resist their destiny?[8]

These are only a few of the questions which can be posed and offered to the future social historian of Victorian and Edwardian Wales. In seeking answers, a historian must use a wider range of evidence than has commonly been employed by Welsh historians. The historian must also be willing to boldly go and examine those areas of human experience which are relatively new for Welsh historical research. One such area is the study of human emotions. Ambition, anxiety, courage, compassion, desire, fear, friendship, generosity, hope, loneliness, love, malice, respect, spite and toleration are powerful forces in the lives of all individuals. To

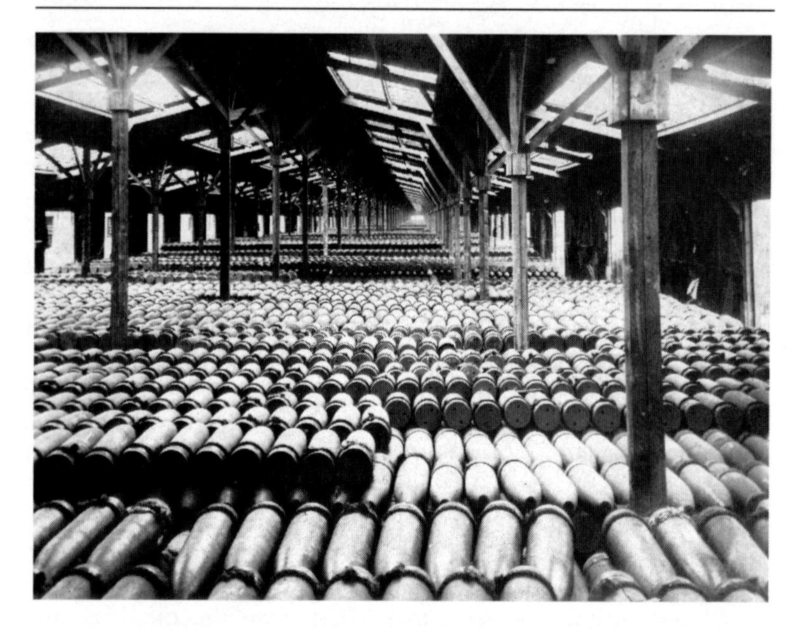

The sinister products of the Pen-bre munitions factory (By permission of Llyfrgell Genedlaethol Cymru/The National Library of Wales)

obtain a complete picture of society, the way that these emotions and forces affected and influenced individuals needs to be analysed, examined and understood. There is nothing new in historians advocating that a more imaginative approach be adopted for the study of human emotions. Since the 1940s a number of French historians have endeavoured to unravel the complex threads of this rich tapestry.[9] In the context, considered here examination of the influence of fear and love in the religious and public life of the nation, and of ambition and respect in economic and class relationships, can yield valuable new insights into the complex totality of Welsh society. They can serve as a key to unlock the door into new areas of human experience and provide insights into the true nature of Welsh society. In order to achieve this we have to equip ourselves as historians with the mental tools which will enable us to understand the concepts, ideas and views of the Welsh people. We have to try to discover the emotions that drove people to act in the way that they did at particular periods in our history in response to particular circumstances and stimuli.

In starting this conclusion, we recalled Gwyn Alf Williams's laconic lament at the lacuna in Welsh history. It is appropriate at the close therefore to repeat his terse treatise. In *The Welsh in Their History* he warns us:

> Before we can start applying any of our brilliant analytical techniques we have to learn the language in which the subjects of our inquiry conducted theirs. We need to cultivate humility before our subjects. We do not stand outside history. We are not gods, we are only apprentices to a craft.[10]

In the cultivation of that humility it is pertinent to note that the language of the majority of the Welsh people in Victorian and Edwardian Wales was the Welsh language. G. M. Young insisted that historians should 'go on reading until they can hear people talk'.[11] Unless we learn the language of the people and discover the meaning and nuances they placed on various words and phrases, we cannot understand their talk. In our apprecnticeship we have to acquire these linguistic skills and sensitivities before we can hope to graduate in Clio's 'sullen craft'. Perhaps then, Welsh History will cease to be history with the Welsh left out.

Notes

Abbreviations

Carm. Ant. *Carmarthenshire Antiquarian*

CROC Carmarthenshire Records Office, Carmarthen

NLW National Library of Wales

Introduction: Private Lives, Public Witnesses: The Individual and Society in Carmarthenshire

1 Lyn Hughes, *A Carmarthenshire Anthology* (Llandysul, 1984), p.xvii.

2 Rhys Davies, *Print of a Hare's Foot* (London, 1961), pp.3–4.

3 'Yr ias a gerdd trwy'n cnawd', D. Gwenallt Jones, 'Sir Gaerfyrddin' in *Eples* (Llandysul, 1951). In his later poem to the county, also entitled 'Sir Gaerfyrddin', published in the volume *Y Coed* (Llandysul, 1969), it is the rural areas of the county which represented the 'true' Carmarthenshire.

4 Both Gwenallt and Rhys Davies had strong family ties with Carmarthenshire. Their relationship with the county and their idealizations of the rural areas of Carmarthenshire are noted in David Rees, *Rhys Davies* (Cardiff, 1975) and Dyfnallt Morgan, *D. Gwenallt Jones* (Cardiff, 1972).

5 This translates as 'The scar which we try to hide/The convenient lie which we sweep under the carpet', Bryan Martin Davies, 'Y Glöwr', in *Darluniau ar Gynfas* (Llandysul, 1970). Please note these translations are provided only to give an indication of the meaning of the original. Considerable care should be taken if they are to be used as a source for quotations. There is a valuable collection of poetry and prose relating to the industrial experience of Carmarthenshire in Huw Walters, *Erwau'r Glo* (Swansea, 1976).

6 The best survey of the county's history is still J. E. Lloyd (ed.), *A History of Carmarthenshire*, 2 vols. (Cardiff, 1938 and 1939).

7 L. Toulmin Smith (ed.), *The Itinerary in Wales of John Leland in or about the year 1536–1539* (1906), pp.59–60.

8 For details of the county's early industrial history, see E. H. Brooke, *The Chronology of the Tinplate Works of Great Britain* (Cardiff, 1944); Michael C. S. Evans, 'The Llandyfân Forges', *The Carmarthen Antiquary*, IX (1973), pp.131–57; idem, 'The Cwmdwyfran Forge,

1697–1839', *Carm. Ant.*, IX (1975), pp.146–76; Terrence James, 'The Carmarthen Tinplate Works', *Carm. Ant.*, XII (1976); M. V. Symons, *Coal Mining in the Llanelli Area*, vol.1 (Llanelli, 1979).

9 The two sides of this historical gulf can be seen through studying the following works: on rural society, David Jenkins, *The Agricultural Community in South-West Wales at the turn of the Twentieth Century* (Cardiff, 1971); David W. Howell, *Land and People in Nineteenth Century Wales* (London, 1978); J. Geraint Jenkins, *Life and Tradition in Rural Wales* (London, 1976); on urban society, see David Smith, 'Wales through the Looking Glass', in David Smith (ed.), *A People and a Proletariat* (London, 1979), pp.215–39; idem, *Wales! Wales!* (London, 1983). Perhaps the differing viewpoint can be seen in sharpest contrast in Dyfnallt Morgan, *Y Wlad Sydd Well* (Llandysul, 1984) and Richard Cobb, 'Coming of Age', *New Statesman* (28 August 1981).

10 P. J. Waller, *Town, City, and Nation: England 1870–1914* (Oxford, 1984), p.239.

11 On the Welsh woollen industry in the nineteenth century, see J. Geraint Jenkins, *The Welsh Woollen Industry* (Cardiff, 1969), pp.249, 287.

12 As the *Cardigan and Tivyside Advertiser* noted, 'within days the pace of business in Newcastle Emlyn and Tivyside has quickened' (1 July 1895). Similar expectations were voiced when a station was opened at Henllan in Pentre-cwrt in February 1912, see Roger Hadfield and Barius Burgess, *The Teify Valley Railway* (Haverfordwest, 1974), p.12.

13 Gwyn Thomas, *A Welsh Eye* (London, 1964), pp.65–6.

14 On the economic and social changes brought about by railways, see Nicholas Faith, *The World the Railways Made* (London, 1990).

15 Several studies are available on the influx of labour into south Wales, for example P. N. Jones, 'Some Aspects of Immigration in the Glamorgan Coalfield between 1881 and 1911', *Transactions of the Honourable Cymmrodorion Society*, I (1969), pp.82–98. For the cultural and social experience of migration, see William D. Jones, *Wales in America: Scranton and the Welsh 1860–1920* (Cardiff, 1984).

16 E. P. Thompson, *The Making of the English Working Class* (Harmondsworth, 1979), p.13.

17 For a fuller discussion of the importance of the individual in history, see Richard Cobb, *Reactions to the French Revolution* (Oxford, 1971); idem, *The Police and the People: French Popular Protest, 1789–1820* (Oxford, 1970); David Smith, 'What Does History Know of Nailbiting?', *Llafur*, 1, 2 (1976), pp.34–41; Theodore Zeldin, *France 1848–1948*, 5 vols. (Oxford, 1979–80); *idem.*, 'Personal History and the History of the Emotions', *Journal of Social History*, 15, 3 (1982), pp.339–47; *idem.*, 'Ourselves as we See Us', *Times Literary Supplement*, 31 December 1982.

[18] Jose Harris provides illuminating comments on these themes in *Private Lives, Public Spirit: Britain 1870–1914* (Oxford, 1993), pp.1–3, 13–17 and 251–6.

[19] For the main themes on the concept of 'total history', see Peter Burke, 'People's History or Total History?' in Raphael Samuel (ed.), *People's History and Socialist Theory* (London, 1979), pp.4–9; Mark Bloch, *The Historian's Craft* (trans. Peter Putnam, Manchester, 1976); Paul Ricoeur, *The Contribution of French Historiography to the Theory of History* (Oxford, 1980); and François Furet, *In the Workshop of History* (Chicago, 1982). See also the contributions to the debate on the 'new history' in the *Times Higher Education Supplement*, 4 November 1983.

[20] For example, Carlo Ginzburg, *The Cheese and the Worms: The Cosmos of a Sixteenth-Century Miller* (London, 1980). The quotation is on p.xxvi.

[21] On the press in Wales, see Aled Jones, *Press, Politics and Society: A History of Journalism in Wales* (Cardiff, 1993).

[22] Carmarthenshire Records Office Carmarthen (hereafter CROC), *Quarter Sessions Papers*, Box 86, and *South Wales Press*, 25 September 1912.

[23] Michael Foot, *Aneurin Bevan* (St Albans, 1975).

[24] Robert Darnton, *The Great Cat Massacre and other Episodes in French Cultural History* (London, 1984), pp.3–5. For a discussion of the themes raised by Darnton, see Lynn Hunt (ed.), *The New Cultural History* (California, 1959), and Keith Thomas, 'History and Anthropology', *Past and Present*, 24 (1963), p.17.

[25] This paragraph has been deeply influenced by the arguments presented in Michel Vovelle, *Ideologies and Mentalities* (trans. Eamon O'Flaherty, London, 1990), especially the essays on 'The Relevance and Ambiguity of Literary Evidence', pp.24–35, and 'Serial History or Case Studies', pp.232–45.

[26] Eugen Weber, *France: Fin de Siècle* (London, 1986), pp.1–7.

[27] M. Vovelle, op. cit.

[28] For a similar approach, see Arlette Frage, *Fragile Lives: Violence, Power and Solidarity in Eighteenth Century Paris* (Oxford, 1993).

[29] These arguments have been well presented by Richard Cobb, *The Police and the People*, and Theodore Zeldin, *France 1848–1945*, *passim*.

[30] L. B. Namier, *Skyscrapers and Other Essays* (London, 1931), p.46.

[31] As John Clive has argued:

> The Victorian subconscious was haunted by fear and worry, by guilt, frustration and loneliness – all the symptoms of the syndrome of the age duly make their appearance in the lives of notable men and women . . . it is foolish to expect to find no contradiction, no

> struggle, no complexity in the individual psyche, it is even more foolish to be able to categorise the age as a whole in clearly distinct social and political terms, to choose obvious 'teams'.

(John Clive, *Not by Fact Alone: Essays on the Writing and Reading of History* (London, 1989), p.247.)

32 Gwyn A. Williams, *The Welsh in their History* (London, 1982), p.7.

33 The survival of such beliefs into the twentieth century was common in all areas of Britain, as Thomas Hardy showed clearly in his novels; see Ruth A. Prior, *Folkways in Thomas Hardy* (New York, 1962), and James Obelkevich, *Religion and Rural Society: South Lindsay, 1825–1875* (Oxford, 1976).

34 Perhaps the best sources for examples of the idealization of the family, as the cornerstone of society, are the nineteenth- century songs and poetry such as 'Y Teulu Dedwydd' by Samuel Roberts and 'Rheolau yr Aelwyd' by Mynyddog. Both these compositions and several others in the same genre are included in E. G. Millward, *Ceinion y Gân* (Llandysul, 1983).

35 See the review of Mary Midgley, *Wickedness: A Philosophical Essay* (London, 1984) in *The Guardian*, 12 September 1984.

36 The most notable contributions to the political and religious history of Wales in the nineteenth and twentieth centuries are Ieuan Gwynedd Jones, *Explorations and Explanations* (Llandysul, 1981); R. Tudur Jones, *Ffydd ac Argyfwng Cenedl: Hanes Crefydd yng Nghymru 1890–1914*, 2 vols. (Swansea, 1981 and 1982); Kenneth O. Morgan, *Wales in British Politics 1868–1922* (Cardiff, 1970); idem, *Rebirth of a Nation: Wales, 1880–1980* (Cardiff and Oxford, 1981); Glanmor Williams (ed.), *Merthyr Politics: The Making of a Working Class Tradition* (Cardiff, 1966); idem, *Religion, Language and Nationality in Wales* (Cardiff, 1979).

37 For some perceptive comments on political apathy, see Gwyn A. Williams, op. cit., pp.1–10; and J. Le Goff, 'Is Politics Still the Backbone of History?' in F. Gilbert and S. R. Graubert (eds.), *Historical Studies Today* (London, 1971), pp.337–55.

38 On Sir John Williams, see Ruth Evans, *John Williams 1840–1926* (Cardiff, 1952).

1 A Sense of Place

1 The Census details are as follows:

	1871	1921
Cardiganshire	73,441	60,881
Carmarthenshire	115,710	175,073
Glamorganshire	397,859	1,252,481
Pembrokeshire	91,824	91,778

Based on L. J. Williams, A *Digest of Welsh Historical Statistics*, Vol.1 (Cardiff, 1985), pp.72, 13, 17, 22.

[2] *Ibid.*, pp.62–7.

[3] Noel Gibbard, *Hanes Plwyf Llan-non* (Llandysul, 1984).

[4] Gomer M. Roberts, *Hanes Plwyf Llandybïe* (Cardiff, 1939).

[5] E. T. Lewis *et al.*, *Local Heritage: From Efailwen to Whitland*, Vol.1, pp.117–20; D. E. Jones, *Hanes Plwyf Llangler a Phenboyr* (Llandysul, 1897); pp.357–62.

[6] Muriel Bowen Evans, 'An Aspect of Population History in Carmarthenshire', *Carm. Ant.*, XIX (1983), p.55.

[7] F. G. Hannell, 'The Geographical Significance of Population Change in Carmarthenshire' (unpublished University of Bristol Ph.D. thesis, 1952), p.15.

[8] Brinley Thomas, 'Wales and the Atlantic Economy' in *The Welsh Economy: Studies in Expansion* (Cardiff, 1962), p.9. See also the same author's *Migration and Economic Growth* (Cambridge, 1954). Gwyn A. Williams, *When was Wales? A History of the Welsh* (London, 1985), pp.173–5. Between 1901 and 1911, Wales experienced a net growth of 98,492 through migration. The growth occurred in just four counties – Flintshire (1,573), Carmarthenshire (10,664), Glamorganshire (92,121) and Monmouthshire (34,408). Every other county in Wales experienced substantial losses of population. See L. J. Williams, op. cit., p.38.

[9] *Census of Population*, County of Carmarthen 1891, p.550; 1901, p.38.

[10] R. M. Thomas, 'The Linguistic Geography of Carmarthenshire, Glamorganshire and Pembrokeshire' (unpublished University of Wales (Aberystwyth) MA thesis, 1967), pp.58–9.

[11] J. E. Southall, *The Welsh Language Census of 1891* (Newport, 1895).

[12] But a notable feature of the Carmarthenshire work forces was a significant number of smallholders in the agricultural areas who tramped to work in the 'coal mountains', F. G. Hannell, op. cit., p.327. For the calculation of sex ratios, see Michael Drake, *Historical Demography: Problems and Projects* (London, 1975), p.24.

[13] Holmes, op. cit., pp.196–9. Jevons, op. cit., pp.667–9.

[14] Hannell, op. cit., p.276.

[15] For the employment of women in tinplate, see *Report on the Conditions of Employment in the Manufacture of Tinplate with special reference to the Process of Tinning* [Cd.6394] 1912, *passim*; see also Gwyn A. Williams, 'Women Workers in Contemporary Wales 1968–82', *Welsh History Review*, 11, 4 (1984), and L. J. Williams and Dot Jones, 'Women at Work in the Nineteenth Century', *Llafur*, 3, 3, pp.20–33.

[16] *Llanelly Mercury*, 25 August 1892.

[17] Huw Walters, *Canu'r Pwll a'r Pulpud* (Denbigh, 1987), p.8.

[18] 'Veritas', 'The Progress of Ammanford during 1889 with hints for its future development', *Carmarthen Journal*, 24 and 31 January 1890.

[19] Gomer M. Roberts, op. cit., *passim.*

[20] *Kelly's Directory of South Wales 1920* (Cardiff, 1921), pp.476–7.

[21] On the drive for local representation and the meaning of politics at a local level, see Ieuan Gwynedd Jones, *Health, Wealth and Politics in Victorian Wales* (Swansea, 1979) and *Communities* (Llandysul, 1987).

[22] Carmarthenshire Records Office Carmarthen (CROC), *Carmarthenshire County Council Minute Book*, 22 January 1902, p.337.

[23] CROC, CCC Minute Book, 22 January and 9 April 1902, pp.338–40.

[24] *South Wales Press*, 9 August 1900.

[25] Harold Carter, *The Towns of Wales: A Study in Urban Geography* (Cardiff, 1966), *passim.*

[26] For the histories of the towns, see: William Spurrell, *Carmarthen and its Neighbourhood* (Carmarthen, 1879); Pat Molloy, *A Shilling for Carmarthen* (Llandysul, 1980) and idem, *Four Cheers for Carmarthen* (Llandysul, 1981); Gareth Hughes, *A Llanelli Chronicle* (Llanelli, 1984); John Innes, *Old Llanelly* (Cardiff, 1902); D. Q. Bowen, *The Llanelli Landscape* (Llanelli, 1980); James Lane Bowen, *The History of Llanelli, Carmarthenshire* (Llanelli, 1886); and James Davies, *Llanelli Trade Directory and Local Guide* (Llanelli, 1897).

[27] *South Wales Press*, 6 August 1897.

[28] *Kelly's Directory*, op. cit., p.348.

[29] *Carmarthen Weekly Reporter*, 17 September 1897.

[30] *Carmarthen Journal*, 2 July 1892.

[31] *South Wales Press*, 11 July 1895.

[32] Ibid., 13 October 1898; *Carmarthen Journal*, 14 October 1898.

[33] Llanelli Borough Council, *Tinopolis and Scene of the National Eisteddfod of 1895, 1903 and 1930* (Llanelli, 1930).

[34] *Kelly's Directory*, op. cit., pp.507–23.

[35] *South Wales Press*, 7 March 1917.

[36] Alfred S. Williams and R. F. Kewer-Williams, *Who's Who in Llanelly and District* (Llanelli, 1910)

[37] *South Wales Press*, 7 March 1917.

[38] Ibid., 2 May 1895.

[39] *Carmarthen Weekly Reporter*, 28 July 1899.

[40] 'The light of the works travelled across the mountains like dawn to awaken the men of Gwynfe to cross the mountain.' Enoch Rees, *Hanes Brynamman a'r Cylchoedd*, 2nd edition (Ystalyfera, 1896), p.8.

[41] On the importance of work in late Victorian society, see Jose Harris, *Private Lives, Public Spirit: Britain 1870–1914* (Oxford, 1993),

pp.123–49 and F. M. L. Thompson, *The Rise of Respectable Society: A Social History of Victorian Britain 1830–1900* (London, 1988), pp.197–245.

42 For the history of the tinplate industry, see W. E. Minchinton, *The British Tinplate Industry* (Oxford, 1957), p.38.

43 The town took great pride in this title well into the twentieth century. In 1936 the official guide was grandiloquently entitled *Llanelly: Port, Industrial Centre, Tinopolis and Scene of the National Eisteddfodau of 1895, 1903 and 1930.* (Despite the many facilities of the town the guide was printed in London!)

44 Aman Tinplate Works 1881; Ashburnham (Burry Port) 1890; Burry Tinplate Works (Burry Port) 1875; Cambrian 1874, Pontarddulais Tinplate Co. 1875; Teilo 1880; Glamorgan Tinplate Works 1872 (Pontarddulais); Hendy Tinplate Works 1889; Morlais Tinplate Works (Llangennech) 1873; Gwendraeth Tinplate Works 1889; Raven Tinplate Works (Glanaman) 1881; Dynevor (Pantyffynnon) 1889. See E. H. Brooke, op. cit., *passim*.

45 Tinplate was also used in the dairying industry and for roofing in the USA.

46 Minchinton, op. cit., *passim*.

47 See Harold Hancocks, 'History of the Tinplate Manufacture in Llanelli' (unpublished University of Wales (Swansea) MA thesis, 1965, pp.163–85). Minchinton, op. cit., pp.77–92; and T. Eurwedd Williams Collection, 'Hanes Llanelli', NLW, MSS 10684C.

48 Ibid. The works were the Welsh Tinplate and Metal Stamping Co. (1891), Garnant Iron and Tinplate Co. (1904), Welfield Galvanising Works (1908), Dulais (1910), Gorse Dafen (1911), Pemberton Tinplate Co. (1911), and Bynea (1912).

49 E. H. Brooke, op. cit.

50 *Royal Commission on Coal*, CMD 360, 1919, p.195. Quoted in Thomas Hughes Griffiths, 'The Development of the south Wales Anthracite Coal Area with Special Reference to its Industrial and Labour Organisation' (unpublished University of Wales (Aberystwyth) MA thesis, 1922), p.61.

51 H. S. Jevons, *The British Coal Trade* (London, reprint, 1969), p.663. Jevons noted that the production of anthracite had doubled during the previous twelve years and that the quality was shown in the high foreign demand. See also G. M. Holmes, 'The south Wales Coal Industry 1850–1914', *Transactions of the Honourable Society of Cymmrodorion*, 1976, p.170.

52 Ibid., p.667.

53 D. T. Rosser, 'A Regional and Economic Survey of the Anthracite Area of Carmarthenshire' (unpublished University of Wales (Aberystwyth) MA thesis, 1948), p.73.

54 The First World War was particularly damaging because of the loss of the industry's major markets, the ravages of the U-Boats and the blockade of European ports. See David James Davies, 'The South Wales anthracite industry with special reference to changes in business organisation since Government decontrol in 1921, and their social effects' (unpublished University of Wales (Aberystwyth) MA thesis, 1930), Chapter II; and Thomas Hughes Griffith, op. cit., pp.78–111.

55 See D. Russell Davies, 'A Social History of Carmarthenshire 1870–1920' (unpublished University of Wales (Aberystwyth) Ph.D. thesis, 1989), Table 2. H. S. Jevons, op. cit., p.665.

56 D. T. Rosser, op. cit., p.86.

57 Aneirin Talfan Davies, *Crwydro Sir Gâr* (Llandysul, 1955), p.277.

58 D. T. Rosser, op. cit., p.66.

59 H. W. E Davies, 'The Development of the Industrial Landscape of Western South Wales During the Nineteenth and Twentieth Centuries' (unpublished University of London (London School of Economics) M.Sc. (Econ.) thesis, 1955), p.73.

60 Ibid.

61 D. T. Rosser, op. cit., p.66.

62 Raymond E. Bowen, op. cit.

63 *South Wales Press*, 20 March 1912; Raymond E. Bowen, op. cit., p.84.

64 Geraint Wyn Jones, 'Dirywiad Dociau Llanelli' (unpublished University of Wales (Aberystwyth) BA thesis, 1984), pp.20–2.

65 Ibid.

66 I. K. Brunel, 'Port of Llanelly. Harbour Improvements Report to the Commissioners', CROC, Mansel Lewis Papers (1857). Also quoted in Geraint Wyn Jones, op. cit., p.2.

67 Clarence S. Howells, *Transport Facilities in the Mining and Industrial Districts of South Wales and Monmouthshire* (London, 1911), pp.14–16. Writing in 1911, Howells noted the problems of Llanelli:

> apart from the tinplate trade and other industries already established, it would be very optimistic to predict any great development of Llanelly as a port. Its bad situation in relation to the open sea, and the failure of engineers to produce a scour sufficient to create a deep-water entrance to the harbour, alike depreciate Llanelly's chance, even if any great extension of dock facilities took place in the future. With Swansea the opposite holds (p.42).

68 House of Lords Select Committee, *Evidence*, 18 June 1896, pp.9–11. For comparable statistics of Llanelli and Swansea, see L. J. Williams, *Digest of Welsh Historical Statistics*, Vol.2 (Cardiff, 1986), pp.45–55.

[69] For Nobel's, see Raymond E. Bowen, op. cit., p.87; and *History of the Ministry of Munitions*, Vol.III (London, HMSO, 1922), pp.172–3.

[70] Llanelly and District Electric Lighting and Traction Co. Ltd., *Prospectus* (Llanelli, 1914), and NLW, *House of Commons Local Government Legislation (Wales). Electric Lighting Orders Confirmation (No 3) Act* [2 & 3 Geo 5] [Ch.CXVI]. For the industry, see R. H. Morgan, 'The Development of the Electricity Supply Industry in Wales to 1919', *Welsh History Review*, II, 3 (1983), pp.317–37.

[71] James Lane Bowen, *The History of Llanelly, Carmarthenshire* (Llanelli, 1886), p.30.

[72] Russell Davies, 'The Importance of Motor Omnibus Passenger Services in South West Wales as Illustrated by the 1935 Bus Strike,' *Carm.Ant.*, XX (1984), pp.87–92.

[73] *South Wales Press*, 14 March 1914.

[74] *Carmarthen Journal*, 6 January 1888.

[75] Roscoe Howells, *Old Saundersfoot: From Monkstone to Marros* (Llandysul, 1977).

[76] The woollen industry has been well served by its historians, particularly J. Geraint Jenkins, *The Welsh Woollen Industry* (Cardiff, 1966). See also Gwenllian Evans, 'The Welsh Woollen Industry: Recent History and Present Position' (unpublished University of Wales (Aberystwyth) MA thesis, 1948), and A. C. Darragh, 'The Welsh Woollen Industry' (unpublished University of Wales (Aberystwyth) Ph.D. thesis, 1980).

[77] 'It is unlikely that there are in Wales another two parishes which produce as much Welsh flannel as these two parishes . . . There are more weavers than ever before, and the majority are fully employed. Almost all the natural energy of the rivers and streams has been tapped to drive the industry's engines. There is almost no spot alongside a river available to locate a new factory or mill.' D. E. Jones, *Hanes Llangeler a Phenboyr* (Llandysul, 1897), p.357.

[78] J. Geraint Jenkins, op. cit., p.256.

[79] Ibid., p.258.

[80] Gwenllian Evans, op. cit., pp.150–5. On the University's extra mural work in the period, see E.L. Ellis, *The University College of Wales, Aberystwyth 1872–1972* (Cardiff, 1972), Chapters 4 and 5, *passim*.

[81] A. C. Darragh, op. cit., p.188.

[82] For the events of 1921 and 1926, see Margaret Morris, *The General Strike* (Harmondsworth, 1976); Christopher Farman, *The General Strike: May 1926* (St Albans, 1972); David Smith and Hywel Francis, *The Fed* (London, 1980); J. Geraint Jenkins, op. cit., p.278.

[83] See, for example, David Howell, *Land and People in Nineteenth Century Wales* (London, 1978), pp.xi–xiv and 148–57. Idem 'Rural Society in Nineteenth Century Carmarthenshire', *Carm. Ant.*, XIII

(1977), pp.72–83; Spencer Thomas, 'The Agricultural Labour Force in some South-west Carmarthenshire Parishes in the Mid Nineteenth Century', *Welsh History Review*, 3, 1 (1966), pp.63–72. See also the following unpublished University of Wales theses: Alan Bainbridge, 'The Agricultural Community in Carmarthenshire c.1876–1896' (Swansea MA, 1975); J. H. Davies, 'Society and Economy in South-West Wales' (Aberystwyth MA, 1967); Muriel B. Evans, 'The Community and Social Change in the Parish of Trelech a'r Bettws During the Nineteenth Century' (Aberystwyth MA, 1980).

84 John Williams, op. cit., p.207.

85 Rhys Davies, op. cit., pp.3–4.

86 For the abandonment of farms see J. W. G. Jasper, 'A Study of the Changes that have taken place in Farm Size in Carmarthenshire since the End of the Nineteenth Century' (unpublished University of Wales (Aberystwyth) M.Sc., 1959), pp.76–82. The struggle to carve out a living from inhospitable land is often the backcloth for the more sinister events of Caradoc Evans' short stories. 'The Way of the Earth', for example, is a mournful portrayal of farmland returning to its uncultivated state before the eyes of its powerless cultivator (Caradoc Evans, op. cit., pp.32–44).

87 John Williams, op. cit., p.228.

88 David Howell, 'The Impact of Railways on Agricultural Development in Nineteenth-Century Wales', *Welsh History Review*, 7, No.1 (1974), pp.40–62.

89 John Davies and Gordon Mingay, 'Agriculture in an Industrial Environment' in A. H. John and Glanmor Williams (eds.), op. cit., pp.292–308. See also A. W. Jones, 'Agriculture and the Rural Community of Glamorgan c.1830–1896' (unpublished University of Wales (Swansea) Ph.D. thesis, 1980), p.561; and David Howell, 'Farming in South East Wales' in L. J. Williams (ed.), *Essays on Modern Welsh Economic History* (Cardiff, 1986).

90 D. Morgan, *The Story of Carmarthenshire* (Cardiff, 1909), p.26.

91 D. Howell, 'The Impact of Railways', p.54.

92 David Howell, *Land and People*, p.70.

93 *Return of the Owners of Land 1873* (c.1097) 1874 LXXII; Vol.2 has the Welsh statistics; John Bateman, *The Great Landowners of Great Britain and Ireland* (1st edn 1876, reprinted Leicester, 1971), p.501. For an analysis of the returns, see Brian Ll. James, 'The Great Landowners of Wales in 1873', *National Library of Wales Journal*, XIV, 3 (1965–6), pp.301–17.

94 Ibid.

95 David Howell, 'Rural Society', *Carm. Ant.*, p.72.

96 A. W. Ashby and I. L. Evans, *The Agriculture of Wales* (Cardiff, 1944), p.96.

[97] Edgar Thomas, *The Economics of Small holdings: A Study based on a Survey of Small Scale Farming in Carmarthenshire* (Cambridge 1927). I am grateful to Dr D. Roberts for this reference.

[98] Ibid.

[99] J. W. Jasper, op. cit., p.52.

[100] For the tradition of 'tramping' to the works, see Huw Walters, 'Gweithgarwch Llenyddol Dyffryn Aman' (unpublished University of Wales (Aberystwyth) Ph.D. thesis, 1985), pp.11–13. In *Yn Chwech ar Hugain Oed* (Llandysul, 1964), D. J. Williams noted the existence of collier smallholders at the turn of the twentieth century in the Aman Valley: '[r'oedd] llawer o 'r gweithwyr newydd adael y tir o'r tu hwnt i'r garreg galch, eraill yn parhau i fyw yn y tyddynnod bach o gwmpas yn cadw buwch neu ddwy a gweithio gartref fin nos pan fyddai angen a chyfle . . .' ('Several miners had just left the land beyond the limestone hills, others continued to live in small cottages scattered about, keeping a cow or two, working at home in the evenings whenever there was a need and an opportunity.') (p.148).

[101] David Jenkins, *The Agricultural Community in South-west Wales at the Turn of the Twentieth Century* (Cardiff, 1971), pp.39–73; idem, 'Trefn Ffarm a Llafar Gwlad', *Ceredigion*, IV, 3 (1962), pp.244–54; idem, 'The Community and the Land in South Cardiganshire at the close of the nineteenth century', *Folk Life*, 8 (1970), pp.5–12; and 'Rural Society Inside Outside' in David Smith (ed.), *A People and a Proletariat* (London, 1980), pp.114–26.

[102] NLW, Glyneiddan MSS 92, p.2.

[103] David Jenkins, *Agricultural Community*, pp.50–3.

[104] Ibid., p.138.

[105] 'Y forwyn fawr' = the chief maidservant; 'yr ail forwyn' = the second servant; 'y forwyn fach' = the young, junior maidservant. NLW, Glyneiddas MSS 92, p.4.

[106] David Jenkins, op. cit., p.58.

[107] 'This was called the payment of harvest debt. The common people were deeply indebted to the farmers in this respect. They had received loads of manure for their potatoes and a few rows of the farmer's field to plant potatoes in, they had also received loads of logs from the woods and loam and peat from the moors, and material for their roofs. Several jugs of milk and oatmeal had also been sent to them, as had thousands of small favours of many types during the year, all these were part of the debt that was outstandong at harvest time.' D. E. Jones, op. cit., p.332. See also D. Parry Jones, *Welsh Country Characters* (London, 1952), pp.98–102; *My Own Folk* (Llandysul, 1972), pp.49–50.

[108] David Jenkins, op. cit., p.53. The payment of labour varied across the county. In the Llanboidy area in west Carmarthenshire it was the custom that:

> Potato ground is given to the labourers, for which women, too, have to pay at the rate of one day's work for every load of manure . . . Men who work in Glamorganshire, but have left their families at home living in such cottages, have to return to work at the harvest.
>
> (*Royal Commission on Labour: The Agricultural Labourer Report* by Mr D. Lleufer Thomas on the Narberth Union [Vol.II, Wales], 1893–4, [c.6894 – XIV] Vol.XXXVI, p.68.)

109 The school log books of the period 1880–1910 are dotted with reports of schools being forced to close because of the harvest. The following is taken from the log book of Nantcwmrhys School, Cynwil Elfed, 22 April 1896: 'Decrease in attendance again today. Several of the families are planting potatoes; weather most favourable.' (CROC, *Education Book*, 154, 2 vols.)

110 Ibid., p.107. Evidence of Nathaniel Williams, tenant farmer, Llandeilo (Q38,652).

111 Ibid., p.113. Evidence of Gwilym Evans, Chairman, Carmarthen County Council (Q38,765).

112 Ibid. Evidence on behalf of the tenants of the parish presented by Thomas Hopkins, tenant farmer, Llangadog (Q39,492).

113 Ibid. Evidence of John Davies, tenant farmer, Llanddeusant.

114 Ibid.

115 Ibid. Evidence of R. Morgan, Independent Minister (Q41,051).

116 See F. M. L. Thompson, *English Landed Society* (London, 1980 edn), G. E. Mingay, *Rural Life in Victorian England* (London, 1977).

117 Quoted in David Cannadine, *The Decline and Fall of the British Aristocracy* (London, 1992), p.16.

118 D. C. Moore, 'The Landed Aristocracy' and 'The Gentry' in G. E. Mingay (ed.), *The Victorian Countryside*, Vol.2 (London, 1981), pp.367–88 and 383–98.

119 David Williams, *The Rebecca Riots: A Study in Agrarian Discontent* (Cardiff, 1971), Chapter 1, pp.3–7; David W. Howell, *Patriarchs and Parasites: The Gentry of south-west Wales in the Eighteenth Century* (Cardiff, 1986), p.13.

120 John Bateman, *The Great Landowners of Great Britain and Ireland*, reprinted with an introduction by David Spring (Leicester, 1971), *passim*.

121 Lord Dynevor also owned 221 acres in Oxford, Wiltshire and Gloucester (Brian Ll. James, 'The Great Landowners of Wales in 1873', *National Library of Wales Journal*, XIV, 3 (1965–6), pp.30–1.

122 Ibid.

123 See, for example, H. M. Vaughan, *The South Wales Squires: A Welsh Picture of Social Life* (London, 1924). A series of articles appeared in

the *South Wales Daily News* between 1909 and 1912 on 'Welsh Country Houses'. In each the ancestry of the family is stressed. See, for example, the entries on Derwydd, 4 September 1911. Through dubious heraldry, Colonel Rice Trevor, fourth Baron Dynevor, was traced back to Hywel Dda (ibid., 26 February 1910). However, it was not until 1917 that Rice was Cymricized to Rhys (*Cambria Daily Leader*, 22 January 1917). The following estates of south-west Wales were featured in the series: Golden Grove, 27 November 1909; Picton Castle, 15 and 22 January 1910; Dynevor Castle, 26 February 1910; Llanarth Court, 9 and 16 April 1910; Glyn Eos, 11 March 1911; Dolau Cothi, 18 July 1911; Edwinsford, 19 and 22 July 1911; and Derwydd, 4 and 9 September 1911.

124 *Carmarthen Journal*, 8 August 1890.

125 On the menu were 'Salmon à la Mayonaise deone, Raised paté's various, Lamb à la Cygre, Spiced Beef, Cutlets à la Rothschild au Aspice, Prawns à la Indurine Garni, Lobster à la Mayonaise, Sweetbread Cutlets aux Truffles, Chicken vardi, Fared Ducks, Pigeon Pies, Sirloin Beef with Horseradish Sauce', and, for those with less cosmopolitan palates, Lamb with Mint Sauce.

126 *Carmarthen Journal*, 21 October 1910.

127 Ibid., 7 September 1894.

128 *Carmarthen Weekly Reporter*, 7 April 1899.

129 *Carmarthen Journal*, 22 July 1899.

130 *South Wales Press*, 20 October 1915.

131 Ibid., 30 July 1915. On the deference in industrial society, see David Cannadine, 'From Feudal Lord to Figurehead', in *Urban History Yearbook 1978* (London, 1979).

132 John Davies, 'The End of the Great Estates and the Rise of Freehold Farming in Wales', *Welsh History Review*, 7, 2 (1974), pp.186–212.

133 There were notable exceptions such as Lady Howard of Llanelli who was a prominent member of the Gorsedd (*Llanelly and County Guardian*, 28 September 1910). For the education of squires, see Bateman, op. cit.

134 *South Wales Daily News*, 29 July 1910.

135 Ibid., 8 July 1911.

136 Ibid., 29 July 1911.

137 H. M. Vaughan, op. cit., pp.32–3; *Carmarthen Journal*, 12 September 1890.

138 Tom Rees, *Racing Reminiscences: Recollections of Hunters and Hunting in west Wales* (reprinted Cwmnedd Press, 1977) pp.37–9. For the Tivyside Hunt, see H. M. Vaughan, op. cit., p.47.

139 Tom Rees, op. cit., p.24.

140 Ibid., pp.3–20.

141 Ibid.

[142] *Carmarthen Journal*, 9 May 1890.
[143] For a biography, see J. Austin Jenkins, *South Wales and Monmouthshire at the Opening of the Twentieth Century: Contemporary Biographies* (Brighton, 1907), p.222. For an assessment of his Rugby career, see David Smith and Gareth Williams, *Fields of Praise: The Official History of the Welsh Rugby Union 1881–1981* (Cardiff, 1980), p.44.
[144] *Royal Commission on Land*, Vol.III, *passim*. The *Calendar* of the Dynevor papers in the Carmarthenshire Records Office, Carmarthen, gives ample evidence of Lord Dynevor's willingness to grant leases.
[145] M. J. Symmons, *Coalmining in the Llanelli District*, *passim*.
[146] Ieuan Gwynedd Jones, *Health, Wealth and Politics in Victorian Wales* (Swansea, 1979), pp.15–21; idem, 'The People's Health in Mid-Victorian Wales', *Transactions of the Honourable Society of Cymmrodorion*, 1984, pp.118–21.
[147] T. Austin Jenkins, op. cit., p.258.
[148] Ibid., p.267.
[149] Ibid., p.306.
[150] Ibid., p.318.
[151] Ibid., p.327.
[152] Ibid., p.334.
[153] Alfred S. Williams and Reginald F. Kewer-Williams, *Who's Who in Llanelly and District* (Llanelli, 1910).
[154] Ibid., p.17.
[155] Ibid., p.19; David Smith and Gareth Williams, op. cit., p.464.
[156] Ibid., p.25.
[157] Ibid., p.29.
[158] Ibid., p.47.
[159] Ibid., pp.21, 45.
[160] Ibid.
[161] *South Wales Press*, 24 February, 23 June 1909.
[162] Ibid., 28 April 1898.
[163] Madame Rose, 'Christmas in the House', *South Wales Press*, 14 December 1899.
[164] *South Wales Press*, 9 October 1917.
[165] K. O. Morgan, *Rebirth of a Nation: Wales 1880–1980* (Cardiff and Oxford, 1982), p.53.
[166] *Carmarthen Weekly Reporter*, 10 April 1903.
[167] Sidney J. Phillips, 'The Abolition of Poverty', *South Wales Press*, 4 February 1914.
[168] See D. Russell Davies, op. cit., Table 4.
[169] John Williams, *Digest of Welsh Historical Statistics*, Vol.1 (Cardiff, 1986), pp.172–3.
[170] Ibid.

[171] W. E. Minchinton, *The British Tinplate Industry* (Oxford, 1957), p.221.

[172] John Williams, op. cit., p.172.

[173] *Carmarthen Weekly Reporter*, 12 March 1915.

[174] Ibid.

[175] Ibid., 13 September 1918.

[176] *South Wales Press*, 22 November 1916.

[177] Colin Bundy and Dermot Healy, 'Aspects of Urban Poverty', *Oral History*, 6, 1 (1978), pp.79–98.

[178] Charles Booth, *Life and Labour of the People of London* (London, 1895), *passim*; Seebohm Rowntree, *Poverty: A Study in Town Life* (London, 1901).

[179] *South Wales Press*, 3 March 1904, 6 March 1912, and 30 July 1903. For the pawnbroker's role in local communities, see Melanie Tibbutt, *Making Ends Meet: Pawnbroking and Working-Class Credit* (Leicester, 1983).

[180] *South Wales Press*, 21 September 1905. Stephen Humphries, 'Steal to Survive: The Social Crime of Working Class Children, 1890–1940.' *Oral History*, 9, 1 (1981), pp.23–33.

[181] *Carmarthen Weekly Reporter*, 10 August 1900.

[182] *South Wales Press*, 18 June 1891.

[183] *Llanelly Mercury*, 17 November 1892; *South Wales Press*, 14 March 1895; *Carmarthen Journal*, 20 July 1894.

[184] *Carmarthen Weekly Reporter*, 15 October 1897.

[185] *South Wales Press*, 22 August 1895.

[186] John Williams, 'The Great Miner's Strike of 1898 in South Wales', *Morgannwg* IX (1965).

[187] See, for example, the synopsis of articles from *The Shipping World* by Major E. R. Jones in the *South Wales Press*, 6 April and 19 May 1892.

[188] Ibid., 14 November 1895; *Carmarthen Journal*, 17 May 1895.

[189] *Carmarthen Weekly Reporter*, 14 March 1902.

[190] David Smith and Hywel Francis, *The Fed* (London, 1980).

[191] For rural deference, see R. J. Colyer, 'The Gentry and the County in Nineteenth Century Cardiganshire', *Welsh History Review*, 10, 4 (1981), p.497: 'In the eyes of the tenants and the poor, the early nineteenth century Cardiganshire squire served the function of leader of local opinion, adviser on all manner of problems, and sympathetic patron in times of distress.'

[192] The granting of rent abatements and the unfulfilled expectations of such abatements was one of the themes of the witnesses before the Royal Commission on Land in 1896 (Vol.III, *passim*).

[193] Although he was a wealthy man. Gwilym Evans gave up the Liberal candidature in 1898 because of its cost.

[194] *Carmarthen Journal*, 28 December 1877.

[195] *South Wales Press*, 28 March 1912.

[196] Ibid., 3 April 1912. The editor of the *Carmarthen Weekly Reporter* noted in his edition of 27 January 1911:

> The crowds of people who throng to the soup kitchen on Friday and Tuesday show how acute must be the misery which exists in certain parts of the town. One may see such a sight as that of a woman with a baby on her left arm, a jug of soup in her right hand, 2 children clinging to her skirts, and a little boy running on eagerly in front with the loaf in his hand – on the way home from the distribution. There must be a tremendous amount of real misery in the town or there would not be such keen competition for such a dole.

[197] Ibid.

[198] Ibid., 21 February 1895. In 1912, the Distress Committee was still in existence, the major donations being Vint's Theatre Ltd. with £20, and James Haggar's Theatre Ltd. with £15.5*s*.

[199] For a fuller discussion of this theme of co-operation between classes, see Ieuan Gwynedd Jones, 'The People's Health in Mid-Victorian Wales', *Transactions of the Honourable Society of Cymmrodorion*, 1954, pp.115–47, especially p.146.

[200] James Walvin, *Victorian Values* (London, 1987), pp.96–108.

[201] *South Wales Press*, 3 May 1888.

[202] *Carmarthen Weekly Reporter*, 27 January 1911.

[203] Ibid., 15 December 1915.

[204] Alun Eirug Davies, 'Poverty and its Treatment in Cardiganshire 1750–1850' (unpublished University of Wales (Aberystwyth) MA thesis, 1968);. M. A. Crowther, *The Workhouse System 1834–1929: The History of an English Social Institution* (London, 1981); Karel Williams, *From Pauperism to Poverty* (London, 1981).

[205] A total institution is an institution which takes complete control of all aspects of an individual's life. Ervin Goffman, *Asylums: Essays on the Social Situation of Mental Patients and other Inmates* (Harmondsworth, 1968). See below, Chapter 2, for a discussion of the Carmarthen Joint Counties Lunatic Asylum.

[206] She was, however, provided for to some extent as she received 1*s*.6*d*. from one of her children, and a daughter was in receipt of £10 per annum plus a pig a year for saving the life of the child (*South Wales Press*, 28 February 1895).

[207] Ibid., Cd.272, 1906, p.4.

[208] Ibid., p.38. The numbers were Llanelli (+ 14), Llandeilofawr (+ 32) and Carmarthen (+ 23).

209 This poem is included in E. G. Millward, *Ceinion y Gân: Detholiad o Ganeuon Poblogaidd Oes Victoria* (Llandysul, 1983), p.43.

210 CROC, Penlan Workhouse MSS 158, *Register of Births at the Workhouse*.

211 CROC, Abercennen Workhouse MSS 178, *Register of Births at the Workhouse*.

212 The average age at the workhouse was over 55 (see CROC, Abercennen 327, *Vagrants Admission and Discharge Book*). Between 1880 and 1913, the average of deaths per annum at the Llandeilo (Fawr) Workhouse is five (CROC, Abercennen 649, *Register of Deaths*). Sons and daughters of elderly people were frequently brought before courts by the Poor Law officers to face charges of refusing to support their parents. See, for example, *Carmarthen Weekly Reporter*, 20 September 1907.

213 *South Wales Press*, 6 January 1909. In Pencader, twenty-three old age pensioners dressed up in their bowler hats and their Sunday best to collect their pensions for the first time (*Carmarthen Journal*, 12 February 1909). In Llanelli over 400 elderly persons crammed into the General Post Office and up to a hundred turned up at sub-post offices to receive the applications forms. There was a scramble at the Registrar's Office to get hold of copies of the Parish Registers to prove longevity (*South Wales Press*, 30 September 1908). Some women even exaggerated their age. Sarah Lewis of Gosport, Llangennech, was fined £2 and £2.1*s*. in costs at the Carmarthen County Police Court for making fraudulent claims for an old age pension (*Carmarthen Journal*, 25 March 1910). After a forty-year courtship one couple now decided that the Old Age Pension provided them with sufficient means to marry (ibid.).

214 In 1897, a vehement debate broke out in the Llanelli Board of Guardians between Mrs Knotts and Mrs Paton. Mrs Knotts had suggested that workhouse girls should be dressed like the other girls with whom they attended school. The Board agreed (*South Wales Press*, 21 October 1897). However, others feared for the young girls' morals as they had to associate with a 'certain class of woman' at the workhouse (ibid., 7 September, 13 July 1899).

215 Millward, op. cit. p.42.

216 *Census of Population of Great Britain, Carmarthenshire*, p.36.

217 Rachel Vorspan, 'Vagrancy and the New Poor Law in Victorian and Edwardian England', *English Historical Review*, XCII, 362 (1977), pp.59–81. D. J. V. Jones, ' "A Dead Loss to the Community". The Criminal Vagrant in Mid-Nineteenth Century Wales', *Welsh History Review*, 8, between the vagrant and crime, see below, Chapter 4.

218 'Though the period after 1870 has been considered as a period of heightened public concern for the plight of the poor and the

unemployed, the social literature of these decades exhibits even more obviously an obsession with the "undeserving segments of society"' (Rachel Vorspan, op. cit., p.81). For the social fear of vagrancy, see Gareth Steadman Jones, *Outcast London: A Study in the Relationship Between Classes in Victorian Society* (Harmondsworth, 1984), pp.127–52.

219 *Carmarthen Weekly Reporter*, 28 January 1910.

220 In November 1898, Llanelli had over 1,700 persons in receipt of Outdoor-Poor Relief (*Return on Poor Law Relief* Cd.272, 1898). For the difficulties of definition, see the report on the Board of Guardians (*South Wales Press*, 17 November 1898).

221 'Bona fides' were people 'genuinely seeking work' (*The Welshman*, 19 September 1913).

222 For the way-ticket system, see *The Welshman*, 20 June 1913; *Carmarthen Weekly Reporter*, 19 May 1916, 26 June 1913; *South Wales Press*, 10, 24 June, 11 November 1914.

223 The tasks to be undertaken varied between workhouses; at Carmarthen two cwt of stones were to be cut so that they would pass through a 2″ grill, at Llandeilo, four cwt of stones; at Llanelli the task was chopping four cwt of stones, at Narberth four cwt of stones; Newcastle Emlyn was harsher with eight cwt of stones; Llandovery three cwt of stones. Breaches of workhouse discipline resulted in the punishment of the offender in the Police Court and transfer to the prison. See CROC, MSS. Abercennen 526, *Punishment Book*, 24 August 1880.

224 CROC, *Board of Guardians Minute Books: Landeilofawr*, Vols.31, 35, 38, 46 and 89; Llandovery, Vols.59 and 18.

225 Vorspan, op. cit., pp.63–4; CROC, Abercennen 327, *Vagrants Admission and Discharge Book*.

226 *Carmarthen Weekly Reporter*, 19 February 1904.

227 *The Welshman*, 20 June 1913.

228 *Carmarthen Weekly Reporter*, 23 October 1903.

229 For Llandeilo, see *South Wales Press*, 11 May 1905; for Carmarthen, see *Carmarthen Weekly Reporter*, 14 April and 14 July 1905.

230 On being sentenced to fourteen days in prison in 1905, a tramp thanked the Carmarthen Magistrates (ibid., 24 November 1905).

231 'The Tramp and His Ways' by 'Amateur Casual', *Carmarthen Journal*, 26 August 1890. On social explorers in general, see Peter Keating (ed.), *Into Unknown England: Selections from the Social Explorers* (London, 1978).

232 'Strange Characters I have met in Llanelly' by 'Amateur Casual', *Llanelly Mercury*, 22 June 1911. For 'The Western Prophet', see *Carmarthen Weekly Reporter*, 3 January 1908; for the 'ballad seller' see ibid., 5 August 1904. See also Councillor Robert Williams, 'How the

Very Poor Live', *Swansea and District Workers Journal*, April 1912, p.12; D. Richards, 'The Casual Ward', ibid., May 1910; and 'Life with "Weary Willy"', *The Welshman*, 10 February 1905.

[233] *Carmarthen Weekly Reporter*, 25 December 1896. Wales had a celebrated tramp in the early twentieth century – W. H. Davies, the self-styled 'Super-Tramp'. See Richard J. Stonisfer, *W. H. Davies: A Critical Biography* (London, 1963), especially pp.44–72. W. H. Davies, *The Autobiography of a Super-Tramp* (London, 6th edition 1926), and *Beggars* (London, 1919), are valuable for first-hand experiences of vagrants and casual labourers. Kellow Chesney, *The Victorian Underworld* (Harmondsworth, 1976), pp.229–69 has a description of the tricks used by beggars.

[234] *Carmarthen Weekly Reporter*, 5 April 1907. The same report gives details of those beggars on the bridge in Carmarthen the previous Saturday:

> A third [man] was even more aggressive. He had only one leg, but he could get about faster on it than most people can do on two. He held his cap in the way of the wayfarers and, if he saw anybody trying to dodge him by going to the other side of the road, he promptly hopped over into their way and presented his cap in front of them.

[235] CROC, Museum Collection 654, *Common Lodging Home Report Book*, Carmarthen 1886–91.

[236] For reports of Ada Thompson's convictions, see *Carmarthen Journal*, 8 November 1901, 13 May 1904, 10 June 1904, 12 April 1907, *Carmarthen Weekly Reporter*, 15 June 1906, 12 April 1907, 19 July 1907, 25 October 1907, 7 August 1908, and *The Welshman*, 7 January 1910.

[237] *Carmarthen Journal*, 23 November 1900. On 28 June 1907 the editor of the *Carmarthen Weekly Reporter* quipped:

> Thank God for Mill Street – otherwise we would not have a Police court. Several languages are spoken here . . . but they don't take any interest in the Pan-Celtic movement. The only approach to that movement made in this neighbourhood is when one Celt hits another in the face with a frying pan. They are quite a harmless lot when they are sober but many of them are drunk from the 1st of January – 31st December.

Confirmation of the Celtic nature of the common lodging- houses of Carmarthenshire is given in a report of the case against John Walsh, a labourer on six charges of assault, criminal damage and being drunk and disorderly at the Prospect Place Lodging House, Llanelli. When arrested he was shouting 'Long Live the Sinn Feiners' and 'Home Rule for Ireland' (*Cambrian Daily Leader*, 2 May 1916).

238 Terry Coleman, *The Railway Navvies* (Harmondsworth, 1981).

239 *Llanelly Mercury*, 30 August 1900; *Carmarthen Journal*, 10 October 1902; *Carmarthen Weekly Reporter*, 23 October 1914.

240 *History of the Ministry of Munitions*, Vol.III (London, HMSO, 1922), p.172.

241 *South Wales Press*, 17 March, 21 April, 8 and 29 May, 18 and 25 August, 1 September, 26 October 1915. So frequent were charges against labourers at the construction site that the *South Wales Press*, in reporting seventeen cases of drunkenness, dubbed them 'The Endless Army' (ibid., 8 December 1915).

242 Ibid., 21 July 1915.

243 Thomas Jones was the person who suffered most damage during the Llanelli riots of 1911 (see below). In several decisions as a justice of the peace he appears to have been hard-headed towards the working classes of the town (*South Wales Press*, 25 March 1908). See also ibid., 18 November 1897 and 5 August 1908.

244 See, for example, J. P. Waller, *Town, City, and Nation: England 1850–1914* (Oxford, 1983), pp.213–16 and Gareth Steadman Jones, op. cit.

245 Millward, op. cit.; Huw Williams, *Canu'r Bobl*. 'Home', 'The Cottage on the Hill', 'My Grandmother's Little Cottage', 'The Little Thatched-Roof Cottage'.

246 For a full text, see Millward, op. cit., p.6. 'I lost my father. I lost my mother in the little thatched-roof cottage.'

247 D. Lleufer Thomas, *Report on the Agricultural Labourer in the Poor Law Union of Narberth*, HC 1893–4 (C 6894-XIV) XXVI, p.63.

248 Ibid.

249 Ibid.

250 *Third and Fourth Reports of the Commissioners on Employment of Women and Children in Agriculture with Appendices* [C 70] 1870, Vol.XIII, p.12. For cottages, see also Royal Commission on Land, Vol.III, *passim*.

251 See Edgar L. Chappell's eleven articles on various aspects of rural housing (*South Wales Daily News*, 22, 23, 24, 25, 26, 28, 29, 30 and 31 August; 1, 2, 4 and 5 September 1911).

252 Ibid., 25 August 1911.

253 Ibid. For another report on rural housing at this time, see D. Lleufer Thomas, *Housing Conditions in Wales* (Cardiff, 1913). D. Parry Jones provides this description of the method of construction of cottages in the Llangeler and Penboyr areas: D. Parry Jones, *Welsh County Upbringing* (London, 1949), pp.83–4.

254 Lleufer Thomas, op. cit. 'On morality and bad housing conditions', see Revd Herbert Morgan, *Housing and Public Welfare: Some Economic and Moral Considerations* (n.d.), *passim*.

[255] *South Wales Daily News*, 25 August 1911.

[256] Lleufer Thomas, op. cit.

[257] CROC, MSS.WWH/3/1, Reports of the County Medical Officer of Health, 1914. A report also appeared in the *Carmarthen Weekly Reporter*, 17 July 1914.

[258] *The Land: The Report of the Land Enquiry Committee*, Vol.II Urban (London, 1914), p.23.

> In 1911, the Housing Committee of the Town Council was informed by Mr Blagdon Richards that 'the poor of Carmarthen were housed in slums and hovels that were not fit for human habitation. I will go further – some of the houses are not fit to kennel a dog in. Some are veritable death traps . . . To provide new homes for the children would be like transporting them to paradise.' His call for improvements and slum clearance was reflected by the Revd Fuller Mills, who questioned whether Carmarthen, unlike large towns, could afford it (*Carmarthen Weekly Reporter*, 15 December 1911).

[259] Quoted in the *Carmarthen Weekly Reporter*, 27 February 1914; CROC, WWH/3/1. Report, Dr Arthur Hughes.

[260] CROC, *Quarter Sessions Papers*, Box 75. *Carmarthen Weekly Reporter*, 28 April 1917.

[261] *South Wales Sentinel and Labour News*, 27 October, 3, 10, 17 November 1911.

[262] Ibid., 27 October 1911.

[263] Ibid.

[264] 'Condition of Water', *Carmarthen Journal*, 14 August 1896.

[265] CROC, WWH/3/1, *Annual Report of the County Medical Officer*, Dr E. Cambrian Thomas, 1913, p.10.

[266] Ibid., *Annual Report*, 1921, pp.23–4.

[267] Ibid., p.24.

[268] Ibid.

[269] Ibid.

[270] *South Wales Press*, 13 July 1893.

[271] For similar improvements in a neighbouring area, see Geraint D. Fielder, 'Public Health and Hospital Administration in Swansea and West Glamorgan since the End of the Eighteenth Century to 1914' (unpublished University of Wales (Swansea) MA thesis, 1962).

[272] Ieuan Gwynedd Jones, op. cit., p.133.

[273] For a discussion of these themes, see *idem* Merthyr Tydfil; 'The Politics of Survival', *Llafur*, 2, 1 (1976), pp.18–31, and *Exploration and Explanations: Essays in the Social History of Victorian Wales* (Llandysul, 1981), part 2.

274 For a discussion, see Russell Davies, op. cit., Chapter 7.

275 S. O. Davies and E. R. R. Lewis (of Tumble), 'Health and Social Conditions', *Llanelly Mercury*, 21 March 1918. For S. O. Davies and Carmarthenshire, see Robert Griffiths, *S. O. Davies: A Socialist Faith* (Cardiff, 1983), especially Chapters 1 and 2.

276 *South Wales Press*, 24 July 1917.

277 *Carmarthen Weekly Reporter*, 3 August 1917.

278 Ibid., 4 October 1907.

279 *Annual Report of the Medical Officer of Health Llanelly Rural Sanitary Authority*, 1901.

280 CROC, Education Book (Ed.Bk) 555/2-3 *Log Books of Glasfryn School Llanfihangel Abercywyn*, 11 November 1881, report on the death of Ann Williams, 6 years of age; 30 June 1884, funeral of William Thomas. In April 1884, the Master of the National School, Llanfihangel-ar-Arth, was forced to close the school because of scarlet fever and scarlatina. CROC, Ed Bk 546/3.

281 *The Welshman*, 28 December 1894. In 1880, Dr H. C. Buckley, in his report on the Health of the district to the Llanelly Local Board of Health, complained of 'the morbid custom of the area to take children to see the features of the recently passed away' (*South Wales Press*, 26 February 1880).

282 'The leopard of industry which pounces suddenly and silently from the centre of water and fire, attacking men at their work.' Gwenallt Jones, 'Y Meirwon' in *Eples* (Llandysul, 1951), p.10. There is a translation of this poem in Tony Conran, *Welsh Verse: Translations By Tony Conran* (Southampton, 1986), pp.280–1. Gwenallt, following the death of his father in an industrial accident, was deeply conscious of the terrifying suddenness of industrial accidents.

283 *South Wales Press* and *Llanelly Mercury*, 30 December 1908.

284 'I never dreamt that I would hear of two contemporaries / puking their lungs red with blood in a bucket . . . The coughing of the five of them, in their turn was heard over the garden hedge. / To cut across our conversation and darken our fun.' D. Gwenallt Jones, ibid., p.10.

285 Registrar General, *Supplement to the Fifty-Fifth Annual Report*, Part I [C 7769], 1895, pp.ixxx, xcv, 594–8. Table 5 gives details of the comparative death rates for the twenty-four major causes of death identified by the Registrar General. This table provides the basis for the following paragraph.

286 Edgar J. Collins and J. Hilditch, *Report on the Conditions of Employment in the Manufacture of Tinplate with Special Reference to the Process of Tinning* [Cd 63–94], 'The tinhouse operative . . . also suffers more than his fellow outside from chest complaints'.

287 The death rates given in this section are crude death rates expressed per thousand deaths. See Russell Davies, op. cit., Table 7.

[288] Registrar General, *Supplement to the Fifty-fifth Annual Report*, p.598.

[289] Ibid. For a discussion of mortality rates in Wales in the mid-nineteenth century, see Ieuan Gwynedd Jones, op. cit., and his *Health, Wealth and Politics in Victorian Wales* (Swansea, 1979), p.9. For the trends in British mortality rates, see W. P. D. Logan 'Mortality in England and Wales from 1847 to 1947', *Population Studies*, 1950, pp.132–78 and J. M. Winter, 'The Decline of Mortality in Britain 1870–1950' in T. Barker and M. Drake (eds.), *Population and Society in Britain* (London, 1982), pp.100–20.

[290] Anthony S. Wohl, *Endangered Lives: Public Health in Victorian Britain* (London, 1983), p.11.

[291] Registrar General, *Annual Report 1908* [Cd 4961], 1909, p.xxxix.

[292] Ibid.

[293] Ibid., p.xliv.

[294] Quoted in F. B. Smith, *The People's Health 1830–1910* (London, 1979), p.67.

[295] Quoted in J. M. Winter, 'The Impact of the First World War on Civilian Health in Britain', *Economic History Review*, 2nd series, XXX, 3 (1977), p.497: *The Daily Telegraph* agreed with the bishop, but for different reasons: 'If we had been more careful for the past 50 years to prevent the unheeded wastage of infant life, we should now have had at least half a million more men available for the defence of the country.'

[296] Lyon Playfair (President of the Health Section of the Social Science Association), quoted in Anthony S. Wohl, op. cit., p.10. On the decline in infant mortality, see Carolyn Dyhouse, 'Working Class Mothers and Infant Mortality in England 1895-1914', *Journal of Social History*, 12, 2 (1978), p.248.

[297] For example, the editor refers to the 'slaughter of the innocents' in an article in the *Carmarthen Weekly Reporter*, 23 July 1915.

[298] Anthony S. Wohl, op. cit., p.11.

[299] *The Thirty-Ninth Report of the Medical Officer of the Local Government Board* notes that Carmarthenshire featured amongst the worst areas for infant mortality, though it did not appear to share the worst features of social deprivation of the large urban areas (op. cit., p.56).

[300] Ibid., p.100. The rate for Newcastle Emlyn is comparable to that of Bombay and Calcutta in the early 1930s. See Anthony S. Wohl, op. cit., p.345, ff 7.

[301] See Russell Davies, op. cit., Table 6 for further details.

[302] *The Thirty-Ninth Report of the Medical Officer of the Local Government Board*, p.36.

[303] *Third and Fourth Report of the Commission on the Employment of Women and Children in Agriculture with Appendices* [PP 1870, c70 1870, Vol.XIII, p.41]. The report also noted that 'boys and girls of

10 or 11 can earn from 4d to 6d a day' in the collieries in south Pembrokeshire.

304 Edgar Collins and J. Hilditch, *Report on Conditions in Tinplate*, 1912, p.15.

305 *Royal Commission on Land in Wales and Monmouthshire*, Vol.III, p.391.

306 Ibid. For a fuller discussion of the diet in this period, see John Burnett, *Plenty and Want* (London, 1966), Chapter 10, and D. J. Oddy, 'A Nutritional Analysis of Historical Evidence: the Working-Class Diet, 1880–1914' in D. J. Oddy and Derek S. Millar, *The Making of the Modern British Diet* (London, 1976). Oddy noted that 'the conclusion seems inescapable that families in the period with an income of less than say, 30 shillings a week, and with a family of growing children might well obtain only 2,000–3,000 calories and 50–60 grammes of protein per head per day . . . It is impossible to envisage how the diverse physiological needs of a manual worker, his wife and growing children could be met adequately . . . under these conditions women and children were under-nourished.'

307 D. Lleufer Thomas, *Report on the Agricultural Labourer in Wales*, 1892, p.63.

308 *Report of the Minister of Health on Investigation in the Coalfield of South Wales and Monmouthshire*, Cmd 3272, Vol.VIII 689, 1928–9, p.6. It is worth noting that in the 'grim and dour' 1930s the maternal and infant mortality rates had improved considerably on their pre-First World War levels. See, for example, Charles Webster's 'Healthy or Hungry Thirties?', *History Workshop*, 13, Spring 1982, pp.110–29. The poor health conditions in Wales in this period were highlighted in the *Report on the Committee of Inquiry on the Anti-tuberculosis service in Wales and Monmouthshire* (London, 1939).

309 CROC, WWH/2/1, Dr Arthur Hughes, *Annual Report of the County Medical Officer of Health*, 1911, p.10. These reports on the health of schoolchildren reveal the serious extent of poor nutrition. Over 90 per cent of schoolchildren had decayed teeth and it was noted in 1911 that 'decayed teeth are so common amongst infants that they have almost come to be recognised as a natural condition' (p.11).

310 CROC, WWH/2/1, Dr E. Evans, *Annual Report of the County Medical Officer of Health*, 1909. Evidence such as this clearly reveals the paucity of the arguments of those Victorians – and they were many – who crudely applied Darwin's theory of the survival of the fittest and argued that the high mortality rates among infants killed off the weak and so created a nation of the strong. The poor physical condition of recruits during the First World War also refuted these arguments.

311 Quoted in Edgar Collins and J. Hilditch, op. cit., p.22.

312 Ibid., p.22.

313 Ibid.

[314] Anthony S. Wohl, op. cit., p.42. 'Malnutrition and severe anaemia adversely influence the course and outcome of pregnancy, affect foetal growth and birth weight and hence contribute significantly to perinatal mortality . . . A rapid succession of pregnancies may aggravate a pre-existing nutritional anaemia, resulting in infants of low birth weight with early iron deficiency'.

[315] See F. B. Smith, *The People's Health* (London, 1981); and Lionel Rose, *The Massacre of the Innocents: Infanticide in Britain* (London, 1986).

[316] Reported in the *South Wales Press*, 26 June 1902.

[317] CROC, WWH/3/1, Dr E. Cambrian Thomas, *Annual Reports of the County Medical Officer of Health*, 1915, p.32.

[318] Ibid., 1916, p.13. (Puerperal fever is a streptococcal infection of the uterus immediately after birth.)

[319] Reported in the *South Wales Press*, 22 December 1904.

[320] Anthony S. Wohl. op. cit., p.15. For the reluctance of the working class to accept social reforms, see Henry Pelling, *Popular Politics* (London, 1968), Chapter 1. On sexual conflict between male doctors and midwives and expectant mothers, see A. Oakley, 'Wisewoman and Medicine Man: Changes in the Management of Childbirth' in A. Oakley and J. Mitchell (eds.), *The Rights and Wrongs of Women* (London, 1976).

[321] Reported in the *South Wales Press*, 23 June 1904.

[322] Anon., *Carmarthenshire Infirmary: A Brief History and Appeal for Funds* (Carmarthen, 1935), pp.10–11.

[323] *First Report of the Welsh Consultative Council on Medical and Allied Services in Wales* (PP.1920, Cmd 703); HC 1920, Vol.XVII, *passim*. One of the areas selected by the Council for enquiry was the area between the Gwendraeth and Loughor valleys.

[324] In the broadcast, Lady Dynevor declared that 'it will come as a shock to many people to be told that there is no hospital accommodation for maternity cases, apart from Public Assistance Institutions, in the whole of Carmarthenshire, and the county is the largest in Wales' (Carmarthenshire Infirmary, *Brief History*, p.10).

[325] *First Report of the Welsh Consultative Council* . . ., op. cit., p.15.

[326] These examples are taken from the press cutting of an article by Dr Arthur Hughes, dated 20 April 1921, entitled 'Fetish in West Wales', found in the *Carmarthen Antiquarian Scrapbook*, XIV, p.211, in the Carmarthenshire Records Office.

[327] Ibid.

[328] Ibid., pp.212–13.

[329] Reported in the *Carmarthen Weekly Reporter*, 27 January 1911.

[330] This was recognized by contemporaries. The editor of the *Carmarthen Weekly Reporter* noted in 1912 that poverty was the only explanation of the county's high infant mortality rate. 'The death of the child of

the mansion was a phenomenon. But the children of the labourer die at an appalling rate', wrote the editor.

331 *Thirty-Ninth Annual Local Government Board 1910. Supplement to the Board's Report. Medical Officer's Report on Infant and Child Mortality* (Cd 5263, PP.1910), p. 138.

332 See E. Lomax, 'The Uses and Abuses of Opiates in Nineteenth-century England', *Bulletin of the History of Medicine*, XLVII, 1 (January–February 1973), p.169; and F. B. Smith, *The People's Health 1830–1910*, pp.97–8.

333 *South Wales Press*, 8 February 1883.

334 W. R. Lambert, *Drink and Society in Victorian Wales* (Cardiff, 1913), *passim*.

335 See, for example, *Carmarthen Weekly Reporter*, 26 June 1902, 8 November 1907 and 22 July 1910.

336 Ibid., 24 December 1909.

337 *South Wales Press*, 22 May 1910.

338 Ibid., 3 August 1899.

339 F. B. Smith, op. cit., p.214.

340 Anthony S. Wohl, op. cit., pp.21–3. The local press is full of reports of prosecutions for selling adulterated milk. See for example the case of S. Reynolds, St Clears, in the *Carmarthen Weekly Reporter*, 15 March 1906. (He was fined £5.)

341 In 1903 although the number had declined, diarrhoea was the second largest killer of infants, accounting for 17,000 deaths of children under one in Britain (ibid., p.23).

342 See, for example, the report of the inquest into the death of an infant in November 1911 in Carmarthen. With only one blanket to shelter it from the cold, the child was fed only cow's milk and died (*Carmarthen Weekly Reporter*, 29 December 1911).

343 *South Wales Press*, 31 July 1918.

344 Ibid., 3 May 1916.

345 On the social welfare provisions of the period, see Derek Fraser, *The Evolution of the British Welfare State* (London, 1973). It is worth pointing out that the passage of an act by Parliament did not automatically mean that either the letter or the spirit of that law was enacted. In 1912, the medical officer of health complained that the Midwife Act of 1908 had still not been adopted by the local county council (*Annual Report of Medical Officer of Health* 1912, op. cit.).

346 The 1921 Census reported that the average size of families in the county had fallen. In the *Registrar General's Report* of 1908 it was reported that the annual fertility rate of Carmarthenshire had declined from 344.1 in 1870–2, to 274.9 in 1900–2 and to 266.2 in 1906–8. Evidence perhaps of increasing economic pressure on family size and an increase in contraception. See below, Chapter 5.

[347] Anthony S. Wohl, op. cit., pp.38–42.
[348] *Annual Report of the Medical Officer of Health*, 1920, p.14.
[349] See, for example, Edward Shorter, *The Making of the Modern Family* (London, 1976).
[350] Personal knowledge.
[351] DROC, Education Books, *Esgairdawe School Log Book*, entries for 31 March 1890 and 11 November 1891. The toilet facilities were also poor (ibid., 31 March 1891).
[352] Ibid., Ed. Book 154, 1, *Nantcwmrhys School, Cynwyl*, entry, 11 April 1897.
[353] Ibid., *Caeo C.P. School Log Book*, entry, 7 January 1894.
[354] Ibid., *Coedmor Log Book*, entry, 12 February 1903.
[355] Ibid., *Berrisbroke Ed. Book*, 179/1 entry, 12 March 1919.
[356] Ibid., *Penwaun Ed. Book*, C84/1 entry, 12 November 1897.
[357] Ibid., *Nantcwmrhys Ed. Book*, 104/1 entry, 2 April 1890.
[358] Ibid., entry, 1 August 1890.
[359] Ibid., entry, 22 October 1907.
[360] Ibid., entry, 20 May 1908.
[361] *Report of the Committee appointed to inquire into the condition of Higher Education in Wales, 1881* [c.3047] 1881, p.lvi.
[362] Rhys Davies, *Cefnarthen: Y Comin, Y Capel a'r Ysgol* (Swansea, 1983), p.132.
[363] Muriel B. Evans, op. cit., p.180.
[364] CROC, *Nantcwmrhys Ed. Book*, entry, 14 June 1895.
[365] Ibid., entry, 21 June 1895.
[366] Ibid., entry, 23 August 1895.
[367] Ibid., entry, 1 April 1896. For labour debts, see above, Chapter 1.
[368] Ibid., entry, 1 May 1896.
[369] Ibid., *Berrisbroke Ed. Book*, 179/19, entry 4 December 1891.
[370] Ibid., *Rhydcymerau Ed. Book*, 5781, entries for the weeks 17–21 June 1874 and 14–18 April 1884.
[371] Ibid., *Cefnarthen Ed. Book*, entry, 30 June 1905.
[372] Ibid., *Cwmdwr National School Ed. Book*, entry, 5 May 1890.
[373] Ibid., *Llanfihangel-yr-arth Ed. Book*, 546/3, entries for 15 January 1889; 15 June 1898 and 27 February 1907.
[374] Ibid., *Rhydcymerau Ed. Book*, 578/1, entry, 15 June 1877.
[375] Ibid., *Coedmor Ed. Book*, entry, 5 November 1915. This school also closed for the Dalis Fair at Lampter (9 May 1921) and for the religious services of both the Unitarians and Baptists (26 May and 1 June 1921).
[376] Ibid., entry for the week 11–15 September 1882.
[377] Ibid., entry, 28 September 1889. (Crug-y-bar School was also closed for this event.)
[378] Ibid., *Rhydcymerau Ed. Book*, 158/1, entry, 27-30 January 1874.

[379] Ibid., entry, 1 June 1894.

[380] Ibid., *Berrisbroke Ed. Book*, 179/A, entry, 2 October 1895. They also complained in 1900 (4 May 1900).

[381] Ibid., *Farmers Ed. Book*, 591, entry, 30 April 1886.

[382] Ibid., *Gwernogle Ed. Book*, 86/1/96, entry, 1 June 1877.

[383] Ibid., 20 February 1880.

[384] Ibid., *Caeo Ed. Book*, 557, 19–23 September 1892.

[385] Beriah Gwynfe Evans informed the Cross Commission that: 'At Gwynfe I never permitted a word of Welsh to be spoken under any circumstances inside the schoolroom or even on the playground. I am to this date ashamed to own that I as a schoolmaster did what was at one time an universal custom, and caned my boys for using in my hearing their mother tongue . . . I shall regret it to my dying day.' Quoted in W. G. Evans, 'Intermediate Education in Carmarthenshire 1889–1914' (unpublished University of Wales (Aberystwyth) MA thesis, 1980), p.49.

[386] CROC, *Ed. Book*, 78/1, 10 October 1887.

[387] Ibid., *Ed. Book*, 584/1, 9 January 1891.

[388] Ibid., *Llanllawddog Ed. Book*, 110, *HMI Report*, 1908.

[389] 'A fart in a jam pot', 'a calf suckling two cows', 'a pot of standing milk'. See David Jenkins, *The Agricultural Community in South West Wales at the Turn of the Twentieth Century* (Cardiff, 1971).

[390] For the role of schools in society, see E. Weber, *Peasants into Frenchmen: The Modernisation of rural France 1870–1914* (London, 1979); and Robert Gielden, *Education in Provincial France 1800–1914* (Oxford, 1983).

[391] CROC, *Ed. Book*, 110, 2 February 1872.

[392] Ibid., *Ed. Book*, 340, 12 December 1877.

[393] Ibid., *Gwernogle Ed. Book*, 30 October 1874 and 14 March 1884: 'Cursing, swearing and slang words', the master noted, 'are carried on in a disgraceful manner'.

[394] Ibid., 6 October 1884.

[395] On this theme, see Eugene Weber, op. cit., pp.325–7.

[396] J. Geraint Jenkins, op. cit.

[397] *Minutes of Evidence Agricultural Depression*, Vol.IV, 1896 [C 7400–IV]. Evidence of D. W. Drummond, p.338.

[398] On light railways, see James Page, op. cit.

[399] T. Moline, *Mobility and the Small Town, 1900–1930*, Department of Geography Research Paper, No.132, University of Chicago (1971), pp.4–5.

[400] *Carmarthen Weekly Reporter*, 25 December 1903.

[401] *The Welshman*, 25 April 1913. For a discussion of the development of these services, see Russell Davies, op.cit., *Carm. Ant.*, XX (1984), pp.87–92.

402 See Geraint J. Jenkins, 'Technological Improvement and Social Change in South Cardiganshire', *Agricultural History Review*, XIII (1965), p.94. For a perceptive view of the social effects of technological change, see Gareth W. Williams, 'The Disenchantment of the World: Innovation, Crisis and Change in Cardiganshire c.1880–1910', *Ceredigion*, IX, 4 (1983). For more on this theme, see David H. Morgan, *Harvesters and Harvesting 1840–1900* (London, 1982).

403 Quoted in Gareth W. Williams, op. cit., p.311.

404 David Jenkins, op. cit., p.258.

405 *The Welshman*, 4 March 1910.

406 See, for example, David Howell, *Land and People in Nineteenth Century Wales* (Cardiff, 1977).

407 'Before the war broke out Wales had changed more within one generation than she had done within an entire century before . . . the patterns of the old world had disappeared for ever.' W. Llewelyn Williams, *'Slawer Dydd* (Llanelli, 1918), p.5, and for similar comment, see p.16.

2 *A Psychic Crisis? The Social Context of Mental Illness and Suicide*

1 Caradoc Evans, 'A Just Man in Sodom', *My People* (London, 1915, reprinted 1953), pp.86–94.

2 Herbert Butterfield, *The Whig Interpretation of History* (London, 1931), reprinted 1973, *passim*; Ian Bradley, *The Optimists: Themes and Personalities in Victorian Liberalism* (London, 1979). For a scathing criticism of nineteenth- century social thinkers, see John Carey's review of Ian Bradley's book (*The Sunday Times*, 10 February 1980); G. F. A. Best, *Shaftesbury* (London, 1964). For Lewis Llewelyn Dillwyn, see Dr Tom F. Davies, 'Bedlam yng Nghymru – Datblygiad Seiciatreg yn y Bedwaredd Ganrif ar Bymtheg', *Trans. Hon. Soc. Cymmrodorion*, 1980, pp.105–22.

3 Reported in *The Carmarthen Journal*, 28 September 1865.

4 CROC, St David's Hospital Collection, Acc 4648, Huw Jones *et al.*, *Centenary of the Joint Counties Lunatic Asylum 1865–1965* (Carmarthen, 1965) pp.1–10.

5 Ibid.

6 CROC, St David's Hospital, Box 17, *Annual Reports of the Committee of Visitors of the Joint Counties Lunatic Asylum, Twenty-Sixth Annual Report of the Medical Officer* 1880, pp.14–17.

7 CROC, St David's No.17, Twenty-Fourth Annual Report, 1888, p.15.

8 CROC, St David's Acc 4648, Huw Jones *et al.*, *Centenary*, *passim.*

9 Ibid. In 1910 the lunacy commissioners declared that 'It is impossible to enter into all, or to point out where repair and renovation is required, in order to properly maintain the Asylum in a condition approaching modern requirements.' *Lunacy Commissioners Report* (HMSO London, 1910) (Report on Carmarthen).

10 *Carmarthen Journal*, 16 May 1870; see also the report in the *Journal* on 23 February 1873.

11 Ibid., 22 March 1873.

12 The results for the three counties of south-west Wales in the election of 1889 were Carmarthenshire, 42 Liberals, 12 Conservatives; Pembroke, 31 Liberals, 15 Conservatives; Cardiganshire, 38 Liberals, 10 Conservatives ('Seneddau Sirol Cymru', *Baner ac Amserau Cymru*, February 1889).

13 CROC, St David's Hospital, Nos.19 and 20, *Papers relating to the dispute at the Joint Counties Lunatic Asylum*, *passim.*

14 *Sixty-fourth Annual Report of the Lunacy Commissioners*, HC [Cmd] 204, 1910, XLI, p307.

15 'Editorial comment', *Journal of Mental Science*, March 1913.

16 CROC, St. David's Hospital, Joint Counties Lunatic Asylum, Agenda and Minutes of the Committee of Visitors, Vol.3 *Fifteenth Report*, 2 April 1915. *Carmarthen Weekly Reporter*, April 2, 1915.

17 Ibid., Fifty-First Report, 3 April 1916.

18 R. W. S. Bishop, *My Moorland Patients* (London, 1922), p.16.

19 CROC, St David's Hospital Joint Counties Lunatic Asylum, Agenda and Minutes of the Committee of Visitors, Vol.4, *Report of the Lunacy Commissioners visit to the Asylum*, 20 July 1906.

20 The sense of imprisonment is shown clearly in O. M. Lloyd's winning sonnet at the Llandybïe National Eisteddfod in 1944. Set in the Cefn-Coed Psychiatric Hospital, Swansea, it took the title 'Carcharorion' ('Prisoners'). The metaphors are those of a locked fortress, 'Mae cadarn glo/Ar ddrysau'r gaer gaeëdig fore a hwyr'. 'There are stout locks/On the doors of this locked farmers morning and night'. See Gomer M. Roberts (ed.), *Cyfansoddiadau a Beirniadaethau Eisteddfod Genedlaethol Llandybïe, 1944* (Llandysul, 1944), p.79. This is also seen in the experiences of Helen, the wife of the poet Edward Thomas, on her visits to the musician Ivor Gurney in the 1920s. See Michael Hurd, *The Ordeal of Ivor Gurney* (Oxford, 1984), pp.167 and 151–78. I am grateful to Dr W. L. Davies for this reference.

21 Mrs M. M. Lewis's recollections were printed in CROC, St David's, Acc 4648, Huw Jones *et al.*, *Centenary*, pp.19–29. This section is based on this source.

22 Ibid., p.21.

[23] Ervin Goffman, *Asylums: Essays on the Social Situation of Mental Patients and Other Inmates* (New York, 1961), especially Chapters 1 and 3.

[24] Montagu Lomax, *The Experiences of an Asylum Doctor: with suggestions for Asylum and Lunacy Reform* (London, 1921), provides this graphic description of fellow inmates who greeted a new patient 'beastialised, apathetic, mutinous, greedy, malevolent – often quarrelling fiercely with each other, at meal times snatching away each other's food, or spitting into each other's plates . . . Into this is brought the man/woman suffering from profound melancholia' (pp.48–9).

[25] For example, Sam Evans, 'The Welsh Prophet', of no fixed abode who was arrested in Station Road, Llanelly, for disorderly behaviour and slapping PC Harries across the face with a herring, ripped his mattress and clothes in the police cell and on committal to the Asylum ripped the uniform to 'atoms' (*Llanelly Mercury*, 5 April 1900). On the treatment of vagrants in Wales, see D. J. V. Jones, 'A Dead Loss to the Community: The Criminal Vagrant in Mid Nineteenth Century Wales', *Welsh History Review*, 8, 3 (1977), pp.312–44.

[26] This point is made forcibly in Montagu Lomax, op. cit., *passim*.

[27] Quoted in Kathleen Jones, *A History of the Mental Health Service* (London, 1972), p.166.

[28] *Carmarthen Journal*, 31 July 1868.

[29] Ibid., 14 January 1870. *Cruelty in Lunatic Asylums. Report of the Commissioners in Lunacy on the cases of Santri Nistri (Hanwell Asylum) and Rees Price (Carmarthen Asylum)* 1870 (c.148), Vol.VII. Reprinted in Irish University Press, *British Parliamentary Papers*, Vol.8, Health, Mental. I am grateful to Dr Paul O'Leary for this reference.

[30] *Carmarthen Journal*, 28 January 1870.

[31] Ibid., 26 June 1874.

[32] Montagu Lomax, op. cit., p.96.

[33] Ibid., p.97.

[34] Kathleen Jones, op. cit., *passim*. Thomas S. Szasz, *Ideology and Insanity: Essays on the Psychiatric Dehumanisation of Man* (London, 1973) and *The Age of Madness: The History of Involuntary Mental Hospitalisation* (London, 1975).

[35] *South Wales Press*, 13 October 1881.

[36] One example from several is the suicide of Ernest Joshua, in the White Horse in Carmarthen. He had served in South Africa and had, since his return, spent two years in the Asylum. The suicide caused a sensation in the neighbourhood when it was disclosed that he had stood in front of a mirror whilst cutting his own throat (*Carmarthen Journal*, 8 April 1904).

[37] D. H. Tuke, *Chapters in the History of the Insane in the British Isles* (London, 1882), p.178. Quoted in M. Rolf Olsen, 'The Foundation

for the Hospital of the Insane, Denbigh'. *Transactions of the Denbighshire Historical Society*, 23 (1974), p.196.

38 *Carmarthen Journal*, 4 April 1873.

39 CROC, Agenda and Minutes, Vol.6, 'Annual Report 1907', p.29.

40 Caradoc Evans, *My People* (reprint 1953), p.14.

41 E. G. O'Donoughue, *The Story of Bethlehem Hospital* (London, 1914). In 1908, during such a trip to the Carmarthen Asylum, a patient went into fits of hysterical laughter at people outside the Asylum's wall. When asked by an attendant why he was laughing, he replied, 'I'm laughing at the likes of them being out and the likes of us being in' (*Carmarthen Weekly Reporter*, 7 August 1908).

42 CROC, St David's, No.17, Annual Reports of the Committee of Visitors, *Twenty-First Report of the Medical Officer*, 1885, p.16.

43 John Dryden, *The Spanish Friar* (1681), 2.1.

44 For a discussion of the development of ideas about the cause of mental illness, see Videa Skultans, *Madness and Morals: Ideas on Insanity in the Nineteenth Century* (London, 1975). The simplistic attitude of contemporaries is seen in the following declarations: 'The insane, moreover, are not the only degenerates – epileptics, eccentrics, habitual criminals and drunkards and prostitutes, are all members of the same family of degeneracy'. ('The Report of Dr Richards', *Carmarthen Weekly Reporter*, 26 April 1912, and 'Crime and insanity are mainly different branches of the same tree', CROC, St David's Agenda and Minutes, Vol.1, *Thirty-First Medical Report*, 10 January 1896).

45 For a full discussion of this theme, see Olive Anderson, 'Did Suicide Increase with Industrialisation in Victorian England?', *Past and Present*, 86 (1980), pp.149–73.

46 Peter Keating, *Into the Unknown England 1866–1913; Selections from the Social Explorers* (London, 1978), is an useful introduction. The threat that this 'degenerate' segment of society offered to respectable society is brilliantly analysed in Gareth Steadman Jones, *Outcast London: A Study in the Relationship Between Classes in Victorian Society* (Harmondsworth, 1984), especially Chapter 6.

47 It is interesting to note that the concept of rural 'purity' and urban degeneracy coloured all contemporary attitudes to town and country as the following anecdote reveals. An old woman of Carmarthen on a visit to Dowlais was supposed to have remarked, on seeing the moon: 'Give me the beautiful little moon we have in Carmarthen not the dull brazen thing you call a moon here', quoted in David Davies, *Reminiscences of My Country and People* (Cardiff, 1925), p.63.

48 Quoted in Dyfnallt Morgan, *Y Wlad Sydd Well* (Llandysul, 1984), pp.26–7.

49. These percentages have been calculated from the *Annual Reports* of the medical superintendent which were presented to the committee of visitors. CROC, St David's Hospital, *Agenda and Minutes*, Vols.1–5, *passim*. The 'Joint Counties' were Carmarthenshire, Cardiganshire and Pembrokeshire.
50. Andrew T. Scull, *Museums of Madness: The Social Organisation of Insanity in Nineteenth Century England* (Harmondsworth, 1982), p.247.
51. CROC, St David's Hospital, *Agenda and Minutes*, Vol.3, *Thirty-Sixth Annual Report* 1907.
52. Charles Booth, *The Aged Poor in England and Wales* (London, 1894), pp.240–3. This breakdown of family ties is also seen in court cases brought by Poor Law authorities for refusal to maintain parents, spouses and children which were frequent in south-west Wales.
53. D J. Williams, *Storiau'r Tir* (Llandysul, 1974). The adverse effects of inbreeding on the mental health of a community was not restricted to south-west Wales. See, for example, R. W. J. Bishop, op. cit., p.67; Robert Dugdage, *The Jukes: A Study in Crime, Pauperism and Disease* (New York, 1960); and Michael Lesy, *Wisconsin Death Trip* (London, 1973).
54. CROC, St David's Hospital, No.14, *Superintendent's Journal*, entry for 18 April 1881.
55. Ibid., entry for 25 November 1882.
56. CROC, St David's Hospital, Annual Reports of the Committee of Visitors, *Twenty-Fifth Annual Report* 1889, p.14.
57. CROC, St David's Hospital, Agenda and Minutes, Vol.4, T*hirty-Ninth Annual Report*, 1904.
58. *Sixty-Fourth Annual Report of the Lunacy Commissioners* [pp.190 Cmd 204], 1910, XLI. 'We have been struck by the relatively large number of patients who are considered as suicidal . . .'.
59. CROC, St David's Hospital, No.17, Annual Reports Committee of Visitors, *Twenty-Fourth Report*, 1888, p.13.
60. CROC, MS WWH/3/1, *Annual Reports of the County Medical Officer of Health*, 1923.
61. Charles Williams, *Religion and Insanity* (London, 1908), p.170.
62. See the Chaplain's Report: DROC, St David's Hospital, Vol.5 *Chaplain's Report*, 10 January 1904.
63. CROC, St David's Hospital, No.17, *Twentieth-Annual Report*, 1884, p.8.
64. Details of the occupations of patients are occasionally given in the medical superintendent's annual reports. The suicides of Ministers of Religion caused considerable disquiet in their locality. See, for example, the reports on Revd H. Lewis (*South Wales Press*, 24 June 1888), and the Revd John Thomas (Ibid., 5 November 1903, and *Carmarthen Weekly Reporter*, 6 November 1903).

[65] CROC, St David's Hospital, No.14, *Superintendent's Journal*, entry for 22 December 1883.

[66] CROC, St David's Hospital, Agenda and Minutes, Vol.5, *Forty-First Annual Report*, 8 January 1906. A powerful warning against the unsettling effects of religious revivals was given by J. S. Bushman in *Religious Revivals in relation to Nervous and Mental Diseases* (London, 1860). For a suicide linked with the revival of 1904–6, see *The Welshman*, 17 February 1905. Anthony Thomas, as a result of his religious delusions in 1906, later committed suicide. See *South Wales Press*, 10 April 1912.

[67] CROC, St David's Hospital, No.17, Annual Reports, Vol.3, *Thirty-Fourth Annual Report*, 7 January 1898.

[68] J. M. Winter, 'The Impact of the First World War on Civilian Health in Britain', *Economic History Review*, Second Series, XXX, 3 (August 1977), pp.487–508.

[69] *Cambria Daily Leader*, 30 March 1917. The press was littered with advertisements of cures for venereal disease, under titles such as 'The Pathway of Safety' (*South Wales Press*, 8 October 1888), and 'How to Ensure Health' (*South Wales Press*, 16 October 1888). Even the religious periodicals carried such advertisements: 'French Remedy' and 'To all those who suffer from the errors and indiscretions of youth . . .' (*Seren Cymru*, 3 January 1890 and 12 September 1884).

[70] CROC, St David's Hospital, No.14, *Superintendent's Journal*, entry for 23 July 1881.

[71] Ibid., 3 February 1882.

[72] Ibid., 15 January 1884.

[73] Ibid., 17 April 1881.

[74] Ibid., 12 October 1881.

[75] Ibid., 12 November 1881.

[76] E. P. Thompson, *The Making of the English Working Class* (Harmondsworth, 1979), p.13.

[77] Olive Anderson, op. cit., pp.166–73. Michael MacDonald, 'The Secularisation of Suicide in England 1660–1800', *Past and Present*, Spring 1986, pp.50–100; Richard Cobb, *Death in Paris* (Oxford, 1978).

[78] *Annual Reports of the Registrar for Births, Marriages and Deaths*, *passim*, 1884–1911.

[79] P. E. Hair, 'Deaths from Violence in Britain: A Tentative Secular Survey', *Population Studies*, XXV (1971), p.15.

[80] See Russell Davies, op. cit., Tables 7 and 8. The following section is based on these tables.

[81] For a discussion of female suicide in literature, see Margaret Higgonet, 'Speaking Silences, Women's Suicide' in Susan Rubin Suleiman (ed.), *The Female Body in Western Culture* (London, 1986), pp.68-83.

[82] Albert Camus, *The Myth of Sisyphus* (New York, 1955 edn).
[83] *Cambrian Daily Leader*, 11 January 1917.
[84] *Carmarthen Weekly Reporter*, 27 November 1909. Their reason was that they were unsure of the legal position and deemed it best to await the arrival of the police. It is interesting to note the following incident which occurs in the opening of Caradoc Evans's short-story, 'The Blast of God':

> Owen Tygwyn . . . was ploughing when his wife Shan came to the break in the hedge crying: 'For what you think, little man? Dai is hanging in the cowhouse. Come you now and see to him.' Owen ended the furrow and unharnessed the horse, which he led into the stable and fed with hay. Then he unravelled the knot in the rope which had choked the breath of his son Dai. (Caradoc Evans, op. cit., p.151).

[85] *Cambrian Daily Leader*, 11 January 1917.
[86] *Llanelly Mercury*, 27 April 1899; *Carmarthen Weekly Reporter*, 5 November 1915; *Carmarthen Journal*, 25 March 1904; *South Wales Daily News*, 25 November 1897; *South Wales Press*, 1 December 1887.
[87] *Carmarthen Weekly Reporter*, 3 November 1916.
[88] *Carmarthen Journal*, 19 January 1905.
[89] *South Wales Press*, 24 August 1910.
[90] *South Wales Press*, 8 February 1900; *Carmarthen Journal*, 8 February 1900.
[91] *South Wales Press*, 5 April 1906.
[92] Ibid., 25 November 1918.
[93] For other suicides linked with marital problems, see ibid., 28 April 1904 and 29 May 1902; *Carmarthen Journal*, 24 October 1902.
[94] *South Wales Press*, 17 December 1917.
[95] Ibid., 11 July 1907.
[96] Ibid., 17 January 1907.
[97] Ibid., 14 June 1900.
[98] *Carmarthen Weekly Reporter*, 4 June 1909.
[99] For a discussion of the treatment of shell-shock and hysteria brought on by the First World War, see Elaine Showalter, *The Female Malady: Women, Madness and English Culture, 1830–1980* (Virago Press, 1987), pp.167–94.
[100] *Carmarthen Weekly Reporter*, 9 October 1914 and 1 December 1916; *South Wales Press*, 17 October 1917.
[101] *Carmarthen Weekly Reporter*, 15 September 1915.
[102] *South Wales Press*, 3 July 1918; *Cambria Daily Leader*, 3 July 1918.
[103] *South Wales Press*, 9 August and 18 October 1916.
[104] *Carmarthen Weekly Reporter*, 17 August 1917.

[105] Ibid., 4 April 1919.

[106] Ibid., 6 November 1903; *South Wales Press*, 5 November 1903.

[107] *South Wales Press*, 24 May 1906.

[108] A. Alvarez, *The Savage God: A Study of Suicide* (Harmondsworth, 1979).

[109] *South Wales Press*, 24 June 1880.

[110] For some of the more unusual methods of death, see ibid., 14 February 1914 (broken glass); ibid., 18 January 1906 (liquid ammonia); ibid., 1 March 1900 (hanging off bacon hook); *Cambrian Daily Leader*, 2 November 1916 and *Carmarthen Reporter*, 24 January 1908 (strychnine).

[111] There is a valuable discussion of the popular songs of this period in E. G. Millward, *Ceinion y Gân* (Llandysul, 1983). The song mentioned is on p.6.

[112] Extracts from the report of Dr Hunter on the Death Rate of the Population in parts of south Wales, *Seventh Report of the Medical Officer of the Privy Council*, 1864. I am grateful to Professor Ieuan Gwynedd Jones for a transcript of this report.

[113] Volume III of the *Reports of the Royal Commission on Land* is concerned with conditions in south-west Wales [HC 1895] XL.

[114] CROC, WWH/3/1, *Annual Reports of the County Medical Officer of Health* 1922.

[115] D. Lleufer Thomas and Rev. Morgan Herbert, *Housing Conditions in Wales* (Cardiff, 1913), pp.9–10.

[116] D. Howell, *Land and People in Nineteenth Century Wales* (London, 1978), *passim*; R. J. Colyer, 'Limitations to Agrarian Development in Nineteenth Century Wales', *Bulletin of the Board of Celtic Studies*, 27, Part IV (May 1978), pp.602–19.

[117] Such attitudes were common throughout Britain, see John Cornwell, *Earth to Earth* (Harmondsworth, 1984), Chapter 1.

[118] Richard Vaughan, *Moulded in Earth* (London, 1951), p.17; there is a valuable study of Vaughan's work by Tony Bianchi, *Richard Vaughan* (Cardiff, 1984).

[119] This is the title of a book by Caradoc Evans published in 1946.

[120] John Davies, 'The End of the Great Estates and the Rise of freehold farming in Wales', *Welsh History Review*, 7, 2 (1974), especially pp.209–11.

[121] Quoted in John Cornwall, op. cit., preface.

[122] The poem commences:

> This is pain's landscape
> A savage agriculture is practised
> Here; every farm has its
> Grandfather or grandmother, gnarled hands

On the cheque book, a long, slow
Pull on the placenta about the neck . . .

in R. S. Thomas, *Selected Poems, 1946–1968* (London, 1973), p.120.

[123] R. W. S. Bishop, op. cit., remarked on rural curiosity, 'it is said that country people will even look down the chimney to see what their neighbours are having for breakfast' (p.3) and on the tedious uneventful nature of rural life relates the following anecdotes of an old man's leisure activities, 'Ah sits and smokes and thinks, sometimes ah sits and thinks and sometimes ah just sits' (p.8).

[124] For the 'ceffyl pren', see David Williams, *The Rebecca Riots: A Study in Agrarian Discontent* (Cardiff, 1971); and David Jones, *Before Rebecca: Popular Protests in Wales 1793–1835* (London, 1973).

3 *'Secret Sins': Crime and Protest*

[1] Thomas Rees, *Miscellaneous Papers on Subjects relating to Wales* (London, 1867), p.33.

[2] David Davies, *Echoes From the Welsh Hills* (London, 1908), p.171.

[3] The extent of the belief in this concept is shown by the fact that amongst the crowd of over 5,000 who had gathered to welcome Princess Christian and her daughter to Llanybydder to open the Alltymynydd Sanatorium were several banners with the message 'Welcome to the Capital of Hen Wlad y Menyg Gwynion' (*Carmarthen Journal*, 26 April 1906). Subsequent historians have accepted this concept without criticism, for example: 'A chyn diwedd y cyfnod [1850–1890] ni phetrusai'r wasg Gymraeg, a hynny heb wag ymffrost, sôn am Gymru fel "Gwlad y Menig Gwynion"' ('Before the end of the period (1850–1890) the Welsh Press justifiably did not hesitate to refer to Wales as "the Land of the White Gloves"'). So wrote T. H. Lewis, 'Y Wasg Gymraeg a Bywyd Cymru, 1805–1901: II Agweddau Diwydiannol a Chymdeithasol' in *Transactions of the Honourable Society of Cymmrodorion*, Part II (1964), p.236.

[4] For example, in 1887 when Mr Justice Field was presented with clean calendars in Cardiganshire, Carmarthenshire and Pembrokeshire, a correspondent to *Seren Cymru* wrote:

> Nid rhyfedd fod yr hen gân adnabyddus 'Hen Wlad y Menig Gwynion' mor boblogaidd, nid yn unig ar gyfrif ei cherddoriaeth uchelryw, ond hefyd ar gyfrif y ffaith gysurus a ddyg i'r cof, sef gloewder ein hannwyl wlad oddi wrth droseddai ('It is not surprising that the familiar song "Old Land of the White Gloves"

is so popular, not only because the music is outstanding, but also because of the comfortable fact that it brings to mind the freedom of our dear land from crime.'). (*Seren Cymru*, 22 Gorffennaf 1887.)

5 *South Wales Press*, 5 July 1900.

6 David J. V. Jones, 'The Welsh and Crime, 1801–1891', in Clive Emsley and James Walvin (eds.), *Artisans, Peasants and Proletarians* (London, 1985), p.84.

7 Quoted in S. H. Jones-Parry, 'Crime in Wales', *Red Dragon*, III (1883), p.524; and David Jones, op. cit., p.101.

8 Caradoc Evans, NLW, MSS 20033C, p.12. In many respects the furore of criticism which greeted the publication of *My People* in 1915 was symptomatic of these conflicting views of Welsh society. For local reaction to its publication, see *The Welshman*, 31 January 1913 (following Evans's articles entitled 'In Darkest Wales' in the *Daily Express*), *Cambria Daily Leader*, 15 and 21 December 1916. For details of Caradoc Evans's upbringing and work see T. L. Williams, *Caradoc Evans* (Cardiff, 1970), John Harris, *Fury Never Leaves Us* (London, 1985); and David Jenkins, 'Community and Kin: Caradoc Evans at Home', *Anglo Welsh Review*, 24, 53 (1974), pp.58–66.

9 Contemporaries and subsequent historians have expressed concern at the figure of unrecorded crime. Some have claimed that crimes brought to trial represented only one in ten of actual crime committed. For a discussion, see David J. V. Jones, *Crime, Protest, Community and Police in Nineteenth Century Britain* (London, 1982), p.2. As early as 1839 the Revd W. Russell stated that: 'The tables cannot show the amount of actual crime, but only of such as have been detected, and become the subject of legal cognizance.' (Quoted in David Phillips, *Crime and Authority in Victorian England: The Black Country 1835–1860* (London, 1977), p.41.)

10 For a fuller discussion on this theme, see Jones, op. cit., pp.16–24.

11 Jones, op. cit.

12 Alternative interpretations of the relative usefulness of national and local criminal statistics are V. A. C. Gatrell and T. B. Hadden, 'Criminal Statistics and their Interpretation', in E. A. Wrigley (ed.), *Nineteenth Century Society: Essays on the use of quantitative methods for the study of social data* (Cambridge, 1972), pp.336–96 and J. J. Tobias, *Crime and Industrial Society in the Nineteenth Century* (London, 1967), pp.14–21. David Phillips's book is, in many respects, a critique of these works and the analysis of this section is based upon his arguments.

13 CROC, *Quarter Sessions Minute Book*, 1878–1891; Box 38, *Quarter SessionsPapers*. The cases are also reported in the *South Wales Press*, 27 October 1881.

14 Ibid.

15 For a discussion of the rising crime rates in Britain, see Lyn MacDonald, 'Theory and Evidence of Rising Crime in the Nineteenth Century', *The British Journal of Sociology*, CXXXIII, 3 (1982), pp.404–21.

16 *Civil Judicial Statistics*, PP.1919, Cmd 1362, 1921, p.78.

17 For the operation of the legal system, see R. M. Jackson, *The Machinery of Justice in England* (Cambridge, 1964); and Carolyn Steadman, *Policing the Victorian Community: The Formation of English Provincial Police Forces, 1856–1890* (London, 1984), especially pp.47–53.

18 CROC, *Chief Constable's Returns*, 30 September 1883.

19 CROC, *Quarter Sessions Papers*, Box 40, *passim.*

20 *Criminal Statistics*, PP.1919, Cmd 1414, Vol.XLI, 1921, 'Assizes and Quarter Sessions in Wales'.

21 Ibid. The figures for the numbers tried at the Assizes in Welsh counties were Anglesey three, Breconshire two, Cardiganshire seven, Carmarthenshire thirty-two, Caernarvon twenty, Denbigh fifteen, Flint ten, Glamgoran 223, Merioneth two, Montgomery six, Pembrokeshire seven and Radnorshire one. This gives a total for Wales of 337.

22 David J. V. Jones, op. cit., pp.5–14.

23 CROC, *County Council Minute Books*, Vol.19, Reports of the Chief Constable to the Standing Joint Committee, *passim.*

24 Ibid., *Report* 1912.

25 He added that 'for the last five years Carmarthenshire has been worse than forty-seven other counties'.

26 *Chief Constable's Report*, 10 January 1913. Quoted in *South Wales Press*, 15 January 1913.

27 See below, Chapter 5.

28 For a history of the police in Carmarthenshire, see Pat Molloy, *A Shilling for Carmarthen: The Town They Nearly Tamed* (Llandysul, 1980); and J. F. Jones, 'The Carmarthenshire Rural Police Force', *The Carmarthen Antiquarian*, Vol.4, 1962. Also of relevance is R. W. Jones, *History of the Radnorshire Constabulary* (Llandrindod Wells, 1959)

29 David J. V. Jones, op. cit., Chapter 1.

30 The criticisms of the public house were frequent and the words of one critic can represent many: 'the youth of our country are corrupted, honesty and virtue are bartered within its precincts, and health and character are drowned in its fatal cup. It is there that . . . deeds subversive of all law and happiness are meditated' (quoted in W. R. Lambert, *Drink and Sobriety in Victorian Wales* (Cardiff, 1983), p.19). For some influential contemporary articles, see Revd J. W.

Horsley, 'Drink and Crime' and Revd H. Horsley, 'The Causes of Rural Crime' in J. J. Thomas, *Nineteenth Century Crime: Prevention and Punishment* (Newton Abbot, 1972), pp.12–16, 16–19.

31 For example, see B. Waugh, 'A Case History' in J. J. Tobias, op. cit., pp.20–4. H. Elwyn Thomas's *Martyrs of Hell's Highway*, (London, 1894) is a fictionalized account of the dissolute habits of a drunken father who sells his daughter Bell to white slave traders.

32 *Carmarthen Weekly Reporter*, 3 February 1899. In 1876, William Hoyle complained that the beer which used to be a beverage accompanying food was 'now mainly used as part of a habit of tippling, which fills the land with drunkenness, crime, pauperism, inanity, and a host of other festering evils'. J. J. Tobias, op. cit., p.12.

33 *South Wales Press*, 16 February 1905. Such public confessions of past guilt and present salvation following conversion to Christianity was a frequent feature of Revival meetings in 1904–5. In Carmarthen in February 1906, 'a massive crowd' turned out to hear the confession of Madame Florence Worth, a former drunkard and ex-actress.

34 W. R. Lambert, op. cit., pp.45–50. For local conflict over the increase or decrease of Sunday drinking, see the *South Wales Press*, 20 December 1888.

35 For Lloyd George's worries about the effects of the drink trade on the war effort, see Arthur Marwick, *The Deluge: British Society and the First World War* (London, 1979), p.56. *South Wales Press*, 9 February 1916, and *Cambria Daily Leader*, 9 February 1916. In the latter, the author of the report concluded that in the first few months after its introduction the drink restrictions in Llanelli were effective 'but this was no longer so'.

36 For the history of prohibition in England and Wales, see A. E. Dingle, *The Campaign For Prohibition in Victorian England: The United Kingdom Alliance* (London, 1980), and Brian Harrison, *Drink and the Victorians: The Temperance Question in England 1815–1872* (London, 1971), pp.196–247. For a study of complete prohibition and its failure in operation see Thomas M. Coffey, *The Long Thirst: Prohibition in America, 1920–1933* (London, 1976)

37 On the social function of alcohol, see below, Chapter 5.

38 K. O. Morgan, *Wales in British Politics, 1868–1922* (Cardiff, 1970), p.43.

39 W .R. Lambert, 'The Welsh Sunday Closing Act, 1881', *Welsh History Review*, 6, 2 (1972), p.175.

40 Ibid.

41 *Carmarthen Weekly Reporter*, 28 June 1907.

42 *South Wales Press*, 28 February 1912.

43 *Carmarthen Journal*, 30 September 1904.

[44] *South Wales Press*, 8 September 1892.

[45] For example, see the *Carmarthen Journal*, 27 July 1894, 17 January, and 14 February 1902.

[46] After raiding the house, the police found two full thirty-six gallon casks of beer, two of the same size partially full and two empty, and a large quantity of wines and spirits (*South Wales Press*, 14 April 1892).

[47] W. R. Lambert, op. cit., p.186.

[48] For the Militia, see below, Chapter 5; and *Carmarthen Weekly Reporter*, 29 June 1906. In 1902 it was reported that 'Sunday is the liveliest day of the week . . . In the morning the militia and band parade through the town to Church. In the evening the Salvation Army and local drunks compete. It is a kind of contest between Salvation and Damnation – in which Salvation comes off a bad second' (ibid., 6 June 1902).

[49] Ibid., 2 August 1901.

[50] For examples of Sunday drinking in Llanelli see *Llanelly Mercury*, 16 June 1894 and 20 April 1899, and *South Wales Press*, 18 April 1901, 23 November 1893 and 25 September 1902. In February 1902, the Revd B. Evans of Lloyd Street complained that 'I have seen men passing by my Chapel on a Sunday morning reeling drunk from the clubs in existence' (ibid., 22 February 1894).

[51] Ibid., 23 June 1915.

[52] Clubs were exempt from the Sunday Closing Act and so their number multiplied rapidly following the Act's passage. On the increase in clubs in south Wales, see W. R. Lambert, op. cit., pp.177–9.

[53] For the 'Cwrw Bach', see below Chapter 5.

[54] This 'Conservative Club' was a considerable embarrassment to the Conservative Party in the county. The frequency with which its name appeared in the press was a constant source of concern (*Carmarthen Weekly Reporter*, 1 July 1904).

[55] The five books were *David Copperfield*, *Lord Listner*, *A History of Wales* and, presumably to help with its legal problems, *Law for the Million*. Failing this they had resort to a higher authority for the club also had a copy of 'The Bible' (*Carmarthen Weekly Reporter*, 1 November 1912).

[56] *South Wales Press*, 27 October 1887.

[57] *Carmarthen Weekly Reporter*, 4 August 1911.

[58] Gwyn A. Williams, *When Was Wales? A History of the Welsh* (London, 1985), *passim*.

[59] *Llanelly Mercury*, 9 February 1911; CROC, *Quarter Sessions Papers*, Box 85.

[60] CROC, *Quarter Sessions Boxes, passim*.

[61] *South Wales Press*, 26 April 1916.

62 Ibid., 12 May and 6 October 1904, 27 January 1907, 14 September 1910, 10 January 1912 and 14 October 1914; *Carmarthen Weekly Reporter*, 24 January 1908.

63 *South Wales Press*, 30 April 1903, 17 March 1904, 24 August 1905 and 23 August 1906.

64 Ibid., 16 February and 2 March 1905, 30 December 1908, 17 August 1911.

65 *Carmarthen Journal*, 23 January 1914.

66 *Carmarthen Weekly Reporter*, 22 July 1914.

67 Ibid., 15 December 1905; *The Welshman*, 7 March 1913.

68 For the operation of the 'Black List', see *Carmarthen Weekly Reporter*, 19 September 1904 and *Carmarthen Journal*, 11 September 1903.

69 Ibid., 19 October 1894 and 25 November 1904; *Carmarthen Weeky Reporter*, 25 November 1904 and 13 July 1917.

70 *Carmarthen Journal*, 5 September 1902.

71 *Carmarthen Weekly Reporter*, 1 March 1907. For his adventures with the Salvation Army, see ibid., 14 June 1901.

72 Ibid., 12 January 1912.

73 *Carmarthen Weekly Reporter*, 15 September 1905.

74 Indeed, the editor of the *Carmarthen Weekly Reporter* remarked sarcastically 'Thank God for Mill Street, otherwise the Police Courts should have no business' (15 September 1905).

75 For an impressionistic history, see Kellow Chesney, *The Victorian Underworld* (Harmondsworth, 1976), pp.32–59, and Henry Mayhew, *London Labour and the London Poor* (selected by Victor Neuburg) (Harmondsworth, 1986), pp.107–26.

76 For such biased views of the Welsh, see Arthur Tyssilio Johnson, *The Perfidious Welshman* (London, 1910) and T. W. H. Crossland, *Taffy was a Welshman* (London, 1912). Both were attacks on Lloyd George.

77 This section is largely based on a study of the Minute Books of the Quarter Sessions between 1878 and 1926. See CROC, *Quarter Sessions Minute Books*, Vol.1, 1878–1891; Vol.2, 1892–1915; Vol.3, 1916–1926.

78 CROC, *Quarter Sessions Minute Books*, Vols.1 and 2. This source has been supplemented with the minutes of the Carmarthen County Council Standing Joint Committee for the period 1905 to 1912. See pp.310–84 for offences in 1909.

79 Ibid.

80 Indeed any item imaginable seems to have been desired and stolen at some time, see ibid., *passim* and CROC, *Quarter Sessions*, Boxes 40–80, *passim*. It is difficult to imagine what some people hoped to do with the goods they stole. Mary Bowen of Railway Terrace, Pontyberem and twelve men were charged at the Llanelli Police Court with the theft of 64 coconuts, 49 boxes of figs, 3 lb of apples,

2 lb of pears and 12 lb of gingerbread of a total value of £1.11*s*. (The men were fined 10*s*.; Mary Bowen was discharged.) The date of the offence, December 1904, may provide some explanation (*South Wales Press*, 15 December 1904). Others were more certain. On 16 September 1901, the *Carmarthen Journal* reported that wreaths and ribbons were being stolen from a local cemetery and then resold. Eighteen years later it seems that the honesty of some of the town's populace had not improved. The collection box of the Royal Institute of the Blind had been broken open and the money stolen (*Carmarthen Weekly Reporter*, 22 August 1919).

[81] Adelina Dodd's case is reported in the *South Wales Press*, 24 January 1907. For other examples, see ibid., 3 August 1905 and 25 April 1907, and *Llanelly and County Guardian*, 26 January 1908. The majority of the thefts of coal were by women, although in 1915 William Henry Samuel, a Labour member of the Borough Council, was severely warned by the magistrate for the theft of 9*d*. worth of coal from the Mynydd Mawr Railway Co. Ltd. Though it was 'enough of a punishment for a man such as you to be heard', said the magistrate who placed him on probation (*South Wales Press*, 4 August 1915).

[82] *Carmarthen Journal*, 10 June 1909.

[83] *South Wales Press*, 20 August 1903.

[84] *Carmarthen Weekly Reporter*, 10 November 1905.

[85] *South Wales Press*, 4 August 1904.

[86] CROC, *Quarter Sessions Papers*, Box 80. Testimony of William Smythe, 23 October 1908.

[87] *Carmarthen Journal*, 19 January 1894.

[88] *South Wales Press*, 10 January 1907; *Carmarthen Weekly Reporter*, 11 January 1907. For the case of another pickpocket, see the case of Hyman Adler, op.cit., 11 July 1907.

[89] *South Wales Press*, 6 December 1906.

[90] Ibid., 18 June 1913.

[91] Ibid., 25 June 1903.

[92] *Carmarthen Weekly Reporter*, 29 July 1904.

[93] CROC, *Quarter Sessions Papers*, Box 62, 1897.

[94] *South Wales Press*, 7 May 1913; *Carmarthen Weekly Reporter*, 12 January 1917.

[95] CROC, *Quarter Sessions Papers*, Box 73, Calendar 4 July 1902.

[96] Quoted in D. J. V. Jones, 'A Dead Loss to the Community', *WHR*, 1977, p.327.

[97] In 1907 for example plain clothes police were employed at the market and on other occasions in Carmarthen. Report of Chief Constable, CROC, *Quarter Sessions Papers*, Box 79, 1907.

[98] Ibid., Box 76, Calendar 5 April 1905.

[99] In the period 1895–1905, sentences were noticeably lighter. William George Harris was sentenced to six months' hard labour for the theft of an overcoat (ibid., Box 59); and Lettitia Davies, aged thirty-three, for the theft of flannel valued at £7 was imprisoned for six months (ibid., Box 43).

[100] Ibid.

[101] Gamini Salgado, *The Elizabethan Underworld* (Gloucester, 1977).

[102] *Criminal Statistics*, 1919, op.cit.

[103] See above, Chapter 3.

[104] CROC, *Quarter Sessions Papers*, Boxes 74 to 86, *passim.*

[105] CROC, *Petty Sessions Records, Llanelli Borough and County Police Courts and Carmarthen Borough and County Police Court Records.*

[106] *Carmarthen Weekly Reporter*, 20 May 1904.

[107] Reprinted in the *South Wales Press*, 9 February 1910.

[108] Ibid., 19 February 1891; a similar report is found in ibid., 6 May 1886.

[109] CROC, *Quarter Sessions Papers*, Boxes 83–6.

[110] For Hopkin John, see *South Wales Press*, 3 May 1916, and John Phillips (ibid., 14 May 1920).

[111] This was how Thomas Jones described John Phillips before sentencing him to nine months' hard labour in October 1909. See ibid., 27 October 1909.

[112] The advantage with brickworks, gasworks and limekilns was that they provided warm shelters. At the Ammanford Police Court in June 1904, a solicitor, Ian Griffiths, defending two tramping labourers who were charged with sleeping out, stated that both were only too willing to pay for lodgings but none were available (*Carmarthen Weekly Reporter*, 24 June 1909). Superintendent Rogers of Llanelli reported to the magistrates in November 1910 that 'all the lodging houses are full' (*South Wales Press*, 9 November 1910).

[113] *Llanelly Mercury*, 2 March 1893. Similar offences are reported in the *Carmarthen Weekly Reporter* on 7 December 1906, 4 May 1910, 24 August and 15 and 29 September 1911.

[114] For example, see the comments of Ernest Trubshaw (*South Wales Press*, 22 February 1906) and William Spurrell (*The Welshman*, 21 February 1913).

[115] William Croon was sentenced to seven months' hard labour for this offence (*Carmarthen Weekly Reporter*, 12 July 1912). John Ruddle was sentenced to two months hard labour for a similar offence (*The Welshman*, 1 August 1913).

[116] See Chapter 4.

[117] See David Phillips, op. cit., p.285.

[118] For poaching, see D. J. V. Jones, 'The Poacher: A Study in Victorian Crime and Protest', *Historical Journal*, 22, 4 (1977), pp.825–60, and

his 'The Second Rebecca Riots: A Study of Poaching on the river Wye' *Llafur*, 2, 1 (1976), pp.32–56. See also Harry Hopkins, *The Long Affray: The Poaching Wars in Britain* (London, 1986).

[119] David Howell, *Land and People in Nineteenth Century Wales* (London, 1978), p.77.

[120] D. J. V. Jones, 'The Welsh and Crime', op. cit., p.102.

[121] David Howell, op. cit. Given its nocturnal nature, it is probably true to state that poaching was far more frequent than the actual rates of committal would suggest.

[122] CROC, *Carmarthenshire County Council Standing Joint Committee Minute Books*, 30 September 1883.

[123] Ibid., 29 September 1887.

[124] CROC, *Quarter Sessions Papers*, 1880–1912, *passim.*

[125] See the evidence given to the *Royal Commission on Land in Wales and Monmouthshire*, Vol.III, 1895, *passim.*

[126] CROC, *Quarter Sessions Papers*, Box 40.

[127] Ibid., Box 43.

[128] Ibid., Box 41.

[129] Ibid., Box 47.

[130] Ibid.

[131] Ibid., Box 48.

[132] Ibid., Box 47.

[133] Reported in the *Carmarthen Journal*, 20 November 1903.

[134] Reported in *South Wales Press*, 27 January 1881.

[135] *South Wales Press*, 14 November 1881 and 16 August 1894.

[136] Ibid., 10 March 1881.

[137] CROC, *Quarter Session Papers*, Boxes 40–51, *passim.*

[138] H. M. Vaughan noted that 'It is an interesting fact that very few Welshmen are gamekeepers' (*The South Wales Squires* (London, 1926), p.193).

[139] *South Wales Press*, 21 November 1881.

[140] CROC, *Quarter Sessions Papers*, Box 41; for reports, see *South Wales Press*, 10 March and 7 April 1881.

[141] Harry Hopkins, op. cit., *passim.*

[142] Quoted in Revd H. Horsley, 'The Causes of Rural Crime', J. J. Tobias, op. cit., p.18.

[143] Quoted by D. J. V. Jones, op. cit., p.96.

[144] *Carmarthen Weekly Reporter*, 4 January 1907.

[145] Griffith Evan Jones, *Confessions of a Welsh Salmon Poacher* (Holborn, 1877), p.7. For earlier views see John Henry Cliffe, *Notes and Recollections of an Angler* (London, 1860).

[146] Griffith Evan Jones, op. cit., p.52.

[147] This phrase was used by Thomas Toplis in evidence reported in the *South Wales Press*, 21 November 1881.

148 Ibid., 19 February 1881.

149 Ibid.

150 Thomas Toplis in evidence (ibid., 21 November 1881).

151 Ibid., 14 November 1881.

152 Ibid., 21 November 1881. One of the gamekeepers, William Toplis, was fined £20 and bound over for twelve months for the use of unnecessary violence, although the justice, Sir Henry Hawkins, remarked that the evidence against his father appeared to be much stronger. The poachers were sentenced to terms of two and three months imprisonment with hard labour (ibid., 12 December 1881).

153 D. J. V. Jones, op. cit., *passim*.

154 See, for example, reports in *South Wales Press*, 30 May 1907, 25 November 1908 and 1 July 1914; *Carmarthen Journal*, 15 May 1884 and 13 June 1902; and *Carmarthen Weekly Reporter* 10 November 1906, 17 November 1906, 15 May 1908 and 1 September 1916.

155 *Carmarthen Journal*, 3 October 1902.

156 See Russell Davies, op. cit., Chapter 5.

157 Between 1893 and 1896 the majority of those accused of assault at the Llanelli County Police Court were from Llan-non, the parish in which Tumble was situated (CROC, *Quarter Sessions Papers*, 1890–7). Tumble 'roughs' appeared in some numbers. In January 1897, seven were charged with assaulting two men from Llan-non; in June 1895, five were charged with assaulting a farmer, William Jones, of Llan-non (*South Wales Press*, 28 January 1897 and 20 June 1895). Injuries inflicted in street fights in Tumble were frequently serious and costly. In November 1894, at the Llanelli Petty Sessions, Lewis Williams, a timberman from Llanarthne, tried to recover £10 from William Henry, a collier of Tumble, for the loss of earnings and doctor's fees after a fight on 20 July at the Tumble Hotel (ibid., 22 November 1894).

158 See D. J. V. Jones, 'The Welsh and Crime', op. cit., p.97.

159 *Carmarthen Weekly Reporter*, 18 November 1907.

160 CROC, *Quarter Sessions Papers*, Boxes 40–51, *passim*.

161 See, for example, the threats uttered in a quarrel between Richard Lewis and Charles Smith, both colliers from Llanedi. The fight arose from their original argument about Cronje's abilities as a commander (*Carmarthen Journal*, 23 February 1900). See also Chapter 4.

162 *Llanelly Mercury*, 18 October 1900.

163 *South Wales Press*, 9 April 1913.

164 Ibid., 10 November 1915.

165 CROC, *Carmarthen County Council Standing Joint Committee Minute Books*, entry for 10 July 1906. For other attacks on the police, see *South Wales Press*, 21 August 1884, 17 July 1902 and 28 September

1905, and *Carmarthen Weekly Reporter*, 30 September 1904 and 28 September 1906. In the latter report, two police officers were thrown over a ten-foot wall into a field by unruly youths in Llandysul.

[166] These occurred in 1879, 1881 (two), 1883, 1884 (five), 1886 (two), 1887 (three), 1893, 1894, 1896, 1897 (two), 1908, 1910, 1911, 1913 (two), 1914 and 1916.

[167] For newspaper reports, see *South Wales Press*, 24 June 1897 and 21 September 1908; *Llanelly Mercury*, 18 May 1911; *Carmarthen Weekly Reporter*, 6 December 1912; *The Welshman*, 25 July 1913.

[168] *South Wales Press*, 27 January 1881.

[169] The following report appeared in the *South Wales Press* on 10 February 1881:

> *WHERE DO THE MAIZEY'S COME FROM?*
> 'Where do the Maizey's come from? This has also been the subject of misapprehension. Kidwelly folk have naturally enough the satisfaction of knowing and making it known that the accused persons were not of their stock; whilst the published statement that they belonged to Llangennech speedily elicited an outcry from the inhabitants of that town. It is now stated in authority that the Maizey's came from Pontarddulais, and it is also known that they lived for some years at Caer Elms in Llanelly.'

The case is also reported in *The Carmarthen Chronicle and Haul Advertiser*, March 1881.

[170] For a brief summary of these events, see the article by Bethan Phillips, 'The Dyfed Murders: Arsenic and Corpse Candles', in the *Western Mail*, 18 November 1987.

[171] William Brice beat and kicked his wife to death in June 1871 and was seen carrying her body across a field to old coal workings near Llanelli. See the *Carmarthen Journal*, 7 June and 19 July 1871.

[172] These events have been well told. See Fred S. Price, *History of Caeo* (Carmarthen, 1904), Susan Beckley, 'A Devil who Cared for his Own: The Dolaucothi Murder Viewed Anew', *Carmarthen Historian*, 14 (1982), pp.78–82, and Bethan Phillips, 'The Dyfed Murders: The Tragedy of a Broken Promise', *Western Mail*, 4 November 1987.

[173] Valuable sources are the Dolau Cothi correspondence (NLW, MSS L10,419), and *National Library of Wales Journal*, XIV, Summer 1965.

[174] For an account of this murder, see J. Towyn Jones, *Ar Lwybr Llofrydd* (Llandysul, 1970).

[175] On Welsh murders, see T. Llew Jones, *Gwaed ar eu Dwylo* (Llandysul, 1974); and Gwylon Phillips, *Llofruddiaeth Shadrach Lewis* (Llandysul, 1986).

[176] The extensive space given to reports of murders in local newspapers clearly illustrates the interest of contemporaries. Every detail of the court proceedings, and especially the clothing and demeanour of the accused, was noted. Although by this period, hanging was no longer a public spectacle, crowds still travelled to Carmarthen to view the lowering of the black flag above the prison. In 1894, a crowd of between two and three hundred gathered at the Castle Wall in Carmarthen on the morning of the Borth murderer's execution (*The Welshman*, 16 November 1894). Subsequently many events or murders were said to be on the anniversary of another dark deed in the county: the death of William Nurse, for example, was said to be on the anniversary of the Dafen murder (*South Wales Press*, 21 November 1881).

[177] For example, the murder of Mary Jane Jones by her ex-boyfriend, George Thomas, in 1893 (ibid., 23 November 1893). See also Bruce Sanders, *Murder in Lonely Places* (London, 1960), pp.35–47.

[178] On ballads, see Ben Bowen Thomas, *Drych y Baledwr* (Aberystwyth, 1958), especially section C, pp.98–103. He lists 232 ballads relating to murders in various collections of ballads.

[179] 'Peaceable Land of the White Gloves/Once Wales was called;/But now Land of the Black Gloves/Is how everyone will refer to her.' Welsh Folk Museum, St Fagans, *Volumes of Nineteenth Century Ballads*, Vol.III, pp.1–63. For other ballads in this collection relating to murders committed in Carmarthenshire, see Vol.II, 1726/LXIX, LXX and LXXII.

[180] D. J. V. Jones. *Before Rebecca: Popular Protests in Wales 1793–1835* (London, 1973), especially Part 3; idem, 'Rural Crime and Protest' in G. E. Mingay (ed.), *The Victorian Countryside* (London, 1981). For a discussion see D. Russell Davies, op. cit.

[181] Donald Richter, 'The role of mob-riots in Victorian Elections 1865–1868', *Victorian Studies*, XV, 1 (1971), pp.19–29.

[182] For details, see *South Wales Daily News*, 1 December 1885; *The Welshman*, 19 December 1885, and *South Wales Press*, 7 January 1886. See also DROC, Quarter Sessions Papers Calendar 8 April 1886. Charges against Wyndham Nurse, William Rees, Rees Bowen, David Morris, Phillips Griffiths, Thomas Phillips and John Hopkins for riotous assembly in Llanelli and unlawful damage to the Conservative Club. For the wider context of electoral violence, see below, Chapter 7.

[183] For an account, see J. P. D. Dunbabin, *Rural Discontent in Nineteenth Century Britain* (London, 1974), and Elwyn L. Jones, *Gwaedu Gwerin: Braslun o Hanes Rhyfel y Degwm yng Nghymru* (Denbigh, 1983).

[184] K. O. Morgan, *Wales in British Politics: 1868–1922* (Cardiff, 1970), p.84.

[185] Ibid. Pamela Horn, *The Tithe War in Pembrokeshire* (Fishguard, 1982), pp.3–5. Revd D. Thomas, *The Anti-Tithe Movement in Wales* (Llanelli, 1891) laid great importance on the agricultural depression as a cause of the anti-tithe demonstration:

> Had they [lay impropriators and clerical appropriators] . . . granted abatements . . . on account of commercial depression . . . they would have paralysed the movement effectually for a time . . . Those who refused any abatement convinced the people that tithe receivers had no sympathy whatever with them in their hardship? (pp.4–5)

For a biography of Revd W. Thomas, see NLW, Glyneiddan MSS.

[186] Revd W. Thomas, op. cit., p.25.

[187] K. O. Morgan, op. cit., p.84.

[188] *Carmarthen Journal*, 7 January 1887.

[189] R. E. Prothero, *The Anti-Tithe Agitation in Wales* (London, 1889), p.12.

[190] Ibid. See also P. Horn, op. cit., p.8.

[191] For Lewis's work, see Revd Robert Lewis, *Reminiscences of the Tithe War in West Wales*, NLW, MSS 15,321, 15,322 and 15,323.

[192] NLW, MSS 15,321, *passim*.

[193] At the sales at Blaen-waun, St Clears, the crowds held up cartoons from the Nonconformist press of 'Robber Lewis and Co.' (*Carmarthen Journal*, 14 September 1888).

[194] NLW, MSS 15,321, p.20.

[195] See, for example, Muriel Bowen Evans, op. cit.

[196] *Carmarthen Journal*, 6 January 1888.

[197] Ibid.

[198] Women were central in the anti-tithe protests throughout west Wales. At Fishguard, Robert Lewis was forced to take shelter from a hostile crowd in a house 'when suddenly without warning, seven or eight women headed by Mrs Havard rushed into the room, sprang at me and began to tear my clothing'. From this depressing experience, Lewis was rescued by police (NLW, MSS 15,321, p.10).

[199] Ibid., p.167.

[200] *Carmarthen Journal*, 14 September 1888.

[201] NLW, MSS 15,323, pp.38–50.

[202] On the burning of effigies, see ibid., p.15. In February 1888 the *Carmarthen Journal* reported a tithe war at Wern-y-groes, Whitland:

> On entering the yard the first thing that struck me was the life-sized effigy of the rector, the Rev. Felix Lewis, in full canonicals and which was placed on a sack of corn. In addition to this was a

large boarding with poor Felix printed thereon. (*Carmarthen Journal*, 3 February 1888.)

The mock sympathy of the crowd rendered little comfort to the vicar whose loneliness must have been acute.

203 NLW, MSS 15,323D.

204 *Carmarthen County Council Standing Joint Committee Minutes, passim.*

205 *Carmarthen Journal*, 26 October 1888.

206 Ibid., 25 August 1893.

207 NLW, MSS 15.321, p.54.

208 *South Wales Press*, 19 January 1888.

209 See, for example, reports on the 'Boy Martyr' (*Carmarthen Journal*, 28 July 1893).

210 'As a mark of respect after suffering imprisonment because I established religion'. *The Welshman*, 26 August 1892; *Carmarthen Journal*, 26 August 1892.

211 Ibid., 2 September 1892.

212 Ibid., 16 November 1894. The paper also delighted in describing the unfounded allegation against the 'Boy Martyr' for stealing apples (28 July 1893).

213 K. O. Morgan, op. cit., p.89.

214 For protests in this period, see *Carmarthen Journal*, 19 May, 27 October and 8 December 1893, 12 January and 11 May 1894; *South Wales Press*, 30 March 1893 and 16 January 1896; *The Welshman*, 25 January and 22 March 1895. Echoes of the tithe riots surfaced again in 1911 in Rhydargaeau when seven calves belonging to three farmers were sold (*Carmarthen Weekly Reporter*, 4 August 1911).

215 In 1913, *The Welshman* reported that after twenty-five years of non-payment of tithe two bailiffs took possession of the garden of the Llanpumpsaint Calvinistic Methodists, confiscated the potatoes and sold them at auction (*The Welshman*, 15 August 1913). As a quarter century had passed, public shock at the events was understandable.

216 CROC, *Quarter Sessions Papers*, Box 40, Calendar of Prisoners 16 July 1884.

217 For similar parallels on the hatred of *cynffonwyr* in north Wales, see R. Merfyn Jones, *The North Wales Quarrymen 1874–1922* (Cardiff, 1981), pp.237–9.

218 *Carmarthen Weekly Reporter*, 19 May 1905.

219 See, for example, *South Wales Press*, 13 December 1894, report of Loughor Riots; CROC, *Carmarthen County Council Standing Joint Committee Minute Books*, p.477, report on riots at Trimsaran when the local colliery manager and under-manager were assaulted. For an eye-witness account of the riots, see *Carmarthen Weekly Reporter*, 27 January 1911 and *The Llanelly Mercury*, 26 January 1911.

CROC, *Quarter Session Papers*, Box 76, Calendar, 12 July 1905 contains report of a case of persistent following against John Hopkins and several others. The case arose as a result of the actions of a crowd of men who intimidated the other workers of the Llanelli Steel Works during a strike in July 1905.

CROC, *Quarter Sessions Papers*, Box 77, Calendar, 19 October 1906. Report of the cases against twelve men (eight colliers, one labourer, a blacksmith, a haulier and a farmer) charged with rioting on 16 June at Llan-non. In all, ninety-three charges were brought against thirty-seven defendants for persistently following workers, see *South Wales Press*, 13 July 1906.

For details associated with industrial disputes, see Hywel Francis, 'The Anthracite Strike and the Disturbances of 1925', *Llafur*, 1, 2 (1975) and idem, 'South Wales' in Jeffrey S. Kelly, *The General Strike of 1926* (London, 1976); Bryn Daniel, 'The Forgotten Riot', Bryn Daniel Papers, Box 1, South Wales Miners Library; and Russell Davies, 'The Importance of Motor Omnibus Passenger Services in South West Wales as illustrated by the 1935 Bus Strike', *Carm. Ant.*, XX (1984), pp.87–92.

220 *South Wales Press*, 9 March 1893.

221 For a brief account, see Noel Gibbard, *Hanes Plwyf Llan-non* (Llandysul, 1984), pp.116–26, and for the methods of working, see J. H. Morris and L. J. Williams, *The South Wales Coal Industry, 1841–75* (Cardiff, 1958), *passim*.

222 *South Wales Daily News*, 27 September 1893. (Letter of John Treharne on the reasons for the riot.)

223 *South Wales Press*, 9 March 1893.

224 *Carmarthen Journal*, 24 August 1893; *South Wales Press*, 6 July 1893.

225 Noel Gibbard, op. cit., p.104.

226 *Carmarthen Journal*, 8 September 1893. A photograph of the lodging house is reproduced in Noel Gibbard, op. cit., p.113.

227 *South Wales Press*, 24 August 1893.

228 *Llanelly Mercury*, 26 October 1893.

229 Ibid., 13 April 1893.

230 The hymn begins: 'Beth sydd imi yn y byd?/Gorthrymderau mawr o hyd!' The hymn, which describes the faithful conquering an oppressor, was set to music by Joseph Parry (see *Y Caniedydd* (Swansea, 1972), p.334).

231 *South Wales Press*, 4 May 1893.

232 Ibid., 13 July 1893.

233 *Western Mail*, 14 June 1893; *South Wales Press*, 22 June 1893.

234 Ibid., 20 April 1893.

235 *Llanelly Mercury*, 6 July 1893.

236 Ibid., 7 September 1893.

[237] *South Wales Daily News*, 6, 7, 8 September 1893.

[238] *South Wales Press*, 7 September 1893.

[239] *Carmarthen Journal*, 8 September 1893.

[240] *South Wales Daily News*, 6 September 1893. In all the damage totalled £173.7*s*.9*d*. (CROC, *County Council Minutes*, 26 October 1893 and 24 January 1894).

[241] *Llanelly Mercury*, 7 September 1893.

[242] Ibid., *South Wales Daily News*, 6 September 1893.

[243] Ibid.

[244] *Llanelly Mercury*, 14 September 1893.

[245] Noel Gibbard, op. cit., p.123.

[246] Following seventy years of silence, the Llanelli riots have at last received the serious historical examination which they deserve. See Deian Hopkin, 'The Llanelli Riots 1911', *Welsh History Review*, II, 4 (December 1983), pp.488–515; and Robert Griffiths, *Streic! Streic! Streic!* (Llandysul, 1986).

The account given here is based on the above and the Court records in CROC, *Quarter Sessions Papers*, Box 85 Michaelmas Quarter Session 1911; the report of the Chief Constable on the riots to the Standing Joint Committee in CROC, *Carmarthenshire County Council Minute Books*, Volume 10, January 1911–January 1912, pp.2195–2201; and the reports of the Riot Damages Act (1886) Committee in ibid., and the reports which appeared in the *Llanelly Mercury, The Llanelly and County Guardian, The South Wales Press, The South Wales Daily News, The Cambrian Daily Leader* and *The Llanelly Star*. It is worth noting that the same reporters provided the story for several newspapers, so that different newspapers contain identical reports.

[247] For details of Churchill's condemnation of other Welsh riots, see David Smith, 'Tonypandy 1910: Definitions of Community', *Past and Present*, 86 (1980), pp.158–60 and idem, 'A Place in the South of Wales', Chapter 4 of *Wales! Wales?* (London, 1984), pp.55–98.

[248] *Parliamentary Debates* (Commons), xxix, col. 2332 ff (22 August 1911). Quoted in Deian Hopkin, op. cit., p.508 and Robert Griffiths, op. cit., p.52.

[249] On 17 August 1911, the recorded temperature in Cardiff was 124.1 degrees in the sun (*South Wales Daily News*, 18 August 1911).

[250] Indeed it is claimed that in Britain 50,000 workers were on unofficial strike before the union leadership took command. Philip Bagwell, *The Railwaymen: The History of the National Union of Railwaymen* (London, 1963), p.291. For a good analysis of labour relations on the railways, see Robert Griffiths, op. cit., pp.1–13, 21–37.

[251] Deian Hopkin, op. cit., p.491. The labour unrest of the period is analysed in George Dangerfield, *The Strange Death of Liberal England*

(London, 1976), pp.195–291 and Henry Pelling, *Popular Politics and Society in Late Victorian Britain* (London, 1968) Chapter 9. For labour politics in Carmarthenshire, see D. Russell Davies, op. cit., Chapter 7.

[252] Deian Hopkin, op. cit., p.492; Robert Griffiths op. cit., pp.41–5.

[253] CROC, *Carmarthenshire County Council Minute Books*, Vol.10, Chief Constable's Report, p.2197.

[254] Ibid.

[255] Deian Hopkin, op. cit., p.498.

[256] *Llanelly Mercury*, 24 August 1911.

[257] Ibid.; *South Wales Press*, 23 August 1911.

[258] Ibid., 30 August 1911.

[259] For more information on John Johns and Leonard Worsell, see the *Llanelly Mercury*, 24 August 1911 and the *Llanelly and County Guardian*, 24 August 1911.

[260] *South Wales Daily News*, 21 August 1911; *South Wales Press*, 23 August 1911.

[261] Ibid. Such was the anarchic activity that one shocked observer claimed, "It was indeed a veritable pandemonium . . . a case of Tonypandy being out pandied' (*Cambria Daily Leader*, 21 August 1911).

[262] D. Hopkin, op. cit., p.500; Robert Griffiths, op. cit., p.48.

[263] *South Wales Press*, 23 August 1911.

[264] *Llanelly and County Guardian*, 31 August 1911.

[265] 'From now on the town will not be regarded as a peaceful place, but as the abode of rioters thieves and drunkards. It is a shame that such infamy has been brought upon the town by a crowd of unemployed hooligans and noisy layabouts.' *Tarian y Gweithiwr*, 24 August 1911.

[266] *Llanelly and County Guardian*, 24 August 1911.

[267] David Smith, op. cit., p.169.

[268] Such was the shame that people in villages with the Llanelli postmark began to use 'near Swansea' instead, lest they should be stigmatized (*South Wales Press*, 13 September 1911).

[269] 'Riots at Llanelli' by 'Junius' (*Carmarthen Weekly Reporter*, 25 August 1911).

[270] Ibid.

[271] Brinley Thomas, 'Wales and the Atlantic Economy', in B. Thomas (ed.), *The Welsh Economy: Studies in Expansion* (Cardiff, 1962); and Gwyn A. Williams 'The Crucible', in *When Was Wales? A History of the Welsh* (London, 1985), pp.173–81.

[272] See above, Chapter 2.

[273] W. E. Minchinton, *The British Tinplate Industry* (Oxford, 1957), p.86.

[274] Ibid.

[275] Ibid., p.83.

[276] NLW, MSS 5919, Llanelli Borough Council, *Petition to His Majesty the King for Incorporation* (1911).

[277] This population growth was concentrated in the south east (see above, Chapter 1). For the statistics quoted here, see L. J. Williams, *Digest of Welsh Historical Statistics* (Cardiff, 1986), p.50.

[278] This section is based upon the information given in James Davies and Co., *Llanelli and District Trade Directory* (Llanelli, 1897).

[279] For photographic evidence of Stepney Street, see the local history collection in Llanelli Public Library and also Gareth Hughes, *A Llanelli Chronicle* (Llanelli, 1984).

[280] See Chapter 1.

[281] CROC, *Quarter Sessions Papers*, Box 85, depositions.

[282] Ibid.

[283] 'The first thing that struck me was the filthy roads, the unhealthy smoke and a tram being pulled by a horse . . . There was no escaping the smoke because all the steel, tinplate and other works were planted in the centre of the place and houses built disorderly around them. Oh such ugly disorder . . .' 'Cwrs y Byd', 'Trwy Spectol Gwenidog', *Llais Llafur*, 14 September 1907. Quoted in Robert Griffiths, op. cit., p.17.

[284] See Russell Davies, op. cit., Chapter 6.

[285] Gareth Hughes, *A Hundred Years of Scarlet* (Llanelli, 1980) and for the town's dedicated support of the Scarlets, see David Smith and Gareth Williams, *Fields of Praise: The Official History of the Welsh Rugby Union* (Cardiff, 1950), pp.11–13.

[286] See Russell Davies, op. cit., Chapter 6.

[287] Ibid., Chapter 5.

[288] *South Wales Press*, 13 September 1911. For a convenient summary, see D. Hopkin, op. cit., p.513.

[289] *South Wales Press* (23 August 1911) and *South Wales Daily News* (21 August 1911).

[290] Ibid.

[291] Ibid.

[292] CROC, *Quarter Sessions Papers*, Box 85. (Depositions relating to the case against Ann Edwards.)

[293] Ibid. (Depositions relating to the cases against Peter Kelliher, Tomas John Edwards, Charles O'Neil, Richard Nurse, Thomas Page, Frederick Williams, James Price and Albert May.) See also Calendar, 20 October 1911.

Quarter Sessions Papers, Box 85. (Depositions relating to David Daniel John.)

[294] Ibid. (Depositions relating to the cases against David Davies, Thomas Davies, David John Daniel, Thomas Evans, David Daniel John, David Jones, Fred Lewis, Thomas Lucas, William Tucker, Gilbert Tucker, William Trimming, and Thomas Williams.)

295 Ibid. (Depositions relating to Albert May.)

296 Ibid. (Deposition relating to William Trimming.)

297 Reported in the *South Wales Press*, 23 August 1911.

298 CROC, *Quarter Sessions Papers*, Box 85. (Depositions relating to David Daniel John.)

299 Deian Hopkin, op. cit., p.506.

300 Ibid., p.507. The majority of people convicted of looting were imprisoned for two months in the second division, which was not harsh compared with sentences passed on people guilty of property theft in the period.

301 For a report of the funerals, see Robert Griffiths, op. cit., p.72.

302 For a fuller analysis on this theme, see David Smith, op. cit., pp.160–9.

303 *South Wales Press*, 5 January 1905.

304 Ibid., 1 February 1894.

305 *Llanelly Mercury*, 3 September 1897.

306 *Carmarthen Weekly Reporter*, 16 October 1903.

307 For some examples, see ibid., 21 June 1901 and 30 December 1904. In the latter issue the editor complained that one old lady had been knocked over and had sustained several cuts as a result of rough treatment. She remarked: 'the police are able to tackle the rogues of the Rhondda Valley, and the revivalists are able to convert them; but nobody seems able to suppress or convert the ruffians who make Carmarthen's streets a terror to the helpless after dark'.

308 J. J. Tobias, op. cit. See also Kellow Chesney, op. cit., David J. V. Jones, op. cit. and David Phillips, op. cit., *passim*.

4 Sexuality and Tension

1 For example Steven Marcus, *The Other Victorians: A Study of Sexuality and Pornography in Mid-19th Century England* (New York, 1977), and Peter Cominos, 'Innocent Femina Sensualis in Unconscious Conflict' in Martha Vicinus (ed.), *Suffer and Be Still: Women in the Victorian Age* (Bristol, 1972)

2 This subject has been perceptively analysed in the work of Peter Gay, particularly in his *Education of the Senses Vol. I: The Bourgeois Experience, Victoria to Freud* (Oxford, 1984)

3 For a discussion of the views of recent historians, see Carol Zisowitz Stearns, 'Victorian Sexuality: Can Historians Do It Better?', *Journal of Social History*, Summer 1985, pp.625–34.

4 *South Wales Press*, 3 November 1898.

5 *Report of the Commissioners Appointed to Inquire into the State of Education in Wales*, 1847, 3 vols. (PP 1847, C 870, 871, 872), XXVII.

For critical commentary on the report, see *Y Diwygiwr*, January 1848, pp.30–4 and March 1848, pp.94–7; and *Y Traethodydd*, January 1848, pp.110–35. The subsequent obsession with the allegations of the Report are eloquently discussed in Hywel Teifi Edwards, *Gwˆ yl Gwalia yr Eisteddfod Genedlaethol yn Oes Aur Victoria 1858–1868* (Llandysul, 1980), pp.84–7.

6 Thomas Rees, *Miscellaneous Papers . . . on Subjects relating to Wales*, (London, 1867), pp.29–37.

7 'Clean Wales, Pure Wales.' For a discussion of these themes, see D. Russell Davies, 'Hen Wlad y Menid Gwynion', in Geraint H. Jenkins (ed.), *Cof Cenedl VI* (Llandysul, 1991), pp.135–60.

8 'It is the homes of Wales which are responsible for the Welsh character . . . And it is the mothers to a great extent who are responsible for the character of the homes.' *Y Gymraes*, 1898, pp.84–5. For a valuable discussion of women's periodicals in nineteenth century Wales, see Sian Rhiannon Williams, 'Y Frythones: Portread Cyfnodolion Merched y Bedwaredd Ganrif ar Bymtheg o Gymraes yr Oes', *Llafur*, 4, 1 (1984), pp.43–56.

9 D. J. Williams, *Hen Dyˆ Fferm* (Llandysul, 1957), translated as *The Old Farmhouse* (London, 1975 edn), W. Llewelyn Williams, *Gwilym a Beni Bach* (Carmarthen, 1896).

10

In a picturesque spot at the side of a hill
We see a small cottage,
Its walls are whitewashed clean
Every spot, inside and out.

——

The Contented Family there
Live fondly and tenderly
And each one is always
Conscientious with his duties

At evening time, they all do meet
And sit around the table,
And for the food, until it arrives
Silently they sit expectant.

When mother brings the food before them
They always seek a blessing,
And after eating of their fill,
Without prejudice they give their thanks.

——

Very early, in heavenly spirits,
They arise for the Sabbath,

To seek God's blessing,
Together, quietly they walk.

——

How sweet their song! How sweet each word!
And oh how insistent their prayer!

And God serenely serves,
The Godly happy family;
It's true that they don't have gold,
Or resplendent silver dishes.

Or expensive carpets in the house,
Or satin bedclothes.

——

But they have the wine and the milk of
Salvation in their house,
And Christ a Brother, and God a Father
And tender provider to them.
They will be saved from all misfortune,
And in His hand He'll lead them,
Until they all reach journey's end
After long suffering.
Each will arrive in his turn,
The perfect glades of paradise,
And there in perfect peace
They will forever rest.

The most convenient source from the complete text is E. G. Millward, *Ceinion y Gân: Detholiad o Ganeuon Poblogaidd Oes Victoria* (Llandysul, 1983). Millward also contains a valuable introduction to the main themes of popular Victorian literature.

11 'Do not be deceived; neither adulterers, nor the worshippers of false gods, or marriage-breakers, or homosexuals, or thieves, or misers, or drunkards will inherit God's kingdom . . . Their place will be in the lake which is consumed by fire and brimstone, this which is the second death . . . undoubtedly if these frightening warnings from the word of God have no effect on you then go away vile man . . . Go away along your vile roadway and prepare to Welcome Hell! Welcome flames! Welcome Devil.' Ewyllyswyr Da (E. Edwards and W. Pryse), *Y Sefyllfa Briodasol: Neu Cyfarwyddiadau a Chynghorion i Wŷr a Gwragedd Er Meithrin a Chynnal Heddwch Teuluoedd* (Newport, 1851), p.19.

12 'to organise the family, upon which good management much depends . . . she should have no time to tell stories, or to wander here and

there, her place is in her home, at the centre of her duties. There are no excuses against this . . .' J. R., 'Addysg y Fam Gartref', *Y Cronicl*, 1849, p.335, quoted in W. Gareth Evans, 'Secondary and Higher Education for Girls and Women in Wales 1847–1920' (unpublished University of Wales (Aberystwyth), Ph.D. thesis, p.25).

13 For the developments in women's education, see ibid.

14 'The requirement of our country is young girls devoted to the high ideals of making the homes of Wales an example to the world for their good housekeeping, purity, and respect for God and mankind.' Anon, 'Addysg Genethod Cymru', *Y Gymraes*, Tachwedd 1909, p.163.

15 See Martha Vicinus (ed.), op. cit., *passim*.

16 'There are some things which women should know that should remain mysteries to the other sex – indeed it would be a sign of weakness in men if they displayed a knowledge of such things. Each of the sexes should excel in the knowledge which is pertinent to their situation.' 'Chwaer', 'Gwersi Angenrheidiol i Ferched Ieuanc', *Y Gymraes*, 3, 28 (1899), p.134.

17 Rhys Gwesyn Jones, *Caru, Priodi a Byw* (Bala, 1886).

18 Preface to the fourth edition, quoted in R. Tudur Jones, 'Daearau'r Angylion: Sylwadau ar Ferched mewn Llenyddiaeth 1860–1900', in J. E. Caerwyn Williams (ed.), *Ysgrifau Beirniadol XI* (Denbigh, 1979), p.197. Other sources of advice for the pursuit of a happy marriage are Edward Foulkes, *Y Pwysigrwydd o Fynd i'r Ystad Briodasol yn Anrhydeddus* (Caernarfon, 1860); and J. Jones, *Arferion a Defodau Priodas Ymhlith Amryw Genhedloedd y Ddaear* (Trefriw, n.d.). Contemporary women's magazines such as *Y Fythones* and *Y Gymraes* frequently contained short essays of advice.

19 R. Tudur Jones, ibid., p.197.

20 M. Hopkins, *Cyn, ac ar ôl Priodi; Ar Fodrwy Briodasol* (Denbigh, 1881).

21 Reay Tannahill, *Sex in History* (London, 1981), Chapter 13, *passim*.

22 Quoted in Keith Thomas, 'The Double Standard', *The Journal of the History of Ideas*, XX, 2 (1959), p.197.

23 Ibid., pp.196–7.

24 A. J. P. Taylor, *Lloyd George: Twelve Essays* (London, 1971); K. O. Morgan, *David Lloyd George* (Cardiff, 1974); W. R. P. George, *Lloyd George* (London, 1985).

25 Caradoc Evans, NLW, MSS 20033C, p.12.

26 On prostitution, see Frances Finnegan, *Poverty and Prostitutes: A Study of Victorian Prostitutes in York* (London, 1979). The reports of the inspectors appointed under the Contagious Diseases Acts stated that the one town in south-west Wales to come under the jurisdiction of the Acts – Pembroke Dock – was an area of 'clandestine

prostitution'. *Reports from Committees, Contagious Diseases Acts*, Vol. (3), Vol.IX, February–December 1882, PP.lxxix.

27 *Carmarthen Weekly Reporter*, 6 July 1906.

28 *South Wales Press*, 22 September 1915.

29 *Tarian y Gweithiwr*, 17 Gorffennaf 1884.

30 *South Wales Press*, 30 October 1902.

31 *The Welshman*, 21 March 1913.

32 *Carmarthen Weekly Reporter*, 28 June 1907. Elizabeth Hughes admitted to having intercourse with John Bevan of Garnant by the gate of Tyllwyd farm (CROC, *Quarter Sessions Papers*, Box 81, 1909). David Griffiths and Ellen Evans, 'a common prostitute', were fined eight shillings each in September 1898 for having intercourse in the People's Park Llanelli (CROC, *Quarter Sessions Papers*, Box 65, 1898).

33 *South Wales Press*, 8 December 1909. The case was adjourned because of lack of evidence.

34 H. Elwyn Thomas, *Martyrs of Hell's Highway* (London, 1896). For a discussion of child prostitution, see Ronald Pearsall, *The Worm in the Bud: The World of Victorian Sexuality* (Harmondsworth, 1983), Chapter 6, pp.358–66; and Deborah Gorham, 'The Maiden Tribute of Modern Babylon Re-examined: Child Prostitution and the Idea of Childhood in Late-Victorian England', *Victorian Studies*, 21, 3 (Spring 1978).

35 *South Wales Press*, 13 April 1913.

36 Ibid., 30 May 1914. The case was the first to be brought in the county under the White Slave Traffic Act. These acts had been passed as a result of W. T. Stead's campaigns in the Pall Mall Gazette. See 'The Maiden Tribute of Modern Babylon', *Pall Mall Gazette*, July 1885, *passim*. For a discussion of Stead's activities, see Ronald Pearsall, op. cit., pp.366–78.

37 *South Wales Press*, 29 August 1907. The local press was full of warnings of what could happen to young women in the great cities. See, for example, M. Jones, 'Peryglon Merched Ieuainc y Trefydd Mawrion', *Y Frythones*, 1888, pp.209–11, 238–9.

38 Thomas Rees, op. cit.

39 Gwilym Davies, 'Cyflwr Moesol Cymru', *Y Geninen*, June and July 1909, pp.201–8, 223–7. For the figures, see Table 10. On Gwilym Davies, see Ieuan Gwynedd Jones (ed.), *Gwilym Davies 1879–1955* (Llandysul, 1972).

40 These figures have been calculated from the Annual Reports of the Registrar General for Births, Marriages and Deaths between 1885 and 1919.

41 T. C. Smout, 'Aspects of Sexual Behaviour in Nineteenth Century Scotland', in Peter Laslett (ed.), *Bastardy and Its Comparative History* (London, 1980), pp.192–216, and idem, Chapter VII of *A Century of the British People 1830–1950* (London, 1986), pp.159–80.

[42] Edward Shorter, *The Making of the Modern Family* (London, 1976).

[43] A summary of Shorter's argument is provided in Theo K. Rabb and Robert Rotberg (eds.), *The Family in History: Interdisciplinary Essays* (London, 1973).

[44] For a discussion of these customs, see E. W. Jones, 'Carwriaeth y Cymry, Neu Cipdre Feddygol ar Flynyddoedd Cynnar y Bedwaredd Ganrif ar Bymtheg yng Ngheredigion', *National Library of Wales Journal*, Summer 1966, pp.1–40. Reprinted in idem, *Ysgubau'r Meddyg* (Bala, 1973) pp.16–40.

[45] David Jenkins, *The Agricultural Community in South West Wales at the turn of the Twentieth Century* (Cardiff, 1971), pp.125–7.

[46] The case against Daniel Rees is reported in the *Carmarthen Weekly Reporter* on 13 November 1905, that of Evan Jones in ibid., 14 December 1906. At the Carmarthenshire Quarter Sessions in October 1909, David Owen was defended on a charge of breaking and entering by William Llewelyn Williams, KC, MP who argued that Owen had been attempting to enter the maid servants' quarters, not to steal but for the 'Pleasures of Noswedd o Garu' – a tradition which, this notable Welsh historian claimed, dated back to the age of Dafydd ap Gwilym in the fourteenth century (*Carmarthen Weekly Reporter*, 29 October 1909). In the *South Wales Press* of 7 March 1907, T. R. Ludford described the practice as the 'traditional courtship procedure on local farms'.

[47] *South Wales Press*, 2 July 1913. John Evans entered the quarters of Hannah Davies, a seventeen-year-old servant of Penboyr, through the coalhouse door (ibid., 31 July 1912.)

[48] Ibid., 7 March 1907.

[49] Quoted in Cyril Pearl, *The Girl with the Swansdown Seat* (London, 1956), p.42.

[50] The historian is continually struck by the number of persons who just happen, whether accidentally or from voyeuristic motives, to turn up at crucial moments. In the case of slander brought by Sarah Ann Hughes against John Evans of Carmel, he admitted that he and four friends were 'carrying on the detestable custom of the area' – 'spotting' with the aid of a glass' (*South Wales Press*, 4 November 1904).

[51] The transcripts of the affiliation orders awarded by the police courts of Carmarthenshire are to be found in the *Quarter Sessions Records* at the Carmarthenshire Record Office (Carmarthen). These official documents only record the award of the affiliation order. They do not contain any information on the personal circumstances of individuals. To obtain the human story behind each order, the reports of court proceedings in the local press have been used. The decisions noted in the following section have been checked against the official records, although in the footnotes only the newspaper source is identified

except where the court record carried personal information in the form of a signed document. In such cases the official source is used.

[52] In her application against Laurence Summers, Mary Rebecca Jones claimed that he had sent her a number of postcards 'depicting the pleasures of married life' (ibid., 30 May 1907).

[53] For a discussion on these themes, see Richard Cobb, 'A View in the Street', in *A Sense of Place* (London, 1975), pp.79–135.

[54] *South Wales Press*, 7 June 1904.

[55] Ibid., 12 March 1907.

[56] Ibid., 16 February 1905.

[57] Other cases in which class or moral prejudices influenced the verdict are: *South Wales Press*, 18 May 1905, 7 and 20 July 1904, 21 July 1904 and 16 February 1905; *Carmarthen Journal*, 6 July 1900; *Llanelly Mercury*, 8 February 1900. The problems that the victims faced are shown in the case of Miss E. A. Davies of Cross Hands. The daughter of an unemployed collier, she had attempted to earn a living through keeping lodgers and charring. Her confinement was financially crippling (*South Wales Press*, 29 January 1913).

[58] *Carmarthen Weekly Reporter*, 6 January 1906.

[59] *South Wales Press*, 31 June 1905.

[60] Ibid., 19 August 1907.

[61] Ibid., 9 October 1918. It was apparently common for mothers in Carmarthen to warn their daughters to keep clear of 'ministerials' on a Sunday night because they were too excited. For other examples, with religious implications, see ibid. 12 November 1913, and 12 March 1920, and *Llanelly Mercury*, 2 February 1911.

[62] *South Wales Press*, 28 February 1907. It was claimed that some men deliberately took up casual labour so that the order made against them would be less (*Llanelly Mercury*, 29 June 1911).

[63] *South Wales Press*, 17 May 1907.

[64] Ibid., 22 November 1906. Indeed some women appear to have been remarkably careless. Fanny Garland had her thirteenth illegitimate child at Carmarthen Workhouse Infirmary on 24 July 1917. (See CROC, Abercennen MSS178, *Register of Births at the Workhouse*.)

[65] *South Wales Press*, 15 September 1904.

[66] Ibid., 4 March 1908.

[67] Ibid., 26 December 1917.

[68] Ibid., 25 September 1912.

[69] Keith Thomas, op. cit., p.215.

[70] *Llanelly Mercury*, 11 August 1904.

[71] See Chapter 3.

[72] *Carmarthen Weekly Reporter*, 30 April 1915.

[73] On the social effects of the war, see Arthur Marwick, *The Deluge: British Society and the First World War* (London, 1979), pp.105–22. For

'War Babies', see idem, *Women at War 1914–1918* (Fontana Edition, 1977), pp.115–26.

74 *Carmarthen Weekly Reporter*, 28 July 1905.

75 *Llanelly Mercury*, 15 November 1900; *South Wales Press*, 15 November 1900.

76 Ibid., 6 November 1906. At the Carmarthenshire Winter Assizes in March 1892, Alexander Miller was found guilty of supplying Catherine Bassett of Llwynhendy with a noxious drug with a view to procure abortion (*Carmarthen Journal*, 25 March 1892).

77 *Carmarthen Weekly Reporter*, 10 August 1906. Several women at affiliation order proceedings admitted that they had taken drugs to terminate pregnancies. Charlotte Davies, a farm servant from St Clears, admitted to terminating two pregnancies (*South Wales Press*, 28 May 1908). After intercourse following the Five Roads Eisteddfod of 1918, Jane Rees became pregnant. When she informed the father, he directed her to obtain three bottles from a Llanelli chemist. Though the mixture made her ill, a child was born in June 1919. It would appear from her evidence that the chemist, who was unnamed, gave her advice on the use of the medicine (*South Wales Press*, 27 August 1919).

78 Alice Jenkins, *Conscript Parenthood: The Problem of Secret Abortion* (London, 1938).

79 The cures were, of course, for venereal disease. Some eight companies advertised in the local press. See *South Wales Press*, 8 October 1888. See also *Seren Cymru*, 1 January 1899, 4 May 1893 and 10 December 1896. In 1918, after wartime experience had eroded the moral opposition, over 1,200 people from Carmarthenshire received treatment for the disease at Swansea General Hospital.

80 Quoted in J. Weeks, *Sex, Politics and Society* (London, 1981), p.71. See also Angus McLaren, *Birth Control in the Nineteenth Century* (London, 1981), Chapter 13. For contemporary condemnation see Anon, 'Quacks and Abortion', *The Lancet*, Vol.I, 1898, pp.1570–1, 1651–3, 1723–5, Vol.II, 1899, p.174 and P. S. Brown, 'Female Pills and the Reputation of Iron as an Abortionist', *Medical History*, 21 (1977), pp.300–3.

81 The Welsh translation ran:

> Pelenau Penyroyal a Steel i Fenywod
>
> Cywira yn gyflym bob afreolwydd. Symuda bob rhwystr, a lliniara yr a rwyddion poenus sydd mor gyffredin i'r rhyw. Mewn blychau 1s.1c a 2s.9c. (cynhwysai dri chymaint o swm) gan holl fferyllwyr. Anfonnir i unrhyw le am dderbyniad 15 neu 34 stamps gan E. T.

> Towle a'i gyf., Gwneuthurwyr, Dryden St., Nottingham. Gochelwch efelychiadau, y rhai ydynt yn niweidiol a diwerth.

The advertisements appeared weekly in *Y Tyst* from 7 July to 27 December 1899.

The advertisements of over thirty companies have been discovered in the local press. For example, Lanchard's *(Llanelly Mercury*, 10 March 1904), Mr T. A. Clair *(Carmarthen Weekly Reporter*, 3 May 1907), Towle's *(Seren Cymru*, 9, 16 September; 13, 20, 27 November 1885). 'Institute of Anatomy', Birmingham (*Seren Cymru*, 25 September 1895); Holloway's (*Seren Cymru*, 22 August 1890); and Southall's (*Y Goleuad*, 20 Mawrth 1895).

An interesting feature is that from 1904 the advertisements were not those of disreputable English companies, but were by disreputable local manufacturers. These included the self-styled 'Baron Watkin of Glancothi' (in reality, Sam Watkins of Llanfihangel Rhos-y-corn), who sold extensively locally, in the United States and in Lancashire (*Carmarthen Weekly Reporter*, 3 November 1905); Mrs Stewart, 'Lady Specialist', 9 Grove Place, Swansea (*South Wales Press*, 1 January 1908); Mrs Huxley, 57 St Helen's Road, Swansea (*Llais Llafur*, 5 March 1911); John Gower MPS, 14 Vaughan Street, Llanelli (*Llanelly Mercury*, 12 January 1911); and the infamous Professor T. W. Price, MH, FBIMS (Medical) Phrenologist, of 50 Station Road, Llanelli (*Llanelly Mercury*, 5 January 1911).

Y Goleuad however could also offer civilized comfort to the problems of women. On 1 January 1887 it advertised:

> TO LADIES ONLY
> Southall's (Patented) Sanitary Towels . . . 1*s*. a doz from Southall Bros, Bareleg, Birmingham. For protection against useless and injurous imitations, the label of each packet bears the signature of each patentee.

82 *South Wales Press*, 20 October 1898: a two-page report and an editorial. Reports of abortions were fairly frequent in Carmarthenshire in the period under review. See, for example *South Wales Press*, 8 October 1885 and 6 December 1888; the *Carmarthen Journal*, 25 March 1892; *Carmarthen Weekly Reporter*, and *South Wales Press*, 10, 17, 24, 31 July 1884.

83 The local press abounds with reports of such distressing behaviour. The following references are only a small selection. For concealment of births, see *South Wales Press*, 5 May, 27 December 1883, 15 October 1885, 13 October 1887, 21 June 1894, 25 January 1895. The details of the suicides of young unmarried pregnant women are

particularly gruesome and distressing. See, for example, *Carmarthen Journal*, 25 March 1904. Reports of the discoveries of infant corpses are very frequent, especially in the period before 1913; *Carmarthen Journal*, 20 April 1877 (found in the Tywi by a fisherman); *South Wales Daily News*, 5 December 1885 (washed up at Swansea); 17 December 1886 (found in old iron mine in Mumbles); 18 February 1887 (in the River Taff); 6 September 1887 (in a bucket in Cilgerran); 14 January 1904 (Maesteg); 24 March 1904 (Narberth); (3 Old Castle Pond, Llanelli); ibid., 15 August 1889 (in New Dock, Llanelli); ibid., 7 January 1907 (in a ditch in Gowerton); ibid., 18 August 1909 (in a blocked drain in Swansea Road, Llanelli); ibid., 3 January 1912 (in the New Dock).

84 Lionel Rose, *Massacre of the Innocents: Infanticide in Great Britain 1880–1939* (London, 1986), pp.93–108.

85 For details of Ellen Johnson, see *South Wales Press*, 10 March 1901.

86 *Carmarthen Weekly Reporter*, 1 and 8 June 1917.

87 For details of other prosecutions of local baby-farmers, see *South Wales Daily News*, 2 December 1905; *Llanelly Mercury*, 25 February and 10 November 1904.

88 *South Wales Press*, 16 June 1893.

89 For the reaction of *The Times*, see Philip Magnus, *Gladstone* (London, 1970), pp.386–91. See also the *South Wales Press*, 27 October and 3 November 1898. It is interesting to note that in each issue of local papers which reported local divorce cases there appeared advertisements for the services of private detectives. See, for example, the *South Wales Press*, 2 May 1898. These village Marlowes thrived on the fear and suspicion which were endemic in married life.

90 *South Wales Press*, 27 October 1898.

91 *Llanelly Mercury*, 12 October 1911.

92 *South Wales Press*, 15 November 1913.

93 Ibid., 16 July 1913.

94 Ibid., 18 May 1910.

95 *South Wales Press*, 18 April 1895. Among the accusations against Thomas was that his wife had found a bill for 'fancy garters, corsettes, chemises etc' which were intended for a young lady, and she found something which Mr. Howell [her Solicitor] said he should not like to mention, and he would have to write it on a piece of paper'. He was ordered to pay a fine of 10*s*. for assault and costs of £1.6*s*.6*d*.

96 'Whoever is without a wife, is without discourse', 'The best wife, is she who has no tongue', 'Three things impossible to obtain: dry water, wet fire and a quiet wife'. H. H. Vaughan, *Welsh Proverbs with English Translations* (London, 1889), pp.171, 172, 316.

[97] *South Wales Press*, 18 July 1907.
[98] *The Welshman*, 9 May 1913.
[99] *South Wales Press*, 6 April 1906.
[100] Ibid., 24 December 1919.
[101] Ibid., 14 June 1883.
[102] Exodus 21: 23–5; *South Wales Press*, 1 October 1919, 18 March 1914.
[103] *South Wales Press*, 23 April 1913.
[104] *South Wales Press*, 25 June 1913.
[105] Ibid., 28 March 1918. Daniel Skinner was accused of assault by Richard Evans, their lodger. In his defence, Skinner replied that although he was quarrelling with his wife, 'Evans had no business to interfere between me and my wife' (CROC, *Quarter Sessions Papers*, Box 91, 1916). The manuscripts and calendars of the Quarter Sessions do not, unfortunately, provide details of many cases, and this is why newspaper reports of the cases have been used in this discussion. These reports have been checked with the official transcipts wherever possible.
[106] *Carmarthen Weekly Reporter*, 18 October 1907.
[107] *South Wales Press*, 3 December 1903.
[108] Ibid., 21 September 1881, 24 August 1910.
[109] For details of the sexual abuse of children, see CROC, *Quarter Sessions Papers*, Box 86 (case against John Mayor); and Box 65 (case against David Jones).
[110] *Carmarthen Weekly Reporter*, 16 May 1913.
[111] *South Wales Press*, 6 April 1910. At the meeting 'a hope [was] expressed that Llanelli, which unfortunately has supplied so many cases of child cruelty and neglect, would give the Society a larger measure of support henceforth than it had afforded in the past'.
[112] *South Wales Press*, 30 November 1910, 3 July 1912.
[113] *Carmarthen Weekly Reporter*, 2 March 1906; *South Wales Press*, 28 June 1916. CROC, *Quarter Sessions Papers*, Box 80.
[114] *South Wales Press*, 9 March 1910 and 5 March 1913.
[115] *South Wales Press*, 28 May 1913, 5 May 1909. Inspector Idris Jones, one of the unsung heroes of south-west Wales, described the house of Mary Ann Holloway as follows: 'The Pantry, the back kitchen and the back yard were no better than open cesspools', CROC, *Quarter Sessions Papers*, Box 86, 1912.
[116] *Carmarthen Weekly Reporter*, 4 December 1914.
[117] *South Wales Press*, 11 November 1919.
[118] *Carmarthen Weekly Reporter*, 31 December 1909.
[119] *The Welshman*, 7 March 1913.
[120] The cases are reported in several issues of the *South Wales Press*, the *Llanelly and County Guardian*, the *Carmarthen Journal* and *The Welshman*, December 1887 and September 1908.

[121] 'Now is not the writing on the walls of public toilets evidence of the low moral standard of many young people in Wales? Wherever you go you will see the English words for the nudity of both sexes written in chalk. I have before now seen a drawing of a naked man and a woman on a hymn book in a Welsh chapel, and on a Testament used in Sunday School! It appears that there is a large number – how many I do not know – of our young men and women whose minds are corrupted by ideas of a carnal nature. Our Chapels are silent, too often fathers and mothers are also silent: they allow their children to grow up enslaved to one of the inherited sins of the Welshman.' Gwilym Davies, op. cit., p.226.

[122] For the controversy over tight-lacing, see Valerie Steele, *Fashion and Eroticism: Ideas of Feminine Beauty From the Victorian Era to the Jazz Age* (Oxford, 1985), Chapter 9, pp.161–91.

[123] H. Elwyn Thomas, op. cit., pp.137–9.

5 Spiritual Skeletons: Religion, Superstition and Popular Culture

[1] Henry Richard, *Letters and Essays on Wales* (London, 1881 edn), p.2.

[2] *Parliamentary Debates*, 3rd series, CCCL, 1265 (20 February 1891).

[3] On the special relationship between the Anglican Gladstone and Welsh Nonconformity, see K. O. Morgan, 'Gladstone and Wales', *Welsh History Review*, 1, 1 (1960), pp.65–82.

[4] Ieuan Gwynedd Jones and David Williams (eds.), *The Religious Census of 1851, A Calendar of the Return Relating to Wales*, Vol.1, South Wales (Cardiff, 1976). For an analysis of the act, see Ieuan Gwynedd Jones, 'Denominationalism in Caernarvonshire' and 'Denominationalism in Swansea and District', reprinted in idem, *Explorations and Explanations: Essays in the Social History of Victorian Wales* (Llandysul, 1981); and David Williams, 'The Census of Religious Worship in Cardiganshire', *Ceredigion*, IV, 2 (1961), pp.113–28.

[5] Ieuan Gwynedd Jones and David Williams (eds.), op. cit., *passim*.

[6] Quoted in Ieuan Gwynedd Jones, *Explorations and Explanations*, p.219.

[7] Thomas Gee, *Moesoldeb Rhyfel y Degwm* (Denbigh, 1891).

[8] Ibid., pp.103–4.

[9] *Report of the Royal Commission on the Church of England and other Religious Bodies in Wales*, Vol.1, *Report* (PP. 1910, Cd 5432), HC 1910; XIV; Vols.2–4 *Minutes of Evidence* (Cd 5433–5), HC 1910, XV–XVII; Vols.5–6 *Appendices* (Cd 5436–7), HC, 1910, XVIII.

[10] Ibid., Vol.II, 1, pp.77–9, Questions 1752–1828; Book II, pp.373–87, Q 29,038–29,520 and Q 30,171–30,435.

11 For the Church's recovery in the nineteenth century, see D. M. James, 'Some Social and Economic Problems of the Church of England in Diocese of St David's 1800–1874' (unpublished University of Wales (Aberystwyth) MA thesis, 1972).

12 *Report of the Royal Commission on the Church . . .*, Vol.1, Part 1, p.20.

13 Ibid.

14 One such influential preacher in Carmarthenshire was the Revd Thomas Johns of Capel Als, Llanelli. See Gwilym Rees, *Cofiant y Parch Thomas Johns D.D. (Taborfryn), Capel Als, Llanelly* (Llanelli, 1929), p.145. See also J. Vyrnwy Morgan, *Welsh Religious Leaders in the Victorian Era* (London, 1905); and Revd T. Morgan, *Enwogion Cymreig 1700–1900*, Vol.1 (Morriston, 1907). On the influence of the Revd G. H. Roberts, Peniel, Carmarthen, S. D. Evans wrote 'ni all neb amau dylanwad mawr Mr Roberts er sobri a gwareiddio yr elfennau gwaethaf yn rhannau o'r dref. Gwelid ef yn aml yn llonyddu'r terfysgwyr ac yn dwyn heddwch ymhlith yr ymladdwyr' ('No-one can doubt the profound influence of Mr Roberts in sobering and civilising the worst types in the town. He was often seen calming rioters and pacifying the fighters,') in S. D. Evans, *Braslun o Hanes Peniel 1886–1936*, CROC, CNC/1.

15 The figure of Carmarthenshire adherents is given in the *Report on the Church of England*, Vol.1, Book II, p.91, Q2,215, quoted in R. Tudur Jones, *Ffydd ac Argyfwng Cenedl, Cristionogaeth a diwylliant yng Nghymru 1890–1914*, Vol.1, *Prysurdeb a Phryder* (Swansea, 1981), p.26. This brilliant book is the most important analysis of the condition of Welsh religion at the turn of the twentieth century.

16 *Royal Commission on the Church of England*, Vol.1, p.20.

17 Ibid., p.438.

18 Of the 47,971 communicants in the Diocese of St David's, the parishes in Carmarthenshire accounted for 19,191.

19 *Royal Commission on the Church of England*, Vol.1, Part 1, p.438.

20 The statistics for Carmarthenshire are given in Vol.1, Part 1, pp.70–93 (Nonconformity) and pp.132–7 (Church of England). The statistics given in this section are taken from the report.

21 R. Tudur Jones, op. cit., pp.25–31.

22 Quoted in Dai Smith, *Wales? Wales!* (London, 1984), p.103.

23 For this argument concerning the Welsh language, see B. Thomas (ed.), *The Welsh Economy: Studies in Expansion* (Cardiff, 1962), pp.1–29, especially pp.26–9, and idem, 'A Welsh Cauldron of Rebirth: Population and the Welsh language in the Nineteenth Century', *Welsh History Review*, 13, 4 (1987), pp.418–37.

24 *Royal Commission on the Church of England*, Vol.1, Part 1, p.55.

25 The statistics presented in this section have been calculated from the statistics on communicants and population given in the Royal

Commission on the Church and the 1901 Census. The twenty-two parishes were:

Rural parishes: Llangynnwr 39.28, Newchurch 36.89, Llanfair-ar-y-bryn 37.4, Pencarreg 42.69, Llansadwrn and Llanwrda 47.24, Cynwyl Elfed 54.8, Talyllychau 56.0, Llangeler 69.68, Tre-lech a'r Betws 75.1, and Cil-y-cwm 75.3.

Urban and industrial parishes: Llandybïe 33.5, Ammanford 48.86, Betws 49.27, Carmarthen 46.89, Kidwelly 47.59, Llanelli Urban 52.80, Llan-non 58.16, Pen-bre 57.18, Abergwili 77.62, Llandeilo Urban 84.79, and Cwarter Bach 60.22.

26 This argument has been put briefly in David M. Thompson, 'The Churches and Society in Nineteenth-Century England: A Rural Perspective', in D. Barker and C. J. Cuming (eds.), *Popular Belief and Practice* (Cambridge, 1972), pp.267–76.

27 *Royal Commission on the Church*, Vol.2, Book 2, p.365, Q28,787–8.

28 Ibid.

29 For general comments on the growth of religion in the nineteenth century, see David M. Thompson, *Nonconformity in the Nineteenth Century* (London, 1976), pp.10–17; David Williams, *A History of Modern Wales* (Cardiff, 1950, revised 1974); K. O. Morgan, *Rebirth of a Nation: Wales 1880–1980* (Cardiff and Oxford, 1982); and E. T. Davies, *Religion in the Industrial Revolution in south Wales* (Cardiff, 1965).

30 'The Chapel gave without prejudice,/In the greenery and rural rain, and in the noise and dirt;/The water on the crown, the ring on the finger, and the resurrection above the coffin.' D. Gwenallt Jones, 'Y Capel yn Sir Gaerfyrddin' in *Gwreiddiau* (Llandysul, 1975), p.41.

31 *Report of the Royal Commission on the Church . . .*, Vol.2, Book 1, p.80, Question 1,865.

32 Ibid., p.69, Q1496. The Revd Walters informed the Commissioners' of the various societies which held meetings at St David's Church most evenings of the week. The societies ranged from the Children's Temperance meeting and Girls' Friendly Society on Monday evening to Choral Singing for men and boys on Tuesdays and Wednesdays, to the Mutual Improvement Society and the Men's Bible Class meetings on Wednesdays and Thursdays.

33 A. D. Gilbert, *Religion and Society in Industrial England: Church, Chapel and Social Change 1740–1914* (London, 1976), pp.69–70.

34 See Derec Llwyd Morgan, *Y Diwygiad Mawr* (Llandysul, 1981).

35 G. M. Roberts, 'Y Cyffroadau Mawr', *Y Goleuad*, 22 October and 24 June 1953, quoted in David Jenkins, *The Agricultural Community in south west Wales at the turn of the Twentieth Century* (Cardiff, 1971), p.244.

36 For a full discussion, see C. B. Turner, 'Revivals and Popular Religion in Victorian and Edwardian Wales' (unpublished University of Wales

(Aberystwyth) Ph.D. thesis, 1971), especially Chapter 5, pp 282–340.

37 This is virtually claimed by Evan Roberts' biographer, D. M. Phillips, in *Evan Roberts a'i Waith* (Dolgellau, 1912), p.57. See also Basil Hill, 'The Welsh Revival of 1904–5: A Critique', in Derek Baker and C. J. Cuming (eds.), *Popular Belief and Practice* (Cambridge, 1972), p.296.

38 In 1901, the editor of the *Y Dysgedydd* noted: 'Mae sefyllfa ein gwlad . . . yn wleidyddol, cymdeithasol, masnachol, a chrefyddol, yn galw'n uchel am ostyniad ac ympryd gerbron Duw.' ' The condition of our country . . . politically, socially, economically, and religiously, calls loudly for people to bow and fast before God.' (Quoted in R. Tudur Jones, op. cit., p.123.) For more on this theme, see ibid., pp.122–5.

39 David Jenkins, op. cit., p.244.

40 *South Wales Press*, 18 February 1897.

41 *Carmarthen Weekly Reporter*, 12 February 1897.

42 Ibid., 30 June 1899.

43 David Jenkins, op. cit. p.223.

44 Ibid.

45 R. Tudur Jones, op. cit. p.127. See also T. Mardy Rees, *Seth Joshua and Frank Joshua* (London, 1926), p.61.

46 For the origins of the revival in Cardiganshire, see Revd Eliseus Howells, 'Toriad y Wawr yn Ne Aberteifi', in Sidney Evans and Gomer M. Roberts (eds.), *Cyfrol Goffa Diwygiad 1904–05* (Caernarfon, 1954), pp.25–39.

47 Ibid. See also D. M. Phillips, op. cit., p.204.

48 For Joseph Jenkins, see W. Morris (ed.), *Deg o Enwogion* (Caernarfon, 1965).

49 W. Nantlais Williams, *O Gopa Bryn Nebo* (Llandybïe, 1967). See also idem, *Y Deugain Mlynedd Hyn: Ychydig o Hanes, Bethany Ammanford* (Ammanford, 1921), pp.29–33.

50 *Y Diwygiwr a'r Diwygiad*, p.33.

51 Quoted in Eifion Evans, *The Welsh Revival of 1904* (Bridgend, third edition, 1987), p.106.

52 Ibid., pp.104, 105.

53 W. Nantlais Williams was a promising eisteddfod poet but gave up composition, preferring to concentrate upon Christ's work. He devoted himself to his own Church. He made a subsantial literary contribution to the Welsh nation, edited *Trysorfa'r Plant*, wrote several hymns, and translated those of Sankey and Moody into Welsh. See Huw Walters, *Canu'r Pwll a'r Pulpud: Portread o'r Diwylliant Barddol Cymreig yn nyffryn Aman* (Denbigh, 1987), pp.194–200.

54 Eifion Evans, op. cit., pp.101–2.

55 *Carmarthen Weekly Reporter*, 23 November and 9 December 1904; *Carmarthen Journal*, 25 November and 9 December 1904.

56 Eifion Evans, op. cit., p.102.

57 Thomas Johns noted in his annual address to Capel Als: 'Y mae llawer mwy o ddarllen ar y Beibl. Mae mwy o brynu Beiblau nag y mae llyfrwerthwyr yn cofio o'r blaen, ni bu erioed yn ein gwlad gymaint o ganu emynau a gweddio ag sy'n bresennol . . . Gwagheir temlau Bacchus, a throir cablwyr yn weddiwyr' ('There is much more reading of the Bible. Booksellers cannot remember so many bibles being sold, there has never been so much hymn singing as there presently is . . . Bacchus' temples are emptied, and liars are turned into worshippers.') quoted in Maurice Loader (ed.), *Capel Als 1780–1980* (Swansea, 1980), p.67.

58 H. Elvet Lewis, *With Christ Among the Miners* (Aylesbury, 1900), p.215. For example, the Old Castle Tinplate Works commenced work with a religious service and the song:

> O'th flaen, O Dduw rwy'n dyfod,
> Gan sefyll o hir bell
> Pechadur yw fy enw
> Ni feddaf enw gwell.

59 *South Wales Press*, 22 December 1904.

60 *Carmarthen Weekly Reporter*, 23 December 1904.

61 *South Wales Press*, 22 December 1904.

62 It was reported that a 'converted Negro' was responsible for some remarkable revival scenes (ibid., 15 December 1905). The *Western Mail* also followed the progress of the missions in the Dock District. See 'Awstin', *The Religious Revival in Wales 1904* (Cardiff, 1905), p.27.

63 Ibid., 29 December 1904.

64 Ibid., 22 December 1904.

65 'Llanelli was hard ground to plough.' Quoted in R. Tudur Jones, op. cit. p.150.

66 W. Anthony Davies, *Berw Bywyd, 1903–1955: Dyddiadur W. Anthony Davies* (Llandysul, 1968), p.21.

67 R. Tudur Jones, op. cit., pp.134–5. D. M. Phillips, op. cit., p.293.

68 See, for example, the *Western Mail*, in which the editor personally attacks Evan Roberts and the 'sham revival'. Such attacks became common after the revival, when large numbers of people began to feel guilty about their previous enthusiasm. This consequent disenchantment is seen clearly in venemous prose in J. Vyrnwy Morgan, *The Welsh Religious Revival 1904–05: A Retrospect and a Criticism* (London, 1909).

69 David Davies, *Reminiscences of My County and People* (Cardiff, 1925), p.61.

70 Allen Raine, *Queen of the Rushes* (London, 1906), p.32.

71 H. Elvet Lewis, op. cit., p.180.

72 For Pastor Howton, see *South Wales Daily News*, 30 April and 1 May 1906.

73 *Carmarthen Weekly Reporter*, 17 and 24 November 1905.

74 CROC, CNC/1. S.O. Evans, op. cit.

75 For Keri Evans, see R. Tudur Jones, op. cit., pp.149, 152 and 201, and R. T. Jenkins and E. D. Jones (eds.), *Y Bywgraffiadur Cymreig 1941–50: Gydag Atodiad i'r Bywgraffiadur Cymreig Hyd 1940* (London, 1970), pp.14–15. Educated at Newcastle Emlyn Grammar School, Evans went to the Carmarthen Presbyterian College, and to Glasgow University where he won the degree of MA in 1888. After a period lecturing in Glasgow he returned to Priordy Chapel Carmarthen. The 1904 revival had a profound influence upon him. For Keri Evans's experiences and beliefs in 1904, see Keri Evans, *Fy Mhererindod Ysbrydol* (Liverpool, 1938), pp.69–91.

76 *South Wales Daily News*, 16 April 1906, for a photograph of Gors-fach.

77 Report on 'The New Revival', ibid., 14 April 1906.

78 For the spiritual condition of Pen-y-groes, see D. Edgar Bowen, *Diwrnod yn y Winllan: Cofiant y Parch William Bowen* (Esher, 1924).

79 *South Wales Daily News*, 13 April 1906. See also D. Huw Owen, 'Chapel and Colliery: Bethel, Cross Hands 1907–1982', *Carm. Ant.*, XVIII, pp.56–8.

80 Ibid., 12 April 1906.

81 Ibid., 14 April 1906.

82 Ibid., 12 April 1906.

83 *Carmarthen Weekly Reporter*, 19 April 1906. Mr Evan Roberts was credited with similar attributes. See R. Tudur Jones, op. cit. pp.137–9.

84 *Carmarthen Weekly Reporter*, 19 April 1906.

85 Ibid.

86 Ibid. Brynmor Thomas, later minister of Milo (Carmel) and Mynydd Seion Pen-y-groes, two chapels profoundly moved by the revival, recalled Sarah Jones in the revival meetings 'Weithiau cerddai'n araf, arall yn ôl a blaen ar hyd ale'r capel gyda'r ystum o fam yn magu'i baban. Yr argraff a gai'r gynulleidfa oedd y Fendigaid Fair yn magu'r Iesu. Siaradai ag ef yn ôl dull mam yn siarad â'i hanwylyd bach gyntafanedig. Canai'n dawel iddo, a'i alw'n "Anwylyd y Tad", "Rhosyn Saron", "Lili'r Dyffrynnoedd", "Eneiniog yr Arglwydd" ' ('Sometimes she would walk slowly, other times she would walk down the aisle with the gestures of a mother holding a baby. The impression the congregation had was of Mary cradling the infant Jesus. She talked in the tones of a mother addressing her dearest first-born child. She sang quietly to him and called him "Father's

Dearest", "Rose of Sharon", the "Lily of the Valley", the "Anointed of the Lord".') (Brynmor Thomas, *Llwybrau Llafur*, (Swansea, 1970), p.96.) For more on Sarah Jones, see R. Tudur Jones, op. cit., p.187, ff123.

87 *South Wales Daily News*, 18 and 21 April 1906.

88 Ibid., 18 April 1906.

89 Ibid., 21 April 1906.

90 Ibid.

91 Ibid., 13 April 1906.

92 Ibid., 25 April 1906. He continued with warnings against spiritualism and mesmerism, and 'strong delusions', which was becoming increasingly powerful.

93 *Western Mail*, 5 June 1906; *Carmarthen Weekly Reporter*, 8 June 1906. People in the county continued to witness remarkable visions well after the stories of 1904 abated. On 1 July 1915, at the Lakefield Mission Room, Llanelli, massive crowds gathered when a vision of 'the man of Sorrows' appeared on the wall. Over a hundred converts were claimed and several spoke in tongues. One of them wrote in the *South Wales Press* with a conviction that was common to them all: 'Do not run away with the idea that we were deceived by a little dampness on the wall; what we saw was a reality. We saw the face of Christ whether you believe it or not' (*South Wales Press*, 15 July 1914). See also ibid., 14 March 1914, and *Cambria Daily Leader*, 29 July 1914. For later scenes of revival activity in the Park Place Mission, see *South Wales Press*, 31 December 1919.

94 Ibid., 2 December 1904.

95 See above, Chapter 2.

96 For studies of the 1904 revival, see C. R. Williams, 'The Welsh Religious Revival of 1904', *British Journal of Sociology*, 3 (1953), pp.242–59; Basil Hill, op. cit.; W. T. Stead, *The Revival in the West* (London, 1905). By far the best acounts are R. Tudur Jones, op. cit., pp.122–228 and the contemporary works of Henri Bois, *Le Reveil au Pays de Galles* (Toulouse, 1905) and J. Rogues de Fursac, *Un Movement mystique contemporain: Le Reveil religieux du Pays de Galles. 1904–1905* (Paris, 1907).

97 See above, Chapter 2.

98 Gareth W. Williams, 'The Disenchantment of the World: Innovation, Crisis and Change in Cardiganshire c.1880– 1910', *Ceredigion*, IX, 4 (1983), pp.303–21, especially p.317.

99 T. M. Bassett, *Bedyddwyr Cymru* (Swansea, 1977), pp.361–2.

100 Evan Roberts experienced most of his spiritual visions in Newcastle Emlyn and perhaps his deepest spiritual experience in Blaenannerch, but his most effective work was undertaken in Loughor. Joseph Jenkins and John Thickens both had experience of preaching a living in the

industrial areas of Wales. For Evan Roberts, see D. M. Phillips, op. cit. Chapter 21; for Joseph Jenkins, see R. T. Jenkins and E. D. Jones (eds.), op. cit., p.411; and for John Thickens, see D. Jenkins, op. cit., p.225.

101 *South Wales Press*, 1 December 1904.

102 *South Wales Daily News*, 27 September 1905.

103 For a discussion of religion and the 1868 election, see Ieuan Gwynedd Jones, *Explorations and Explanations*, Part 3, pp.217–98.

104 Quoted in I. J. Salmon, 'Welsh Liberalism 1868–1896: A Study in Structure and Ideology' (unpublished D.Phil. thesis, University of Oxford, 1983, p.176).

105 On disestablishment, see Kenneth O. Morgan, *Freedom or Sacrilege?* (Cardiff, 1966).

106 Idem. *Rebirth of a Nation: Wales 1880–1980* (Cardiff and Oxford, 1938), pp.37–8.

107 For the Carmarthenshire County Council, see Russell Davies, 'A Social History of Carmarthenshire 1870–1920', unpublished Ph.D. thesis, University of Wales, Aberystwyth, 1989), Chapter 7.

108 Thomas Johns had been a member of the council since its inception. See Revd Gwilym Rees, op. cit., pp.151–2. The Revd William Thomas of Whitland had been influential in the county council committees in opposing the presence of police at tithe sales at ratepayers' expense. See above, Chapter 3.

109 For Carmarthenshire's opposition to the Act, see Leslie Wynn Evans, *Studies in Welsh Education: Welsh Educational Structure and Administration 1880–1925* (Cardiff, 1974), especially Chapter III, 'The Carmarthenshire Enquiry', pp.117–82.

110 Ibid., p.159.

111 C. R. Williams, op. cit., *passim*.

112 *Carmarthen Weekly Reporter*, 22 March 1901.

113 Ibid., 8 December 1905.

114 See E. G. Bowen, 'The Baptists in Carmarthen Town, 1867–1967', reprinted in *Geography, Culture and Habitat* (Llandysul, 1976), pp.103–4.

115 *Carmarthen Weekly Reporter*, 17 April 1896.

116 *South Wales Press*, 14 February 1907.

117 Ibid., 17 December 1913, 15 October 1913.

118 *Carmarthen Weekly Reporter*, 17 May 1907. For the difficulties of the Independents in attracting young people, see R. Tudur Jones, *Yr Undeb* (Swansea, 1975), p.127.

119 R. Tudur Jones, *Ffyd ac Argyfwng Cenedl*, Vol.2, especially Chapter 1, 'Dryswch y Deallusion', pp.7–44.

120 For examples of petty squabbles between individuals and rival chapels, see *South Wales Press*, 20 July, 7 September and 23 November 1893, 23 May 1894, 28 February 1895, 3 and 31 March and 31

April 1904, 8 July 1908, 24 February 1909, and 13 July 1910, and *Carmarthen Journal*, 17 February 1888, 1 July 1892, 21 July 1893, 8 September 1893, 13 September 1895, 26 December 1902 and 31 January 1908.

121 On the Pentecostal movement, see W. J. Kollenweger, *The Pentecostals* (London, 1972). For the Apostolic Church, see T. N. Turnbull, *What God hath wrought* (London, 1959).

122 This was particularly true in School Board elections where adherence to a religious denomination took precedence over educational interests and abilities. For disputes in Llwynhendy between rival Baptists, see D. Russell Davies, op. cit., Chapter 7.

123 *Llanelly Mercury*, 11 January 1906.

124 *Carmarthen Weekly Reporter*, 8 and 22 December 1905.

125 E. Cefni Jones, *Gwili: Cofiant a Phregethau* (Llandysul, 1937), p.100. For Gwili, see J. Beverley Smith, 'John Gwili Jenkins, 1872–1936', *Transactions of the Honorary Society of Cymmrodorion*, 1974–5, pp.191–214.

126 For an immediate contemporary account, see A. T. Fryer, 'Psychological aspects of the Welsh Revival, 1904–05'. *Proceedings of the Society for Psychical Research*, Part 51, Vol.19, (December, 1905), pp.80–161.

127 Henri Bois, op. cit. and J. Rogues de Fursac, op. cit. The passage that follows is a gross simplification of their argument. For a better summary, see R. Tudur Jones, op. cit., pp.203–11.

128 E. Keri Evans, op. cit., p.77.

129 Henri Bois, op. cit., pp.53 and 73.

130 R. Tudur Jones, op. cit., p.211, especially pp.125 and 225.

131 *Carmarthen Weekly Reporter*, 2 December 1904.

132 H. Elvet Lewis, op. cit., p.197.

133 'Thank him for Remembering the Earth's dust;' 'Love as deep as the oceans'. Ibid.

134 'Me, me to remember me, O such overwhelming Love to remember me'. Quoted in D. Gwenallt Jones, *Ffwrneisiau: Cronicl Blynyddoedd Mebyd* (Llandysul, 1982), p.82.

135 James Williams, *Give Me Yesterday* (Llandysul, fifth edition, 1980), p.86.

136 'The Lord has done great things in our midst.' *Y Tyst*, 1 February 1904.

137 'After years of the sounds of the earth, the sounds of Heaven are heard in our land. We no longer have to ask the meaning of the heavenly noise of seraphs . . . because we have heard it ourselves . . . The Lord has done marvellous things to us, and for these we rejoice.' E. Cefin Jones, op. cit., p.100.

138 *South Wales Press*, 8 December 1904.

139 D. P. Williams, *Souvenir: The Apostolic Church Commemorating the Opening of the Apostolic Temple* (Llanelli, 1933), p.9.

140 '. . . without doubt, the Spirit of the Great Awakenings flowed in all its power down and worked powerfully upon the masses.' D. Gwenallt Jones, op. cit., p.83; James Griffiths, *Pages from Memory* (London, 1969), p.11; D. J. Williams, *Yn Chwech â'r Hugain Oed* (Llandysul, 1964), p.158

141 For an example of this belief, see the comments of Seth Joshua at the Swansea Central Hall: 'The Devil is raising a counter revival . . . we want to ring an alarm, for there is a dangerous thing in the air and spreading all over the country. It is a mixture of spiritualism and mesmerism, and it will need a strong hand to keep it down and a strong voice to denounce it. In the last days there are to be "strong delusions" and even the "elect" will only just escape from their power' (*South Wales Daily News*, 21 April 1906).

142 For example, see *Pulpud Cymru*, 1, 3 (March 1887), pp.45–8; 1, .5 (May 1897), pp 65–74; and 2, 21 (September 1889), pp.129–41.

143 D. M. Phillips, op. cit., pp.212–21; Phillips noted sixteen different experiences by Evan Roberts in late 1904, all involving supernatural powers, including a battle between Christ and the Devil. The vision of the Devil was seen on a Sunday in a Newcastle Emlyn garden between 4 and 5 p.m. Pondering on the low state of religion in Wales, Roberts heard scornful laughter and saw the Devil's face in the hedge (ibid., p.217). See also *South Wales Daily News*, 19 December 1904.

144 Jessie Penn-Lewis and Evan Roberts, *War on the Saints* (First Edition 1912; unabridged ed., New York, 1974). In this they continually warn that 'the time of the "Baptism of the Spirit" was a time of special danger' (p.54).

145 For example, the thunderings of Brutus against superstitions in the 1840s were ineffective because they offered no practical alternative except prayer to the effects which the superstitions were designed to cure.

146 For the links between Christianity and superstition in the nineteenth century, see James Obelkevich, *Religion and Rural Society: South Lindsey 1825–1875* (Oxford, 1976), especially Chapter 6, pp 259–82.

147 On the links between religion and superstition, Alfred Russell Wallace was positive. The people of Carmarthenshire, he recalled:

> As might be expected from their ignorance . . . are exceedingly superstitious, which is rather increased than diminished in those who are able to read by their confining their studies almost wholly to the Bible . . . Witches and wizards and white witches, as they are called, are firmly believed in, and their powers much dreaded. (Welsh Folk Museum, St Fagans, MSS 1173)

For similar views relating to superstition and conformity in France, see Theodore Zeldin, *France 1848–1945: Taste and Corruption* (Oxford, 1980), p.47.

148 Obelkevich, op. cit., p.281.

149 John Rhys, *Celtic Folklore: Welsh and Manx*, Vol.II (London, 1907), p.559.

150 Wirt Sikes makes this point in *British Goblins: Welsh Folklore, Fairy Mythology, Legends and Traditions* (Boston, 1881), p.4.

151 John Rhys, op. cit., p.571.

152 Edmund Jones, *A Relation of Apparitions of Spirits in the County of Monmouth, and the Principality of Wales . . .* (Newport, 1813 edition), p.72.

153 NLW, MSS 10,551, *Mary Thomas's Notebooks, Pantyclochydd.*

154 There is a problem in using the term 'bwci' for it appears to be a hold-all term covering all phenomena which manifested themselves at night.

155 Wirt Sikes noted that 'the Spirit of a suicide is morally certain to walk and hence [suicides are] unpopular as tenants of graveyards (Sikes, op. cit., p.146).

156 Ibid., pp.153–4.

157 For more on this theme, see Eugen Weber, 'Fairies and Hard Facts: The Reality of Folktales', *Journal of the History of Ideas*, XLII, 1 (1981), p.101.

158 *Carmarthen Journal*, 26 December 1902.

159 *South Wales Press*, 30 March 1899.

160 Ibid., 24 January and 7, 21 and 28 February 1917.

161 This story is retold in Gomer M. Roberts, 'Ysbrydion', in *Y Geninen*, 27, 3 (1977), pp.130–2.

162 Wirt Sikes, op. cit., p.337.

163 On the revival of spiritualism in Llandysul, see the *Cardigan and Tivyside Advertiser*, 3 June 1903. Dr Charles Williams outlined his experience in seances in south Wales and described the progress of the spiritualist movement. He claimed that the Spiritualist movement was widespread with local libraries stocking its magazine (Charles Williams, *Spiritualism: Its true nature and results* (London, 1910), p.41).

164 NLW, MSS Dolau Cothi Correspondence, L5138. She also assisted John Rhys on various points regarding superstitions and spirits (see NLW, MSS L9169, 9171 and 10,084).

165 These beliefs were also common in neighbouring counties. See Edward Laws, *The History of Little England beyond Wales and the Non-Kymric Colony Settled in Pembrokeshire* (London, 1888), p.412, and D. Rhys Phillips, *A Romantic Valley in Wales . . . The History of the Vale of Neath* (Swansea, 1925), p.579 ('the belief in ghosts has not yet taken wing').

166 Wirt Sikes, op. cit., p.2.

[167] Jonathan Ceredig Davies, *Folklore of West and Mid Wales* (Aberystwyth, 1911), p.148.

[168] On fairies, see Hugh Evans, *Y Tylwyth Teg* (Liverpool, 1944) and John Owen Huws, *Y Tylwyth Teg* (Llanrwst, 1987).

[169] See W. Jenkin Thomas, *The Welsh Fairy Book* (London, third edition, 1912), pp.221–2, 268–71. See also P. H. Emerson, *Welsh Fairy Tales and Other Stories* (London, 1894); idem, *Tales from Welsh Wales, Founded on Fact and Current Tradition* (London, 1894); and Joseph Jacobs, *Celtic Fairy Tales; Comprehensive Edition* (first ed., 1891; reprinted London, 1970).

[170] W. Llewelyn Williams, *'Slawer Dydd* (Llanelli, 1913).

[171] 'Cardi', 'Cardiganshire Customs and Superstitions', *By-Gones*, 29 September 1897, p.209.

[172] For changelings, see J. Ceredig Davies, op. cit., p.116, and Wirt Sikes, op. cit., pp.56, 75, 88. On infanticide, see Chapter 4.

[173] John Rhys, op. cit., pp.160–1. He bases one of these traditions upon Wirt Sikes' evidence. He also adds that a mermaid was reportedly caught off Fishguard in 1858, adding another element to maritime superstition.

[174] W. J. E. Wentz, *The Fairy Faith in Celtic Countries: Its Psychological Origin and Nature* (Rennes, 1909), p.16.

[175] R. C. Bosanquet, 'Corpse Candles in Carmarthenshire', *Trans. Carm. Ant.*, LVIX, 25 (1934), pp.72–4.

[176] George Borrow, *Wild Wales; Its People, Language and Scenery* (London, first edition 1856, 1977 ed.), p.301.

[177] Gomer Roberts, op. cit., p.131.

[178] See Edward James, op. cit., p.412. Corpse candles were also seen in neighbouring counties. The last corpse candle in the Neath Valley was seen outside the Star Inn, Crynant (D. Rhys Phillips, op. cit., p.597). In Pembrokeshire, they were known as 'fetch candles'.

[179] Mary Curtis, *The Antiquities of Laugharne, Pendine and their Neighbourhoods* (London, 1880), p.216.

[180] Ibid., p.217.

[181] Ibid., p.218.

[182] 'I remember Mother would shake with fright if she heard a cockerel crow at night or a dog howl. Everyone believed in corpse candles: if a small light was seen in the darkness it was a sign that a child would die, and a stronger, brighter light foretold the death of older people.' H. G. Davies, *Edrych yn ôl: Hen Atgofion am Bentref Gwledig* (Liverpool, 1958), p.66.

[183] Jonathan Ceredig Davies, op. cit., p.182. He noted that 'I was informed at Llanynog five years ago that spectral dogs still haunt that part of Carmarthenshire; and more than one of my informants had seen such apparitions themselves'.

184 The Revd Elias Owen noted in 1897 that 'We have in Wales the "deryn corff" or corpse bird, a bird said to flap against the window of the room of the sick' (*By-Gones*, 29 December 1897, p.270).

185 For 'Gwrach y Rhibyn', see *Cardigan and Tivyside Advertiser*, 16 December 1932.

186 Marie Trevelyan, *Folk Lore and Folk-stories of Wales* (London, 1909), p.202.

187 Sikes, op. cit., pp.220–1.

188 Obelkevich, op. cit., *passim*.

189 D. G. Williams, 'Casgliad o Lên Gwerin Sir Gaerfyrddin', *Trafodion Eisteddfod Genedlaethol Llanelly 1895*, pp.351–7.

190 Ibid., p.351.

191 Ibid., p.353.

192 *South Wales Press*, 5 February 1908.

193 *Cambrian Daily Leader*, 5 November 1918.

194 *South Wales Press*, 19 September 1917.

195 Their advertisements are to be found in the columns of the local newspapers. See, for example, ibid., 23 February 1905.

196 For Harries, Cwrtycadno, NLW, Cwrtmawr MSS. Jane Pugh, *Welsh Witches and Warlocks* (Llanrwst, 1987) and Kate Bosse Griffiths, *Byd y Dyn Hysbys* (Talybont, 1977).

197 *South Wales Daily News*, 3, 4 and 5 November 1904.

198 L. Winstanley and H. J. Rose, 'Collectanea: Scraps of Welsh Folklore', *Folklore*, LXXXVI (1926), p.167.

199 NLW, Cwrtmawr MSS 97A, *The Book of Harries, Cwrtycadno*.

200 D. G. Williams, op. cit., pp.337–9.

201 Major Francis Jones declared that 'at the close of the nineteenth century and in the first half of the twentieth century, the well cult had survived all attempts to destroy it' (Francis Jones, *The Holy Wells of Wales* (Cardiff, 1954), p.87 and ibid., pp.163–72).

202 They were also used to solve local mysteries. The wise man of Gwernogle guided searchers looking for the body of a farmer from Llanfihangel Rhos-y-corn who had been missing for a long period. The body, when it was eventually found, had been almost totally devoured by dogs. He also found straying cows (*Carmarthen Journal*, 4 July 1892).

203 Marie Trevelyan, op. cit., p.321. W. Llewelyn Williams, the historian and politician, recalled that in his boyhood, 'roedd llawer o ddoctoriaid bôn clawdd yn yr ardal. Yn Llansawel yr oedd doctor esgyrn; yn Llangadog trigai g˘r oedd yn berchen ar eli llosg-tân digyffelyb; yn Nhal-y-llychau yr oedd gof a chanddo eli ardderchog at wella'r ddarwden (ringworm) a fflamwydden (erysipelas); ac yn y Plough Inn ym mhentref Caeo yr oedd gan Morgans y tafarwnwr eli digymhar at wella cancr' 'There were several quack doctors in the

area. In Llansawel there was a doctor who set bones; in Llangadog there lived a man with a special healing cream for burns; in Talley a blacksmith had a wonderful cure for ringworm and erysipelas; and in the Plough Inn in Caeo, Morgans the publican had an unrivalled cream to cure cancer.') (W. Llewelyn Williams, *'Slawer Dydd* (Llanelli, 1913), p.31).

204 *South Wales Press*, 7 March 1907.

205 For industrial superstitions, see Lyn Davies, 'Aspects of Mining Folklore in Wales', *Folklife*, 9 (1971), pp.79–107.

206 A cockerel crowing after dark was considered to be particularly unfortunate, matched only in terms of bad luck with a cuckoo singing on ploughed land. Welsh Folk Museum, St Fagans, MSS 2111–19. For omens of good and bad luck in Carmarthenshire, see D. G. Williams, op. cit., pp.330–6.

207 Caradoc Evans, 'The woman who sowed Iniquity' in *My People* (London, second ed., 1953), p.78. Evans plays on the theme again, when Rhys Shop questions the possibility that her sudden change in clothes signifies an impending wedding.

> 'Iss, iss, Rhys Shop,' Betti answered, and in her ostentatious pride, she lifted her frock and displayed the skirt of her white petticoat.

In the story it is clear that Betti's pride did come before and that her fall, when it inevitably came, was severe.

208 D. J. Williams, 'Blwyddyn Llwyddianus', *Storiau'r Tir* (Llandysul, 1979 edn)

209 Obelkevich, op. cit., p.309.

210 For a discussion of the main themes in Caradoc Evans' short stories, see John Harries' introduction 'The Banned, Burned Book of War', in Caradoc Evans, *My People* (Bridgend, 1987), pp.7–48 and idem, *Fury Never Leaves Us* (Bridgend, 1985).

211 On these themes, see Keith Thomas, *Religion and the Decline of Magic* (Harmondsworth, 1978), *passim*.

212 Obelkevich, op. cit., p.304.

213 David Jenkins, for example, argued that the fundamental social divisions in south-west Wales were between 'Buchedd A' and 'Buchedd B' people. The 'buchedd' of a person was determined by a person's membership or non-membership of a religious denomination. See Elwyn Davies and A. D. Rees *et al.* (eds.), *Welsh Rural Communities* (Cardiff, 1960), pp.12–23, especially pp.13–15.

214 Beriah Gwynfe Evans was for a time a schoolteacher in Gwynfe and Llangadog. He later worked on the staff of several newspapers and was one of the pioneers of Welsh language drama. See *Dictionary of Welsh Biography*, p.205. For an assessment of his dramatic work, see

John Gwilym Jones, 'Dramâu Beriah Gwynfe Evans (1848–1927)', in Dyfnallt Morgan, *Gwy^ r Llên y Bedwaredd Ganrif ar Bymtheg a'u Cefndir* (Llandybïe, 1968), pp.255–67.

215 Ibid., p.261.

216 Reported in *Seren Cymru*, 25 February 1898.

217 T. J. Morgan, *Diwylliant Gwerin* (Llandysul, 1972), p.47.

218 T. J. Morgan, *Peasant Culture* (Swansea, 1962), p.18.

219 Elfyn Scourfield, 'Astudiaeth o Ddiwylliant Lleol a Thraddodiadau Llafar Ardal Tre-lech' (unpublished University of Wales (Swansea) M.A. thesis, 1969), p.273).

220 For Gwylfa, see Alfred S. Williams and Reginald F. Kewer-Williams, *Who's Who in Llanelly and District* (Llanelli, 1910), pp.42–3.

221 Pennar Griffiths, *Cofiant Watcyn Wyn* (Cardiff, 1915), p.95.

222 See Russell Davies, op. cit., Chapter 7.

223 *Celtic News*, 4 May 1923. Quoted in Elfyn Scourfield, 'Rhai o Eisteddfodau Lleol Cylch Caerfyrddin', *Transactions of the Honourable Society of Cymmrodorion*, 1976, p.231. It would seem that behaviour in competitive meetings held in chapels was no better.

224 D. Gwenallt Jones, *Ffwrneisiau*, *passim*. One of his complaints was that the adjudicators at Eisteddfodau frequently chose religious topics as the subject for *awdlau* and *pryddestau*. This put the worker-poet, as compared with the teacher-poet, at a disadvantage. As one of them remarked, 'Mae'r canu Beiblaidd 'ma yn gani peiriannol, yn ganu pell oddi wrth yn bywyd ni heddi. Pam ddiawl na fydden nhw yn rhoi testune tidi? Fe fydd barddoniaeth Gymrâg yn siwr o ddarganfod y cnawd rywbryd; ac fe fydd yr awen yn darganfod fod gan ddyn goc . . .' 'This singing of biblical themes is artificial and irrelevant to our daily lives. Why the hell don't they choose sensible titles! Welsh poetry must discover the flesh some time; and inspiration must discover that man has a prick.' (ibid., p.100).

225 For Amanwy, see Gomer M. Roberts, *Caneuon Amanwy* (Llandysul, 1956). For a study of this bardic tradition, see Huw Walters, *Canu'r Pwll a'r Pwlpud: Portread o'r Diwylliant Barddol Cymraeg yn Nyffryn Aman* (Denbigh, 1987), especially pp.276–9.

226 For this tradition, see Cecil Price, 'Portable Theatres in Wales 1843–1914', *National Library of Wales Journal*, 9 (1955–6).

227 Ibid., pp.84, 91.

228 *Llanelly Mercury*, 23 March 1910. On William Haggar, see David Berry, *Wales at the Cinema: The First Hundred Years* (Cardiff, 1994), pp.44–62.

229 Quoted in Cecil Price, op. cit. Arthur Mee claimed that members of religious denominations who frequented the theatre were excommunicated.

[230] *South Wales Press*, 8 March and 3 May 1916. During the war, however, censorship was relaxed. In its advertisement for the film 'The Kaiser: The Beast of Berlin', the Popular Cinema declared that 'the mind cannot grasp through word medium the hellish hideousness of the arts of the super devil. He out "devils" the devil himself . . . To have a graphic idea of this beast, to see the soul of this human monstrosity stripped naked of all its contemptible hypocrisy, see the soul stirring drama, "The Kaiser: The Beast of Berlin" at the Popular next week' (*South Wales Press*, 23 October 1918). The immediacy of the cinema was clearly shown in October 1916 when Mrs Wilson, watching the official war film 'The Battle of the Somme' recognized her husband as one of the corpses (ibid., 10 October 1916). Sensationalism such as this ensured that the cinemas would be 'much frequented' (ibid., 7 March 1917).

[231] *Carmarthen Weekly Reporter*, 22 September 1905.

[232] Ibid., 11 November 1904. For Sir Lewis Morris, see Douglas Phillips, *Sir Lewis Morris* (Cardiff, 1981).

[233] *Carmarthen Weekly Reporter*, 11 November 1904.

[234] David Smith and Gareth Williams, *Fields of Praise* (Cardiff, 1980).

[235] *South Wales Press*, 19 October 1905. He had played it twice weekly and advocated healthy exercise. For Iona Williams, see Alfred S. Williams and Reginald F. Kewer-Williams, op. cit., p.47. At the Llanelli Market Hall in 1906, George Clark, in a talk on 'The Christian Athlete', observed that 'man had a body, mind and soul and should look after all three' (ibid., 24 May 1906).

[236] *Carmarthen Weekly Reporter*, 22 December 1905.

[237] For Llanelli, see Lynn Hughes, *One Hundred Years of Scarlet* (Llanelli, 1981).

[238] *South Wales Press*, 3 January 1907.

[239] Cricket was, however, widespread, most of the towns and villages having teams. In 1897, Laugharne, Lampeter, Llandovery, Llanybydder, Pencader, Llandeilo, St Peters (Carmarthen) and St Clears all had teams which played in a competitive league (*Carmarthen Journal*, 23 July 1897).

[240] *South Wales Press*, 11 October 1906 and 21 February 1912. Boxing was frequently condemned by the religious denominations. See, for example ibid., 3 September 1919.

[241] For the Newcastle Emlyn Lawn Tennis Club, see above, Chapter 2.

[242] Tom Rees, *Racing Reminiscences* (1st edn, n.d., reprinted Cwm Nedd, 1977). On the development of gambling, see Ross McKibbin, 'Working Class Gambling in Britain', *Past and Present*, No.82, 1979, pp.147–78.

[243] *Carmarthen Journal*, 23 March 1894.

[244] *South Wales Press*, 30 October 1912. So popular had the races become

that in 1915, Captain Morton Evans harangued 'hundreds of young men' at the Llanelli race meeting as to why they were not in khaki. Fifty were subsequently detained for further questioning by the police (*Carmarthen Weekly Reporter*, 15 September 1915).

245 Ibid., 25 February 1892.

246 *Carmarthen Journal*, 23 February 1894, reported that ploughing competitions were spreading across the county.

247 For a typical report, see ibid., 3 October 1890. See also Elfyn Scourfield, op. cit.

248 There was an otter hunt based at Llandeilo (*Carmarthen Journal*, 24 August 1888). Another hunt was based in Glansevin (ibid., 12 September 1912). For fox hunting, see above, Chapter 2.

249 For a report on the Burry Port regatta, see *South Wales Press*, 6 August 1902.

250 Brian Harrison, *Drink and the Victorians: The Temperance Question in England 1815–1872* (London, 1971), pp.40–1.

251 *Report of the Royal Commission on Labour: The Agricultural Labourer*, Vol.2 (London, 1893), p.20.

252 For these traditions, see Elfyn Scourfield, *Macsu Cwrw yn Nyfed* (Cardiff, 1983).

253 D. J. Williams, op. cit., p.62.

254 Many writers complained at the unfairness of the fact that though the police kept vigilant watch over the 'cwrw bach', they did not intervene at weddings at local mansions where larger quantities of alcohol would be drunk (*Carmarthen Weekly Reporter*, 10 March 1899).

255 'No-one was censured at the chapel for going on the cruise in a little beer – because although it did harm to oneself it did do some good for others.' W. Llewelyn Williams, op. cit., p.84. Drinking on the 'cnap', at the fair and at auction were however fined.

256 *Cambria Daily Leader*, 18 March 1910.

257 CROC, *Quarter Sessions Papers*, Box 75, Llanelly Temperance League submissions.

258 Ibid.

259 *South Wales Press*, 27 October 1915. For the temperance movement in Wales, see W. R. Lambert, *Drink and Sobriety in Wales c.1820–1895* (Cardiff, 1983).

260 W. R. Lambert, op. cit., p.65. The Llanelly Temperance Society used to meet in the long room of the Wheat Sheaf public house.

261 Quoted in James Walvin, *Leisure and Society 1830–1950* (London, 1978), p.38.

262 On theft, see above, Chapter 3, and on prostitution, see Chapter 4.

263 'Election' was a horse which was running on 25 October (*The Welshman*, 14 November 1913).

[264] The case against Edwinsford is reported in *Carmarthen Journal*, 11 August 1899; against the Albion Inn in *South Wales Press*, 6 March 1902; against the New Inn in *Llanelly Mercury*, 28 June 1900; and against the Jubilee Hotel in *Carmarthen Journal*, 16 January 1903.

[265] *Carmarthen Weekly Reporter*, 12 February 1909.

[266] *South Wales Press*, 31 January 1917.

[267] Daniel Roche, *The People of Paris: An Essay in Popular Culture in the Eighteenth Century* (translated by Marie Evans, Leamington Spa, 1987), p.259.

[268] For a discussion of these themes, see George Orwell, *Down and Out in Paris and London* (Harmondsworth, 1980 edn).

[269] 'Treating' was the custom of purchasing drinks for soldiers on leave. Great resentment was caused when people were fined for buying drinks for soldiers who had just returned from the front. See, for example, *South Wales Press*, 16 October 1917.

[270] The moralists and temperance campaigners frequently complained of the dancing and singing which took place in public houses. See, for example, *Llanelly Mercury*, 23 November 1911.

[271] For just a few examples, see *South Wales Press*, 5 January 1905; *Carmarthen Weekly Reporter*, 14 August 1896, 1 February 1900, 21 June 1901, 16 October 1903, and 30 December 1904; *Llanelly Mercury*, 3 September 1897; and *Carmarthen Journal*, 27 September 1895.

[272] For the visit of Italian organ-grinders to Carmarthen, see *Carmarthen Weekly Reporter*, 15 April 1904.

[273] For 'Jim Pais's activities', see ibid., 8 July 1898.

Conclusion: Carmarthenshire and Welsh Society

[1] This point is explained in David Cannadine, 'The way we lived then', *Times Literary Supplement*, 13 July 1990, p.935.

[2] I think this is stated in Gwyn A. Williams *The Welsh in their History* (London, 1982), 'Introduction'.

[3] This statement was made in a television programme.

[4] D. Gwenallt Jones, *Gwreiddiau* (Llandysul, 1959), p.47.

[5] On this theme, see Gareth Williams, op. cit., *passim*.

[6] On politics in Carmarthenshire and the level of corruption in Carmarthen town affairs, see D. Russell Davies, 'A Social History of Carmarthenshire 1870–1920' (unpublished Ph.D. thesis, University of Wales, Aberystwyth, 1989), Chapter 7.

[7] *South Wales Press*, 27 June 1895.

[8] For a brilliant approach to history based on such themes see Theodore Zeldin, *An Intimate History of Humanity* (London, 1994).

[9] In 1941 Lucien Febrre published a paper entitled 'Sensibility and history: how to reconstitute the emotional life of the past'. This is republished in Peter Burke (ed.), *A New Kind of History from the Writings of Febrre* (Rudan, 1973), pp.12–26.

[10] Gwyn A. Williams, op. cit., p.10.

[11] Quoted in Ieuan Gwynedd Jones, *Towards a Social History of the Welsh Language* (Aberystwyth, 1994), p.17.

Index

abortifacients, 172–3
abortion, 172–4
affiliation proceedings, 167–70
agriculture, types of farming, 34–9; hardship, 39–40
alcohol, given to babies, 77–8; as the cause of crime, 116, 122; prohibition against, 117; women drinkers, 120–1; as a cause of family problems, 177–8; popular customs, 226–30; social functions of, 228–9
Ammanford, Sunday drinking in, 119; religious revival, 195–6
anthracite, mining of, 29–30; economic depression, 53–5

baby farming, 174–5
Barker, Thomas, 47
Beith, Robert (manager Great Mountain Colliery), 140–2
Benjamin, Walter, 5
Bird in Hand, Carmarthen, 162
birth control, 171–4
Bishop of London, 71
Blackberry Fair (Carmarthen), 23
Bois, Henry, 207
Borrow, George, 213
Bowen, C. A., 47
Bowen, Revd William, 201
boxing, 224
Buffalo Bill's Wild West Circus, vagrants at entrance, 126; mentioned in affiliation order, 169
Burry Port, 21, 30

Caeo, murder, 134; school, 83; immigration of children from Patagonia, 84
'canwyll corff', *see* corpse candles
Carmarthen, development and character of the town, 22–4; middle classes of, 45–6; insanitary housing, 64–5; Sunday rowdiness in, 119; abortion, 174; prostitution, 163; religious revival, 196, 199
Carmarthenshire County Council, urban powers, 21
'caru yn y gwely' (courting in bed), 165–6
Cawdor, family, 41
change in rural life and customs, 86–8
Chaplin, Charlie, impersonation competitions, 223
Chappell, Edgar, 63
Churchill, Winston, and Llanelli riots, 143
cinema, 222–3; tension with chapels, 205
coming of age ceremonies, 42–3
concealment of birth, 174
corpse candles (*canwyll corff*), 213–14
corruption (in elections), 236
Cowell-Stepney, Sir A. K., 41
Crwys (William Crwys Williams), 108
crime, professionals, 124; frequent transgressors, 125–6
crime rates, 113–14
cruelty, to wives, 178–81; to children, 182–4; to parents, 184
'cwrw bach', 227–8

'Danws' (Daniel Jones), 121
Davies, Bryan Martin, 1
Davies, Catherine, 48
Davies, Gwilym, complaints at immorality of Carmarthenshire, 164, 184
Davies, Jonathan Ceredig, 212
Davies, Revd David, 112
Davies, Rhys, 1, 233
Davies, S. O., 67
Davies, W. Anthony, 197
Davies, Walter, 47
death rates, 70
de Fursac, J. Rogues, 206–7
Devil, the, 209–10
divorce, 176
docks, Burry Port 30; Llanelli New Dock, 30–1
Dolau Cothi, 43; murder, 134; spirits, 212
domestic servants, 49
double standard, 161, 170
'dyled cynheua' (harvest debt), 38
Dynevor, Lady, 1935 radio appeal, 75
Dynevor, Lord, 41

education, 12; bad condition of schools, 79–80; non-attendance in rural areas, 81–3; problems of teaching English, 83–5
Edwinsford, 41
eisteddfodau, 220–1
emigration, to the USA, 53; to Tuscany, 54
emotions, history of, 11, 237–8
epidemics, 68–9
Evans, Caradoc, 89, 97, 110, 113, 161, 218
Evans, Gwilym, 24
Evans, Keri, 199, 207

farmers, harsh living conditions, 72–4, 108–9
fortune-tellers, 215–16
freemasons, 45, 46, 47

gambling, 225
Gee, Thomas, and the tithe war, 135; religious census, 187
gentry of south-west Wales, land holdings, 40–7; sporting pursuits, 44–5; links to industry, 45
ghosts, 211–12

Gladstone, W E., 186
Goodall, Dr, 93–4, 99
Gwenallt (D. Gwenallt Jones), 1, 69, 209, 221, 235
Gwynne-Hughes, J. W (of Tre-gib), 41

Haggar, William, 221–3
Harding, A., 48
Harries, John (Cwrtycadno), 216
harvesting, 37–9
'Hen Wlad y Menig Gwynion', 112–14
Hills-Johnes, Charlotte, 212
Hills-Johnes, Sir James, 134
Hopkins, Dr, 173–4
Hopkins, Revd M., 160
horse racing, 44, 225
hospitals, 75
housing conditions, rural, 62–4; urban, 64–6
Howard, Lady Stafford, *see* Stepney, Catherine Muriel Cowell
Howard, S. V. S., 42
Howton, Pastor, 199
Hunter, Dr, 1864 report on health, 108
hunting, 44

illegitimacy, 164–6
indecent assault, 170–1
infant mortality, high rates, 71–4; causes, 75, 78–9
Inniskillen Dragoons, in Tumble, 143
insanity, growth in number of people suffering, 97–9

Jenkins, Revd Gwili, 206, 209
Jenkins, Joseph, 195–6, 203, 207
John, John, 145
Johns, Revd Thomas, 112, 192, 204
Joint Counties Lunatic Asylum, building, 90; funding dispute, 90–1; overcrowding in, 92–3; discipline, 93–4; cruelty, 95–6; home location of patients, 98–9; suicidal tendency of patients, 99–100; and religion, 100–1; syphilis in, 101; superintendent's journal, 102–3
Jones, F. A. G. (of Pantglas), 41
Jones, Morgan (of Llanmilo), 41
Jones, Revd Professor R. Tudur, 190
Jones, Rhys Gwesyn, 160
Jones, Sarah, 199–202

Jones, Thomas, 61, 144–6, 149–51, 153
Jones-Davies, Henry, 37–8
Joshua, Seth, 195, 206

Kelly's Directory, 20

Leland, John, 2
Lewis, Charles Prytherch, 45
Lewis, Mrs M. M. (asylum attendant), 93
Lewis, Peggy (tithe martyr), 138
Lewis, Robert (tithe collector), 136–9
Llandybïe, trades in the parish 20; colliery violence, 139
Llandovery, bad housing conditions, 66
Llanelli, rapidity of development, 148; development and character of the town, 24–6; tinplate industry, 27–8; docks, 30–1; *Who's Who* in Llanelli, 46–9; and the National Society for Infant Mortality, 79; violence of some areas, 132–4; 1911 riots, 143–53; Stepney Street, 149; NSPCC, 181, 183; religious revival, 197; theatre, 221–2; public houses, 228; National Eisteddfod, 236

Maizey family (Kidwelly murder), 133
Maudsley, Henry, 99
Mee, Arthur, 221–2
Mill Street (Carmarthen), 60, 121–2, 132, 229, 232
milk production in Tywi valley, 34
miracles, 202
murder, 133–5

Namier, Sir Lewis, 10
Nevill, R. T., 42
newspapers, as historical sources, 7; censorship of, 223
NSPCC, 182–4

O Lwch y Lofa, 221

Pantglas, 41
Parry-Jones, Daniel, 87
paupers, 56–7
pawnbrokers, 52, 181
Peel, Miss, coming of age celebrations, 42
Pen-y-groes, revival in, 199–202; pentecostalism, 209
personal experiences, 8–11
phantom funerals, 213–14
Phillips, J. B., 46
Phillips, Sydney J., 50
poaching, 128–31
poor relief, 55
popular culture, 220–31
population, growth of, 14–21
poverty, 50, 56–8
prostitution, 161–4
puerperal fever, 74–5

Rae, George (of Mill Street, Carmarthen), 60, 121
Rees, Revd Thomas, 156
religion, attendance, 186–91; services of religion to the community, 192–3; 1904–5 revival, 193–209; causes of the revival, 203–9; class divisions in chapels, 205
Rhys, Sir John, 210, 211
Richards, H. E. B., 46
Roberts, Evan, 193, 195, 197, 199, 208–9
Roberts, Samuel, 'Y Teulu Dedwydd', 157–9
Roberts, Revd Dr Gomer, 193, 212, 214, 221
Roderick, William Buckley, 45
rugby, 224

sanitation, 67–8
separation and maintenance orders, 176–82
sex ratios, 18–19
Sikes, Wirt, 215
Simon, Sir John, 71
Southall, J. E., 18
sport, 223–5
Stepney, Catherine Muriel Cowell, (later Lady Stafford Howard), 48, 79
Stepney Motor Wheel Co., 47
streetcorner culture, 230
strikes, Tumble, 139–43; Llanelli, 143–53
suicide, in Carmarthenshire, 103–8; First World War, 106–7; and religion, 107; suicide notes, 107

Sunday Closing Act 1881, 117–19
superstition, 210–19
syphilis, presence in asylum, 101; mentioned in separation order proceedings, 181–2

Teifi Valley, woollen manufacturing, 3
theatre, 221–2
theft, 122–3
Thickens, John, 195, 203, 207
Thompson, E. P., 4
Thomas, Gwyn, 3, 234
Thomas, H. Elwyn, *Martyrs of Hell's Highway*, 163
Thomas, R. S., 110
Thomas, Revd W. (Whitland), 135, 137–8, 204
tinplate industry, general development, 27–8; depression in, 53–4; bad working conditions, 72
tithe wars, general outbreak, 135–9; martyrs, 138–9; problems of tithe collectors, 138; role of Nonconformist ministers, 137–8
'Tommy Mammy', 121
'torri y llech', 76
tramways, in Llanelli, 32
Trevelyan, Marie, 217
Trevelyan, G. M., 231
Tumble, population growth in, 19; typhoid, 68–9; riots, 142–3; strike, 139–43; violence, 141
'tylwyth teg' (fairies), 212–13

vagrants and tramps, numbers in the county, 58–61; punishment of, 127
Vaughan, H. M., 44

Waddel, George, and Tumble riots, 139–40, 142; divorce, 176
wages, 51
Weber, Eugen, 8
Welsh speakers, 18
Wilkins, Henry, 144, 150
Williams, D. J., 99, 157, 209, 218, 225, 227
Williams, D. P., 209
Williams, David (phrenologist), 48
Williams, Gwyn Alf, 231, 239
Williams, James, 208
Williams, Sir John, 12
Williams, William (Pantycelyn), 193
Williams, William Llewelyn, 88, 157, 212, 227
Williams, W. Nantlais, 195–6, 208
Williams-Drummond, Sir James, 41
wise men, 216–17
women, their place in the home, 159; in public houses, 120–1
woollen manufacturing, 3, 33–4
Worsell, Leonard, 145

youth, complaints at behaviour of, 154; streetcorner culture, 229–30